The Way of the Cross Leads Home

Religion in North America

Catherine L. Albanese and Stephen J. Stein, Editors

The Way of the Cross Leads Home

THE DOMESTICATION OF
AMERICAN METHODISM

A. Gregory Schneider

Indiana
University
Press

BLOOMINGTON AND INDIANAPOLIS

The paper used in this publication meets the minimum requirements of American National Standard for Information Sciences—Permanence of Paper for Printed Library Materials, ANSI Z39.48-1984.

Manufactured in the United States of America

∞™

Library of Congress Cataloging-in-Publication Data

Schneider, A. Gregory.
The way of the cross leads home : the domestication of American Methodism / A. Gregory Schneider.
p. cm. — (Religion in North America)
Includes bibliographical references and index.
ISBN 0-253-35094-8 (hard)
1. Spirituality—Methodist Church—History—19th century.
2. Methodist Church—United States—History—19th century.
3. Methodist Church—United States—Membership. 4. Family—United States. 5. United States—Religion—19th century. I. Title.
II. Series.
BX8237.S36 1993
287'.673'09034—dc20 92–23087

1 2 3 4 5 97 96 95 94 93

TO

Lloyd Richard Ellison
Lila Ellison Goertzen
Franklin Wright Schneider
Roberta Klooster Schneider

Fathers and Mothers in the Gospel

CONTENTS

FOREWORD

In this important new book, A. Gregory Schneider takes a revisionary look at Methodist piety with narrative strategies that combine the chronicler's dexterous sweep and the analyst's critical vision. Schneider draws us almost seductively into the early Methodism of the Ohio Valley as it experiences its youthful growing pains and gradually transforms itself into a staid middle-aged denomination. In Methodism's frontier setting, he demonstrates the presence of a social and religious world in the process of distinguishing itself and setting itself apart. Using the language of the people he studies, Schneider locates his fledgling Methodists in the comparative context of the patriarchal establishment of the old South. Here a culture of honor flourished, with gaming and dueling like twin antipodes, to mark its limits. Birth and breeding counted, slaves obeyed masters, women deferred to men, and men deferred to other men. The church was the high church, and all knew their place and station.

By contrast, in the new Methodist communities formed by the class system, religious converts discovered themselves to be a family. The stern and authoritative patriarch, now become superintending bishop or circuit-riding preacher, had shed much of his harshness for a rule of gentleness and love. The free exchange of testimonials, the flow of feeling and emotion, the language of "melting times" and "love feasts," these set Methodists apart as a public religious culture that implicitly, and sometimes explicitly, challenged the old culture of honor. In a post-Revolutionary context of reforming zeal, Methodists managed to incorporate the intimacy of domestic settings as they freely confessed their failings to one another and immersed themselves in the new democracy of grace and salvation. Yet even as they seemed to destroy the old and rigid formalism of a hierarchical culture of honor, Methodists introduced a new rule that, in its own way, was as demanding as the rule of the world and the flesh had been.

The new rule was the way of the cross. Its ascetic discipline laid Methodists open to measurement by requirements that guaranteed the social scrutiny of fellow believers and the "familial" correction that relatives extended to one another freely. Its continuing summons was to a life of self-denial in the service of a gospel that ordained death as prerequisite for life. Methodists, thus, interwove the sentimental piety of intimate home and family with the iron strands of an exacting code. Democracy and sentiment, it turned out, meant the taut organization of evangelical order and the explicit, totalistic demands that it imposed. The early Methodist sweep of the frontier could be explained in the gift for combining charisma and order, organization and the passional closeness of an extended family.

Or, to put all of this in the sequence that Schneider's title and narrative trajectory suggest, the ironclad austerity of Christian life in the shadow of the cross hid a surprising softness beneath. Looking at Methodist piety this way, we begin to see the connections between a rigid facade of Christian asceticism and an interior of "sweetness" and sentimentality. Indeed, we discover that the much-noticed "feminization" of nineteenth-century American culture and religion is, here, the ironic counterpart of a time-honored religious requirement of self-sacrifice and self-surrender. Instead of a northeastern coalition of liberal ministers and female authors trading authority for consumer satisfaction, we have a new western coalition of evangelical preachers and converts who "methodize" and "feminize" at once. That both of these led to the domestication (read "taming," "settling," and "middle-aging") of Methodism—that is, to its domestication in a second sense—is a final irony of Schneider's account. The consumption in which Methodists engaged was a consuming of themselves.

Intrinsically absorbing as it unfolds, Schneider's story is part of a new wave of scholarship on the Methodists that is effectively marking the differences between Methodist and Calvinist piety. Until the present and the new wave of work, scholars in American religious history have not particularly attended to the sharp and discernible differences between the pieties of separate "camps" within the Protestant mainstream. Perhaps they have not done so because they have had to attend, first, to other scholarly things, because they have been busy delineating the shape of organizations and the structure of thought, the machinations of politics and the vectors of denominational change.

What is clear from Schneider's success, however, is that methodological pluralism plays a distinct and important role in the explication of complex cultural identities and connections. And the explanation of such identities and connections is what leads to a viable understanding of different kinds of religiosity. Schneider's interdisciplinary approach, with its combinations of rhetorical analysis, psychological insight, phenomenological epoche, and historical narrative, is masterfully integrated into the tale he tells. Deceptively simple in its playing out, this approach represents a multileveled and sophisticated reading of the evidence from a rich collection of primary sources. Schneider has used these to advantage to immerse himself in the "thick description" of a world that encompasses anecdote after personal anecdote. But he has immersed himself, equally, in worlds of methodological and interpretive strategy that he knows through and through. The results are something of a scholarly feast, even as they are a literary one.

Catherine L. Albanese
Stephen J. Stein
Series Editors

PREFACE

This is a story of how God, Mother, and Flag joined forces in American popular culture. It is not so conventional a topic as it might sound. At least, this is not a conventional treatment of that topic. A few generations ago, God, Mother, and Flag were compelling images by which to grasp and control human experience. Now, by becoming cliché, these images obscure from us the tears and laughter, passions and purposes of those who first used them. I intend here a partial archaeology of this lost world of feeling and motive. I write for all those who can lay aside prejudices about this world and appreciate some of the people who made it.

In particular, I write for fellow students of religion in American history in order to contribute to a growing interest in the upstart populist religions of the National period. Within this growing community of professional scholars and educated nonexperts, there is a group interested especially in the evangelical and fundamentalist traditions in America. I court their attention by revealing some of the deeper roots of the current conservative Protestant strivings that Grant Wacker has aptly characterized as "searching for Norman Rockwell."[1]

I write also for students of domesticity and of gender in American history. Although I do not count myself as a full member of these networks of scholars, I have drawn gratefully on their work. I hope that my contribution to their efforts will be a deeper appreciation for the role of religious discourse in the cultural processes they seek to understand.

All my readers should know that I aim throughout the book more to comprehend than to criticize. This is a message especially for that category of readers with whom I share common cultural roots in Methodism. The next few paragraphs are especially for them.

I began this study as a quest for a usable past. I am neither a Methodist nor the son of a Methodist, but I am the child of an indigenous American Protestant sect and subculture founded upon, among other things, Methodist sensibilities.[2] With the founding and early growth of the new republic, says Sydney Mead, Americans espoused "the gospel of individualism."[3] The Methodist Age in American religious history began in the same period, and Methodism has been firmly associated with images of heroic individualism ever since. These images are not false, but they are oversimple. One of the several paradoxes that appear in this study is that these individualistic Methodists were also very communal. The usable past I sought to recover was a communal and socially reformist one that might counter what I believed, and still believe, to be the excessive individualism of our times. The largely sympathetic tone of this study stems in part from this initial quest for a usable past.

I have sustained such sympathy, however, out of a growing realization that the early Methodist community is more an *instructive* past than a usable one. It is instructive to see how the psychology I have labeled "the way of the cross" was used to forge a paradoxical synthesis of individualism and communalism. At its best, the way of the cross created strong individuals with great energy and initiative. It enabled them to live orderly and productive lives and to build strong communities and institutions. At its worst, this way created dependent people easily manipulated by authoritarian or demagogic leaders and a censorious community itching to find scapegoats both within and without. It is instructive also to contemplate the ambiguity and irony in this early American effort to bring self, community, and society into a synergy that would, as the Methodists put it, "reform the continent." At the end of the story I tell here, this effort had been both domesticated and bureaucratized, and this outcome was as much an unfolding of the inner logic of the community as it was a conformity to outer pressures.

My initial eager search for a usable past, then, has ended in what I hope is a more balanced appreciation for ambiguity, irony, and paradox. Some readers, identified perhaps with the broad Wesleyan tradition, will wish for a celebration of early Methodist piety and power as markers of a strong time to which we might wish to return. Other readers, many of them also Methodists or cultural heirs of Methodists, will wish for a critical treatment that reflects their own distaste for early Methodists' naivete, crudeness, and excesses. I will not fulfill either wish in this book. I will remain sympathetic to these followers of the way of the cross, but not because I would recommend them as models for contemporary living. Rather, I believe that those of us who are their cultural heirs must both acknowledge them and let go of them. I believe we will achieve this better by an analysis that is sympathetic than by a repugnance that is analytical.

In twenty years I have incurred more scholarly and professional debts than I can remember. I will remember those I can.

Jerald C. Brauer and Martin E. Marty held seminars on revivalism, forms of community, and other topics in American religion and thereby created the atmosphere where the ideas for this book received their first hearing. As counselors on scholarship and advisors on the writing of a dissertation, they were extremely generous in sharing not just their knowledge but also their enthusiasm and support for my project. Don. S. Browning was similarly enthusiastic and supportive. He was especially helpful in teaching me the virtues of clear conceptualization and organization in any scholarly project. All three have my thanks for their remarkable openness to the ideas and perspectives of disciplines not strictly their own. My gratitude extends beyond these three, furthermore, to the whole remarkable community of scholars in and around the University of Chicago Divinity School. Their combined openness and care nurtures a great deal of creative scholarship.

At Pacific Union College I have been fortunate to find good colleagues. I thank my colleagues in the Department of Behavioral Science for their openness to my wide-ranging interests in religion and history. Thanks are due also to several college administrators and to Terry Trivett, who have helped me find time and space for my research and writing. Eric Anderson deserves special mention for the support he has given this project. From the time it was merely an overlong and overdue dissertation through the times when it needed funding for its development and a hearing from other scholars and potential publishers, Eric has been its loyal aid and advocate. Ginger Hanks-Harwood read and commented on a part of the manuscript. Mary Jacobsen and Larry Davidson, two student research assistants, made my work one summer a special delight. Thanks are due to the Pacific Union College Research and Honors Committee for grants that paid Mary's and Larry's wages and for the indexing of this book.

The support of a Fellowship for College Teachers from the National Endowment for the Humanities gave me a year off to do research and writing that did much to make a dissertation into a book. The editorial criticism and counsel I have received more recently from Catherine Albanese and Stephen Stein have also contributed much to that makeover. I am especially grateful to Donald G. Mathews for plowing through the dissertation years ago and writing out both his enthusiasm for the ideas and his exasperation at the verbiage. Others who have read portions of my manuscript in various versions and given useful criticism or helpful support are Carolyn Deswarte Gifford, Jean Miller-Schmidt, Russell E. Richey, Richard D. Shiels, and Grant Wacker.

Of course none of these people are responsible for the remaining errors of fact and argument or infelicities of style and expression. For these I alone am responsible.

Among many librarians and archivists I have met, Kathleen Weibel of Ohio Wesleyan University merits high praise for her ability both to care for the treasures in the Archives of Ohio United Methodism and to allow me virtually unlimited access to these documents during my all-too-short stays in Delaware, Ohio. The staff at the United Library on the campus of Garrett Evangelical Seminary in Evanston, Illinois, have been very helpful over several years and many visits. Among them, special thanks go to Alva Caldwell and David Himrod. Kenneth Rowe and the staff at the Methodist Center at Drew University, Madison, New Jersey, have rendered valuable service and encouragement. Additional thanks are due to the staffs of the Tennessee State Library and Archives, the Upper Room Library, the Library of the Methodist Publishing House, the Library of the Baptist Commission on Archives and History, and the Heard Library of Vanderbilt University, all in Nashville, Tennessee. Thanks also go to the staffs of the Southern Historical Collection at the University of North Carolina at Chapel Hill; the Manuscripts Department at the Duke University Library in Durham, North Carolina; the Ohio Historical Society in Columbus, Ohio; the DePauw University Library in Greencastle, Indiana; the Indiana State Library and Archives in Indianapolis; the Illinois State Library and Archives in Springfield; the Library of the Southern Baptist Theological Seminary in Louisville, Kentucky; the Filson Club, also in Louisville; and the Huntington Library in San Marino, California.

It is conventional for married authors to thank their spouses for things like patience and emotional support. All the conventional thanks are entirely appropriate to give to my wife, Candace Lord-Schneider. As it happens, however, she deserves far greater thanks than these. From the time it was a dissertation, this project has benefited immensely from Candy's energy and skills as research assistant, proofreader, and prose critic. I am especially grateful for her willingness to trek around the country with me to a dozen and a half libraries and archives during two summers. Now that this book is done, I have begun to make good on a promise that we would take a few real vacations.

Deep thanks are due also to Luther and Margaret Lord, whose care for our sons made our joint research tours possible. To David and Darren I render my thanks and admiration for the tolerance they have shown us while we were away, for the aplomb with which they have handled our absences, and for the openness with which they have welcomed us back.

In the dedication of this book I am pleased to keep a promise I made some time ago to another set of family members, regretting only that the fathers did not live to see the fulfillment.

INTRODUCTION

The Rise of Methodism and Domesticity

Wilson Lee was one of the pioneer Methodist circuit riders in the Ohio valley region, which in the first half of the nineteenth century was called "the West." He was a solemn man, but sometimes his pastoral experiences were enough to unbalance even his gravity.

At one of his preaching appointments on a Kentucky circuit, he preached from the text "Except a man deny himself, and take up his cross, he cannot be my disciple."[1] With "melting voice and tearful eyes" he urged his unlettered congregation to take up the cross, whatever it might be for any one of them. Among his listeners were "a very wicked Dutchman and his wife." We are not told how they were wicked except that the wife was a notorious scold who kept her husband "always in a perfect fret so that he led a most miserable and uncomfortable life." Mr. Lee's message reached their hearts that day, however, and they saw their lost condition. Weeping aloud, they both resolved to take up the cross—whatever it was—and do better. The whole congregation was "deeply affected," and Mr. Lee exhorted them and prayed for them until the time drew near when he had to leave for another preaching appointment some distance away. He dismissed the congregation, got a little to eat and drink, saddled his horse, and rode on.

As he rode, he saw ahead of him a rather small man carrying a large and heavy woman. Supposing that the woman was a cripple or had hurt herself, he wondered how he might help. He was surprised to find that it was the Dutchman and his wife. What happened? he asked. You told us that we must take up the cross and follow the Savior, replied the heavily burdened man, or we could not be saved or go to heaven. "[A]nd dish woman is de createst cross I have in de whole world, and I does take her up and pare her, for I must save my soul."

After a few moments of perplexed reflection, Lee told the man to put his wife down. He dismounted and sat down with them on a log next to the road. He took out his Bible, read several texts, and expounded "the way of the Lord more perfectly." He discussed the nature of the cross of Christ and how it was to be taken up and borne. After he had taught and advised them for some time, he prayed with them, leaving them again "deeply affected," and rode on for his evening appointment.

His pastoral care worked well. The Dutchman and his scolding wife were converted long before Mr. Lee came around the circuit again. She was cured of her scolding; he was clear of his cross. "They lived together long and happily, adorning their profession, and giving ample evidence that religion could cure a scolding wife, and that God could and did convert poor ignorant Dutch people." Indeed, the Dutchman often "told his experience in love-feasts." He almost always melted the congregation into tears with his story, and once led virtually everyone to break out into a loud shout.[2]

This story, once the amusement passes, must surely pique our curiosity. What was all the melting, weeping, and shouting about? What sort of meeting was a love feast? How, once the preacher had ridden on, did the Dutch couple get converted? Most important, what was the cross Mr. Lee bade his people bear, and how did it lead to the domestic bliss implied in the story? The answers to these questions are the substance of this book.

Here at the beginning, however, some more general questions claim priority: Who were these Methodists, and why write a book about them? Why, furthermore, does this book about the Methodists focus also on domesticity?

The Methodists whose stories enliven these pages were spiritual children in America of English preacher, theologian, and religious founder, John Wesley. John Wesley was both spiritual and physical child of a scholarly Anglican rector named Samuel and a strong-minded lay theologian and domestic disciplinarian named Susanna. Susanna became legendary in the stories American Methodists told themselves about the power of mothers and homes to make men good, perhaps great, and thereby to save society. There is no doubt about the greatness of her son. In the religious currents of Atlantic culture in the eighteenth century, John Wesley stands out as the single most important progenitor of the Evangelical Revival. References to the English phase of the revival often bear his name—the Wesleyan Revival.

Some even claim that he saved English society. Almost a century ago, French historian Elie Halevy suggested that the Methodist movement helped spare England its own version of the convulsions of the French Revolution. He sparked a long and lively discussion about the social and political significance of Wesley's movement in England.[3] Because of the comparable success of Methodism in North America, it is plausible to expect that a similar discussion might have gone on here. It has not really happened, however. Students of American religion tended for a long time to talk mostly about the Puritans and their descendants when searching for the formative influences in American culture and society. Scholarly attention has been shifting away from this preoccupation, however, and this book represents part of that shift.

John Wesley absorbed many of his mother's habits of discipline and authority. Susanna Wesley's influence contributed to the methodical religious practice by which John and his followers sought to be holy. This piety earned them the name "Methodist," an epithet of derision that they later proudly adopted. And just as Susanna never let it be doubted who was in charge in her house, her son maintained an exclusive rule over his household of faith, letting the thousands of preachers in his movement know that they were never more than his "assistants" or "helpers." Such lawfulness and control might have been deadly had it not channeled great vitality and energy. John Wesley was an immensely energetic man, and he led an immensely energetic movement. It was a movement made up largely of common people who did not count for much in eyes of established authorities of the time. This humble constituency nevertheless produced many strong individuals who made their own unique marks upon Methodism and society. It is testimony to Wesley's genius that he fashioned a movement that so often successfully combined authoritarian control and populist vitality. Perhaps Susanna Wesley provided precedent for this also in her management of a household of ten lively children.

What seems certain is that John Wesley's genius for both nurturing and controlling religious vitality was epitomized in one of his social inventions: the *class meeting*. The class meeting was the basic unit of pastoral oversight and discipline and a vital center of fellowship within the local religious "societies" of the Methodist "connexion" in England and, later, of the Methodist Episcopal church in America. A class was supposed to consist of twelve members of the society, one of whom was chosen by the circuit preacher to be leader. Classes were to meet once a week. The leader would inquire of each member how he or she was keeping the rules of the Methodist society and how he or she was growing in inward spiritual experience. This scrutiny by and among peers could be uncomfortable, even terrifying. The anxieties were generally overridden, however, by the love and joy that members came to feel as they told the stories of their spiritual lives and discovered the liberty and life that came of speaking from heart to heart.

It is likely that the "poor ignorant Dutch" people discussed above had their religious ignorance as well as their contentiousness cured in their local class meeting. The love feasts they subsequently enjoyed were larger meetings, usually held quarterly, that were open to all members of the many classes on a circuit. During love feast, members ate bread and drank water as a symbol of their fellowship and then had opportunity to testify to the work of God in their hearts and lives. The rigors of inquiry and self-scrutiny appropriate to class meeting were relaxed, but the purpose of creating a community of feeling through the sharing of Christian experience was the same. In America, evangelical Protestants in general came to refer to a variety of similar meetings as "social meetings" or "social religion." Their usage will be followed in this book.[4]

The spiritual experience that Methodists shared in their social meetings was guided by Wesley's distinctive weaving of many strands of Christian theological heritage. With the Calvinists, for instance, he affirmed the absolute sovereignty of God and the utter need of humankind for God's grace and salvation. Against them he denied the doctrine of predestination and its corollaries. God's grace was free to all. It was given even before they turned to God so they might indeed have freedom to turn. It was not reserved to a special elect, nor was it irresistible. People could choose against God's grace, and even when they had chosen for it, they could fall away. People could feel and know, furthermore, the *assurance* of their salvation; they could have the *witness of the Spirit* that they were the children of God. They did not have to wonder if they were among the elect. With the Moravian Pietists he affirmed that faith was to be heartfelt and that it must be nurtured in fellowship. Against them he denied the quietist tendency to do no good work that was not motivated by pure faith in God. There were degrees of faith, and the love of God might be obtained in greater or lesser measure. Methodists must strive therefore to perfect the love of God in their souls; they must go on to *perfection* and be holy.

Wesley had practical purposes for weaving these and many other theological strands into his Methodist movement. He constructed a working theology for a movement that he hoped would be distinguished more by its practice of the love of God and humankind than by any formal creed. His theological learning was prodigious, but it was constantly informed by the experiences of the people he led and dedicated to their spiritual prosperity. In his theologizing as in his organizing, Wesley devoted his talents and authority to the interests of the people. It should be no surprise, then, that his people, empowered by his spiritual leadership, sometimes moved in advance of his actual control and administration. It was so with the beginnings of Methodism in America.

Lay people introduced Methodism to America in the 1760s. Although later Methodists debated strenuously whether New York or Maryland had the honor of the very first Methodist society, it seems clear that early American Methodism first flourished as a movement in the Chesapeake region, including portions of Maryland, Virginia, and the Delmarva Peninsula.[5] An unordained local preacher named Robert Strawbridge raised up the first Methodist societies in this region and recruited members who later distinguished themselves as pioneer preachers. He was one of the first of many "local preachers" who led the way in establishing Methodist societies that then accepted the leadership of the Methodist connectional system and were organized into classes and circuits. The strong-willed, Irish Strawbridge did not so readily fall into line with the system as did most subsequent lay leaders, but he evinced a pattern of lay initiative that vitalized the Methodist movement long afterward.

In the 1770s, Wesley sent several formally authorized emissaries to help organize the American wing of his movement. The most famous of these was Francis Asbury, who suffered through the upheaval of the War for Independence and stayed on to become, more than any other man, the father of American Methodism. At the famous "Christmas Conference" of 1784, Asbury met in Baltimore with about sixty of the eighty-one American Methodist preachers and, assisted by three other Englishmen sent by Wesley, organized the Methodist Episcopal church. This new organization became a vessel that both contained and spread a major portion of the remarkable spiritual effervescence that flowed from what is called the Second Great Awakening in America.

This Awakening marked the transition from the "Puritan Age" to the "Methodist Age" in American church history. There is a simple statistical reason for such a statement. In 1784, on the eve of the great revivals in Kentucky that began the Awakening, the Methodists were a small and insignificant sect. By 1850, when the Awakening's evangelical ethos had reached maturity, there were more Methodists in America than any other kind of Protestant.[6] There is also a more sophisticated reason for the statement. When historians speak of the nineteenth century as the Methodist Age in American religious history they refer to a popular religious style that characterized Methodists but was not limited to them. Indeed, this style of religion penetrated virtually all of Protestant church life and virtually every region in America. Its most prominent representative, Charles G. Finney, was a Presbyterian who took old Methodist revival techniques and promoted them as the "New Measures." Finney's Methodist-style revivalism set western New York spiritually aflame in the 1820s and later triumphed in great eastern cities like Boston, New York, and Philadelphia.

Most of the features of this popular religious style were represented in Wesley's theology and organizational style: an affirmation of human ability to seek and secure salvation, a stress on emotional religion of the heart, a belief in perfection, a practical concern with results. Especially important was the readiness to make revivals happen by the right use of the organizational means at hand.[7] Best known was the strong emotional sermon combined with a call to sinners to come forward to the "anxious bench," where they would sit in front of the congregation and be prayed for. Just as important, however, was the use of class meeting and love feast or their analogues to help generate strong religious feeling among the faithful and thus motivate them to work for souls. These social religious meetings were also used to engulf sinners in a tide of religious feeling that helped precipitate their conversions. Likewise, lay people, returning home, would turn traditional family worship into a similar time of social religion, catching up unconverted relatives in the contagion of their heartfelt gospel.

The Methodist style influenced American Protestantism just about everywhere. The Methodist Episcopal church, however, which was the numerically largest denominational expression of Methodism until the 1840s, attracted its greatest numbers in the West. Moving out from its cradle in the Chesapeake region, the infant church marched into the Ohio valley with the early waves of settlers in the 1780s. It kept pace with the great westward rush of migration better than almost any other denomination. Only the Baptists, with their independent farmer-preachers, matched the Methodist circuit riders and local preachers in meeting the religious needs of the frontier. The institutional precipitates of Methodism's great westward flow were still in evidence almost two hundred years later. On a 1970 map showing the dominance of various denominations on a county-by-county basis, Methodist counties marked a bold pattern from the eastern shore of Maryland through the Old Northwest to Iowa, Kansas, Nebraska, and eastern Colorado.[8] The analysis that follows will concentrate on the western Methodism that laid down this durable institutional pattern in the Ohio valley and the Old Northwest during the first half of the nineteenth century.

The first of our preliminary questions asked who the Methodists were who helped to transform the domestic life of the Dutch couple whose story opened this book. To sum up, these Methodists were American proponents of John Wesley's great revival, the pioneers of a popular religious style that dominated the nineteenth century, and the builders of the denomination that became the largest Protestant body in the country. Relatively little, furthermore, has been written very recently about the social and cultural impact of their movement in America. This answer should be sufficient justification for writing some sort of book about them. The other preliminary question still stands: Why write about domesticity?

The simplest answer is to observe that domesticity was a major preoccupation of the people and practices of Methodism. When the Methodist Episcopal church developed a popular press, for instance, their domestic preoccupations commanded much ink. Their weekly *Christian Advocates* in various cities included frequent parents', ladies', and children's departments and, beginning in 1841, they published American Protestantism's most successful monthly magazine for women, the Cincinnati *Ladies Repository and Gatherings of the West*. They added to these periodicals many tracts and manuals on family matters. Domestic sentiments saturated their pages.

"The family circle is of divine origin," read the preface to the *Methodist Family Manual*, "and is stamped with signal holiness and beauty." The three-fold cord of conjugal, parental, and filial affection holds the family together, while in it we also find "an epitome of all rule, authority and power." The hopes of earth and heaven are founded in the family's training of children. "The patriot, the statesman, the minister, and all other philanthropists" must therefore have an incalculable interest in the formation and government of families.[9] A young lady sounded a more tender note in her article entitled, simply, "Home." "Life's choicest blessings center all at home," she sighed. She declared that all who have had to leave home have found that the world may reject them, but the family circle opens joyously to receive them. Here they may safely pour out their story of grief to sympathetic ears.[10] The *Ladies Repository* made it clear that at the center of this sacred domestic haven was to be found a creature of unique holiness and spiritual power: Woman. Like the violet that sheds its mild fragrance only in the shade of its native wood,

So woman: born to dignify retreat
Unknown, to flourish; and, unseen be great;
To give domestic life its sweetest charm;
With softness polish, and with virtue warm;
Fearful of fame, unwilling to be known,
Should seek but Heaven's applause, and her own;
Should dread no blame, but that which crimes impart
The censures of a self-condemning heart.[11]

Such retiring modesty was the secret of her power. "In declining to mingle with the mob, or direct the popular assembly . . . woman acquires a sovereignty more absolute than that possessed by the conquering hero or the sceptered monarch."[12] How this could be true was part of the paradox of the way of the cross.

If domestic sentiments and images like these were only an idiosyncratic preoccupation of the Methodists, noting and analyzing them might be left as just a curious sidelight of denominational history. But the Methodist Age of American church history coincided with what might be called the "domestic era" in the history of white American middle-class popular culture. In the first half of the nineteenth century, especially after about 1830, images of the home that today are cliché came to be widely shared. The idea of the family as belonging to a private sphere of affection and moral discipline that was to be set over against a public sphere of competition and self-interest became widespread. This private sphere, moreover, was the proper sphere of Woman, while the worldly sphere belonged to Man. Domesticity became a form of religion with its own sacred symbols and cultus. Womanhood came to be defined as "naturally" religious.[13] According to Mary Ryan's prize-winning study of one local community, this domestic ideology was the principal way in which the emerging white middle class defined itself.[14]

It was no mere coincidence that Americans were caught up in the periodic revivals of the preeminently Methodist Second Great Awakening at about the same time that the ideology of domesticity was taking root in the culture of the American middle class. There is a connection to be made between the Awakening and the ideology. A vital part of that connection may be found, as Ryan observes, in the forms of voluntary association promoted by evangelical Protestants. In this study it is further argued that the essential element of connection is evident in class meeting and similar rituals of social religion by which the Methodists and other evangelicals propagated their revivals.

The central argument of this book, then, is that the forms of social religion in American Methodism laid the foundations in white people's experience for the adoption of an evangelical version of Victorian domestic ideology.

The metaphor of "foundations" avoids a potential distraction from the aim of explicating the domestic significance of Methodist religious practice. One might try to argue that the ideology of domesticity had its *origins* in Methodist evangelical religion. A set of ideas and images as widely diffused in a culture as Victorian domesticity came to be, however, is likely to have had many origins. Important scholarly efforts to locate these origins show no consensus. What this scholarship does show is that the ideals of privacy, individualism, and affection that were essential to Victorian domesticity were well established in segments of European societies before they became popular in America.[15] There will be no search in this book, therefore, for the origins of the domestic ideal. It is one thing to originate a particular set of images and ideals; it is another to persuade people to adopt those ideals as their own. Methodism changed people, persuaded them to view themselves, their society, and their families differently and to organize their experience in accord with these new views. The task of the argument is to describe *how* it changed people and then to show how these changes inclined people to adopt a domestic ideology.

To specify white people's experience in the formulation of the argument is to draw attention to an important limitation of this study: it does not purport to describe black religious experience, black visions of domestic life, or the relationship between them. American blacks were a part of the early Methodism that, for whites, helped to undermine older understandings of family life. But blacks transformed the evangelical vision of liberty according to their African heritage and their oppressed social position. It would seem, in fact, that the black churches finally embodied that vision and its meaning for American society more adequately than their white counterparts.[16] It is not clear, however, what nineteenth-century blacks made of the trends toward domestication and respectability that became part of later white Methodism and undergirded its evangelical domesticity. The question deserves examination, but the evidence and argument presented here cannot illuminate it save as elements of background for comparison and contrast. This study raises the question of the relation between evangelical religion and domesticity. Only a different study supported by long immersion in different sources can answer the question for the black Christians in America.

We have considered who the American Methodists were and why a book about them might also appropriately be about domesticity. It seems wise to consider one more preliminary matter before proceeding to the substance of the book. This is the question of what sort of book this is and how it ought therefore to be read. The first step in answering this question is to say what the book is not. It is not history if by history is meant the conventional form of telling a story that traces, one after another, the course of human events. Some degree of historical storytelling is necessary, of course. The above account of who the Methodists were shows as much.

Further accounts of the course of events will be necessary at various points below. Even the overall argument has a certain narrative structure to it, as the roughly chronological order of the chapters suggests. The title of the book encapsulates the narrative: *The Way of the Cross Leads Home*. The fact remains that this book is primarily a work of analysis, an analysis that attempts to connect the inner life of an important religious group to an important aspect of American culture. The appropriate sort of reading for such a book asks at each new chapter not "Then what happened?" but, rather, "What is the next step in the argument?" An overview of the argument will allow the reader to follow its steps as they appear through the following chapters.

The argument may be broken down into three main phases. First comes a stage-setting phase that makes clear the views of self and society that people held prior to Methodism's rise in influence and advances some explanations of why many were ready to change their views. The second phase describes and analyzes the religious experiences and the methods of promoting them that characterized Methodism and by which Methodists identified themselves. The third phase shows how the domestic ideology that Methodists eventually adopted and promoted was a logical extension of Methodist identity and practice.

Phase one of the argument begins with the understanding that any idea of change implies a set of conditions that existed prior to the change. The idea that Methodist social religion facilitated a change to middle-class domesticity implies that people held other views of self, society, and family prior to the change. Following current scholarship in early American history, I call the culture that fostered these earlier views "the culture of honor." This culture characterized the Chesapeake region in the last half of the eighteenth century and persisted among many Americans even as they pulled up roots and moved West. Chapter one introduces the culture of honor. Throughout the book this account of the culture of honor will be a foil against which the concerns of Methodist evangelical culture will be more sharply revealed.

Four elements of contrast and continuity emerge from this discussion of the culture of honor. The first is that this culture tended to define the family primarily in terms of patriarchal sovereignty rather than in terms of mutual affection. The second is that the family was experienced and understood as one point, albeit a fundamental one, in a single sphere of social life. The various institutions of society were not sharply differentiated from one another. Of particular interest for this study is the fact that domestic life was not yet sharply defined as the private sphere set apart from the public sphere. The third is that judgments of personal worth were made primarily on the basis of external appearance and physical or verbal performance in relatively small face-to-face settings. Norms of privacy were not well developed, nor was solitude generally sought or respected. Control of behavior was based more on awareness of community judgments and avoidance of shame rather than on internalized conscience and fear of guilt. These three elements represent important points of contrast between the culture of honor and the culture that Methodist evangelicals helped construct.

The fourth element, however, was a point of continuity, albeit with an important change in significance. This fourth element consisted in a cultural configuration deeply lodged in the minds and hearts of the Anglo-Americans to whom the Methodists addressed their religious message. It was an image of a sacred feminine space to be protected from encroaching, polluting forces. As a man considered his estate, on which he founded his very self, he felt the most precious and most vulnerable part of it to be this secluded space that was identified first with wife and children, then with hearth and home, then with community and nation. The man of honor had to be a hardened warrior ready to give up his life in defense of this soft, life-giving inner sanctum. The Methodist rituals of social religion, in their separation from the world and their familial patterns of communion, echoed this image. They endued it with new meaning, however, when they generated a spiritual energy that seemed to turn the tables on the encroaching world, overcoming it and spreading holiness throughout the land.

With the beginnings of these points of contrast and continuity established, phase one of the argument continues with the understanding that the idea of change also implies a set of events or situations that dispose people to let go of their prior way of life. Something led people to be dissatisfied with the culture of honor and with the perceptions of themselves, their society, and their families that it fostered. Chapters two and three focus on the social and ideological upheavals of the American Revolution and of the great migrations West as explanations for why some people became less attached to the culture of honor and ready to adopt different views and practices. The reader who is eager to know the Methodists better is urged to be patient with these early stage-setting chapters. The knowledge of the Methodists that is relevant to the book's argument requires an awareness of the cultural situations they attempted to encompass with their religious strategies.

Phase two of the argument, however, turns directly to the Methodists themselves and to an analysis of their religious experience and ritual practice. The overall point is to show how Methodism changed people. Chapter four begins with the religious experience Methodism promoted among whites and the worldview and way of life that such experience implied. This discussion lifts up the "way of the cross" as a pattern of perception, thought, and feeling in which believers mortified their passions and weaned their affections away from Earth in order to attach them to Heaven. Such mortification came from within. It was an internalizing of control that had powerful rewards for those who adopted it. Just as the crucifixion of

Christ resulted in resurrection and new life, these constant little crucifixions of earthly human nature issued in peace, joy, vitality, and intense moral striving.

After analyzing the experience Methodism promoted, the argument turns next to analysis of the methods by which they promoted it. Chapter five describes the ways in which Methodists recruited people to their cause, focusing on the meanings that the itinerant ministry embodied and on the family-centered methods of recruitment that the itinerants employed. Chapters six, seven, and eight take up the main rituals of social religion that were Methodist distinctives—class meeting and love feast—and analyze the processes by which they transformed people into followers of the way of the cross.

The theme that runs throughout the second phase of the argument is Methodism's subversion of traditional honor and patriarchal sovereignty and its promotion of a moral individualism that required a new community founded upon mutual affection and located in a sphere separate from the world. The Methodist itinerancy, the methods of recruitment that the itinerants employed, and the ritual practices they fostered all aimed to transform people's sense of who they were. Identity may be rendered in terms of a metaphor of place and in terms of a metaphor of story. Class meeting and love feast taught believers that their place in the universe was ultimately within the sacred space that was separate from a threatening outside world, but that also had power to overcome that world. Within that space believers learned to tell their stories, which were all variants of a single story. That story was of the way of the cross, a story of the dying life that led not only to the repose and security of the secluded space but to the evangelistic zeal that propelled them into the world again in order to reform the nation and spread holiness. Discipline, separation, and boundary setting combined with testimony and intense communion to create a sort of fusion reactor of the spirit. The resulting reactions generated remarkable religious, psychological, and social energies.

Phase three of the argument shows how these energies transformed thinking and feeling about family life. This phase is founded on the understanding that Methodists tended to transfer their religious ways of organizing experience to other important regions of their lives. Since, for instance, believers addressed one another as sisters and brothers, mothers and fathers in the gospel, and since they spoke of their class meetings as being like families, it was easy for them to develop the expectation that literal family life should resemble relationships within the family of God. Chapter nine builds the case for this influence of the metaphorical family of God upon the literal families of believers. Again, Methodist believers came to expect that traditional household rituals should take on the character of their religious rituals. Chapter ten describes how, under the superintendence and prodding of preachers and lay pastors, the traditional rituals of family worship and the deathbed came to reflect the patterns of separation, testimony, and communion that characterized Methodist social religion.

Phase three continues by showing how the popular Methodist domestic literature that burgeoned in the 1830s and 1840s incorporated the two basic patterns by which Methodists identified themselves. Those patterns, to repeat, were the narrative pattern of the way of the cross and the spatial pattern of a sacred space separate from, but overcoming, the world. Chapter eleven analyzes Methodist domesticity and shows how it may be seen as part of a general trend toward consolidation that began to characterize American culture generally at the time. The once subversive way of the cross was domesticated and made to refer primarily to conduct in the private sphere of life. The secluded-but-transformative religious community was identified increasingly with the home circle. The domestic ideology in general was contained within a conservative evangelical version of the republican ideology that had guided the founding of the American nation. According to this conservative Christian republicanism, the self-abnegating virtue that a people needed in order to govern themselves in a republic was safeguarded by the evangelical churches. The Christian home circle with the pious wife and mother at its center was the special agency through which evangelical religion would insure the virtue of husbands and of the rising generation, thus securing the republic. The practice of the way of the cross at home would chasten the naturally indulgent affections of family members and infuse them with sterner moral fiber.

Chapter twelve considers what men made of the domesticated way of the cross for women and what women made of it for themselves. The vision of woman propagated mostly by men elevated the passive, often victimized, but still virtuous wife and mother. This woman, an icon of the suffering Savior, would inspire active self-discipline and moral striving in her husband and sons. Women's piety could not be contained within this consolidating ideology and its passive iconic role for women, however. The way of the cross required the passion of self-sacrifice, yes, but it also demanded strong individual moral agency. As successive generations of women grew up in the disciplines and piety of Methodism, they sought more and more to find their own callings and create their own opportunities for moral achievement. At the end of this chapter, we move a generation or two beyond the main temporal and topical limits of the book to describe examples of women who followed the way of the cross as it turned back on itself and led them away from home into a world that cried out for reform. The way of the cross could leave home as well as lead there.

The argument ends with a return to the class meeting and an explanation for its decline in the middle decades of the nineteenth century. The reasons reflect the story encapsulated in the book's title: *The Way of the Cross Leads Home*. Methodists learned the way of the cross in class meeting, and they learned that this way led to a home that was ordered according to patterns similar to class meeting. Once home was ordered along these lines, they found that it was a more appropriate agency than class meeting for inculcating the moral individualism and self-control that were the outcome of Methodist discipline and piety. The work of self-knowledge and self-control could be carried further and accomplished with greater subtlety in the domestic crucible—if the domesticated believers would indeed continue to pursue the way of the cross in private. Ultimately the home took priority over the church as the main agency for the salvation of souls. The church became a nascent bureaucracy made up of specialized agencies and programs designed for denominational self-propagation and for the melioration of societal ills.

The bureaucratization of the church elicited a countermovement in the middle and late nineteenth century. This movement elevated the old Wesleyan doctrine of holiness as a means of restoring vital godliness to the church. Its meetings for holiness echoed the old class-meeting and lovefeastthemesin a new key. That, however, is a different story for a different time.

The Way of the Cross Leads Home

1

Patriarchy and the Culture of Honor

American Methodism began as a religion of the Upper South and then moved west with the Southerners. Some further observations may give weight to this assertion. During its first forty years, 1784 to 1824, the Methodist Episcopal church always held its general conferences in Baltimore, except for one meeting in New York. Most of its circuit riders, local preachers, and presiding elders during this time were of southern background. Its membership was concentrated where its organization and leadership were. As he rode around the nation keeping watch over his wandering flock, Bishop Francis Asbury came to refer to parts of Ohio in the early 1800s as "New Virginia." When the Western Conference drew together circuits in Ohio, Kentucky, and Tennessee in 1804, two thirds of the circuit riders for which there are records of origin had come from southern states. It is important to note that much of the southern population that this conference was to superintend settled in states that later would be counted as northern: Ohio, Indiana, and Illinois. The divisions of the Civil War should not be read back onto these earlier patterns of migration and settlement. The people whom the Methodist itinerants followed and served in these states of the Old Northwest were mostly Southerners in origin and in culture.[1] Certain elements of their southern culture, moreover, survived a long time. Domestic outlooks of women and men of the Midwest in the 1850s, for instance, overlapped significantly with those of the culture of honor.[2]

It is unwise to overemphasize Methodism's southern accent, however, lest the reader wonder how this religion could have prospered in New England, in the middle states, and among the many non-Southerners who also migrated west. The patriarchal social order and the hierarchical worldview discussed below were only variants of norms and values that persisted throughout the early republic. New England patriarchs, for instance, might have been less impulsive or sensual, more pious, and more communally minded than the southern gentry, but they were patriarchs just the same. Their authority and outlook were subject to erosions similar to those suffered by the Southerners. The communities they led were also susceptible to Methodist subversion. That Methodism did not flourish so abundantly in their territory is probably testimony to the New Englanders' ability to co-opt the Methodist populist impulse rather than evidence that their social situations were radically different from those of the South. Methodism, imported from England and shaped in the Upper South, devised some powerful strategies for encompassing the human situation, powerful enough to touch and transform lives throughout the new American nation.[3]

This study, however, is about Methodism at the center of its strength. An overview of southern patterns of family and community is an essential first step in understanding that strength. This chapter therefore has two purposes. The first is to establish a beginning point from which to trace a process of change from a hierarchical to an egalitarian ethos. This change was in progress throughout the American colonies before Methodism arrived and continued everywhere at an accelerated pace through the Revolution and into the National period. Subsequent chapters will show how, in one sense, Methodism was simply engulfed in the process, while in another sense, it augmented the change. The second purpose of this chapter is to provide the appropriate background with which to compare and contrast the early American Methodist community. The Methodist spiritual family reflected this background and defined itself in opposition to it. A clear understanding of both the nature of early American Methodism and of its contributions to change in the early republic depends upon a grasp of its original southern background.

The social order of the South in the eighteenth century oscillated between two different principles: patriarchy and the market. Pure patriarchy counts as wealth the particular personal ties that obligate dependents to show submission, render service, and supply needs. By contrast, market relations based on money imply an impersonal scale of value that transcends particular personal ties. The gentry patriarch stood at the center of webs of dependents—slaves, bond servants, children, wife—who were tied to him not by impersonal wage-for-labor contract but by the conditions of living under his "roof" and partaking of his "Meat, Drink, or Wages." On this condition they owed him deference and service. To strike him down was not mere murder but petit treason. As God was Father, so the king was Father, so the head of the household was Father. The highest level of cosmology incorporated the everyday experiences of dependence and deference and sanctified the authority of the planter patriarch. These were archaic ideas and patterns, very foreign to the modern individualistic society and capitalistic economy that were America's near future. Nevertheless these patriarchs did seek wealth more through the sale of cash crops than through the propagation of networks of dependence and patronage. Furthermore, when it served their interests, they could convert headrights, land ownership, and the labor of bond servants into money through sale. The impersonal market was changing the meaning of the land and labor the patriarchs controlled.[4]

The opposing principles of patriarchy and the market, held in tension, produced a general order that still based authority on traditional criteria like family lineage, but that developed a broad sphere of powers exercised on the basis of personal judgment and interest.[5] The social geography of Virginia evinced the gentry's exercise of this authority through their roles as justices of the county courts. They governed the layout and maintenance of the roads and bridges; the siting of warehouses, ferries, courthouses, and churches; the licensing of taverns and mills; and the appointment of tobacco inspectors whose judgments could turn a farmer's crop into cash or trash. A map of the roads in a given neighborhood could be read as a diagram of the needs and power of the leading planters.[6]

The patriarchal household in this context was as much a political and economic unit as a familial one. Participation in the southern political order depended upon land ownership: only freeholders could vote. This stipulation was only the legal means of identifying and recognizing those men who had "permanent common interest with, and attachment to, the community."[7] Their essential characteristic was their status as heads of families, but families in a sense quite different from the twentieth-century notion of parents and children living, but not working, under a single roof. Americans of the eighteenth and early nineteenth centuries still understood their families as estates: all those dependent on the productivity and order of the farm, plantation, or business as an economic and social unit. Each responsible freeholder headed a hierarchy of his own and enjoyed the privileges and responsibilities of the paternal position. The early Americans, then, conceived of the social and political order as made up of family units, each under the paternal authority of one man.[8]

Some patriarchs, of course, were more patriarchal than others. The gentry, by force of custom, mutual support, and established law, were "fathers" of their communities who established their county courts as self-perpetuating bodies largely independent of control by either provincial government or the common ranks of freeholders. They determined either directly or indirectly the persons to occupy all local offices whether political, spiritual, or military. Through the county court itself they dominated local legislative, executive, and judicial functions. Finally, with the elective consent of the freeholders, whose votes they had ample means of influencing, they spoke for their county "family" in the affairs of the entire colony or state.[9]

The evangelical sects did not directly contest this political and economic dominance. Instead they opposed the style of life, the manners and morals, and, implicitly, the worldview whereby the gentry legitimated their dominance. From the time of the First Great Awakening, New Side Presbyterians, Baptists, and Methodists waged a battle against the self-indulgent, self-assertive lifestyle of southern planter society. This lifestyle was evident in a network of cultural performances, a ritual economy of court days, elections, militia musters, horse races, dances, and the like, in which the people acted out their values, purposes, and self-understandings and, in so doing, induced one another to identify with those values and understandings. Indeed, the very nature of southern community at the end of the eighteenth century was defined and dramatized in these events.

At the most general, philosophical level, the colonial Southerners, like many other colonists, understood the cosmos to be a vast continuous hierarchy of parts, each with its own degree of honor. In terms of the nature depicted in this vision, fathers were by nature of greater honor than children, men were by nature of greater honor than women, whites of greater honor than blacks, and gentry of greater honor than common planters.[10] This genteel philosophical vision, however, overlaid and elaborated a more archaic vision of the world and human relations. A fundamental attitude of pessimism lay beneath these patterns: the world was insecure, subject to whims of fortune and fate largely beyond human control. The prevalence of sudden death from pestilence or war, the unreliability of fellow humans, and the ephemeral nature of prosperity and human achievement all led to an attitude of stoicism and an attachment to the familiar, the tried and true.[11]

Basic conditions of belonging in the community of honor included having a white skin and being a legitimate father; a white man with a family could be at least minimally trusted to protect the welfare of the community in which his children would pursue their fortunes. Women and children by law and custom were virtual possessions of the head of the household. Tied to the possession of a family was ownership of property. Selfhood, family identity, moral position, and, as freehold voting requirements made clear, legal recognition were all tied to one's land and estate. Once such basic conditions were established, a man must, when circumstances demanded, demonstrate his honor in personal bravery, especially in defense of family and community. He showed his capacity and potential for such bravery in his physical appearance, ferocity of will, and prowess in skills akin to combat. It follows that personal identity and self-worth depended upon how one appeared to others, on the opinion of the community. The honorable man sought fame and avoided shame. This last psychological pattern of honor is one of its most obvious contrasts with the evangelical ethos; the pious man sought righteousness more than fame and feared guilt more than shame.[12]

The world the gentry made in the mid-eighteenth-century Upper South combined both the genteel and the more archaic elements of honor in periodic events that constituted southern community. Community in the South occurred in and through events. Where New Englanders defined their community spatially in towns built around church and commons, and peoples of the middle colonies organized themselves into a pluralistic mosaic of affinity-group neighborhoods, the Southerners defined and dramatized their community by events like weekly worship at the parish church and monthly meetings of the county court.[13] The gentry owned their own pews at the front of the church, and they exhibited their superiority of property and social standing as they entered in a group just before services began, walking past the common sorts in regal self-assurance. In one church, space was so limited that only the greatest families could sit all together. "Lesser gentlemen represented the honor of their houses in single places, while their wives were seated further back."[14] Recitation of liturgy from the Book of Common Prayer and the rank-ordering of seated personages constituted a powerful representation whereby the people might discern and internalize the divine hierarchical ordering of their lives. However, the meaning of such worship also derived from what happened before and after church. Sundays were not Puritan Sabbaths. They were times for a variety of diversions for all ranks of society. Church itself was a place for gentlemen and their ladies to show off their clothes, discuss tobacco prices, debate the relative lineages and qualities of their favorite horses, and invite one another home to dine. Worldly worship forged an identification of church and world. Residing at the top of the community hierarchy, the gentry embodied the spirit of the community, and in their public acts at church they identified themselves and their world with the spiritual realm.[15]

Gentlemen demonstrated their honor at the county court as well. At the courthouse they sat, wigged and finely dressed, on a raised bench, hearing the swearing of solemn oaths and settling disputes over land and money, the very means of livelihood. In their dignity and superior legal knowledge they seemed the very embodiment of the law, and they brooked no sustained challenge to their prestige or authority.[16] Out on the courthouse green, events occurred that might soften but not diminish this dignity. Some peers of the current justices, likely men who had served on the bench themselves, might be treating freeholders of all ranks to a barbecue and rum punch. Even more likely would be a horserace or cockfight in which the gentry took leading roles as owners of the best animals, placers of the largest bets, and general promoters of the contests. Their reputations were enough to attract sufficient participants to make the events absorbing pastimes. In the nearby "ordinary" or tavern, the planters would play rough games of dice, billiards, or cards where extravagant bets would be matched by extravagant banter that sometimes led to blows.[17]

Horseraces, cockfights, gambling, drinking bouts, verbal banter, and occasional duels were not, save for the duels, the sole province of the gentry. The common planters engaged in such contests too, as time and fortune allowed them. Their version of the duel, however, was the rough-and-tumble fight where even eyes might be gouged and genitals dismembered. All these rituals of contest were tests of the wealth, skill, stamina, and basic manliness of those who took part. In a world where there was always some threat to community and family (if not from the Indians, the French, or the British, then from the blacks they held in bondage), these men required proof of manliness from one another. Constant vying for honor cultivated toughness and steeled the nerves of potential warriors. Contests in peacetime were moral equivalents of war; men who had tested one another here could trust one another as brothers in time of battle. The event in a southern community that most clearly communicated this basic brotherhood of potential warriors was the militia muster. Even here the local gentry were the chosen commanders and trained the common ranks in discipline and deference. After drill, however, they provided the rum that helped bind high and low alike into a martial brotherhood.[18]

In the context of patriarchy, the sort of competitive display in which the gentry engaged had a rhetorical quality. In striving to acquire, maintain, and display their fine clothes, elegant houses, fast horses, and copious flow of gambling money, the top ranking southerners were imitating one another. Competition in general can be seen as an effort to "out-imitate" one another. This sort of activity stimulated a conformity of ways and cohesiveness of sentiment. Although the common ranks were excluded from the higher levels of competition, their witnessing of the elite performances invited them to partake of the masculine self-assertive principle of the patrimonial hierarchy. These contest pastimes had a persuasive function, then, because the gentlemen most convincingly embodied this principle, and the lower ranks gave assent to their continuing subordination through their presence and interest in the proceedings. If the implicit rhetoric of competitive display were translated into explicit appeal, it might read "Watch and imitate us as we out-imitate one another," and then, reflecting on the community thus established, "Now, see how we are all made of the same substance; though some of us are more substantial than others."[19]

However, the sense of inclusion that lower and middling ranks of men felt came not just from imitation but from moments of mutuality that all communities must provide if they are to sustain the selfhood of their members. The ritual center of this mutuality was the viva voce voting in Burgess elections at the county courthouse. There the freeholders walked up one by one and faced the sheriff, several of the justices of the peace, and the candidates, all of whom were among the most distinguished of the local gentry. The sheriff called out the name of the voter and inquired for whom he voted. The voter then looked over the faces of the candidates and announced, "I vote for Mr. Byrd and Mr. Jarratt." Whereupon the favored candidates replied, perhaps while standing and bowing, "Thank-you sir!" or more elaborately, "Mr. Smith, I shall treasure that vote in my memory. It will be regarded as a feather in my cap forever." If the general bustle of court day festivities drew the freeholder into the texture of community life, this center-stage moment allowed him to feel himself a special part of that life.[20]

The election ritual was a culminating moment in a rhythm of patronage and deference, of favors given and favors returned, that characterized this largely face-to-face society. As vestrymen of the parish churches, the gentry could make life easier or harder for hard-pressed families by providing poor relief. They could lend money to strapped farmers. In addition to forging such economic dependencies, they provided somewhat more subtle inducements to loyalty and friendship. The gentry knew their neighbors of all ranks and called them by name; at home and at community gathering places, they were fond of company and strove to be masters of sociability. Treating at the muster ground, on the courthouse green, or at entertainments given at home might be combined with warm greetings and offers of hospitality while traveling. All these moments of sociability helped the rich and powerful establish an "interest" among freeholders of all levels in their neighborhoods. A man's friends were his interest, and friendship in this context meant an expectation of mutual services or favors.[21]

It may be difficult for modern sensibility to comprehend these sorts of ties as either friendship or as mutuality. Mutual recognition by face and by name fulfills a basic psychosocial need, however, and this element of ritual lay at the heart of these exchanges. Such exchanges undergirded a vital sense of selfhood by communicating both a sense of inclusion and a sense of specialness. The confrontation of gentry with their inferiors in personal, face-to-face sociability provided nurturing mutuality even across the social distance enforced by the norms of hierarchy. Indeed, it is probably a mistake to imagine such distance as necessarily a hindrance to enlivening social ties. A sense of belonging and distinctiveness may be imparted by an idealized presence whom one may "look up to."[22] The gentry fathers, in their social, economic, and political elevation engaged in a rhetoric of uplift that communicated a sense of the rightness, even goodness, of their elevation. Their rhetoric communicated the conception of a hierarchical cosmos in a ritual interplay that enlivened the participants and made them feel like themselves.

However, a basic tension did exist within the organizing metaphor of patriarchal honor. On one hand, the community was made up of a brotherhood of all those who could make the claim to basic free manhood; on the other hand, the community was founded on an essential distinction between men of rank and men of common circumstances. Fraternity versus patriarchy yielded contradictory imperatives: every man was supposed to seek place and position for himself and his family and, at the same time, defer to those of superior rank. This tension, like that between patriarchy and money, helped define the direction of social and cultural change as the eighteenth century gave way to the nineteenth.[23] Methodism would be among the forces that would exploit these tensions and help subvert traditional patriarchy in the first decades of the new American nation.

The place of women in the man's world of the Upper South, was at least as plagued by paradox as that assigned to the deferential yet self-assertive man. Men of honor understood themselves to be assertive and bellicose not simply for themselves but for their families, especially their women. A sexual configuration even more powerful than the image of hierarchical cosmos informed their imaginations. They pictured a moral world constructed of an interior space that was soft and vulnerable surrounded by an exterior boundary that had to be hard and strong in order to protect the vulnerable interior from the encroachments of a threatening world. Women belonged to the soft vulnerable interior space and were charged with the duty of sanctifying it and making it receptive. Men belonged in the world and were charged with the duty of protecting the inner sanctuary where their women abode. Helpless women and children at the hearthside were the sacred realities for which men might gird up their loins in self-sacrificing martial virtue, ready to fight to the death whatever foe threatened them. To threaten a man's wife, or mother, or sister, or child, or home was to threaten his very self, the most vulnerable part of that self. Nothing could evoke greater fury. Paradoxically, women were also expected to stir their husbands and sons up to warrior virtues, to demand that they fight and die honorably. In this complex configuration of sentiment was founded the southern tradition of both the worship and the weakness of woman.[24]

The woman's subordinate role functioned as a reflector to highlight the man's dominance, his possession of the traits and properties most valued in their culture. Men were hard and strong, women soft and delicate. Men had a commanding public presence, women a becoming modesty. Even minor matters of dress could symbolize these polarities: when women rode out from their homes, they covered their faces with kerchiefs to protect their delicate complexions; men went forth bold-faced. But this minor incident of clothing symbolized more than the dominance of male over female. It also symbolized the moral order by which men and women understood their natures to be different, yet indissolubly linked.[25]

In general, women were not to frequent the courthouses, ordinaries, and muster fields where men proved themselves to be men. There was one arena of competitive display, however, where women, especially those of marriageable age, might be allowed a brief place in the sun: the hospitable celebrations that happened at home. A man's plantation and house were extensions of his very self, a public self that had little sense of home as a private domestic circle. Southern planters liked to live their lives in the presence of servants and guests. In offering hospitality to travelers and neighbors, they found yet another outlet for convivial self-assertion. The genteel households entertained guests in refined rituals of dining and toasting and in "sitting" together for conversation. The common planters' houses did not have the specialized spaces for such refined entertaining and little is known of their patterns of hospitality. For them, a move to a new house, a homecoming, a christening, wedding, or funeral were occasions for opening the plantation to neighbors and other guests for merrymaking. The wealthy did not require such momentous occasions for their balls; mere inclination might suffice.

The center of these celebrations was the dance. The gentry had ballrooms and hired dancing masters to train their children. The commoners must have danced more rustic steps. In either case, the opportunity to strut and show off seems to have appealed greatly to these Southerners' competitive passions. Performances on the floor were closely watched and informally judged by onlookers. Nor were the stakes necessarily lower here than at horse races where large sums of money were wagered. Dances provided one of the few occasions where young men and women were visible to each other. The atmosphere was generally heavy with courtship, and the proving of prowess in the dance might lead to a fortunate match. In the case of the well-to-do planters, this could mean the acquiring or securing of a literal fortune. These play times of the planters could be very serious affairs indeed.[26]

The everyday life of women was less exciting. They lived in a world rigidly segregated by sex. By the age of six or seven, girls were segregated with their mothers, female relatives, and, in the case of wealthier families, servants, while fathers took their sons off to work by their sides and learn the ways of men. Young girls also learned their work and their roles by observation and participation at their mothers' sides. Together they discharged the domestic tasks of food growing and preparation, spinning, sewing, cleaning, child rearing, and childbearing. With the exception of some wealthier planters, girls' parents seldom saw formal education as necessary, and even then they sought for their daughters only elementary skills in reading, writing, and math followed by training in the softer, feminine skills of drawing, dancing, and needlework. A father took charge of his daughter's education and emphasized the learning of grace, charm, and an agreeable disposition that would attract genteel suitors.[27]

Segregation created a special feminine social world of close and relatively egalitarian friendship focused on the mother-daughter tie and extending to other female kin and some non-kin friends. Father-son ties, burdened with concerns to maintain patriarchal power and the honor of family lineage, tended to be more distant, didactic, and condescending.[28] Women maintained a network of friendship through visiting. Often while the man of the house was away at county court, the woman would be off at a sister's or mother's house for an extended visit. Crisis occasions like childbirth, illness, or death would also bring women together. Women had their own social world with its own norms of sociability, a world that often allowed for considerably more intimacy and affection than male social life afforded.[29]

This female world of friendship was the major compensation for the monotony, boredom, loneliness, and lethargy of women's life and work on southern plantations and farms. Men were frequently away from home. Even when they were not, the segregation of the sexes and the polar definitions of sex roles made relaxed, informal contact between the sexes difficult. Women's work was probably not harder or more fatiguing than men's, but it was certainly less varied and more all-consuming. It left women little time to themselves and mired them in a daily and weekly cycle of drudgery with some seasonal variations. Their men did little to lighten the burden of their role; men knew little of what women did and placed less value on it. Women themselves spoke of their world in self-denigrating terms: "my narrow sphere"; "my humble duties"; "my little Domestick affairs." The society gave little recognition to women's contributions to the public good. Being a housewife was an end in itself, and a rather unimportant one that provided little support for feminine self-esteem. The best a woman could hope for was to be "notable," a commonly used term that meant having a reputation for managing the day-to-day affairs of her husband's household with such frugality and industry that she might save and even augment his earnings and thus promote his interests in the world.[30]

The Revolutionary experience changed some basic understandings of life and social order in the South. In particular, the hierarchical cosmos would lose much of its power over American imaginations. Women's place in the social order would not really change, but the meaning assigned to it would. The configuration of an inner softness protected by outer hardness would retain, perhaps redouble, its power, but with a changed meaning in both political and religious imagination.

2

Republicanism and Reform

Methodism's spiritual battle with the culture of honor was joined before the first shots of the Revolutionary War were fired. In fact, the shooting war itself was a setback for Methodism because of its ties to the Church of England and because John Wesley was not only a Tory but a Tory who published his unsympathetic views of the American struggle. Englishman Francis Asbury had to remain in hiding for much of the war. Some American Methodist preachers were persecuted for their pacifism. American independence, however, and the constitutional settlements that followed it set the Methodists at liberty to pursue what their first bishops declared was God's design for them: "to reform the continent and spread scripture holiness over these lands."[1]

The republican ideologies that legitimated and motivated the war may have contributed to temporary hard times for the Methodists, but, in the long run, republicanism helped them by undermining the authority of their detractors, whether they were Anglican gentry or Calvinist clergy. The patriarchal principle as a basis for integrating society had been widely shared from the North to the South. Republicanism and revolution sounded its death knell, though for many it lived on as a basis for defining the family. Southern gentry may have retained much of their prominence, but they could no longer command deference as the fathers of their communities. Reformed clergy of the middle and southern states, along with their New England counterparts, attempted to reclothe their customary patriarchal authority in republican garb but generally failed in their attempt to impose virtue from the top down. Meanwhile, other republican discussions were suggesting new roles for women and for the churches in the new nation. Methodists at the end of the eighteenth century cheerfully took advantage of the weakened condition of traditional authorities in order to promote their own community and cultural vision. Not until two or three decades into the nineteenth century, however, did they appropriate the themes of republicanism and begin to articulate their own vision of the roles of women and religion in the nation.

In the earliest years of the American nation, the Methodist orientation was not to the new polity so much as it was to the geographic entity of the continent and to the communities that were springing up all over it. The liberty they celebrated was more spiritual than temporal. But as they acted out this liberty in the events of their worship, they powerfully conveyed their vision of how the continent and its various communities were to be reformed. As they established their strongholds in the Upper South and Midwest, their message clashed with the libertarian republicanism widely shared by the planters and yeomen of this region. Many Southerners still cherished ideals of life, liberty, and the pursuit of happiness that were more in harmony with the culture of honor than with the emerging evangelical culture. The Methodists, however, were at war with the world, the flesh, and the Devil and would not rest until Zion triumphed.

This triumph was a catalyst of change, according to our argument, to a vision of family as a domestic circle of affection rather than an estate under the rule of patriarchal sovereignty. The undermining of patriarchal authority and the ascendancy of republican themes were important steps in the process of change. The discussions of this chapter describe these steps and portray Methodism's relationship to them. Occasionally, discussion ranges beyond the main southern focus of this study because the ideological currents in question were pervasive and significant throughout the nation. Another reason is that the proponents of a religious community and theological tradition to which it is useful to contrast Methodism, the Reformed, had their institutional center of gravity further north, even though they were also influential in the South.

During the last third of the eighteenth century, the struggle for independence established republican ideology in American consciousness. Republican ideas and outlooks set the terms of debate even among groups that radically disagreed with one another.[2] Among the most basic of these terms of debate were power, liberty, and virtue. History revealed a constant struggle between power and liberty. Power became personified in republican rhetoric. It was a masculine aggressive entity, ceaselessly grasping, always seeking to encroach beyond its proper bounds. Liberty was power's necessary victim. Republican ideologues defined liberty as the individual's right to his own life and property, his power over his own sphere of action. Personified in rhetoric, liberty became a passive, feminine entity in need of protection.[3] Thus did republicanism tap the deep feelings of pride and anxiety associated with the archaic imperative that honorable men must defend their women and their homes.[4]

Virtue, the other major term in republican ideology, reinforced the associations of politics with women, home, and family. This richly ambiguous term could implicitly connote feminine virginity while republican speakers and writers explicitly discoursed on the necessity of virtue to the protection of liberty and the maintenance of a republic. Public virtue meant the readiness of the citizens of the republic to sacrifice their private interests to the good of the whole society. It was synonymous with patriotism. Public virtue depended in turn upon private virtues like industry, frugality, temperance, simplicity, and charity. A man beset with selfish lusts of greed and envy was incapable of serving the public good. He had no sense of order or benevolence.[5]

The centrality of the virtues of industry and frugality to republican thinking reveals not only economic but also moral and religious concerns. The idea of industry was a legacy of the Puritan conception of the calling. The Puritan saint fulfilling a calling would labor to provide necessary goods or services to other saints for the glory of God and the prosperity, not of the individual, but of the community of the saints. The idea of frugality reflected the traditional Puritan beliefs that it was difficult to be wealthy and live without sin and that prosperity was God's reward to faithful societies, rather than to individuals. Puritans measured one's personal success in one's calling by one's usefulness to society and by a frugal temperament that made one content with one's circumstances.[6] By the more secularized late eighteenth century, industry and frugality had become ways to resist the allurements of a monarchical style of social life and government. Monarchy was the culmination of the patriarchal principle. A patriarch measured wealth and influence by the network of people who had become dependent upon his estate and were required therefore to defer to him and serve him. A monarch's estate was the whole of the realm, and he sought to subordinate all the other patriarchs and their estates to himself. The monarchical style of influence seemed to rely on luxury and conspicuous consumption in dress, equipage, furniture, and the like displayed at balls and horse races and similar events. According to republicans, the availability of such luxury, and the emulation among all ranks that its display engendered, created all manner of vice: dependency, debauchery, dissipation, extravagance, effeminacy, and idleness. Such devotion to luxury made men dependent upon the lords and rulers who had power and wealth and who gave the preferment and patronage that would support such a style of life. Thus would monarchical government make men slaves and sycophants to those on whom their fortunes came to depend.[7]

To lose autonomy in this way was to become like women, who had no selves of their own, were confined to constricted spaces, and were given over to insignificant, ornamental pursuits. It was also to remain like children, in perpetual dependence, subject to parental tyranny, and receiving no recognition of a capacity for a rational, self-governed moral life. Under the new terms of Lockean empiricism and Scottish commonsense views of human nature and family life, parents who failed to rear their children to this sort of rational moral autonomy were self-interested tyrants. The widely read novels of the eighteenth century popularized these views and helped fuel revolutionary rhetoric that reviled Mother Britain and her Father monarch, King George, for their unfeeling and antirational tyranny. A still further evil of dependency was that it exposed men to the rapacious power of the rulers who were always ready to tax their dependents to serve their own luxury and vice. Frugality and self-denial, therefore, were not only necessary to the proper character of republican citizens, they were especially important qualities to demand of one's rulers in order that the rulers might resist the temptations of power.[8]

Given the austere Puritan themes of republicanism, one might expect that it would call into question many elements of the ethos of southern honor. Indeed, as the revolutionary crisis broke upon the colonies, the southern gentry worried in public print and private writing about the conspicuous consumption, high living, indebtedness, and dependence their style of life seemed to engender.[9] Where displays of wealth and prowess had once been the norm, equally public displays of virtue took their place. Prominent gentry wore homespun as a sign of their frugality. Many electors repudiated the norms that required burgess representatives to treat the electorate. Representatives who had voted to oppose the actions of the British government were reelected by acclamation rather than required to prove the strength of their interests in the normal contest of a poll.

Republicanism and the Revolution were the beginning of the end for patriarchy as an inclusive metaphor for organizing public life in the South and in the rest of the nation. The gentry of the Upper South had been local patriarchs who jealously guarded their prerogatives against encroachment from above by Crown or Church of England and from below by popular New Light sects. The Revolution forced them to join forces with the lowly in the interests of resisting the much more present threat of feudal dependence imposed from above.[10] The republican ideology in terms of which they forged their alliance exalted not the gentleman patriarch, but the independent yeoman farmer as its ideal citizen. It also bore the stamp of a rhetoric that required fathers to nurture their sons for independence. Both visions were hostile to the webs of dependence, patronage, and deference implied in the patriarchal metaphor. There was room for the gentleman planter in the cultural and political consciousness of Southerners after the Revolution, but he was no longer a breed apart from all the other free white men. He was at best a local first among equals.[11]

The Revolution also changed the self-understanding of women. It is true that there is little evidence of actively feminist thought or action among women of the Revolutionary period. But the political culture of mob action, days of fast and of thanksgiving, celebrations of the repeal of parliamentary acts, and especially the nonimportation agreements raised women's political consciousness. Women's traditional industry and frugality in domestic production became politically significant as their husbands wore homespun and inveighed against dependence on imported British luxuries. In such a rhetorically charged ambience, some women enjoyed unprecedented community attention as they held public spinning bees to demonstrate their patriotism and rally support for the American cause. The disruptions brought on by the war itself resulted in women taking responsibilities they had not shouldered before and gave them a sense of their own capacities and patriotism. As a result, many women found a new place for themselves in the widely shared republican visions of the new nation.[12]

The Revolutionary experience of women and of men in relation to women issued in new ideological themes in postwar publications. Female authors began to dispute the pejorative connotations of the traits commonly attributed their sex, arguing that men suffered as much from such traits or that they were positive traits not to be despised. They suggested in republican language and imagery that marriage was less vital to their being than commonly thought.[13] They turned a long-standing cliché about women influencing the virtue of their men into a justification for a new political role for women and into an argument for new educational opportunities. The education of the republican mother was their most important idea.

If the survival of republics depended upon the virtue of their citizens, and if women made men virtuous, then women held the fate of the republic in their hands. Some writers of the postwar period seemed to hold both premises of this syllogism to be true and did not shrink from propounding the conclusion. Magazines of the 1780s and 1790s began to fill with articles on the influence of female "society" upon men, on the benefits to national character and prosperity of women who forbore to dress according to extravagant European fashion and instead exercised economy, frugality, and industry in their dress and in household management. Many magazines solicited material celebrating women's republican virtue and declined material condescending to women.[14] Women were urged to open their arms only to devotees of republican liberty. Women's "approbation" was often the principal reward of "the hero's dangers and the patriots toils." Ladies of virtue, by discountenancing vice and dissipation, could restrain and even reform the men who sought their company.[15]

The late eighteenth century saw the rise on both sides of the Atlantic of a new appreciation of the feeling side of human nature. With it came a growing awareness of the power mothers exercised over the characters of their children through their supposedly greater capacity for tender feeling. Propagated by evangelical publicists, the ideal of the "moral mother" wed itself naturally to the evangelical versions of republicanism in America.[16] The republican mother guaranteed the continuance of the republic by teaching civic virtue in all its dimensions to her sons. In this way the hand that rocked the cradle might rule the nation. Such recognition of a publicly significant mother-son tie departed from older prescriptions of child rearing that emphasized the role of the father in training sons in wisdom and virtue and believed females to be irrationally inclined to indulge children. Women were now regarded as capable of a self-control fully adequate to keep them from spoiling their children. Fathers receded almost entirely from consideration in such literature.[17]

Women's newly recognized political role required that they be educated. It is not clear whether American women generated the ideal of the republican mother for themselves or whether it was thrust upon them. Those exposed to it took it to heart, however, and constructed their self-understandings around it. This fact made possible the beginning of a long-term trend of establishing "female academies" that would fit women to be good republicans, or at least the makers of good republicans.[18] Advocates of female education held the Lockean view that the ignorance, weakness, or irrationality often attributed to the feminine nature were in reality products of environment and might be readily eliminated by improved education. They constantly confronted the counterargument that learning in women would unsex them, make them masculine and untrue to their natures. Their compromise with this point of view reveals the continuing hold of traditional conceptions of male and female natures. Female education would not unsex women, they held, because it would be designed to make them better wives and mothers, not to make them statesmen, judges, or soldiers. The curriculum proposed for women furthered this argument, stressing practical, vocational skills, rather than theoretical or professional intellectual training.[19] The republican mother, then, was an ambiguous ideal. At the same time it conferred new public significance upon women, it bound their identity to gender and to the domestic sphere all the more tightly.

The Revolutionary experience of women impelled them to undertake other reforms beside those in education. In 1787, the historian Hannah Adams published a pamphlet with a title that might have suggested to some a radical break with women's traditional constraints: *Women Invited to War*. In fact, Adams was inviting women to be Christian soldiers in spiritual warfare against the Devil. Her pamphlet is a convenient example of what Linda Kerber calls the "deflection of women's patriotism into benevolence." Kerber suggests that such deflection may have been necessary before patriotism could seem plausible to the millions of women whose lives were defined by domestic responsibilities. Piety had long been a component of ideals of feminine character, and the evangelical movements of the late eighteenth century made it a practical tool in the tasks of character formation assigned to women in their domestic sphere. Domestic piety impelled women like Hannah Adams to form associations for the relief of widows and orphans or for the support of missionaries.[20]

These early organizations constituted themselves more or less on the lines of a famous association of Philadelphia women who aimed at forming a national association to conduct a house-to-house canvas for funds to support the Continental Army. The financial success of this effort and the pamphlets that publicized and rationalized it made it a model of active and organized female patriotism. Women's associations for religious benevolence drew inspiration from this model and provided the beginnings of political and organizational education even as they justified their activities in terms of women's domestic and religious responsibilities. These associations and the female academies began a trend of female education, association, and activism that would lead to the flourishing of reform movements in the nineteenth century.[21]

Republicanism never was purely political. As the stress on virtue suggests, it was also a moral vision, even a religious one. At the end of the eighteenth century, however, there were a variety of republicanisms, some more wed to Christian faith than others.[22] One variety of Christian republicanism was that propounded by a family of denominations that were among Methodism's main detractors and competitors, the Reformed. Outside of New England, Presbyterians, mainly of Scots-Irish descent, were the chief representatives of this tradition. The College of New Jersey, later Princeton, was a major institutional center where a generation of Reformed clergy learned the tenets of Scottish commonsense philosophy along with their Calvinist theology. Based on this philosophy, Reformed leaders articulated a political theology in which their version of Christianity was understood to be an indispensable feature of the republic. The early Methodists, on the other hand, did not much concern themselves with questions of politics or of religion's role in it. They had other priorities. Eventually they would make their own contribution to republican religion, however, and a comparison of early Methodists with the Reformed will make possible a better appreciation of Methodism's distinctive contributions to the alliance of God and country.

The Reformed may be distinguished from the Methodists on three counts: They held, first, millennial interpretations of American nationhood; second, an understanding of religion as necessary to the republic due to its capacity to instill virtue from the top of the social order down; and third, a commitment to the reform of public opinion for the sake of securing properly religious leaders and citizenry.

The Reformed of the middle and southern states as well as of New England preached a millennialism that identified America as the sacred place in which Christ would initiate his thousand-year reign over the world. Americans were God's holy people who resisted the evils of England and the other despotic nations of Europe, nations that Reformed preachers identified with the beasts, idols, and harlots in the apocalyptic books of Daniel and Revelation. The recent history and near future of the American nation, therefore, was the sacred time through which God would create a new, perfected civil and religious order—New Heavens and New Earth.[23]

Millennialism, especially American civic millennialism, was largely absent from American Methodism in the early years of the nation. Contrary to the interpretations of American Methodist apologists a generation or two later, the early Methodists do not seem to have attended the wedding of religion and republicanism in the earliest years of the republic.[24] Bishop Francis Asbury did present an address to George Washington on the occasion of the new president's first inauguration in an effort to communicate the Methodist Episcopal church's approval of the new Constitution and allegiance to the new government. This gesture, however, was more like dropping in at the wedding reception to pay one's respects before returning to more pressing business.[25]

The bishops defined that more pressing business in their explanatory notes on the *Discipline* in 1796. Their one aim, they said, was to raise "a holy people crucified to the world and full of love to God. . . . "[26] The republic was but one aspect of the world. During the war, early Methodists, tarred with the Tory brush of John Wesley and the Church of England, suffered persecution at the hands of the republic. They later professed they were grateful to God for providing the order and liberty that came with the republic. They also were submissive to it according to the scriptural command to be obedient to whatever powers reigned, but they gave it little spiritual significance beyond that. They were first and foremost citizens of Zion, the polity of holy people whom God had raised up not only in America, not only within Methodism, but in all the world and in all the evangelical churches and sects. Methodist preachers spoke of God's increasing the "prosperity of Zion," "enlarging the boundaries of Zion," and "building up our Zion." Although they frequently meant their own denomination, they also used the term to refer to religious events and communities beyond their own. Indeed, the symbol of Zion allowed Methodists to connect their religious experience, evangelism, and church organization with the whole of God's redemptive activity on Earth. Zion was the place, people, and polity where one could see and feel God working to bring the entire world under the reign of Christ. With this symbol, Methodists could lay claim to all the biblical images that filled the rhetoric of the Reformed clergy. The New Israel for the Methodists, however, was not the American republic, but the universal church. The millennium might be on its way, but neither America, nor England, nor any other civil power figured as Redeemer Nation in their imaginations.[27]

The nature of Zion was displayed in Methodist symbolic action. They gathered weekly in "class meetings" where a leader would inquire into the religious experience and practice of the members and all would rejoice and weep with one another as they shared their trials and triumphs. Quarterly meetings and camp meetings reflected this community of intense feeling with greater opportunity for outsiders to witness the love the Methodist people had for one another.[28] Even outside such focused events, fellow Methodists addressed and often treated one another as members of a family, reflecting their love of God and affection for one another. These practices and the explicit language of the Methodists as they reflected on their experience and practice all divided the cosmos into the realm of

Christ, the church, and the believer versus the realm of Satan, the world, and the infidel. Zion was a refuge from the world. Believers might retreat to class meeting or quarterly meeting and know firsthand the experience of being a part of a truly holy people.

Methodist ritual fellowship, then, may be interpreted as a manifestation of a sort of Christian utopia. Utopian conceptions of time and space are different from millennial ones.[29] Millennialism imagines sacred space in a particular place: Massachusetts for the early Puritans, America for republican religionists, Melanesia for cargo cults. Utopianism, derived from a word meaning "no place," finds sacred space anywhere or nowhere. The Methodists' holy fellowship might occur in English coal fields, in rude Virginia cabins, or out in the wilderness forest under the open sky. Sacred space was anywhere the saints gathered apart from the world to worship and share their experience. The millennial vision sees God working through nations and peoples to bring history to the fullness of time, to a special crisis moment, to what the early Christian writers called *kairos*. *Kairos* is distinguished from another sense of time, *chronos*, which sees and feels time as a continuity rather than a crisis. In *chronos*, one moment is much like another. Utopianism has little or no expectation of special crisis moments in history. Its vision of time is that of *chronos*.

Methodism was not entirely devoid of a sense of *kairos* moments. Individual believers came to see how God's grace had brought each of them to his or her special crisis point of conversion. Such stories were the substance of class meeting and love feast rituals. Preachers came to know the moment to call people forward to seek religion during their sermons. The people on a circuit had a sense of when the time was right to hold a camp meeting. But these sacred moments were not often tied explicitly to a biblical, prophetic scheme of history, still less to one that focused on the American nation as the center of the redemptive drama.

There is, however, an affinity between the *kairos* of the individual conversion narrative and the *kairos* of the millennium. That affinity inheres in the fact that both conversion and the millennium come about through a progression from affliction to exaltation. Eventually, by mid-nineteenth century, this affinity brought the Methodists around to millennial thinking about the national destiny. It also led them to echo the claims of the Reformed that only religion, albeit their own brand of Methodist religion, could insure that the abasements and anxieties of the nation would not overwhelm it but lead eventually to its millennial exaltation.[30]

The second point of Reformed contrast with Methodism lay in the Reformed vision of Christian faith as the guarantor of virtue in the republic. Reformed clergy capitalized on the idea of virtue in the language of republicanism in order to argue for the necessity of religion to the preservation of American liberty. John Witherspoon and his son-in-law Samuel Stanhope Smith, successive presidents of the Presbyterian College of New Jersey, used the lens of Scottish commonsense philosophy to discern a basic natural law of politics: the prosperity of nations depended upon the virtue of their citizenries. As one might expect, they also discovered that only religion might sustain virtue in the people. The Christian religion involved both worship and instruction in moral principle. Worship cultivated the habits, affections, and passions of virtue: adoration of the Divine elevated the tone of moral feelings; thanksgiving confirmed the affectionate motives of duty and obedience to God; confession armed the soul against its own weaknesses; supplication reminded people of their dependence on God and awakened the sentiments of piety. The Christian religion also taught the moral law and the existence of an afterlife in which duty would be rewarded and laxness punished. All of these acts and their consequences for human beings were part of the natural order of God's creation. God was unaffected by worship or by obedience; he merely maintained the natural order.[31]

The virtue portrayed in this vision of God and humanity is highly deferential; it echoes the social convictions of the Reformed clergy. They, like the eighteenth-century southern gentry, believed the moral order of a community was constituted from the top downward. Ministers and magistrates were, as they ought to be, the wealthier and socially more prominent "fathers" of the community. The manners and morals of the elite would leaven the whole, just as the regenerative influence and rational instruction of parents insured order, piety, and civic virtue of the family. The key to the character of the nation, then, would be its leaders. The Reformed vision of the virtuous society, accordingly, was conservative. The sort of society to be perfected with the coming of the millennium would not be very different from the one that currently existed. Social ranks would still exist, but every person would be content with his or her station. Ministers, in particular, would be better respected.[32]

The Methodists, of course, had no use for the rational, deferential religion of the Reformed. Nor did they carry the Reformed clergy's burden for conserving established American institutions. Their early ideological links to the republic were forged out of a rhetorical contrast that exploited the ambiguities of the term "liberty." Everyone knew that republicanism and revolution had secured civil liberty for the people of America and that the Constitution and Bill of Rights had codified a religious liberty that allowed each person to believe and worship according to conscience. Methodist evangelicals, however, strove for a spiritual liberty that led to heaven.

William McKendree, at the 1808 General Conference, preached a famous sermon that used the idea of liberty to put both the American republic and Methodism in their proper places. He took as his text Jeremiah 8:21–22 where the prophet bewails the condition of the Jews and asks: "Is there no balm in Gilead?" The heart of his message was what evangelicals called "experimental religion." This deep heart-wrenching experience was the balm in Gilead that God had provided for the "healing of the nations." This "sovereign balm for every wound" caused those who experienced it to express their joys with shouts. This holy noise offended the taste and sense of decorum of many of the respectable part of the community. McKendree, however, noted the "shouts of applause" so often uttered at celebrations of American liberation from slavery to Britain and her King. Then he thundered: "How much more cause has an immortal soul to rejoice and give glory to God for its spiritual deliverance from the bondage of sin!" This master stroke overwhelmed his audience and elicited the sorts of shouting he had talked about. The sermon was so effective that it won him election as bishop, a post in which he became almost as legendary a figure as Francis Asbury.[33]

McKendree's sermon is the classic example of the rhetorical contrast that simultaneously likened Methodist spirituality to the concerns of the nation and proclaimed the priority of the spiritual. The analogy stresses the distance between Christian liberty and republican liberty. McKendree did not identify the Christian hope with the establishment of an earthly republic. As high as the heavens are above the earth was the liberty of Zion above American civil liberty. A generation later, Methodist writers were still making the contrast. A hymn for Sunday school children to sing on July 4 pled with Christ for "A Liberty more blest, more high," that would enable them to live in his service and in his "righteous cause die."[34] Another hymn underlined the heavenward direction of Christian liberty:

> Father, O! prepare us better
> For the blessing richly given,
> Break off every sinful fetter,
> Purge out every sinful leaven.
> Independence
> Then shall clear our path to heaven.[35]

Even as Sunday school youngsters were singing these hymns, however, Methodists were learning to make claims for the conservative political significance of their spiritual liberty. As they did so, they came to sound very similar to their Reformed brethren, who in the meantime had learned to sound a lot more like Methodists. These developments were still in the future, however. At the beginning of the nineteenth century, the contrasts between the Reformed and the Methodists were still strong, and those contrasts comprised differences of both religious experience and social standing.

Spiritual independence from sin in Methodist experience was not the same as spiritual regeneration through the reasoned instruction favored by the Reformed. Methodist-style evangelicalism fostered a greater sense of individual moral autonomy than that envisioned by the Reformed of the early republic. As Methodists learned to pray their own prayers in prayer meeting and to tell their own stories in class meeting, they learned to be more their own persons under God. The shouts and tears by which Methodists expressed their divine joy or godly sorrow elicited disdain from cultured Anglicans or learned Presbyterians who expected to set the moral tone for their communities. But Methodist liberty of expression in worship also signified liberation from the fetters of demeaning social norms that consigned certain categories of persons to low regard. Whatever virtues Methodist conversion experiences might instill, humble subjection to one's supposed social betters was not among them. The respectable classes might scorn the "shouting Methodists"; but just as the early English Wesleyans had taken the epithet "Methodist" and made it a means of self-affirmation, so American Methodists wore "shouting Methodist" as a badge of distinction.[36]

The third point of contrast between the Reformed and the Methodists lay in their two different routes to reforming the nation.

Early in the experience of the new nation, both the New England clergy and the Reformed of the middle and southern states saw that public opinion was the force in a republic that determined the character of the nation's rulers. They were distressed that neither the new Constitution nor the national leadership, especially Jefferson and those who followed him, made explicit avowal of God's providence over the affairs of the nation. They deplored the national policy, instituted in 1810, that required delivery of mail on Sundays. At a more local level, they deplored the Sabbath breaking, gambling, horse racing, cockfights, drunkenness, and profane swearing that seemed generally prevalent in many places. They realized, however, that these crimes of omission and commission were suffered to continue by magistrates who reflected the influence of public opinion. If they wished government to discharge its proper obligations to God, they would have to control public opinion so that proper Christians would be elected who would be properly responsive to the piety of their constituencies.[37]

The tools for this reform were a host of voluntary societies aimed at a variety of causes. Associations like the American Bible Society, the American Sunday School Union, and the American Tract Society were to facilitate the instruction of the public, especially the poor, in basic Christian knowledge. Other, more local, societies were for the "Suppression of Vice and Immorality." They intended to prod magistrates to enforce laws against Sabbath breaking, horse racing, drunkenness, and profane swearing and to support those magistrates who were effective by giving the approbation of "the most worthy part of the community." The apologists for such organizations were alarmed that the population seemed to be outgrowing both the capacities of the denominations for Christian education and the capacities of local communities for the informal surveillance that kept people's behavior in line. They felt this problem to be especially acute in the cities, where the poor were increasingly concentrated. Thus they formed Sunday and infant schools to teach the poor to read, so they could understand their Bibles. They instituted visitation programs to substitute for the missing social control of the local community. The vice and sloth of the poor were threats to the republic, and religion was the means of cultivating among them industry, frugality, and contentment with the social position that Providence dealt them. In this way a Protestant elite sought to preserve the sober deferential order they believed essential to the republic and the coming millennium.[38]

Although it is probably impossible to chart with precision the impact of these societies on national life, it is known that some of their actions, especially those of the societies dedicated to suppressing vice, drew sustained protest and opposition. This was true even in northern and middle states, locations where Reformed influence was the strongest. The general populace wanted ministers to mind their own business and resented their intrusion upon individual liberties and upon commonly accepted habits of business and sociability. Growing individualism was simply not compatible with the corporate deferential vision of family and community morality that at first inspired the Reformed associations.[39] These efforts at social control also seem to have required deference to the leading, "most worthy" part of the community while taking away the means of sociability, like drinking and contests, that made deferential contact bearable. New social conditions required a new mode of control.

If the deferential republicanism of the Reformed elite proved ill suited even to neighborhoods in the northern and middle states, still less did it speak to the condition of most people in the Upper South where Methodism first thrived. In that region, even the elite eschewed much of the sort of virtue favored by the Reformed. Despite their brief brush with Puritan asceticism in preparation for the Revolutionary War, the white planters of the South generally held to a libertarian republicanism that stressed local autonomy and the widest possible room for the exercise of personal freedoms, including the right to own slaves. They disliked strong central government and distrusted efforts to integrate the nation commercially. The gentry leadership tended to be secular, hostile to clergy, and acquainted with enlightenment ideas from France and Scotland. Both gentry and common planter lived rural lifestyles, and they held to the ideal of the independent yeoman freeholder as the source of public virtue. The ethos of honor continued to shape their moral sentiments and behavior. They were eager to migrate west, goaded by intimations of a mythic "garden of the world" beckoning from just beyond the mountains with vague promises of boundless liberty and prosperity.[40]

This individualistic yet vaguely utopian orientation may have helped Methodism to have its greatest success among southerners. The Methodist Zion, after all, was something like a utopian community. And this Zion was the Methodist agency of reform, not the condescending associations of the elite. Zion was a visible community of saints that testified of a heavenly world, a realm set apart from the worldly concerns of politics and society. Yet worldly activities provided some metaphors for communicating the nature of Methodist life together. The republic had only recently emerged from a war of liberation that had required solidarity and struggle. Citizens of Zion fought another war, a cosmic war against the world, the flesh, and the Devil. Worldly people had demonstrated their momentary solidarity in resistance to England by deferentially acclaiming defiant gentry as their representatives. The citizens of Zion demonstrated a solidarity of mutual love in resistance to persecution and ridicule from worldly citizens of the republic. Zion's citizens declared themselves not by wearing homespun in the face of English taxation but by wearing simple apparel in the face of worldly fashion and pride.

The war of Zion against the world had taken precedence over the war of the republic against England, and many Methodists had suffered for their lack of participation in the latter struggle. But their refusal to participate in the rituals of revolution was consistent with their wider dissent from basic patterns of the society they lived in. Their reform efforts were implicit in their quest to be a holy people, a people set apart. Unencumbered by interests in established institutions and privileges, they persisted in their efforts to reform the continent. Their social placement, further down the status ladder than most of the Reformed, precluded any illusions of accomplishing reform by mobilizing "the most worthy part of the community." Their reform efforts had to come to terms with prevailing ways of perceiving, thinking, and feeling among more common folk even as they tried to transform the meaning of these ways.

Their exploitation of the term "liberty" is again a case in point. Rhetoric of liberty moved evangelical audiences because for generations they remembered the Revolutionary War. "It was wonderful," reflected Indiana circuit rider Joseph Tarkington, "how long the animosities of the War of Independence lasted in the hearts of the good people."[41] Particularly among Southerners, the idea of liberty remained a synecdoche for the agrarian republican ideal and its associations with static images of virgin land and mother earth, receptive and restful, fertile and fruitful, vulnerable and in need of defense. Methodist rhetoric exploited these images.

Samuel Parker, a Kentucky preacher, forged a likeness between the heavenward flight of the dying Christian and the homecoming of a young Kentucky volunteer. The young patriot had left his homeland to defend her liberties against the British in the frigid regions of the Great Lakes. With battles fought and victory complete, the heroic soldier pressed southward. Nearing Cincinnati, he strained for a glimpse of the rolling blue hills of home. As he crested one more hill, his homeland revealed herself. He swept off his hat and cheered in ecstatic yearning, "Hurra! Hurra! Hurra! for Old Kentucky forever!" With these images Parker overwhelmed his fellow Kentuckians; saints and sinners alike all wept. Parker's image made manifest what their old Kentucky home must mean to them: she was worth all the suffering, hardship, and pain they might have endured fighting for her. At the same time, Parker's parable implied a spiritual lesson: heaven was worth all the self-denial, scorn, and suffering they might have to endure in order to be members of the family of God, and to defend that churchly family from the world.[42]

The family of God frequently did need defending in the early years. Methodist symbolic action in worship reflected in its own way the configuration of feminine liberty associated with secluded space in need of defense. The Methodists frequently gathered apart from the world in their quarterly meetings and camp meetings. The place where the saints sat to hear preaching was typically bounded by some sort of rude fence. Within the circle of this enclosure they would shout and cry in response to the preacher. Penitent sinners within would go forward to the altar to be prayed over and struggle for conversion. Hardened sinners without would mock and sometimes disrupt the proceedings. James Finley showed the associations such gatherings had in his mind as he told of how he and some fellow ministers overcame hostile gangs who attempted to disrupt and scatter the saints at worship. At one camp ground, the gang miscalculated the response of the Methodist men. As Finley recounted the story, the local Methodist husbands and fathers felt themselves faced with a choice: either they resorted to violence or suffered their wives and daughters to be insulted by the rowdies. Finley remarked dryly, "It did not take them long to decide." Fine points of Christian teaching about meekness and turning the other cheek were forgotten as the male saints gave the rowdies a sound thrashing for their impertinence. The next day, Bishop Asbury, who happened to be present on the camp ground, warned the bruised remnants of the gang that his Methodist brethren were not all sanctified yet, and he could not be responsible for what might happen if they were provoked and the Devil got into them.[43]

At a later camp meeting plagued by similar disorder, Finley found a way to bring to his aid an authority more legitimate than whatever muscular Christianity his fellow believers might muster. He precluded further trouble with a sermon on civil and religious liberty. He invoked the myth of the Pilgrim forefathers who endured danger and hardship that they might "Leave unstained what they found—freedom to worship God." He appealed to any who had the blood of the patriot sires of '76 to come over to the side of the saints and protect them from the rabble. His appeal moved a local magistrate to rise and declare that he had fought for such liberty as Finley and his people desired and that he would enforce the laws of the state to the utmost against any who tried to disturb them in their worship. "From this on," Finley reflected, "the meeting was the most orderly one I had attended."[44]

Attacks like these were common in the early days of the republic, and what Finley called "the rabble" might well have been nonplused to find themselves counted among the enemies of liberty. It is likely that they arranged their attack with precisely the opposite self-understanding. Their ideas of life, liberty, and the pursuit of happiness simply did not agree with the style of life outlined in the General Rules of the Methodist Societies.

On the trans-Appalachian frontier, where the events of Finley's stories took place, there was a continuing community of freeholding yeoman "patriarchs." The controls of a self-assured gentry elite were gone, but concern for honor among one's peers persisted. Virtue for men continued to have the connotation of martial valor that was validated in peacetime by the patterns of contest that settlers brought with them from the East. Indeed the frontier seemed to require an exaggeration of these manly qualities. The society of yeoman farmers on the frontier was fragile. Competitive pastimes, social drinking, and the carnival atmosphere of election days fostered the hail-fellow feeling necessary for social cooperation. Such cooperation was vital for carving a community out of a wilderness. The very precariousness of the yeoman fellowship made its demands impossible to ignore. To refuse to participate in the traditional forms of community was to oppose the community.[45]

Yet refuse to participate was exactly, in large measure, what Methodist evangelicals proposed to do. The spiritual unity enjoyed by the saints was contingent upon observing the rules of the Methodist societies, and those rules proscribed especially those evils most commonly practiced by the world. Gambling, horse racing, drinking bouts, profane swearing, and other patterns of traditional male camaraderie were now evils to be shunned rather than means of demonstrating manly virtue. The family of God required self-restraint and eschewed both the self-assertion and the deference required by the brotherhood of patriarchs. Camp meetings and other forms of Methodist worship appealed to all to join in the new forms of religious community and ascetic self-discipline. They therefore seemed a direct threat to the archaic forms of male camaraderie and to the republican liberty that many believed to be founded on this traditional fellowship of yeoman farmers.

If the Methodists rejected the norms of archaic manly virtue in the southern version of republicanism, they also rejected the deferential virtue of the early Christian republicanism of the Reformed. While their behavioral prohibitions of gambling, drinking, dancing, and profaning the Sabbath had much in common with the Reformed, their emphasis was different. They saw these vices as dangers more to spiritual than to civil existence. They valued industry and frugality like the Reformed did, but more as indications of growth in grace than as preconditions of public virtue. While they were not hostile to hierarchy as such—witness their episcopal church organization—they ascribed merit to the leaders of their Zion more on the basis of holiness than on the basis of learning, social eminence, or political position. The fathers of their Zion were those instrumental in converting them and serving their spiritual growth rather than those who commanded worldly prestige.

Zion's citizens, then, constructed a fellowship of the lowly whose spiritual liberty and virtue had only analogical relations to the other varieties of liberty and virtue sought by citizens of the new American republic. In time, they would grow from a small and despised sect to a prominent denomination in the mainstream of American life. Along the way they would develop a sense of a more direct tie between themselves and the fate of the republic. They would also arrange a variety of temporary truces and strange amalgamations with the archaic ethos of honor. All this lay in the future, however. As the republic moved into the nineteenth century, the populations with which the Methodists were most identified began to move west in huge numbers. Republican liberty, always associated with land ownership, began to mean freedom to pursue prosperity and plenty on the western lands over the Appalachians. This new liberty raised problems of meaning and belonging that the Methodists were well equipped to address.

3

Migration

PERSISTENCE AND CHANGE

Republicanism helped undermine the hierarchical world of eighteenth-century American society, but there were other undermining forces at work as well. Migration was one of the most important of these. Americans moved west in huge numbers in the late eighteenth century and all during the nineteenth century. The waves of migration referred to here are those from the Chesapeake societies into what became Kentucky and Tennessee and, from there, into what is now called the Old Northwest, especially the states of Ohio, Indiana, and Illinois.[1] The frontier created by these migrations became the setting for some of the enduring popular legends of American culture and the focus of some influential interpretations of the nature and meaning of American society. Methodist circuit riders and camp meetings have become part of these legends and interpretations, attaching the aura of the "wild frontier" to the common perception of early American Methodism.

An important strand of historical interpretation has elaborated this perception into a depiction of American Methodism as a "frontier faith." A frontier faith implies a democratic religion adapted to the egalitarian frame of mind and democratic institutions newly grown up on the frontier.[2] "Democratic" is a dubious adjective to apply to an organization so authoritarian and unrepresentative in its polity as was Methodism throughout most of the nineteenth century. "Egalitarian" or "populist" are more accurate, for even the autocratic bishops of early Methodism had their spiritual roots among the people. Whatever egalitarian tendencies the movement had are not to be attributed to the frontier, however. Methodism began its formative conflicts with the patriarchal gentry system and its culture of honor well before the settlement of the trans-Appalachian frontier. When the Chesapeake Southerners moved west, so did the conflict between the culture of honor and the Methodist evangelical culture. Methodism may be accurately described as a frontier faith only in the sense that migration was one of a number of forces that attenuated older social ties and ritual patterns and thus allowed the new faith to present its alternatives with greater power and plausibility. These changes are the burden of this chapter.

Many Americans were lacking in a sense of meaning and belonging even as they enjoyed their new freedom to move west and seek their fortunes. This sense of lack could affect their most intimate relationships. The story of James B. Finley illustrates how the fathers of the local community of honor, even literal fathers, were displaced by new metaphorical fathers and a new metaphorical family. This new family could seem more family-like than one's literal family.

During the 1790s, James B. Finley migrated with his parents from Virginia to Kentucky and then to Ohio. While in what was then called the West, he had to try twice before he finally got religion in a way that stayed with him. Soon after his second experience, he went to a camp meeting where William McKendree conversed with him about his religious experience and whether or not he felt called to be a preacher. "I wept like a child," Finley recalled, "and [told] him I was ignorant, and lived in the wilderness where there was no one to guide me." This was a curious confession from a married man of twenty-six whose father, a Presbyterian minister who had turned Methodist, was still living close by. McKendree's reply to the tearful complaint was just as curious: "My son, be of good cheer," he soothed, "God will supply you with fathers and mothers in the Gospel."[3]

What was Finley's problem? Why did he need fathers and mothers in the gospel? Why should not McKendree have counseled the young man to seek the guidance of the literal father whom God had provided at conception and birth? The short answers to these questions are, first, that he had spent several years of his youth and young adulthood in painful confusion about who he was, to whom or what he belonged, and what his life meant. Only recently had he discovered that he belonged to God, to the Methodist family of God, and to the cause of advancing the interests of that family. Second, he did not know very much about what these new belongings meant. Third, his father could not tell him because his father had joined the Methodists even more recently than had James and still struggled with a sense of belonging to the Calvinist tradition that he had long served. James Finley, in sum, had a problem of meaning and belonging, the sort of problem with which many others in his time and place also struggled.

Problems of meaning and belonging always take place in and reflect a particular social order. Before we can understand the sort of problem Finley had, it is useful to distinguish between two dimensions of social order.

There are what might be called the "hard" sociological structures through which people accomplish together the basic tasks of physical-biological living. Such structures include divisions of labor and the economic classes derived from them, political institutions and the social power structures inherent in them, and the size and composition of households and families. On the other hand, there are the "softer" psychosocial patterns of interaction that communicate an enlivening sense of commonality with a social group, an equally vital sense of recognition to each individual, and a sense of the transcendent legitimacy of the whole common effort. Such patterns, when most effective, will induce a society's members to want to do what they must do and to feel a basic sense of identity among themselves, their community, and the order of the cosmos. The more-or-less specialized social patterns that accomplish this task are everyday ritualizations and periodic rituals that may or may not be self-consciously religious. Young James Finley's problem related chiefly to disruptions in the softer dimension of social order, disruptions aggravated by migration.

The power of westward migration to effect social change should not be overrated. Efforts to assess its impact on the "hard" dimension of social order suggest that the frontiers of Kentucky and the Old Northwest did not significantly alter the social structures settlers brought with them. Divisions of labor and their concomitant economic and social inequalities remained much the same. Political and social elites in the West were composed of the same people or the same sort of people as those in the East.[4] There were some important continuities between East and West on the "soft" dimension of social order as well. James Finley's accounts of camp meeting violence, for instance, suggest that the ethos of honor survived both the advent of nationalist republicanism and the trek west.

Perhaps no phenomenon communicates the persistence of norms of honor better than precisely the one that many suppose to be evidence of a "modern" personality: migration in quest of better fortunes. Such a quest for wealth can be interpreted as a rationally self-seeking economic individualism, and evidence suggests it became just that over the course of a few generations in the nineteenth century.[5] Much of the earlier movement west, however, was undertaken for more traditional reasons. Prestige in the community of honor depended upon such manly things as having a family and the property on which to sustain them. Only by means of property, especially land ownership, was honor and virtuous republican independence sustainable. The quest for property might then be a quest for honor in the eyes of the watching community rather than an expression of modern economic individualism.[6]

The migratory quest for the basic conditions of honor did, however, contribute to the decline of the metaphor of patriarchy as the organizing principle for community life. Cultures in the process of migration tend to reduce their range of normative options and evolve a mode of social control that depends upon community consensus and demands for a rather narrow conformity to popular expectations. This sort of consensual democracy set the limits for whoever might attain to positions of titular authority in the community. Leadership no longer belonged to a learned and cultured elite who were able to insure by their elevated status the effectiveness of legal and political institutions. The fellowship of all white yeoman patriarchs was the social reality from which flowed authority and control.[7]

Under such circumstances, the reciprocal ties between higher and lower ranks of society that had once been embodied in rituals of deference and patronage began to wither away. In their place considerable antagonism, a sort of war of all against all could emerge. The early years of Kentucky saw such a circumstance. Big land speculators assumed leadership at the state level, and an unreliable set of leaders at local levels tried and often failed to supply the services of the traditional gentleman justices. The common level of planters worried over their insecure land titles and distrusted their leaders. Each group strove for its own advancement, and each was suspicious of the other. These conditions probably contributed to the disorientation James Finley felt as he tried to establish himself on the frontier. His parents had lost their dispute over land claims and had been forced to move from Kentucky to Ohio.[8]

The scramble for land often encouraged a one-sided resolution of that basic tension inherent in the ethos of honor: the tension between honor as deference to superior rank and honor as the duty to achieve place for oneself and family. Circumstances like those in early Kentucky led to a stress on the latter and a breakdown in the cohesiveness once supported by the former. According to one critic of American culture, such developments exaggerated the right of the individual to acquire and possess property out of all proportion to the counterbalancing reciprocal responsibilities that classes had once owed each other. Inequalities persisted while the psychosocial patterns that had once conveyed a sense of meaning and belonging among the classes were disrupted. The coherence and stability of the social order was thereby lost.[9] One might also claim, of course, that individual freedom was enhanced.

Whatever one's evaluation of these developments, it seems clear that the older hierarchical style of courtship between classes gave way to a different rhetoric. Once the elite had appealed to the middling and inferior ranks across an assumed line of division: "Watch and imitate us as we out-imitate one another." The common sorts were not included in the circle of genteel honor, but they were lured to give their allegiance to its members by means of a variety of rituals in which the gentry led out. Now the upper classes exuded a more egalitarian appeal: "Let us all out-imitate one another." They added, however, the inevitable reflection on the divisions created by such competition: "Now see how some of us are more substantial than others." Where the traditional rhetoric had begun with a principle of division (the hierarchical cosmos) and sought some sort of merger, the egalitarian rhetoric started with a principle of merger (the brotherhood of all white yeomen) and created division.

These divisions were becoming visible even in the settled eastern areas in the late eighteenth century. Southern hospitality and the conception of the open, nonprivate house that went with it were on the wane. Where country gentlemen had once actively sought out strangers to entertain, they were now much more selective in their invitations. Increasing refinement dictated more and more specialized spaces in the homes of wealthier members of the community. One did not walk immediately into the communal hall on crossing the threshold of a planter's home; a passage or antechamber intervened. This architectural change signaled an increasing conception of domestic space as something to be shielded from a vulgar world. A similar sort of separation of the home from the world was already underway in evangelical circles where houses of believers were being transformed from centers for convivial hospitality to places of prayer. In either case, one meaning of such turns to privacy was an increasing social distance between people of all classes.[10]

If this was the case in the South, where the ideal of the "Cavalier" gentleman planter persisted, it was much more so in the cities and towns of the Northwest. Although a relatively stable elite leadership established itself in most centers, the high rate of population turnover outside of leadership groups precluded the development of stable deference-patronage ties. Instead, the "booster" ethos so ably portrayed by Daniel J. Boorstin pervaded the towns of the Old Northwest. Growing population, rising real estate values, and increasing personal wealth all supported the rhetoric of "Let us all out-imitate one another."[11]

The degradation of traditional rituals that sustained people's sense of inclusion and legitimacy in the culture of honor is suggested by the contrast between election rituals before the Revolution and the image conveyed by the following observation of an election ritual in the early republic. In 1804, Samuel Williams observed an election of national and state representatives in Kanawha county, Virginia (now West Virginia) that had many of the marks of the traditional ritual. Voters stepped before the election officials and candidates and announced their choices viva voce. The candidates voiced their thanks directly to their supporters. Friends of the candidates rolled in supplies of food and drink and treated their candidate's voters just outside the polling place. Other things were different. Although the freehold qualification for voting was still law in Virginia, so few were freeholders that the qualification was waived "by common consent." Not only were all white males of lawful age allowed to vote, but minors ("mere boys"), travelers passing through, and homeless transients were brought in to vote without objection. Williams remembered leaving work—minus his coat, his shirt sleeves rolled up, and wearing a dirty apron—and being hurried to the courthouse to vote for a man who was being hard-pressed by his opponent on the third and final day of the election. The candidate's friends recruited whomever they could find; it did not matter that Williams was only eighteen at the time, nor that he seemed to know little about the candidate.[12]

These irregularities do not seem to have threatened the power of the county elite; allowing them may rather have enhanced their popularity. But Williams's reminiscences of the county courts in Kanawha suggest a decline in the ability of the gentry to convey in their persons the transcendent legitimacy of local institutions. Williams's dominant memories were of the drunken Squire Donnelly who had to be hurried from the bench by his mortified son, of Squire Cobb who enjoyed his meals so well that he used his time on the bench for "*siesta*," and of the horse race outside the court in which one of the contestants fatally fractured his skull in a fall.[13] Williams was a witness to a disenchantment that many began to feel with respect to the traditional "fathers" of the community. People from the middling ranks, like Williams, began to establish through religion their own patterns of community that offered a different sense of identity from that provided by traditional patterns. In so doing, however, they still drew upon archaic models that were very much a part of the traditional culture of honor.

Even with the loss of the "fathers," men still felt the duty to protect the life and property of their households. The legal means to accomplish this protection in newly forming communities on the frontier and elsewhere did not always meet the felt needs of the brotherhood of virtuous yeomen. The old county court system was dependent upon the legitimating aura of patriarchy for much of its effectiveness. The new federal government derived its authority from a written document embodying a contract, thus providing the pattern for viewing all law as rationalized, written code rather than traditional custom. This change was just one more way in which the republic undermined the prestige and authority of local gentry who had once represented the law to their inferiors.[14] The collective virtue and consensus of local citizens was all that was left to give legitimacy to legal proceedings. What many viewed as lawless elements, however, often corrupted the consensus. Peter Cartwright, another Kentucky pioneer, remembered that Logan County was called "Rogues' Harbor" when he was a child. "Murderers, horse thieves, highway robbers, and counterfeiters" had fled there from every part of the Union. "The honest and civil part of the citizens" prosecuted the rogues to no avail because "they would swear each other clear" and thus successfully defy the law. They carried on such "violence and outrage" that the honest sorts eventually resorted to vigilantism.[15]

Cartwright's vigilantes were but one of many antebellum groups who modeled themselves on the example of the colonial South Carolina "regulators" in a conservative effort to secure their lives, families, and property from what they perceived as serious threats from the lawless. Typically, such movements were expressions of consensus among upper- and middle-class groups who found among poor people and various "outlaw" elements the scapegoats necessary for a demonstration of the behavioral boundaries of the respectable community. Often lacking the resources, willingness, and patience to build an effective system of legal justice, local community leaders secured their property and position from two different threats: the lawless and the local tax rates. The libertarian republicans of the Upper South had always been suspicious of formal government and the power to tax property. In vigilantism they avowed their belief in the moral consensus of the community as a superior—and cheaper—governor. Sometimes, however, vigilante movements failed to attract or hold the consensual support of the respectable majority. In such cases they often stimulated countermovements and embroiled communities in protracted conflict and anarchy. Community consensus in the culture of honor could be a fragile affair. An index of that fragility is the fact that vigilantism was general in Tennessee, Kentucky, Indiana, and Illinois throughout the antebellum period.

Both vigilantism and related patterns of social control like charivari and lynch law reflected the basic configuration of a secluded sacred space to be protected against some form of pollution from without. The respectable members of communities where such actions took place came into frequent conflict with the outcasts of the social order. These outcasts might be criminals, or persons considered lazy or shiftless, or political or religious deviants, or blacks. Usually they were believed to have committed some crime against the values of property or family morals. In any case, the loathing and repugnance that these scapegoats aroused was evident in they way they, or their dead bodies, were treated. Whippings of up to a thousand lashes spread out over days, hangings, slow burnings, and mutilation and display of corpses were the more serious actions of lynch law proceedings. In the milder charivari, the community imposed only a figurative death by shame in the procession out of town on a rail, the application of black tar with feathers, or repeated dunkings in a nearby pond. The outcasts became the concrete embodiments of negative identity—what one most emphatically must not be—for the respectable. A rhetoric of killing, either real or figurative, marked the boundary between those who belonged within the honorable community and those who did not.[16]

The Methodists and similar evangelicals resonated deeply with the image of a purified community, but their rhetoric called for a more spiritualized killing. Where citizens of honor purified their community by purging it of persons who polluted or threatened to pollute the sacred space of property and family, the evangelicals directed the purging motive inward into individual hearts as the precondition of true community. Individuals gained admittance to the sacred space of the family of God by means of purging their souls of impure passions; they found their scapegoats within. The boundary of the community of honor ran between those who had proved the self through honorable assertion and those who had violated or disgraced the self through dishonorable assertion or simple lack of assertion. For the evangelical community, on the other hand, the boundary lay between those who had mortified the self and those who still sought to assert it. The difference and the kinship between these two modes of control are equally important. Just as the evangelical motive of self-purging might lead some to condemn actions like lynching, it might lead others to condone and even participate in such actions. The drama of mortification might be internalized or projected outwards with resultant actions that seemed very different, but had, at deeper levels, similar meanings.

Both the growth of the evangelical family of God and the growth of the republican brotherhood of the yeoman farmers were manifestations of a broad-ranging disenchantment with patriarchal fatherhood. This disenchantment was part of a general shift in Euro-American culture from a paradigm of family relations based on sovereignty to a paradigm of family relations based on affection and self-interest. It is not surprising, then, that some sons should become disenchanted with literal fathers as well. Literal fathers were, after all, links in the great patriarchal chain of being that, in the traditional worldview, held all communities and societies together. This worldview was dying and the relations of literal fathers and sons did not escape the current of change.[17]

Young James Finley and his father seem to have participated in this general shift. James had tried to follow his father's guidance in the selection of a life's calling and had trained for medicine. But his association with Indians on the frontier and his love of hunting in the wilderness had well-nigh overcome his sense of filial duty; his parents feared he would go off with the Indians and become one of them. He did not join the Indians, but he did not practice medicine either. He took up hunting for the supply of frontier neighborhoods instead. About the same time, he married a young woman against her father's will and set up a cabin on the outskirts of settlement.

James's move to a life of frontier hunting and farming was more than just a choice of a way to make a living. It represented also his ambivalent relationship with the rough-and-tumble variant of the ethos of honor that sprang up like a weed on the frontier in the absence of the more civilized ethos cultivated by the old gentry families in the East. In his account of his early years, he sometimes yearns nostalgically for the simplicity of pioneer life, but mostly he conveys a troubling incoherence of mood in the midst of uncertainties and loneliness. In connection with problems of Indian warfare, he depicts a pioneer people who were "deeply depressed" when in danger and then, when the danger was over, exultant at the trials through which they had passed. It was a life made up of constant alterations of hope and despondency. Frequent scenes of blood and carnage so brutalized the people as to make them somewhat indifferent to suffering and at the same time reckless of danger. His own life as a hunter was beset with periodic seasons of melancholy. When alone in the woods and unexcited by the chase he was often filled with terrible imaginings, fears, and temptations. Only some stirring adventure of the hunt would rouse him out of "the dead sea of thought" and calm his "whirlpool of passion." Despite the uncontrollable mood swings of life in the woods, he still preferred the single-mindedness of the hunt to the distractions of youthful company in the farming settlements. All the "huskings, quiltings, dancings and plays of all descriptions" he regarded as "calculated to produce dissipation of thought." But his choice of hunting for a living gave him no real alternative to this rustic community of yeoman farmers. For seven years he hunted in the winter and farmed in the summer. Eventually, however, the growth of settlement broke up his hunting grounds and faced him with the choice of finding a different livelihood or moving on to less settled regions.[18]

Finley's observations find an echo in the analyses of antebellum southern social life offered by Bertram Wyatt-Brown. The gregariousness and conviviality of southern life had their hidden dark side. Behind the readiness to have good times together lay the fear of being left alone, bored, and depressed. Distances between houses and settlements, low levels of education and literacy, scarcity of books and intolerance for those who wished to be alone with books or for any other reason, the drive for social standing and reputation, and the largely oral, face-to-face nature of the patterns by which this quest was to be satisfied: all these traits of southern society set the threat of isolation and ennui starkly against the hope for enlivening social contacts.[19] The curious thing about James Finley is that, in the hunt, he actively sought to wrestle with isolation rather than succumb to the giddy round of southern rural sociability.

His effort to resist the frontier version of the ethos of honor reflected a struggle with the God of his father. Finley provides us with little information about his father, Robert W., and so precludes much psychological speculation about their relationship. It seems clear, however, that the elder Finley had not found a way to communicate his own Calvinist faith to his son in a way that undergirded a sense of firm personal identity. Robert himself had shown friendly inclinations to the Methodists early in James's childhood, for which his parishioners had reviled him, and he joined the Methodists not long after his son's conversion.[20] It is unlikely that the Presbyterian pastor himself held a very tight grip on Calvinist orthodoxy. This religious ambivalence seems to have exposed young James to all the terrors of bad conscience that an eroding orthodoxy can inflict. The doctrine of unconditional election and reprobation aroused morbid fears that God had decreed him to commit some crime and hang for it, exposed to shame and death before the eyes of the whole world. His father's Calvinism exacerbated his depressed swings of mood, frequently sinking him into a despair in which he felt his "lost and undone condition as a sinner." He struggled with this conviction for several years before coming to the rebellious conclusion, at age fifteen, that the orthodox doctrine was wrong. God would not damn anyone, he thought. So merciful was He that He would eventually redeem even the denizens of Hell.

James's universalist heresy created quite a stir in his neighborhood. Many of his peers were delighted with his new stand and his aggressive attempts to propagate it. The adults of his father's church were scandalized that the pastor's son should become a renegade from the faith of his fathers. One local Presbyterian elder tried to face down the young heretic at a logrolling only to be discomfited by James's sharply reasoned replies. The elder swore that he would beat such nonsense out of the youngster were he his own son. This overthrow of the local fathers and of their stern patriarchal deity did little to resolve James's nagging sense of sinfulness or his uncertainty of what life held for him. It only isolated him from the responsible adults of his religious community and threw him back on his own resources and the resources of his peers. "I thought if God had brought me into the world, without my consent, for his own purposes, it was no concern of mine, and all I had to do was to be honest, enjoy life, and perform the errand of my destiny." He was no closer to knowing that destiny, however, and his new doctrine only allowed him to enter "fully and freely into all parties of pleasure." He entered so fully and freely into the typical rituals of the ethos of honor, in fact, that he earned himself the sobriquet, "the New Market Devil." Often in moments of calm reflection, he feared the thought of death and eternity, recognized his life was immoral, and resolved to reform. "Thus I lived thoughtless and wicked, resolving and resolving upon amendment, but continuing the same, or rather, growing worse and worse, till I arrived at the twentieth year of my age."[21]

It was in his twentieth year, 1801, that James decided upon his mate for life and his career as a hunter. The latter choice, he implies, was a direct response to his discomfort with the adolescent community of honor that his universalism had led him fatalistically to accept five years earlier. The God of his fathers would not let him rest content. Indeed, this was also the year in which he attended the great sacramental meeting at Cane Ridge, high point of the Great Revival in the West. He went to mock, full of pride in his physical and mental strength which he believed would allow him to resist whatever influences these much publicized revivals were exerting over weaker souls. The holy tumult of the camp ground threatened to unman him, however, and he soon repaired to a nearby tavern for a dram to fortify his nerves. The drunken revelry, gambling, horse trading, and fighting that he saw there revolted him. He quickly took his drink and left, feeling as close to hell as he ever wished to be in this world or the next. He left for home hastily, as if fleeing both God and the devil. He could not escape. The meaning of the campground and its contrast with the tavern overcame him. He saw that if he did not quit his course of wickedness the Devil would surely get him. In anguish he slipped from his horse and tried to pray, falling prostrate on the ground, crying aloud for mercy and salvation. An old Swiss German Pietist living near the trail heard Finley, took him to his cabin, and prayed and sang over him until the young man felt his guilt removed and a sense of God's love flowing through his soul. He cried, laughed, and shouted for joy.

His joy was short-lived. His friends and neighbors opposed and persecuted him for his new religion. He could not find an acceptable religious community to belong to. Worst of all, he resisted a growing conviction that he should preach the gospel, confirmed in his resistance by the counsel of a Presbyterian minister that he should study theology for three years before trying to preach. He lost, therefore, the comforts of his new religion. He gave up his religious exercises of prayer and Bible reading and even returned briefly to his old companions and their worldly conviviality. "I felt no more compunction of conscience, and concluded I might as well live like other people, and that there was no harm in indulging in innocent amusements; and if there was, we would all go to hell together in accomplished and genteel society."[22] He failed to be persuaded by the nervous bravado of this inner lecture to himself. He chose the solitary life of the woods and struggled there in his backslidden state for both physical and spiritual sustenance for seven years. Although Finley does not explicitly draw the connection, his backwoods melancholy, of which he speaks earlier in his account, seems to have been as much a product of bad conscience as it was of isolation.

Eventually his depression became so dark as to lead him to the conclusion that he was a reprobate and that he might as well end his life rather than live on to earn yet deeper punishment in hell. Alone, deep in the woods, on what he thought would be his last hunting trip, he prepared his gun for suicide. He was interrupted, however, by a new thought. "My heavenly Father, in mercy," he asserts, "interposed a thought of my family. 'How,' thought I, 'will my dear wife and parents feel when my body is found, perhaps mangled and torn by wild beasts?' " Even more reassuring thoughts followed, "as sensibly as if audibly pronounced: 'There is yet mercy with God, if you will seek it.' "[23] Constrained by the ties of affection for his family, he heard not a sovereign Deity but a heavenly Father bid him seek mercy.

This heavenly Father, furthermore, had a church family on Earth, and circumstances—or the Father's providence—conspired to get James adopted into it. James's wife, sensing a changed mood in her husband since he had returned from the woods, entreated him to go with her to a nearby Methodist class meeting. He consented reluctantly. The Methodist saints eyed suspiciously the man who had earned the name, "New Market Devil." He was on their ground, however, and they went ahead with their family affairs. James was deeply moved as he listened to them recount their experiences with God, and he wept when the leader inquired into his own experience. The class members prayed for him tenderly. His second conversion followed soon after this meeting.

Again James felt the prompting to preach the gospel. This time, thanks to the family of God, he had a better idea of how to respond to the call. He began by telling his neighbors about his experience and starting prayer meetings in his home. He joined the Methodist church and soon earned an appointment as a class leader. He was instrumental in the conversion of several neighbors and family members. Within a few weeks the circuit preacher had him take a text and preach. He had good results, especially when he told of his own conversion experience and the abiding sense of God's presence that it had brought to him. At the next quarterly conference on the circuit, the presiding preacher called on Finley to exhort, which he did with good effect. The next day he attended the love feast where person and after person arose to tell what God had done for their souls; he shouted for joy in response.

Young Finley had found, in short, a new family. It provided a wealth of gratifying recognition and confirmation of his new identity as a Methodist called to preach the gospel. He was part of God's action in the world, and the people called Methodists, their leaders, and even the sinners they attracted to their meetings all had ways of giving him the sense that he was a special part. They conveyed a precious sense of separateness transcended and distinctiveness confirmed. No longer did he suffer from a sense of irresolution about his future course of life. It was settled for time and eternity. The sense of transcendent legitimacy for this new identity, however, came not from the blessing of his father, not from the fathers of the religious community of his boyhood, not from the fathers of the wider community of honor, nor from his youthful peers. All these had lost their magic. Indeed, the son had turned around the direction of grace and spiritual nurture; his conversion and ministry led to the conversion of his father.

At the end of the chapter in which he tells of his conversion and call to ministry, Finley makes clear the structure of his new identity and shows why he needed metaphoric fathers and mothers in the gospel to guide him, rather than his literal father. At one meeting of the local Methodist society, his father tried to reconcile the "Calvinistic notion of imputed righteousness with Wesley's teaching, and put a construction on Wesley's words which . . . was not Methodistic" according to his son's notion of things. James rose from the congregation after his father had finished and declared:

> Father, you can no more reconcile Calvin and Wesley than you can darkness and light, or error and truth, and there is no use of your trying to do so. Permit me to say, if you are a Methodist be one, and if you are a Calvinist be one, for I want truth to prevail everywhere, and every man to be really what he is.[24]

James had discovered what he was by means of a profound transformation. The chasm between Calvinism and Methodism had, for him, been agonizingly deep and wide, and he would not accept his father's easy bridging of the gap. A man's affirmations and repudiations had to be clear, as far as James was concerned. It was necessary that truth prevail everywhere in order that men may be what they are. It was also necessary for men to be what they are in order for truth to prevail. In this reciprocity is true identity. Yet truth and identity have their price. James admitted he felt "somewhat unpleasant" about his attack on his father; but he had "great zeal for truth" that made him free. A text came to his mind: "He that loveth father or mother more than me, is not worthy of me."[25] It cannot be altogether coincidental that Finley invoked this text in his autobiography just before the chapter in which he tells of his entry into full-time itinerant preaching.

A father might be expected to give moral guidance and confirmation to his son, especially a son who has chosen to follow the same calling as his father. James's attack dramatized the fact that his father could not provide such guidance for him. The Methodist movement overcame this hiatus in the sequence of generations through its own fathers in the gospel. William McKendree was James's most important spiritual father. He first saw McKendree at an 1807 camp meeting when the older man stood up on the preachers' platform. Finley was immediately impressed. It was as if a supernatural being were about to speak. It seemed to this spiritually orphaned young man that McKendree prayed as if he were talking face-to-face with God, as a child with its father. James was drawn to the elder preacher as if by a spell. In the afternoon, McKendree called the younger man to his tent. Finley felt greatly embarrassed upon approaching the elder preacher, but McKendree's cordial and caring manner banished all his fears. "He then conversed with me as man never did before, and as man never can again. There was an overpowering sweetness in his manner and words, that filled me with love and reverence for the man that lasted all through his life." It was then that James wept like a child and McKendree soothed him with promises of fathers and mothers in the gospel. Finley declares that no man except his own father ever had so strong a hold on his heart as McKendree. He knew of no one in whom he might "so implicitly confide" or whom he felt himself "so implicitly bound to obey" as this "amiable minister of Jesus."[26]

In some ways, things had not changed all that much for James Finley. He had not so much given up the hunting profession as he had turned from hunting animals to hunting sinners. The former he had slain with a gun; the latter he would slay with the word of God. He had not so much rejected the God of his father as he had transformed Him. God was no longer an alien sovereign who inscrutably and unresponsively decreed the fate of his creatures. He was instead a heavenly Father with whom one might talk as a child does with its father. Neither had he simply outgrown the need of an earthly father. He still relied on his fathers and mothers in the gospel to nurture and guide him, and many besides McKendree did exactly that.[27] It is important to stress the transformations as much as the continuities, however. Hunting humans with the Word is very different from hunting animals with a gun. An affectionate heavenly Father is very different from an arbitrary sovereign God. Having fathers *and mothers* in the gospel is very different than depending on the patriarchal fathers of the local community. Not only had the means of grace and guidance on earth come to include women as well as men, but the nature of the ties changed from deference and patronage to a more mutual affection.

Moreover, being an itinerant son in the gospel meant taking a good deal of independent initiative in promoting the cause of one's heavenly Father and being constantly on the move among many different sorts of people. There was no possibility in such a life of building up ties of patronage with one's literal father or the fathers of any particular local community. It is true that the charismatic bishops like Asbury and McKendree and many other leading preachers forged remarkable psychological ties with younger men, but these dependencies were sustained only in occasional contacts widely spaced in time. The primary dependence that all pious believers strove to feel constantly and ever more deeply was dependence upon their Savior, Christ, and upon their heavenly Father. The itinerants, as an old song declared, possessed "no foot of land." While this declaration ought not to be taken too literally for most of them, itinerancy attenuated the tie between land and a man's identity as a man. The community of honor in the antebellum period was still attached to land and locality. The family of God was not.

In sum, James B. Finley and his family had passed into a new form of community life centered on a different spirituality and psychology. They were not an isolated case. This new life would play a significant role in transforming the meaning of the family in nineteenth-century America.

4

Experimental Religion and the Way of the Cross

If the culture of honor furnished the main images by which early Methodists defined what they were not, what images defined what they were? If republicanism and westward migration aided Methodism by undermining patriarchal honor and authority, what did the Methodists propose to put in their place? Previous chapters have suggested answers to these questions. This chapter lays the foundation for a systematic attempt to fill in those suggestions.

Methodism was, before all else, a movement that led people to "experimental religion." The modern rendering of this phrase might be "experiential religion." The point is that early Methodists insisted upon the heartfelt experience of religion. The image of the repentant sinner bowed down in sorrow for offenses against God and then leaping up in joy at acceptance through Christ was central to Methodist self-definition. A Methodist was one who knew that he or she had become a child of God. Methodist theology declared that such children could stray and be lost unless they strove constantly to become perfectly devoted to their heavenly Father and his Son. Hence the need to follow the way of the cross; that is, to crucify daily those motives that threatened to separate one from the family of God in heaven and on earth. On this earth the forces of God and the Devil had their particular territories, regions that verged on heaven and hell respectively. Only the way of the cross could lead one aright through these regions. That way began with and was epitomized in the experience of conversion.

Experimental religion and the way of the cross, then, were the essence of what it meant to be Methodist in the early decades of the nineteenth century. These patterns of thinking, feeling, and acting were the center of Methodist identity and the mainspring of the Methodist salvation machine. They were also embodied in images of family that evoked sentiments of mutual affection. These patterns, images, and sentiments infused the forms of ritual and ideology that are the topics of later chapters.

The Methodist movement pursued and propagated experimental religion with a single-mindedness unmatched by any of the other prominent Protestant denominations. Baptist churches required a conversion experience for admission to their fellowship, but they also required assent to some elaborate church constitutions and doctrinal statements. Baptist congregations lavished much energy upon the formulation of such statements and on the conflicts and schisms they provoked.[1] Such issues of polity and creed were not Methodist priorities. The Methodists distinguished themselves from Presbyterians, their other major competitor in the Ohio valley, on similar grounds. They had neither the burden nor the privilege of sustaining the high tradition of systematic Calvinist theology, and they were glad of it. The Presbyterians had a tradition of revivals in which youth who were brought up Reformed and were thoroughly catechized might refresh the spiritual tenor of a congregation with a new seriousness about religion. These "times of refreshing" occurred under the tenacious assumption that growth in grace proceeded no faster than growth in rational understanding. Major divergence from this assumption before the 1820s generally led to schism.[2] Only the Methodists seemed ready to promote experimental religion as both the necessary and the sufficient condition of Christian identity.

The conversion experience in early American Methodism, however, did not differ in form from conversion in many other Christian traditions. Nineteenth-century Methodist accounts of conversion are structurally the same as those of Puritans two hundred years earlier. It was the context and consequences of the experience that changed over the generations and that gave American Methodism its distinctive historical significance.[3]

Experimental religion meant not an exercise in mystical hypothesis testing but an experience of the truths of Christianity applied in heartrending, visceral reality to one's own individual case. The convert had to learn and feel personally the cosmic facts: each person is guilty of sin, polluted by it, condemned by God, and exposed to eternal death because of it, and yet may be saved from it and its consequences by Jesus Christ. This deeply felt learning experience had a three-stage progression: (1) awakening, (2) conviction, (3) conversion.[4]

Awakening involved some cognitive understanding of the alarming facts of sinfulness and the need to live a better life. Whether this understanding was but a haunting remembrance of childhood lessons in a nominally religious family, or the burden of constant moralizing and social restraint in a very pious one, there were few who became experimentally religious who did not have a prior understanding of Christian tenets upon which gospel appeals might work.[5] Even those from the most pious backgrounds, however, were made aware of the fact that Christian upbringing and the moral life it produced were not sufficient to meet the real needs of the human condition. One might appear moral to the superficial of this world, but only a change of heart would really suffice for salvation.[6] "Awakening grace" moved potential converts to a restless dissatisfaction with their current ways of life, whether overtly wicked or conventionally moral. It led them to begin seeking for the deep experiential knowledge of the gospel that would change the heart.

Awakening grace developed into "repenting and reforming grace" in the stage commonly called conviction. This stage often began with frustrated efforts to act out the new and unfamiliar behaviors expected of a Methodist Christian. Unlike the Baptists, the Methodists did not require conversion for probationary admittance to their fellowship, only an expressed desire "to flee the wrath to come" and a promise to abide by the rules of the society. The rules required giving up worldly practices like dancing. They also required spiritual practices like prayer, reading Scripture, attending preaching, prayer meeting, and other "exercises." These provisions reflected a canny understanding of how required actions might lead to desired feelings. The church held, said one commentator on its rules, that if probationers were not converted when received into the church, the blessing would come to them as they walked in the way of obedience.

Methodist probationers repeatedly confirmed what the church held as they found that trying to act like a Christian only served to convince them that the "carnal mind is enmity against God: . . . they that are in the flesh cannot please God." (Romans 8:7, 8.) They could not keep up with the requirements of the Christian life as the Methodist rules defined them, and this failure made them *feel* what they had learned: they were guilty of sin, polluted by sin, and condemned by God. These feelings were exactly the point. If one really knew one's spiritual condition, one would be filled with fear of the wrath to come, with abhorrence of self and of one's sins, and with despair at one's guilt, pollution, and condemnation.[7] When Jacob Young was convicted, therefore, he lost the power of speech, cried uncontrollably, and fell trembling to the floor. After regaining his strength, he wandered for hours in the woods, "moaning like a dove that had lost his mate." He returned to the house where he had felt the onset of conviction and fell to the floor again while the pious family of the house sang and prayed for him. He lay there for hours, conscious of nothing save his own darkness and distress of mind.[8]

Such despair was only the darkness before the morning, however. Toward midnight, reports Young, "God, in mercy, lifted up the light of his countenance upon me, and I was translated from the power of darkness into the kingdom of God's dear son, and rejoiced with joy unspeakable and full of glory."[9] He had experienced the third stage of experimental religion; repenting and reforming grace had transmuted into "justifying and converting grace." Young's despair had never been entirely unalloyed by hope. His Christian acquaintances had been praying for him and with him all along. The Bible spoke of God's mercy and love and of the sacrifice of Jesus Christ by which it was possible to become adopted as child of God rather than to remain an object of his condemnation. Faith was the action of the heart that claimed the promises of God and the grace of Christ for each individual who exercised it. With faith the converted felt clearly that their guilt was removed, they were pardoned rather than condemned, and their pollution was washed away sufficiently to avoid eternal death. The painful emotions were removed and a new, pleasurable class of affections and principles took their place. Most significant among these was a lasting feeling that, in accord with Romans 8:16, one had been adopted into the divine family: "The Spirit beareth witness with our spirit that we are the children of God."[10] It was this persisting sense of God's adoption to which the pious referred when they spoke of retaining or losing the "comforts of religion."

Conversion, then, started in the awakening of an uneasy awareness of sin and judgment that led to the terror and despair of conviction. By its very intensity, this negative condition of feeling cried out for a transformation into a condition in which an ecstasy of joy led to peace, hope, and love.[11] Metaphors of depths leading to heights, heaviness to lightness, and especially darkness to light fill accounts of the change the believers felt. Jacob Young recalled rising early after the night of his conversion, standing on a "high eminence," and facing east: "The morning was cold, clear, and beautifully bright . . . the earth and heavens all appeared new—reminding me of the 'new heavens and new earth' wherein dwelleth righteousness."[12] Young felt himself to be a new creature. A new creature implied a new creation. The conversion experience required a new world in which believers might live out their lives in a manner coherent with their transformative experience.

Chauncey Hobart remembered that the first local preacher to visit his family on the Illinois prairie was an uneducated Southerner named Levin Green. He could barely read and he murdered the King's English, but, "to him, God, eternity, death, the resurrection, the judgment, Heaven and Hell, were vivid and solemn realities. In his many discourses, he spoke as if these were actually present, being seen and felt by him."[13] Good evangelicals sought to be much like Levin Green. They cultivated an awareness of and sensitivity to another order of existence that they believed transcended, yet included, the everyday world. Such spiritual sensibility implied a style of life in harmony with this extramundane reality. Experimental religion was more than just experience; it was ontology and ethics, worldview and ethos as well.

Opposed to the world of time and sense, in evangelical imaginations, was the world of eternity, the setting of two sharply opposed and endlessly evocative images: heaven and hell. The two great heads of these eternal realms, God and the Devil, were at war with each other, working through temporal events to win individual human beings to their respective sides. These efforts yielded two opposite regions of life on earth: "the church" versus "the world." Each of these earthly regions had its characteristic mode of persuasion aimed at securing the allegiances of persons through appeals to their "passions" and "affections."

According to an early writer of "Meditations on the Happiness of Heaven," the defining characteristic of God's abode was the absence of disorder, the negation of evil. The happiness of heaven was uninterrupted by (1) the misery arising from the disorder of material creation, (2) the disordered state of the human body, (3) the miseries arising form the corruption of human society, (4) temptation, and (5) impurity of heart. Heavenly life banished natural disaster, disease, social ills, threats to personal integrity, and all the interior divisions of human beings against themselves.[14] The writer found the presence of order, the positive nature of heaven's happiness, harder to talk about. Indeed, he claimed, human nature is so imperfect that we hold only an imperfect ideal of what heaven is really like.[15]

The Methodists specialized, however, in one cluster of analogies and images by which they conveyed the positive delights of heaven—the imagery of home, family, and friendship. In 1803, James Quinn, then a young itinerant preacher, declared to his beloved friend and spiritual father, Daniel Hitt, that the friendship of Christians was permanent and lasting. Nothing could dissolve it save a "declention [*sic*] of religion."[16] Years later, as an old man, he reminisced in print about the friendships he had enjoyed and asked, "Shall not those tender ties and sympathies be renewed and perpetuated world without end?" His solution to the loneliness he felt in finding most of his old friends gone to heaven was "by faith, [to] hold converse with the intellectual world of light, and love, and immortality, where perfect love and the sacred sweets of endearing friendship shall reign for ever and for ever."[17] Daniel Hitt himself was a Virginia-born Methodist itinerant who had many loving correspondents among Methodist clergy and laity in the 1790s and early 1800s. Another of Hitt's correspondents, whose declarations of friendship were ardent almost to the point of being erotic, wrote: "If retrospection [of our times together] is thus sweet to the Soul, then what shall the full enjoyment of an immortal friendship be?"[18] A writer for the *Western Christian Advocate* expressed similar sentiments regarding the family. "How short," he declaimed, "is the earthly history of a family!" The family circle is scattered in a few years; a few more, and both parents and children pass from the earth. How can such ephemeral beings, he asked, engage all our love? Why should not our feelings for them be as "feeble and unsatisfying as they?" The fact that our feelings are not so feeble, he implied, is evidence of what believing Christians know by faith: the ties of domestic love will be resumed "under far happier circumstances, in the region of everlasting love and bliss."[19]

The Methodists often exploited familial images of heaven to win people to their way. One preacher entitled a sermon "Zion Travelers" and envisioned a mother, father, son, daughter, brother, or sister coming down to the eternal banks to welcome home a cherished kinsman. His yearning peroration implored, "Fathers—mothers—sons—daughters—brothers—sisters, go with us to meet, in bright glory, the dear loved ones, who have gone before us. . . . O, go with us—we are on our journey home."[20] James Finley had a vision while on his sick-bed in which an angel took him to heaven and showed him, among other wonders, a family—a man, a woman, and a "blessed child." He yearned to take the child back to bereaved mothers on earth to show them they need not mourn their infants who had died, but the child flew away on cherub's wings singing praises to the Lamb of God. He woke from his vision shouting God's praises and, he said, was instantly healed of his illness. He shared what he saw with the saints at a camp meeting shortly thereafter, and their shouts of glory echoed through the forest.[21]

Exploitation of family sentiment could grow very oppressive, as a letter from an irate husband and self-professed infidel to George Washington Maley illustrates. Maley was a veteran circuit rider in early Ohio. It seems the infidel's wife—who had buried her only child, a nine-month-old, just ten days before—had attended a Methodist love feast out of curiosity. In his remarks to the assembly, the husband alleged, Maley had dug the departed infants of the women present "out of their peaceful graves" and presented the babes' deaths in "a more horrible and terrific manner than it really was in the first place." As he aroused the people's emotions, Maley claimed that God was working on them more at this time than at any other. The incensed infidel gave Maley a brief lesson in theology, reminding the preacher that God does not change, implying that the unchanging God does not work on people more at one time than at another. Maley, of course, and the pious sisters whose dead infants he had pictured in his appeals had felt and believed in a different deity. When they had seen the infidel's wife shed a few tears over her own child, they had importuned her to come to the altar and seek religion. The woman's husband assured Maley that, had he been present, he would have "regulated" the preacher for meddling in his family matters. He declared that his wife was disgusted by the meeting and advised Maley to abandon his "base theatrical performances" and "vile impostions [*sic*]" in the future. The preacher was unmoved; underneath the address of the letter he scrawled, "another howl from an infidel."[22]

The central quality of friendship and family ties that Methodists celebrated again and again was affection. Affectionate love came from God, guaranteed harmony with fellow Christians, and made them members of the same spiritual family. James Henthorn was a Methodist layman and one of Daniel Hitt's closest friends in the gospel. "Christ is the cement of union," Henthorn observed, "so that while we abide in him, we shall be one in heart."[23] Divine love, he rhapsodized, was "the misterious [*sic*] cement of the soul, sweetener of life, and consolidater [*sic*] of Society." Its depths could not be fathomed in this life, but when the saints got to heaven and bathed in the immensity of love at the Father's right hand, they would tell of love in all its various branches and channels and contemplate what it had done for the apostate children of Adam. "It is enough," Henthorn sighed, "to dissolve the most flinty soul into tears of deep contrition."[24] Devout Methodists had all passed through tears of contrition to join the family of God. They called each other brother, sister, father, and mother in the gospel. Benjamin Hitt, one of Daniel's brothers, blessed the Lord for the measure of love he felt in his soul and asserted that God's people were his people and he wanted God's ways to be his ways. He signed himself to his brother Daniel as "your most affectionate brother, both by nature and Grace."[25] Many referred to their fellow believers as "the friends."[26] In their rhetoric, heaven, the church, friendship, and family were all identified with one another through the common denominator of love and affection. The order of heaven, then, was a harmony of affection.

For the Methodists, as for Jonathan Edwards before them, the affections were the seat of religion in human nature. They placed strictures, of course, on Edwards's Calvinist rendering of religious experience, but they agreed that the key dimension of human nature that drew persons beyond this world and involved them in eternity was the capacity for affection. People also had passions, however. Often Methodists used "passions" and "affections" interchangeably, but the terms still retained connotations that distinguished them from each other. "Affection" connoted a tying, pulling, drawing quality of motivation; "passion" connoted qualities of impulsion, drive, possessiveness, and peremptoriness. Passion demanded; affection implored. Affections might be "fixed" on proper or improper objects; passions were "excited" by various holy or unholy causes. Because all humanity was corrupted in nature, affections tended to settle on earthly objects and passions tended to be excited by worldly causes. Passions in general were often ungovernable, "stormy," and warlike. Only the work of God's grace, only His love "shed abroad in the heart" could change this natural bent toward evil.[27]

Persons who failed to avail themselves of this grace were bound for hell. The Methodists wrote about hell less than they wrote about heaven. They much more commonly dwelt upon "the world" as the antithesis of heaven. It is true that they were not above threatening judgment, hellfire, and damnation. Satan already ruled the world, however, and they need only cast his dominion in the light of God and heaven to reveal its hellish character. James B. Finley felt himself as close to hell as he ever wished to be when he sought out a tavern and a dram to drown the impressions he received at the Cane Ridge sacramental meeting. The drunken revelry, card playing, horse trading, quarreling, and fighting at the tavern, when seen in the light of the sacramental meeting's holy tumult of preaching, praying, crying for mercy, and shouting salvation, seemed to invest the tavern with infernal meaning.[28]

The author of "Meditations on the Happiness of Heaven" provided some reflections that Finley might easily have applied to his own experience of the world. The world, wrote the meditator, was full of social corruption in which men oppressed their fellows to gratify ambition, pride, and cruelty. National jealousies appealed to a thirst for power and vainglory and provoked war. Covetousness gave rise to fraud and injustice. Still worse, all these corruptions induced the writer to feel and act in the same way; they found an answering chord in his own impure heart. Indeed his heart generated its own evil desires: excess appetite, pride, vanity, envy, anger, malice, and covetousness. All these actions and motives led to death. "A flood of misery sweeps them [humanity] down the stream of life, until they pass the gulf of death."[29]

Evangelical literature used images of death to convey what both hell and heaven were really like. Methodist periodicals were full of deathbed scenes in which saints' faces lit up with a heavenly glow, or in which they shouted for joy that they were going home to heaven at last. Their religious principles and motives led them to a peaceful and triumphant end. Occasionally, an account would appear in print that portrayed the end to which worldly motives led. Such was the story Maxwell Gaddis, Ohio itinerant and successful author, told of an acquaintance from childhood, a man of "Herculean strength, [who] seemed to take much pleasure in gaming and fighting." Untroubled by guilt, he had a reputation for violence and blasphemous defiance of the Almighty. Gaddis adduced to his story several Old Testament maledictions on the vanity and vulnerability of the wicked; then he announced that sickness brought this blasphemer to his deathbed in the midst of his worldly prosperity. The man was alarmed and called for religious neighbors to pray for him, but "the ruling passion was strong in death." He had never cultivated the proper religious affections, and so he could not be moved to the proper attitude of penitence. "The Holy Spirit," said Gaddis, "at last left him without one good emotion."

His deathbed behavior provided a vivid portent of the wrath to come. He declared that he was working out "his own damnation with greediness" and told his friends he could feel the fire of hell burning within him. He was so convulsed that his friends had to tie him to the bed by wrapping him in girthing from chest to feet. His profanity, ribaldry, jesting, and vulgar songs drove his wife and all other female attendants from his room. Sometimes he would make hissing sounds like those of "infuriated cats at night in a garret." With red and fiery eyes he stabbed his gaze around the house, and his piercing look "struck terror into every heart." Gaddis himself left the man's house when he began to curse each member of the Trinity "in the most awful manner." Shortly thereafter, perhaps in an echo of rough and tumble fights he had won, the reprobate placed his upper teeth upon his lower lip, bit it off, and attempted to swallow it. It strangled him.

Gaddis's narrative demonstrated with special touches of horror the fruition of his acquaintance's worldly motives. In contrast to evocations of affectionate family harmony as the essence of heaven, this story showed the worldly man's progressive isolation from God, friends, and family; the derangement of his mental and emotional faculties; his reduction to hissing animality; and, finally, a self-mutilation that brought death. Here was a man whose essence was self-assertion through violence. When all means for the expression of that essence were taken from him, he destroyed himself. In his end the essence of evil and the character of hell were manifest.[30]

In the ends of the saints, on the other hand, the essence of good and the character of heaven were manifest. When the editors of the *Western Christian Advocate* titled their obituary column the "Biographical Department," they revealed something fundamental about their religion. Christianity, for them, was preparation for death, an effort to steal a march on death by living a dying life. All were born into a dying world and had to confront the reality of death. Because God in Christ had died and risen again, all who identified with Him were included in the new life and new creation he brought into being through His death and resurrection. Identification with Christ came by acceptance of spiritual death—a crucifixion—that was followed by spiritual life—a resurrection. A preacher at a Tennessee camp meeting dramatized the relation of death to salvation by appearing on the preachers' stand clad in a long white gown. These were his grave clothes, he explained. His friends had made them for him years ago when they thought he was dying. He had recovered from his illness, but now he was going to preach the gospel to the crowd in these grave clothes. He chose as his text, 1 Kings 18:21, where the prophet Elijah calls upon Israel to choose between the Lord God and the idol Baal.[31] People had to choose between the world, the flesh, the Devil, and hell, on one hand, and the church, the Spirit, Christ, and heaven on the other. Death, as the preacher's shroud so starkly symbolized, marked a person's passing to one realm or the other.

The idea of death as the pivotal point between heaven and hell is essential to the understanding of evangelical psychology because the two realms cut through the heart of every individual. "I must pass through the agonies of self-mortification," asserted the author of meditations on heaven. "I must be crucified with Jesus Christ that I may live with him. The old man must die in me, that the new man may be raised up in all his vigor and strength."[32] Self-mortification meant the elimination, the "slaying" of the motives belonging to the "old man" and the cultivation of the motives belonging to the "new man."[33] It all began with the conversion experience, but dying with Christ never ceased in this life. The dying and rising conflicts of conversion were the model for the recurring skirmishes of the soul.

The battle continued in one form or another until believers finally triumphed in the "happy deaths" so often lavishly described in the *Western Christian Advocate*'s "Biographical Department." As Polly Jennings, a cousin of James Henthorn, put it to her spiritual mentor, Daniel Hitt, "I know, if ever I get to heaven, it will be by the way of the cross: and blessed be GOD, the heavier the cross the brighter the crown."[34]

The way of the cross began with a discipline of outward behavior that avoided identification with the world in its popular habits of dress and amusement as well as in its grosser forms of evil. But discipline went deeper than that. A truly religious person needed to be regularly "engaged" with the heart. To know one's spiritual standing, to maintain the witness of the Spirit that one was adopted by God, it was necessary to scrutinize one's motives. The apostle Paul admonished Christians to examine themselves to see whether or not they were in the faith. Good Methodists complied, looking for a living faith within that worked by love to purify the heart and produce good works. If one had an ever-present enjoyment of the witness of the Holy Spirit "to the exclusion of unbelief, the dominion of sin, of all angry or bitter feelings, the willful neglect of any known duty, and in a word, whatever is contrary to the love of God and men," then one was prepared to conquer death. The dying life would triumph over the grave.[35]

The reading of Scripture aided the work of self-examination by making the believers sensitive to the standard by which to judge thoughts, words, and actions. Private prayer implored the guidance of the Holy Spirit to allow believers to see themselves aright. Another significant help was exposure to the biographies of Christians who had already attained the witness of the Spirit. The lives of saints with all their conflicts, sufferings, and triumphs—including the triumphs of the deathbed—provided powerful models for the religious exercises of younger believers.[36] Indeed, Methodism excelled in providing such models. Its weekly class meetings and quarterly love feasts centered around testimonies that could be models for the less experienced and encouragements for the more experienced. Where these meetings were faithfully observed, new converts were constantly exposed to the stories of persons who were struggling to be Christians. As literacy increased and publishing flourished in America, the printed biographies and autobiographies of famous Protestant saints became another useful tool of spiritual discipline. Circuit preachers were all agents of the Methodist publishing effort, and did much to recommend such reading.

The ongoing work of self-examination with its attention to inner feeling states, urges, and temptations could be discouraging work. Seely Bunn, a pastor in western Pennsylvania, confided to Daniel Hitt that he found it necessary to warn young converts of the discouraging temptations they would face in times to come. He observed that many "who have been in such raptures have fainted in time of tribulation" because they thought their conversion insured that they would never have such troubled minds and feelings again. If, however, "they are impressed with the idea, that they must suffer with Christ as well as serve him, they are more apt to struggle hard in time of temptations."[37] Earlier in his own life, Bunn himself had cried out: "Alas! my heart is hard, and very deceitful; I feel that every inordinate affection is not brought in sweet subordination to my Master's will; but there is [*sic*] many things within me yet contrary to holiness." He asked his friend to pray for him that he would not stop short of "full salvation."[38]

As Bunn's desire for full salvation suggests, the point of the struggle was more than just the maintenance of the witness of the spirit. The point was to bring about the further progress of grace in the heart. Although delivered from the guilt, condemnation, and eternal consequences of sin, converts remained in some degree polluted by sin. Such pollution manifested itself in the inward dominion of sin in the life, in a continuing "love or desire to sin." The graces of awakening, conviction, and conversion, then, led on to the graces of sanctification.[39] Sanctification meant the progressive purging of such impurities as pride, vanity, envy, anger, and malice from the believer's motives.[40] It also meant the infilling of love until the believer was enabled to love God with a whole heart. Loving God with the whole heart was a special doctrine and experience for the Methodists. They called it by a variety of names—holiness, perfection, sanctification—but the label that seems most appropriate is "perfect love."[41] Although a long process led up to it, it was also a discrete moment that resembled the conversion experience. Just as the awakened sinner's seeking of religion issued in the conversion experience, so the converted believer's seeking for perfect love issued in experiences similar in structure and even in intensity to the conversion experience.

The conversion experience began in passions of terror and hatred—hatred turned against the self. These dark passions eventually gave way to peace and love, not self-love, but a sense of God's love for the self. The two poles of the experience were a tormented self-abhorrence and contented self-abandonment. The sovereign God of wrath drove the seeker to self-hatred; but the converted believer abandoned himself to the crucified God of love. This emotional process was the structure through which evangelicals organized the whole of their experience. So long as they remained religious, their fear, their self-hatred, and their love never left them. The love they felt was both the love of God for the self and the reciprocal love of the self for God. Love to man followed from the fact that it was the love of God for all human selves that was shed abroad in the heart. The believer still feared God, with a reverential awe rather than a preconversion terror; but the chief motive of the believer's life came more and more to be love in response to God's love.[42] Self-hatred persisted, but it was hatred for a self that was not sufficiently moved by the love manifest in the sacrifice of Christ, by the yearning of God to be one with man. It was hatred for a dull, unresponsive self that would not live up to its privileges of full and constant communion with God but clung to its pride and self-sufficiency and would not humble itself fully so that it might be raised fully into God's love.

The love of God was not only a thing of comfort, then; it was also a consuming fire. It worked within the soul of the believer to more and more mortify the motives of the "old man" and cultivate those of the "new man." Spiritual life was a series of small crucifixions. Believers endured sore exercises of mind as they struggled to yield to God's demand that they die to some impure desire, bad habit, neglect of duty, angry feeling, or just a cold, careless state of mind. In yielding was victory, and the state of mind that followed was one of peace, love, and joy.[43] Thus Rebeccah Morgan entered into a lengthy bemoaning of her unfaithfulness in a number of unspecified duties and especially in failing to write to her friend and pastor, Daniel Hitt. She went on to lament how far she and her husband lived beneath their "gospel privileges." But then her moaning merged into rejoicing: "O! what happy people, the people of GOD might be; O! how happy are the faithful people of GOD.—O! brother while I write, I feel the flame of Love to glow in my heart to GOD & his people, tho' they are despised and reproached by the world.—O! Lord grant that the flame may increase to eternity." After this crescendo her passions died down again and she asked Hitt to pray for her and her husband; they had a great many enemies in the world, she said, but the worst were their own wicked hearts.[44]

The enemies in the world often worked in concert with the enemies in the heart to create trials and temptations. A pious and disciplined Christian met with a submissive spirit the frustrations and sufferings imposed by life in this fallen world. By a submissive spirit the Christian might "sanctify the evils of the present world to his . . . promotion in virtue and piety."[45] Itinerant Learner Blackman sanctified to his own good a very trying assignment to the Holston district in the mountains of southwest Virginia. He invoked the scriptural pattern of Romans 5:3–5 to speak of how his difficulties caused "mortifications," that worked "patience," that gave "experience," that led to "hope, " and "hope maketh not ashamed because the love of God is shed abroad in the heart by the Holy Ghost." When his soul was happy in the Lord, "this rough . . . , this disagreeable and mountainous country seemed a plain."[46] Biographical sketches of dying saints depicted them suffering their terminal illnesses with great fortitude and patience, showing the power of religion over the human mind under the most trying of circumstances. On the other hand, bereavement might be interpreted as a chastening of overfond attachments held by the living and urged as an occasion for setting affections on heavenly things and paying greater attention to religious duties.[47]

The Psalmist encapsulated the basic pattern of experimental religion:

For his anger endureth but only a moment,
in his favor is life;
weeping may endure for a night,
but joy cometh in the morning. (Psalms 30:5)

The pattern, if not the particular scripture, pervaded evangelical thought, feeling, and action. The death and resurrection of Jesus were its theological foundation. A tenacious disposition to expect affliction to yield comfort, sorrow to bring joy, pain to lead to spiritual pleasure, depression to give way to exultation, and discouragement to rebound in renewed courage was its psychological result. "Strange as it is, it is very true," marveled James Henthorn, "the lower we sink, the higher we rise." The Love of Jesus, he declared, leads to this fountain of meekness and of joy.[48]

While sometimes this emotional pattern could lead to some rather bizarre reactions,[49] labor historian E. P. Thompson goes too far when, in his analysis of early English Methodism among the working classes, he charges Methodist religiosity with a wholesale disorganization of the human personality. Every impulse, he asserts, was twisted into its opposite: joy was associated with guilt and sin, pain with goodness and love.[50] The important rhetorical feature of the way of the cross, however, was not the *association* of pain with pleasure but the *sequence* or *progression* from pain and suffering to pleasure and joy. Pious Methodists lived by the paradox that momentary pain, sorrow, or suffering would be transformed, by the grace of Christ, into lasting pleasure, joy, and comfort. Thompson seems to operate with an associationist psychology that obscures this diachronic, narrative element in Methodist piety.

In addition to the pattern in which suffering yielded to joy, experimental religion evinced a paradoxical pattern of active passivity. One anonymous contributor to a weekly newspaper felt she lacked power to maintain the "resignation, meekness, fortitude, and patience" that she felt a thorough Christian experience required. She actively sought such power in persevering prayer, seeking to humble herself before God while feeling it was right for Him to be hiding his face from her. She "contended hard and long" for the right degree of faith. The turning point came when she resolved to wait patiently until God restored to her "the joys of His salvation." She felt a change of mind in which her "enemies"—presumably the impulses of her fallen nature—were gone. Peace possessed her soul, peace that increased for two weeks and culminated in a wonderful season of deep communion with her Savior. "Solemn awe, and humble love" filled her whole soul. "The Spirit and the Word" showed her that the blood of Christ had cleansed her heart from all unrighteousness. Her soul soared "as on eagle's wings," and she felt that now Satan had nothing in her.[51] Elizabeth Kauffmann and George S. Phillips were two Ohio-born Methodists who became husband and wife and served the Methodist church in the Midwest and the Far West during the middle decades of the nineteenth century. In their courtship correspondence, they wrote more about their respective quests for God's perfect love than they did of their love for each other. Elizabeth suggested an insight that George seized upon and later turned to his advantage in his spiritual quest. She observed that her greatest blessings had always come to her while she was praying for sanctification and wondered if it was simply a failure of faith not to call these blessings *the* blessing. Soon after these reflections, George announced to her that he had received perfect love. He had been unusually blessed in his private devotions in the early evening and had recalled her remarks about doubting God's willingness to bless. He had endeavored to believe and had been enabled to exclaim, "Lord I believe." His experience was not ecstatic, but a "deep peace and unshaken confidence." "The Spirit bore witness with my spirit," he wrote, "that it was perfect love."[52] Both Phillips and the anonymous lady had to still their strivings and doubts before they received the blessing. They were patients of the experience, not agents. But only their persistent and energetic agency brought them to the point of the proper trusting patience.

A further psychological result of divine love in the soul was a quality of interior life that suggested the configuration of a sacred place set at a distance from a threatening environment. A short untitled poem in a popular Methodist women's monthly, the *Ladies Repository*, evoked such an image:

> What, what is virtue, but repose of mind
> A pure ethereal calm, that knows no storm;
> Above the reach of wild ambitions wind,
> Above those passions that this world deform.[53]

A generation earlier, a theorist of "Vital Religion" insisted that religion elevated the soul above "the glare of riches, the tinsel of honor, the gaudy show of pleasure" into the "calm regions of resignation and peace divine." The mind of the godly is undisturbed by "that influence which sets the world of the ungodly in high fermentation." Instead, "the temper becomes mild, the dispositions assume a heavenly frame, the passions are reduced to order and harmonious operation and a fountain of pleasure is opened within, springing up into eternal life."[54] These images resonate also with the object lesson on holiness included in the *Methodist Family Manual*. A bowl of water represented the holy person, a bowl of gunpowder the unholy one. Water extinguished the fiery spark of temptation, but the gunpowder exploded in response to it.[55] The calm and order the Methodists sought are presented here not only as positive things in themselves but as states that exist in opposition to evil states that threaten them and above which they rise. Just as the world was the dark background against which visions of heaven shone with starkly contrasting light, so the stormy passions of fallen human nature contrasted with the harmonious quiet of the Christian soul.

The ideal state of the soul was not simply retreat and repose, however. Withdrawal into heavenly repose issued in renewed activity and advance. Learner Blackman, while laboring on his Lexington, Kentucky, circuit in the early 1800s, determined to preach more assiduously the doctrine of sanctification. As he preached the doctrine and several on the circuit professed to find the blessing, the "pleasure of sanctifying love" revived in his own soul. This gave him greater calmness and resignation to the will of God, but it also gave him "a greater zeal for the promotion of the glory of God. A greater struggle for the salvation of souls and a greater willingness to suffer, travel, and die in the field of Battle."[56] George S. Phillips filled his diary and letters with earnest yearnings and prayers to be useful and to do much good in the church. It was toward this end that he prayed to be made holy; holiness and usefulness were reciprocal blessings in his vision of ministry. Indeed, his choice of helpmeet was clearly predicated on the understanding that she and he would enhance each other's usefulness and aid each other in the pursuit of holiness and that their joint attainment of holiness would further increase their usefulness.[57]

The psychological pattern of self-denial leading to joy, peace, and spiritual labor was not, of course, the sole property of Methodism. Baptist and Presbyterian documents of the period display similar sorts of emotional patterning.[58] There is a certain quality in some biographical and autobiographical materials from these Calvinist traditions, however, that rarely, if ever, appears among the Methodists. A clear example of this quality appears in the story of a young man who, in the course of telling his experience to his Baptist congregation, shocked his hearers by saying he was willing to go to hell. He testified that he saw that God was wholly just in sending him, as well as the greater part of humanity, to hell. He had no desire for God to change, and he saw no reason why God should favor his own particular case more than any other person's. He also saw that God might be just in saving sinners through his Son, but without that consideration, he was willing to be damned. Silenced by this terrifying but, on Calvinist grounds, irrefutable logic, the congregation voted to admit him to membership.[59] There is little evidence that Methodists developed such capacity to glory in the untrammeled, imperturbable sovereignty of God. Belief in such sovereignty did give comfort, however, to people like the old-side Presbyterian layman who inveighed against the Cumberland Presbyterians for insisting that God cannot save those who are unwilling. He asserted that God made them willing. If the Cumberland faction were right, then Christ was only half a savior and there was room left for human boasting. Only this firm belief in an unchanging sovereign Providence could give him a sense of security in the midst of the transitory objects of temporal life.[60]

In the young Baptist's willingness to be damned for the glory of God it is easy to recognize something of the "universal otherhood" that Benjamin

Nelson has delineated in his classic historical study *The Idea of Usury*. God, for the magisterial Reformers and for Calvin in particular, was the fount of all equity, justice, and universal love. He did not treat any sort of person differently from any other, nor could He allow his creatures to treat their "brothers" differently from those whom they regarded as "others."[61] Thus a conscience attuned to the ethic of universal otherhood required that even the convert be willing to go to hell, because all humankind were justly deserving of it. Methodist piety might grant the justice of universal damnation, but it was founded on an emotional pattern that dictated terror rather than detached satisfaction in response to the judgments of God. Only when the sovereign God of Sinai became, by grace, the affectionate Father in heaven could the Methodist be satisfied. It seems appropriate, even at the risk of caricature, to describe the Calvinist piety as emphasizing a deity of universal sovereignty and justice, and Methodist piety as emphasizing a deity of universal love and affection. The difference was, of course, only one of emphasis. Methodists did not bask in the love of their heavenly Father without first tasting the bitterness of His righteous wrath, and Calvinists did not glory in the omnipotent righteousness of their sovereign God without the support of His love in Christ. The difference mattered, however—especially when it came to construing the significance of earthly family ties.

In summary, the psychology of experimental religion involved basic ways of organizing experience that may be described in terms of a narrative pattern and a spatial image. The narrative pattern was the way of the cross. It involved the death of affections and passions that bound the believer to the world and the rebirth of these feelings into righteous attachment to God, fellow believers, and their style of living. The ideal Methodist life story evinced the pattern in both continuous and crisis modes. The daily mortification of worldly motives was the continuous mode, while conversion and sanctification were the crisis events to which mortification led. The deathbed was the final crisis point for which the whole of the believer's faithful, dying life had prepared. How did the Methodist saint die? "As she lived; the one was a fitting sequel to the other."[62] In addition, the narrative pattern led the saint into a particular location, as it were, in the spatial image. The pious Methodist resided in a sacred place set over against a threatening environment. Virtue, peace, resignation, love, and joy all pervaded that place and elevated the believer above the stormy passions of this world. Sometimes, in class meeting, love feast, or camp meeting, this spatial image would be incarnate in the physical arrangement of people and buildings. At other times the image would be conveyed through the language of believers about their inner lives. In either case, the reciprocal tie of the narrative pattern to the spatial image was implied: the way of the cross led to a sacred place that was identified with heaven and homeland, family and friends.

This was a different kind of place than the kind of place found in a hierarchical body politic under the headship of a sovereign patriarch. Many who had been entangled in this traditional hierarchy found in the examples and appeals of Methodist itinerants and laypeople a persuasive invitation to relocate.

5

The Salvation Machine and the Subversion of Patriarchy

While images of the cross and resurrection best conveyed the inner dynamic of Methodism, Methodist preacher George Cookman found in the visions of the prophet Ezekiel the best image to convey its organizational form:

> The *great iron wheel* in the system is *itineracy* [*sic*], and truly it grinds some of us most tremendously; the *brazen wheel*, attached and kept in motion by the former, is the *local ministry*; the *silver wheel*, the *class leaders*; the *golden wheel*, the *doctrine and discipline of the church*, in full and successful operation. . . . Let us carefully note the admirable and astounding movements of this wonderful machine. You will perceive there are "wheels within wheels." First, there is the great outer wheel of episcopacy, which accomplishes its entire revolution *once* in *four* years. To this there are attached *twenty-eight smaller wheels*, styled *annual conferences*, moving round *once a year*; to these are attached *one hundred wheels*, designated *presiding elders*, moving *twelve hundred other wheels*, termed *quarterly conferences*, every *three months*; to these are attached *four thousand wheels*, styled *travelling preachers*, moving round *once a month*, and communicating motion to *thirty thousand* wheels, called *class leaders*, moving round *once a week*, and who, in turn, being attached to between *seven* and *eight hundred thousand wheels*, called *members*, give a sufficient impulse to whirl them round *every day*. O, sir, what a machine is this! This is the machine of which Archimedes only dreamed; this is the machine destined, under God, to *move the world, to turn it upside down*![1]

Thus apotheosized, the Methodist organization was an awesome sight, filling some with pride, others with loathing.[2] The modern reader, so well acquainted with the frustrations of bureaucracy, might share the loathing and think of another of Ezekiel's visions, the vision of the valley full of dry bones. The early American Methodists, however, lived before bureaucracy threatened to turn the Holy Spirit into a ghost in the machinery. The early believers felt and saw God working powerfully through their organization. And they did indeed turn at least a part of the world upside down,

The world they upset was the world of patriarchal honor, with which Methodism had both affinities and crucial tensions. These affinities and tensions may be more clearly revealed by a comparison that addresses two fundamental elements of any culture: ways of constructing the self, and ways of constructing hierarchies of selves. Methodism's and honor's ways of constructing the self are made manifest in a comparison of the legendary saints of the frontier camp meeting and the mythical Davy Crockett, hero of the frontier community of republican yeomen. The two ways of constructing hierarchies of selves become clear in a comparison of the circuit riders, the Methodist spiritual "elite," with the traditional gentry hierarchy. The point of these comparisons and contrasts is to demonstrate that the logic of Methodist religion pointed toward a new level of individual self-control and autonomy and toward a different understanding of community and family to go with it. The patterns of recruitment pursued by the early Methodists through their great salvation machine focused on family units and evinced the new logic of self-control, subverting patriarchal authority in the process.

A soul seeking to make its way home to heaven by the way of the cross needed to separate itself from the community of honor. The Methodist *Discipline*, if nothing else, seemed to demand it. It commanded the member of the Methodist society to abstain from all manner of evil, "*especially* that which is most generally practiced," and, lest there be any doubt, it listed these common sins:

> the taking of the name of God in vain; the profaning of the day of the Lord, either by doing ordinary work thereon, or buying or selling; drunkenness, buying or selling spirituous liquors, or drinking them . . . fighting, quarreling, brawling . . . Uncharitable or unprofitable conversation . . . doing what we know is not for the glory of God, as the "putting on of gold or costly apparel;" the taking of such diversions as cannot be used in the name of the Lord Jesus . . . softness and needless self-indulgence; laying up treasures upon earth.[3]

It took little imagination to turn this list of proscriptions into a blanket condemnation of the most visible aspects of the culture of honor. Early Methodist converts consistently portray such activities as the way to hell that they were pursuing before God saved them. Peter Cartwright confessed to being a "naturally wild and wicked boy" who delighted in horse racing and cards. When convicted of his sinfulness and of the need to seek religion, he gave up his race horse and brought his pack of cards to his mother, who threw them in the fire.[4] Jacob Young also became addicted to dancing, horse racing, and worse: "Seeking the deepest and wildest shades," he testified, "I spent the Lord's holy day in gambling." Even while laboring under conviction, he could not well resist the enticements of such rituals of contest. "All the powers of darkness rallied," he recalled, and lured him into keeping a horse race appointment with one whom he characterized as "a desperately bad man." He nearly lost his life in the race. He avowed that he often trembled when reflecting on that day, knowing what his eternal fate would have been had he died in a horse race. The race track and similar scenes became, for Young and many like him, concrete reminders of diabolical powers and the nearness of damnation.[5]

To understand the horror that people like Young felt in the presence of the ethos of honor, it is important to notice the similarities as well as the differences between honor and the Methodist way of organizing experience. Catherine Albanese has provided a convenient analysis for undertaking both tasks. Her comparative study of the Davy Crockett myths and evangelical camp-meeting rituals may be taken as an explication of the cultural contrasts and continuities between the ethos of honor and the family of God. The mythical Crockett was the hero of the egalitarian community of republican yeomen, a community that rejected gentry hierarchy but that sustained other norms of honor among its members. The Crockett stories modeled the grandiose way of constructing the self characteristic of honor. The legendary camp-meeting saints were founders of the American Methodist family of God, a community that replaced gentry hierarchy with a different sort of hierarchy and that rejected the norms of honor. The actions of the saints on the campground modeled the idealizing way of constructing the self characteristic of the family of God. Both Crockett and the saints, however, evinced a cosmology in which overpowering transcendence might at any time oppress the individual. Both dealt with this oppressiveness through a strategy of fusion or identification with the transcendent power. Both the mythical Davy Crockett and the historical camp-meeting converts lost control of themselves in ecstatic union with transcendence, and, for both, this loss of control was a technique for attaining power, control, and order in their lives.[6]

Davy Crockett encountered transcendence in the wildness of the frontier itself—the physical land, its animals, and its natural humans, the Indians. Crockett identified with this wildness by self-expansion, a kind of savage grandiosity. His name was thunder and lightning, he crowed, and anyone who got in his way might look out for a scorching. Tamer of bears, alligators, wolves, he was also conqueror of "niggers" and Indians in hand-to-hand combat in which he gouged, scratched, and bit like wild animal. The paradox of Crockett's savagery and wildness was that it led back to civility and order. He claimed once to have tamed his wild animal pets to such an extent that they listened to one of his Fourth of July speeches with more civility than members of Congress accorded each other. Crockett's order, however, was the order of the *polis*. Its patterns of interaction were those of politics, and the style of politics was founded on the norms of honor. The difference between the mythical Crockett and the historical gentry of the pre-Revolutionary South is that Crockett deferred to no one. Mastery was no longer a gift received, in submissive temper, from legitimate sources of transcendence like God and king. It was something to be taken in one's teeth.

Evangelical religion, on the other hand, required submission and self-abnegation. Crockett became master in the midst of his ecstasy; the evangelical convert agonized first in an ecstasy of helplessness and gained self-mastery only after yielding up the self. Mastery was once again a gift, but now a free gift of grace available to all in the same measure, regardless of rank in the eyes of the community and, for the Arminian Methodists, without restriction in the mind of God. It is true that the camp-meeting converts sank into a wildness and savagery of their own. Shouts, groans, shrieks, jerks, weeping, running, falling, dancing, barking, and many other "exercises" characterized them. Their loss of control, however, issued not in self-expansion and assertion, but in self-mortification and submission. Their brush with savagery, like Crockett's, led back to civilization and order, but their order was that of the family of God, not that of the polis.

The very closeness of the mythical Crockett and the legendary camp-meeting saints made their followers feel hostile to each other when it came to their essential point of difference—their ways of constructing the self. The Crockett character asserted and expanded the self in a grandiose manner to incorporate and master the wilderness. The evangelical character suppressed and contracted the self while idealizing and identifying with a transcendent Other who overcame the wilderness. These two ways of constructing the self, grandiosity and idealization, are but flip sides of the same coin; but to a person who is committed to one way, persons committed to the other way can seem the personification of darkness and perversity.

Human cultures need not only to establish how selves are to be constructed, they also seem bound to prescribe how selves are to be ranked, thus posing the problem of hierarchy. In their response to hierarchy, the Methodists evinced another similarity to aspects of the culture of honor with another crucial difference. Although early Methodists defined themselves in opposition to a hierarchical gentry society, social class distinctions and hierarchy per se did not repel them. Their form of church organization, an inheritance from English churchman John Wesley, was itself a very hierarchical and authoritarian affair. They showed little inclination to condemn the existence of high social stations. If the wealthy, respectable families in a neighborhood were sympathetic to the Methodist cause, Methodist preachers often voiced satisfaction and appreciative words, even if those highly placed personages did not themselves join the church.[7] Peter Cartwright was pleased to see that pride did not prevent many "fine, wealthy ladies from town" from coming forward to the altar as seekers at a Kentucky camp meeting he held. He boasted of the increase in members, usefulness, and "religious respectability" that the Methodist church gained at this camp meeting and put the wealth of the fine ladies in perspective. "*Sanctified* wealth," he declared, "will always prove a blessing to the Church of God; but unsanctified wealth . . . never fails to corrupt and curse the church." He decried great expenditures on ornamental churches that made "a vain show" and gratified "pampered pride," but he lauded generosity for Gospel missions.[8] Even the popular evangelicals who stressed free grace, then, did not seek to overturn socioeconomic hierarchy. They only wanted to sanctify it. It was the self-expansive spiritual style of pride, assertion, and display against which they warred.

Their war was by no means insignificant. In the culture of honor, recognition, rising in society, and authority came by means of the proving of prowess in gaining wealth and connections. Prowess led to the establishment and perpetuation of a family lineage that was expected to have in its blood the qualities that had made for greatness. Among evangelicals, recognition, rising in the religious society, and spiritual authority came by divine call, spiritual giftedness, and an ever deepening experience of mortification. The process of becoming a Methodist preacher and rising in the church hierarchy, at least in the early history of the denomination, exemplifies the evangelical inversion of the principles of hierarchy in the culture of honor.

Concomitant with or shortly after conversion, nearly every evangelical preacher received a conviction or "call" to preach the gospel. The call itself was like a special version of the conversion experience. The conviction of being called produced mental anguish and self-deprecation. An inner struggle eventually allowed the Spirit of God to overcome one's natural fleshly resistance to the call and to lead to an exercise of trust in God. Peace, joy, and renewed energy followed on the resolution of the conflict. William I. Fee felt that his mental and moral qualifications were wholly inadequate to the task of preaching; he professed to be so naturally timid that he would sooner die than try to lead a soul to Christ. He suffered so much strain in resisting his call to preach that his health really did begin to fail, and his friends predicted an early grave. He had taken to his bed, ready to die, when the reflection came to him that his resistance was foolish. If he tried to preach and failed at it, the responsibility was God's, not his. He agreed to preach if God sent the opportunities. God did, apparently, and Fee spent a long life in the ministry.[9]

This special crisis point was a necessary introduction to the preacher's high position in his religious community. Indeed there seems to have been a kind of logic of humiliation involved in the Methodist spiritual hierarchy wherein advancement in position was undergirded by "advancement" in humility. J. B. Finley followed this logic when promoted to the position of presiding elder. He felt "great depression of mind" as he entered his wider field of service. He realized more deeply that his trust could only be in God and prayed for a deeper baptism of the Holy Spirit. He then felt the divine power reconsecrating his heart to God. "O the ineffable richness and extent of divine love!" he exclaimed. "May my soul ever bask in its infinite ocean."[10]

The practice of the itinerant ministry itself exemplified the way of the cross. If men of honor modeled the code of honor in a demeanor that permeated all their dealings with others, the itinerant preachers, the spiritual elite of the Methodist community, also promoted their way by living it out. The rigors of circuit riding required self-denial, suffering, and stern self-discipline. A preacher who did his duty on a typical four-week circuit in the early days might preach thirty times or more at almost as many locations spread out over a hundred miles. He traveled over bad or nonexistent roads in all types of weather in all seasons and was dependent for bed and board upon the settlers he served. Church policy allowed less than a hundred dollars a year as pay, and the members of the circuit were often so poor or stingy that the preachers frequently lacked even what the church allowed. In the earliest years, most preachers abstained from marriage, sparing themselves an anxiety familiar to their successors, but still sacrificing one of the main claims to identity in the culture of honor—a family and property by which to provide for it. No antebellum itinerant, married or unmarried, could get very attached to his land, because the bishops seldom allowed any preacher to stay on a particular circuit for as long as two years.

The early itinerant preacher, then, was a specialist in the dying life, and this identity conferred upon him great rhetorical power and spiritual authority in the community of the faithful. The famous Indiana preacher John Strange repeatedly declined offers of land and a home with the comment that nothing could persuade him to give up the privilege of singing the lines that were "the master passion" of his life:

> No foot of land do I possess,
> No cottage in the wilderness;
> A poor wayfaring man.
> I dwell awhile in tents below,
> And gladly wander to and fro,
> Till I my Canaan gain.

His biographer recalled seeing Strange step from the pulpit on many occasions and sing these lines to his congregation. His face seemed "radiant with light divine," and he sang with such "pathos and power and sweetness" that the hearts of thousands of his hearers were moved as the trees of the forest are moved by a mighty wind.[11]

Bishop Francis Asbury was the prince of the itinerants, and Jacob Young remembered him as the greatest exemplar of "piety, benevolence, regularity, industry, and economy." He never had time to marry, buy a farm or build a house. Like St. Paul he counted all things as loss for the sake of knowing Christ. "He presented his manly form and giant mind as a sacrifice, holy, acceptable unto God."[12] James Finley, remarking that some of his fellow ministers would bear equally lively recollections, recorded an incident that illustrates how this chief of the fathers in the gospel exercised the authority of the dying life. Finley, encouraged by a remark of the bishop himself, had requested a particular appointment that would have been very convenient for his family. When he received an assignment far in the opposite direction from where he had asked to be moved, he remonstrated with the bishop. " 'Well,' said he, smiling and stroking my head, 'be a good son in the gospel, James, and all things will work together for good.' " Finley's reflections on this incident, far from being resentful or even wry, are a small tirade against preachers who pray for particular appointments as he had done.[13] His sense of the rightness of the bishop's authority turned whatever resentment he might have felt into hostility toward people with motives like his own.

There was something about the itinerancy that made it seem close to the core of Methodism for most of its preachers and members. One preacher spoke sentiments echoed by many others in many different settings. The itinerancy, he claimed, was the great spring that kept the whole machine going, the vital principle that animated the whole body. To destroy the itinerancy would be to destroy Methodism; the life and power of godliness would depart.[14] It seems that the itinerancy allowed certain men to embody in their way of life a meaning that the majority of believers touched only periodically in the intense ritual moments of the Methodist family. Both the itinerant way of life and the ritual fellowship of lay believers asserted the fundamental spiritual value of all human beings before God. They affirmed this value regardless of and prior to any social meaning that accrued to a person by virtue of appearance, possessions, family, or any other social status or role. Such spiritual equality was to be acted out and experienced more than talked about, and the itinerancy was a primary way of acting out this truth.

The itinerant, like his Savior, was poor and often without a home. While on the circuit, at least, he engaged in a degree of mendicancy, living on the hospitality of the people he served. He was constantly on the move, always just passing through, both literally and, as John Strange's favorite song made clear, figuratively. With regard to worldly social structure, he was an outsider, having set himself apart from the normal roles and statuses of the communities he visited. His lack of land and often of family was a pivotal lack in the ethos of honor, where a man's claim to be someone in his community rested upon his possession of land and of a family. In his own religious community, he was located up the organizational hierarchy, but this very hierarchy, founded upon self-sacrifice, was an inversion of the worldly hierarchy founded on self-assertion.

The early itinerants understood the material and social costs of their calling. What made it worth the cost was the repeated experience of being owned by God, by the people of God, and, as Russell Richey has made clear, by their brethren in the ministry.[15] Early Methodist meetings frequently were moments of an intense fellowship of feeling, a communion of hearts and minds founded upon the truth that all were precious in God's sight. This basic form of human relatedness, unmediated by standard social labels, both confirmed the distinctiveness of each person present and overcame his or her separateness. The people and the preachers felt an enlivening power in such moments, a power that they could only attribute to the presence of God. The itinerant preacher was a master ritualizer whose calling it was to facilitate and supervise the ritual moments in which this essential divine-human relation might be intensely realized. The condition of its realization was an authentic surrender of the worldly self. Only those who sank to utter humility before God and humankind and yielded up all claim to special privilege, status, recognition, or pride were able to enter into this communion. The preacher himself was a specialist in such self-surrender and was thus best prepared to lead others into these holy moments of mutuality. The voluntary lowliness of the itinerant facilitated community and in community many felt the life and power of a godliness that would depart if the itinerancy were abandoned.

There was, however, a crucial ambiguity in the Methodist inversion of hierarchy. At the same time that Methodist itinerants and their followers relativized the claims to greatness and recognition made by the worldly, they made their own claims to recognition. They established their own world with its own order of status and its own routes to status elevation. Just as the great planters of the gentry had seemed to many common folk to be a bit more than ordinary human beings, the best of the preachers came to seem to many as if they occupied a plane above that of common humanity. Just as the middling and common planters might enjoy the "uplift" of being addressed and treated at muster field and courthouse by the great men of the neighborhood, so the laity of Methodism might know the joy of being "lifted up" by the address and company of the great men of the ministry. It may be that one of Methodism's major assets in the early years of the republic was its ability to maintain a sense of this hierarchical appeal among a people long used to a deferential social order. Yet Methodist holy men were taken from the levels of the common folk themselves; they regularly descended from the pulpit to ordinary levels to sup with the common folk; and the common folk knew they themselves were not hindered by birth or privilege from sharing in the same principles of the cross that gave the preacher his special status.[16]

In true American middle-class fashion, Methodism affirmed an equality of opportunity and an inequality of results in its organizational forms, with an assurance of the basic equality of all humankind in terms of opportunity for salvation. There were even hints here and there that heaven itself held higher rewards for those who distinguished themselves in the way of self-denial. As Polly Jennings proclaimed to Daniel Hitt, "the heavier the cross the brighter the crown."[17] One Rev. Jonathan Stamper reported a dream in which the dead itinerant John P. Finley came to him and exhorted him never to leave the itinerancy, declaring that he would shine brighter in heaven the more he traveled and suffered the peculiar privations of itinerancy on earth.[18]

The subtle invitations to status-striving contained in the Methodist manner of organizing experience should alert us to another important difference between the Methodist hierarchy and that of the gentry in the traditional culture of honor. The Methodist hierarchy was organizational; the gentry hierarchy was cosmological. The customary distinctions between the great families of Virginia, on one hand, and the lower and middling sorts, on the other, had seemed only instances of a principle of order that most people took for granted well into the eighteenth century: the cosmos was made up of many strata of orders of being, each graded according its own degree of honor. The rule of the gentry "fathers" over the affairs of the county and parish had seemed as natural as the rule of biological fathers over their offspring. The point of being a gentry father was, in a sense, to act out with honor his role in sustaining the whole divine order and its exemplary institutions. In such an arrangement, the individual existed for the family lineage and for the life of the community in which the family acted its part. The Methodist hierarchy, on the other hand, was part of an organization that existed for only one purpose: to create and sustain a holy people by bringing individuals to the perfect love of God and humanity. The point of being a "father in the gospel," then, was actually an instrumental one; it was to nurture one's spiritual children in self-surrender in order that they might find their way home to heaven at last. The organization, in principle, existed for the individual and for the special divine-human communion that the way of the cross made possible. It is this essential difference between the two hierarchies that dictates a judgment that Methodism, despite its great authoritarianism, sided with the revolt against patriarchy that Jay Fliegelman has discovered in the Anglo-American world of the late eighteenth century.[19] The agitation within Methodism for lay representation and other reforms, and the eventual schism of the Methodist Protestant Church in the 1820s and 1830s suggests that this movement was complicated and ambivalent. The majority of Methodists clung persistently to the spiritual patriarchy of their community.[20] But the course toward personal autonomy was laid, and succeeding generations followed it.

The differences between the two hierarchies are apparent also in the ways in which metaphors of the family shaped relationships in each. In the traditional understanding, the family as an economic and social estate was the metaphor for all larger social relations as well: as the patriarch was to his household, so the gentry fathers were to the community, and the royal father was to his subjects. In all such pairings, inferiors depended upon superiors not simply for material sustenance but for a sense of identity as well. One derived one's being from the patriarch, be he father of the kingdom or of the immediate family line. This dependence, and the norms of deference that followed logically from it, kept in check the self-expansion and self-assertion that were otherwise encouraged in the ethos of honor.

In the evangelical understanding, the family also served as metaphor for larger social relations—brothers and sisters in Christ, fathers and mothers in the gospel. The evangelical metaphor, however, stressed not the sovereignty of the paternal head, but the mutual love of all members of the family for one another. Such love was not the natural outworking of creation. It was the supernatural gift of redemption in Christ, given to each individual who sought such redemption. The self-aggrandizing motives native to the culture of honor were not merely subordinated in deference to one's betters, they were thoroughly mortified. Even the affections thought natural to family life were to be chastened and purified by the way of the cross, as later chapters will show. The individual's encounter with God, unmediated by agencies of human creation, was logically prior to the constitution of any community, even the community of the church or the community of parents and children. One became a child of God first, then joined the family of God. The natural family was to model itself after the family of God in the hope that it might lead its individual members to become children of God. For Methodist evangelicals, the family was no longer a dance of dominance and deference meant to evince the order of the cosmos. It was a drama of moral influence that was to reflect the felicities of heaven, emulate the mutual affection of church members, and shape the motives of individuals until they were fit for the holy intercourse of heaven and homeland.

In the frontier years of the Ohio valley, the growth of Methodism in a given neighborhood often began not with a representative of the great iron wheel of the itinerancy but with one or more faithful Methodist families from a Methodist society in an older region of settlement. The heads of such families, or at least the wives and mothers, felt the need for "religious privileges" and the obligation to share such privileges with the neighbors they could interest. They faithfully attended to daily family prayer and opened their homes for weekly prayer meetings that often attracted those interested in religion and even those merely curious souls in search of whatever sociability an isolated farming community might afford. If the head of the family was a local preacher (an officially licensed preacher who did not itinerate and had no responsibility for the administration of discipline), he might range a day's journey beyond his neighborhood in search of other pious families, setting and filling appointments for preaching in their homes. The itinerant preachers relied heavily on such lay initiative and occasionally rebuked those who neglected to do their part in assembling congregations for the circuit rider's preaching efforts. Society after society was formed through such efforts. The veteran western itinerant James Quinn reflected that local preachers and private members had very often preceded the travelling preachers in many parts of the Old West and "raised the Macedonian cry" from their primitive log cabins, welcoming the itinerants with, "Come in thou blessed of the Lord."[21]

The preachers and the lay families of Methodism formed an especially close bond in the early years of the nineteenth century. Through this bond, the family lives of a broad segment of the American population were incorporated for a brief but critical time into the ritual order of Methodism. Woven through the formal organization of Methodism—its bureaucracy on horseback—was a network of rituals that communicated the spirit and power of the movement to its members and that served as the patterns of recruitment to the church. The family was a major nodal point in this network.

It should hardly surprise us that the family became a major point of Methodist influence. Consider the work of the itinerant preacher. As he traveled around his circuit in sparsely settled lands, with whom and where was he to spend his nights? Occasionally the answer was alone, under the sky, or in a tavern with other travelers of the most varied spiritual conditions. The former accommodation gave little comfort to the body, while the latter was likely to give much vexation to the soul and still not do the body much good. The place of choice and of necessity, then, was the home of some family, a Methodist family where possible, otherwise any family that would take the preacher in.

In the homes of the devout there would be ample "religious conversation." James Finley's heart, like those of the disciples talking with their Lord on the road to Emmaus, "burned within" him as he talked with an old German couple who were isolated from religious privileges but who maintained their own prayer meetings and class meetings. He thought they talked like "natives of heaven." Another older lady was a "mother in Israel" who "walked with God" and who opened her home freely to the preachers. During one of Finley's visits she invited another couple over to her home to spend the afternoon, and they all "had a comfortable time" as they mingled their prayers together, "resolved to live for God, and strive for heaven."[22] The son of a prominent Methodist layman, Samuel Williams, recalled that the ladies gladly entertained the preachers and never asked any compensation: "His religious conversation and prayers were a full remuneration for their labor." In the more established circuits, in fact, the preachers had favorite stopping places that became known to church members and nonmembers alike as "the Preachers' Home."[23] In at least one locality, some unfriendly neighbors spread the word that "the man who would give the Methodists a home, would soon have none for his family."[24]

Devout Methodists, however, sought foremost a home in heaven for themselves and their families, and so they eagerly opened their homes to the heavenly influence of the preachers. Chauncey Hobart's mother, at eighty-nine, was still telling the story of how God answered her prayers that her raw frontier neighborhood would somehow afford her family the means to maintain a religious life. God sent first the uncultured but devout local preacher, Levin Green, and then a succession of circuit riders and additional religious families. As religion flourished in the neighborhood, the Hobart home entertained many godly people who talked together of their religious experience—"their trials, conflicts and victories." Young Chauncey got as near to them as he could, feeling some close relation to them. He felt that he too would eventually find "all that these so joyfully narrated."[25] Children of pious parents frequently reported the salutary effect of the religious conversation carried on by preachers and other believers around their childhood hearthsides.[26] Joseph Tarkington observed, "The preachers and the people struggled together, each knew the other's trials, and truly, each, in their way ministered to the other."[27]

Another aspect of the mutual ministry of preachers and people was the role the congregations played in the selection of new candidates for the ministry. Often, when a young man had been converted and had testified to his experience in his class meeting or love feast, he would receive messages both subtle and direct from his fellow church members that they believed him to be called to preach. The circuit preachers and presiding elders would also get the message and arrange for the young preacher-to-be to lead class, exhort, fill a preaching appointment, or otherwise participate in church leadership. A young man's success at these endeavors determined whether the brotherhood of itinerant preachers would give him a more extensive trial. It was, of course, the laity in the classes and congregations who, by their collective response to the youngster's efforts, determined whether he would rise to the itinerancy. By means of this informal community consensus the people helped to choose the sort of persons who exercised ministerial authority over them.[28]

These operations of community consensus and the countless vignettes of spiritual socializing that appear in Methodist documents are evidence of the continuing vitality of social norms and practices whose foundations antedated the circuit riders by generations. In a society still organized around oral patterns of discourse, there was a constant search for occasions in which to exchange the words and gestures that conferred a sense of identity and status. In the farming neighborhoods served by the circuit riders of the Ohio valley region, such occasions ranged from traditional gatherings at militia musters and county seats through the rustic forms of mutual aid like corn huskings and cabin raisings to the more novel performances of the pious at preaching appointments and camp meetings. The visit of a preacher or of fellow church members to one's home was another small opportunity to escape solitude and to exchange those ritual words that mutually conveyed a sense of selfhood. On the other hand, the preachers might even be described as exploiting the norms of "southern hospitality" in order to gain not only accommodations but also opportunities to recruit permanent contributors to the wealth and numbers of their intrusive organization. Certainly the talk in one community that giving a home to the Methodist preachers meant eventually having none for one's own family suggests such a suspicion. Both the welcome from church members and the suspicion from others underscore a basic characteristic of the norms of southern hospitality: it was a kin-centered system. Non-kin strangers were likely to enjoy much less of a welcome than legends of southern hospitality might lead us to expect. The fact that preachers enjoyed the welcome they did from fellow Christians seems due to their spiritual status as brothers and/or fathers in the gospel.[29]

Incorporation into the family of God, however, did effect important changes in the nature of temporal family life. It is likely that these changes were the sort of thing intended in the observation that the Methodist preachers did so much to lay the foundations of society in the Old Northwest.[30] George Walker observed "a great social, moral, and religious change" in his family when his parents converted from Roman Catholicism to the Methodist church. The principal change was in the nature of the ritual events in the home: "The party of pleasure, and worldly amusements, and the sound of the violin were superseded by the Methodist prayer meeting and by itinerant preaching. Family prayer was also instituted, and kept up regularly." Walker further believed that these new ritual patterns had a salutary effect on all members of a household.[31]

The ritual permanently identified with the family was, of course, family prayer. Praying in their families was a duty to be enforced upon all Methodist heads of families. It was also a ritual in which faithful itinerant preachers led no matter in whose home they happened to be visiting. In the homes of believers, family prayer was often an occasion for the religious conversations that so many believers young and old found so satisfying and invigorating. The *Discipline* enjoined strict attention to family religion and especially to the pastoral care and instruction of the "rising generation."[32]

Leading in family prayer seems to have been the chief means of observing the spirit, if not the letter, of the *Discipline*'s injunctions. Henry Smith recorded many visits in which he prayed with the families and led them to promises of reform, tears of contrition, and shouts of joy. At one of these visits he sang and talked about Jesus with the family in such a heart-warming manner that all of them together were melted in tears that eventually gave way to a shout of joy.[33] William Fee remembered George Washington Maley, the preacher who received him into the church, as a particularly impressive pastor. "The whole family where he visited would often be bathed in tears. He appeared to understand the character and the peculiarities of every child. He prayed for all, and we thought he prayed for everything."[34]

Praying in families changed emphasis from spiritual instruction to evangelistic recruitment as preachers found themselves among nonprofessing families. Bishop Asbury set an appropriate example to James Quinn as they traveled together along the Little Kanawha River in the mountains of Virginia. Quinn remembered calling with the bishop at several farmhouses and praying with the residents even though they were not Methodists.[35] John Kobler recorded in his journal his settled custom of visiting as many families as possible as he rode his circuit. He believed that from the "small matter" of a friendly conversation on the work of salvation and a parting prayer "incredible results" were accomplished. Later in his journal, he made note of a "nice looking family" who regularly attended worship at one of his appointments and who were "much affected" at his recent preaching service. He spent an hour and a half in conversation and prayer with them the next day at their home.[36] James Finley depicted approvingly the family pastoral care provided by many of his colleagues, but his eulogy of Russel Bigelow provided an ideal image of a Methodist pastor in a family setting. Bigelow would speak to the head of the family about "God's goodness, man's accountability, a parent's influence, a Saviour's love, and approaching judgment, and when he bowed down to plead with God for his friend, it would seem as though the heart of stone must melt." Bigelow's name, declared Finley, "still sheds fragrance from a thousand family altars."[37]

Family prayer and visitation, then, was a ritual not only of spiritual sociability but also of socialization, not only of religious instruction but also of evangelical recruitment. It was one of the chief means of involving the family in the organization and culture of Methodism. Another means was prayer meeting, which was usually a lay-led gathering of believers simply for the purpose of praying together. It too was naturally associated with the home of some prominent or conveniently located lay member. The supplications of the saints reached not only God's ears but those of all in attendance and served as confirmation to the faithful and conviction to the curious sinners as well. This ritual too served the purposes of both sociability and socialization.[38]

Even preaching services, as George Walker mentioned, often took place in the homes of church members or other friends of religion in a neighborhood. The alternatives were usually courthouses, schoolhouses, or the open air. Church buildings came later. A preaching appointment drew churched and unchurched, Methodists and other Christians, because it was one of the occasions where people might come together to see and be seen and act out the social patterns of an oral culture. It might take several rounds on a circuit before the gospel message sank in deeply enough or spread widely enough, but the constant expectation was that enough people would become subjects of grace to warrant the founding of a society in the neighborhood. When the critical mass was finally reached—often the required number was less than a dozen—the preacher would "open the doors of the church" and invite those who wished to "flee the wrath to come" to publicly declare their intent to join the church. He would then read the "General Rules" to the new members, and form the new members into a *class* for which he appointed a *leader* who was charged with meeting with the members once a week to see how their souls prospered in the inward and outward work of religion. One effect of proceeding in this manner was that many Methodist families in the early years had their local church founded right in their own homes and subsequently had the weekly meetings of the class occur in the midst of their own domestic space.[39]

The conjunction of hospitality and various forms of worship under one roof helped to create the great bond of union between preachers and people. One preacher felt the force of the habit of house preaching to such an extent that he disparaged the atmosphere created by many of the church buildings that characterized the later and more prosperous years of his service in Indiana. He confessed he had more "true religious enjoyment" standing behind a split-bottomed chair in some private house on a week day and preaching to twenty-five or thirty "simple-hearted people" than he had from preaching to hundreds in the finest of churches. And then, to meet the class after preaching, which was customary for the circuit preacher, as they were seated in "the good brother's house" which has become for this event God's own house, was "the very next thing to heaven itself."[40] Clearly, in this preacher's experience, the necessity of the early Methodist church in making domestic space one of its chief ritual arenas had become one of its greatest virtues.

To invert the formula, the virtue of concentrating recruitment upon the family was a rather obvious necessity. For all their theological individualism, evangelicals of all stripes knew implicitly that individuals become who they are in and through a community. So long as some portion of an individual's most significant community—husband or wife, father or mother—remained outside the church community, the individual's hold on grace, and the church's hold on the individual, was likely to be slippery. Beyond this realization, itinerants knew that the conversion of whole families gave them a better chance to establish the church's influence in the community at large. Although they were proceeding to change the meaning of the idea, evangelicals understood that the family, not the individual, was the basic unit of civil and religious society.[41] Finally, evangelicals sought to convert whole families because they knew that generations of pious offspring were likely to be the fruit of a family's union with the church. James Quinn, among others, celebrated several sets of devout parents whose children, grandchildren, and even great-grandchildren had proved faithful to the Methodist gospel they had learned from the cradle on up. Most notable was White Brown, the venerable "Patriarch of the Scioto Valley" who was survived at death by eight children, sixty-five grandchildren, and eighty-five great-grandchildren, almost all of whom were subjects of grace and members of the church.[42]

The evangelical stress on the affectionate ties of family and friendship as the key images for grasping the meaning of heaven suggests another, more theoretical, reason for a recruitment focus on family units. Family as a sphere of morally and spiritually pure affection and heaven as the eternal perpetuation of right affection were powerful symbols in religious thought and feeling. It follows that the conversion of a family *as a family* or the unbroken transmission of experimental religion from generation to generation would have been an effective realization of the moods and motivations evoked by these symbols. When Russel Bigelow, therefore, spoke to heads of families of man's accountability in a coming judgment and then slipped in references to "a parent's influence," he was turning the power of familial ties to the church's own ends. Parents who wished always to enjoy their attachment to their children, he implied, must not take them for granted; they must secure their children's affections and their own affections first of all to the heavenly realms.

The symbiosis worked the other way as well: as the church turned the power of family ties to its own ends, families used the church and its exercises to put themselves in order and unity. "In those days," observed William Fee of the 1820s and 1830s, "parents took their children to camp-meeting, that they might be converted."[43] Once there they were likely to participate in scenes that, as James Finley put it, "would have made an angel shout and weep." Finley portrayed a campground covered with parents and children "clasped in each other's arms, rejoicing together, that the 'dead was alive and the lost found.' " A preacher might address the heads of families on the importance of family religion and then invite parents to bring their children into the altar to make a dedication to God. Finley celebrated the solemnity and efficacy of one such scene, noting that many of those whose parents had offered them on that occasion were, at his writing, still "pillars in the house of God."[44] Finley's allusion to the parable of the prodigal son—"the dead was alive and the lost found"—may be read as a reflection of the sort of anxiety Finley's own parents felt for him when he was a wild young man bent on hunting and in danger of being lost in the "far country" of the Indians. Evangelicals constantly offered their gospel as a safeguard against youthful prodigality in the midst of strange and unformed lands, and in the midst of new and uncertain times.

The manner of family recruitment among evangelicals, however, underscored the fact that their vision of the family unit in society had very different implications from the traditional patriarchal vision. For the evangelicals, the individual member was logically prior to the social whole. When each family member was converted, they together became an eternal unit bound together by their sanctified affections. In the traditional understanding, the stress was on the family as a corporate unit represented by the sovereign father; the whole was logically prior to the individual members. In colonial Virginia, one county court so respected the sovereignty of the father that it disallowed the objections that an Anglican woman voiced at having her children reared in the faith of her Quaker husband. The court forbade her interference with the education of her children, going so far as to instruct her not to expound the scriptures to them without her husband's consent. In view of the establishment of the Anglican church in the colony, this was a remarkable adherence to patriarchal principle.[45] The Methodists, however, when it came to the propagation of their gospel, had no such scruples.

Methodist literature of the antebellum period is dotted with righteous, even gleeful, anecdotes of how children defied parents and wives defied husbands in order to get religion and then eventually converted their recalcitrant relations. Peter Cartwright told one of the more entertaining tales of this genre. A set of parents tried, but failed, to dissuade their adolescent children from attending a Methodist camp meeting. They went along with the children instead to keep an eye on them. When two of their daughters went into the altar to pray and be prayed for, their mother took her seat just outside the altar enclosure and, when she thought Cartwright was not looking, kicked the girls to force them up off their knees. Cartwright intercepted her foot, gave her a strong push backward, and tumbled her over into the benches. "Being a large corpulent woman, she had some considerable tussle to right herself again." She still managed to hustle the girls out of the altar into the family tent while Cartwright was engaged with other mourners. Undaunted, Cartwright gathered up a few singers and praying persons from the faithful laity and invaded the tent. He held a singing service and then exhorted the parents to kneel and pray for their children. At first they refused; but, as their remaining three children all joined the first two daughters in the throes of conviction, they were overwhelmed with alarm and began to weep bitterly. "You may be sure," Cartwright remarked, "the whole tent was in a mighty uproar." The singing, praying, and exhorting went on nearly all night until four of the family (Cartwright does not say which four) were converted. They all joined the Methodist church, and, so far as Cartwright knew, "walked worthy of their high vocation."[46] The pattern of children leading their parents into the Methodist church seems to have been a frequent one, at least in the earlier years of the church. James B. Finley, Jacob Young, Maxwell Gaddis's older brother, and Samuel Williams are all examples of young men whose fathers followed their lead in joining the Methodists.[47]

An even more popular story pattern was one where a wife overcame her husband in matters of religion. Typically, the persuasive power of a pious woman, her religious exercises, and often her patient suffering under persecution were sufficient to eventually win over her husband's soul.[48] Sometimes, however, a wife needed the help of some Christian muscle. At an Indiana camp meeting, a woman of "good reputation" in the neighborhood came to the altar and was converted. As she began to loudly praise God, her husband roused himself from simply observing the proceedings, rushed into the altar, and dragged her violently to the rear of the encampment where he began to abuse her for "disgracing the family." He was a strong man who defied the saints who tried to remonstrate with him. They sent for their own champion, local preacher James Jones. Jones's efforts to reason with the man failed; so, he peremptorily commanded the infuriated patriarch to get down on his knees and pray. The husband only laughed and cursed the preacher. It was a challenge, and the preacher took up the gauntlet.

> "But you shall pray," said the preacher; and seizing him, he brought the fellow to his knees, and then flat on his face, and seated himself upon his back. . . .
>
> "I will not pray," said he, "if I go to hell the next moment."
>
> "But you must pray or you cannot arise from this place," said the preacher.
>
> Mr. Jones then called on the trembling wife to pray for her angry husband, which she did in great tenderness and faith. Then others prayed with great feeling and earnestness. . . . Next Brother Jones prayed, still sitting on . . . his victim. . . . While he prayed he felt the muscles of the man's arm begin to relax, and other signs that victory was coming. This increased the faith of all present, and every heart began to pray. Soon the man himself began to weep and cry out, "God be merciful to me a sinner," and soon the shout of victory came. There stood that rejoicing wife and that conquered husband rejoicing and praising God together.[49]

Evangelicals, in perpetrating or recounting such incidents, intended no encouragement to general insubordination among wives or children. They still believed in the headship of the father in the family. It was just that they also believed each man, woman, and child had to meet the sovereign God individually and struggle through on his or her own to a saving faith in an affectionate heavenly father. In fact, neither the preacher nor the wife had, in principle, conquered the husband. It was he and not they who had first raised the shout of victory. He was conquered by the grace of God in his heart that gave him the victory over himself. It was the sort of victory that denizens of the culture of honor would have scorned as weak and feared as emasculating. This husband, however, had had a new order revealed to him, an order with no room for his self-assertive motives of pride, anger, and violence. The new order demanded instead a personal, self-abnegating love of God and humankind. Then it demanded a sanctified affection for his wife, who had struggled through on *her* own to a saving love of God and fellow humans. Their marriage then was to be founded on this mutual love that came from God. Divine love took precedence over the legal sovereignty and ownership that still came with his position. His victory let him enter the new order. Now he could stand up and resume his legitimate authority in a new way—governed not by honor's conflicting demands of deference and self-assertion but by the mutual affection mandated by the way of the cross.

This emotional logic of self-surrender did subvert traditional understandings of authority, or, more accurately, it inverted them. Experimental religion conferred greatest spiritual power and moral authority on those who most embodied the traits that had characterized Christ: humility, suffering, and renunciation of property and temporal power. Someone who led another to religion, for example, retained a special kind of authority in that person's life, an authority symbolized by phrases like "father in the Gospel" or "mother in Israel." Preachers, of course, were major beneficiaries of this logic. Women, however, might be said to have benefited even more because they already were located at a lowly position in the social structure and because the wider culture already defined them in terms of submissiveness as well as in terms of the sort of emotionality that characterized experimental religion. A movement that granted recognition and some authority on these bases could be an agent of a particular sort of liberation for women. The evangelical gospel, then, did tend to undermine traditional understandings of family life and of patriarchal authority.

The understandings that it tended to establish in their place are implied by the interpretation of the way of the cross offered so far. Class meeting and love feast, however, the principal rituals of social religion in Methodism, were the exercises in which the early church members might most readily learn the new ways of organizing their social worlds. A search for the new patterns of family life implicit in the way of the cross must next turn to these rituals.

6

Discipline and the Rhetoric of Separation

It has been a commonplace of American church history to identify early Methodism by its "frontier" camp meetings. The weekly *class meeting*, however, was the one form of association that nearly all good Methodists shared until at least the third decade of the nineteenth century, and that they experienced more frequently than any other kind of religious meeting. Class meeting, furthermore, was tied directly to the love feast, the spiritual heart of the circuit's quarterly meeting. The quarterly meeting, in turn, was the precursor of the camp meeting. There was an infrastructure of meetings for "social religion" in Methodism that undergirded its more flamboyant public events. If we are to understand how early Methodism reproduced itself in the minds and hearts of its members and if we are to understand what difference it made, it is to these ritual forms that we must attend.

The class meeting arose early in the Methodist movement in England as John Wesley groped for a means to provide pastoral oversight for the growing numbers of those who sought the salvation he proclaimed. He found what he desired by a sort of happy accident. In 1742, he met with some members of the Methodist society at Bristol in order to consider how to pay off the debt on their new chapel. As the oft-told story went, a Captain Foy suggested that every member contribute a penny a week until the debt was paid. When someone objected that many members were too poor to manage that amount, the captain proposed to have ten or twelve of the poorest put under his charge. He would collect what they could give each week and pay the penny for them if they could not afford it. Several other members agreed to follow the same plan.

This financial expedient soon developed into a permanent pastoral structure. The leaders who went out looking for contributions discovered husbands quarreling with wives, others who were the worse for drinking. When they reported these things to Wesley, he asked them to start inquiring into behavior and spiritual condition as well as into finances. Later it became convenient to ask members and leader to meet weekly in class rather than to ask the leader to visit each individually. The result was not only a new level of pastoral care but also a new depth of fellowship. Wesley invoked the witness of the New Testament church to describe what occurred: "They began to bear one another's burdens and naturally to care for each other. . . . Speaking the truth in love, they grew up into Him in all things who is the Head, even Christ, from whom the whole body is fitly joined together."[1]

The class-meeting structure came to America as an integral part of Methodism. Attendance at class was officially a condition of continued good standing in the American Methodist societies, though it appears that this stipulation was not so consistently observed in America as in England. Class leaders in America became subpastors under the circuit preachers. The meeting also retained its financial function. The decline of class meeting as a condition of membership and as a widely shared experience of American Methodists happened at various times in various places but seems to have been well underway in many places by the 1830s. The reasons for that decline will occupy us at the end of this study. Here it is sufficient to note that the class meeting was at the center of the ordinary life of local Methodist societies for three or four generations of early American Methodism.

The analysis that follows explicates the experiences afforded by rituals like class meeting and explains how such experiences shaped the outlooks of participants. We must understand this shaping if we are to see that participation in such rituals laid the foundations in experience for the adoption of an evangelical version of the nineteenth-century ideology of the home. This chapter in particular will attend to the ways in which class meeting and love feast separated believers from "the world." This separation was an essential step in the process that established an evangelical Christian identity and distinctiveness. It was also an important element in the power of the Methodist community to overcome and transform the world—or, if not the world, then many of the worldlings.

A Methodist "society," according to the *Discipline*, was a company of people "having the form and seeking the power of Godliness." They united to pray together, receive exhortation, and "watch over one another in love" in order to help each one of them to work out his or her salvation. The way they helped one another was to divide into small groups of twelve called classes.[2] Classes were to meet together weekly, and the member of the class who had been chosen as its leader—by the circuit preacher, not the class—

was to "inquire how their souls prosper." The inquiry had two essential foci: the individual's observance of the outward rules of the societies, and his or her growth in the knowledge and love of God.[3]

The sort of questions asked in class meeting could be direct and uncomfortably personal. Class-meeting inquiry ought to be "close and searching," urged one writer.[4] Another alluded to the questions listed in the *Discipline* under the rules for Band societies—smaller, more intimate groups for fellowship and inquiry that thrived in John Wesley's England but that survived more in the paper memory of the *Discipline* than in the practice of American Methodists. He noted that the questions seemed designed to "cut to the quick and search to the bottom," and he therefore proposed to adopt these questions for his own mode of class-meeting inquiry.[5] The list of questions included the following:

> 1. What known sins have you committed since our last meeting?
> 2. What temptations have you met with?
> 3. How were you delivered?
> 4. What have you thought, said, or done, of which you doubt whether it is sin or not? . . .
>
> 1. Have you the forgiveness of your sins?
> 2. Have you peace with God, through our Lord Jesus Christ?
> 3. Have you the witness of God's Spirit with your spirit, that you are a child of God?
> 4. Is the love of God shed abroad in your heart?
> 5. Has no sin, inward or outward, dominion over you?
> 6. Do you desire to be told of your faults? . . .
>
> 11. Is it your desire and design to be on this, and all other occasions entirely open, so as to speak every thing that is in your heart without exception, without disguise, and without reserve?[6]

While it is unlikely that most class-meeting inquiries were this intense, questions on forgiveness, peace with God, the witness of the Spirit, and the like seem to have been standard repertoire for seriously pious persons. These questions on the "inward walk" were to be complemented by questions on the "outward walk," the keeping of the rules of the Societies. In theory, a member might at any time be asked if he drank or gambled, kept the Sabbath, or prayed secretly and in his family.[7]

Writers on class meetings expected the leader's inquiry to discover cases where persons were especially afflicted or were at crisis points in their experience. They recommended special attention be focused on such individuals, even to the point of interrupting the normal flow of events and holding a special prayer service for the "afflicted, tempted, or agonizing individual."[8] On the other hand, persons who were discovered to have violated the rules of the society were to be reproved, and, if they did not mend their ways, finally separated from the society. The class leader, then, was an ally of the circuit preacher in the delicate task of administering the *Discipline*. He was a member of the quarterly conference that supervised the various business affairs of the circuit and was therefore likely to serve on "moral courts" that ruled on complaints and appeals regarding administration of the *Discipline*.[9]

Class meetings, then, held great potential for social embarrassment. Articles in the Methodist press suggest that members often acutely felt such embarrassment and that many societies resisted the division of their class in order to secure the safety of numbers against the searching inquiry of class leader and circuit preacher.[10] By the time the major Methodist weekly newspaper in the Ohio valley region, the *Western Christian Advocate*, began publication in 1834, the class meeting as a condition of Methodist membership was already on the decline. Many articles on class meeting were attempts to deal with a general falling away from faithful class-meeting practice. Writers alluded to familiar complaints from members: "It is a great task to speak in class." "It is hard to get my mind into such a state." "I am too weak to perform." "Does not class meeting tempt people to tell falsehoods?" "I've been away so long, I'm ashamed to go." "Brethren have lost confidence in me." "I've none in them." "Some have nothing to give in the class meeting collection."[11]

These objections confirm the impression given by the recommended class-meeting inquiry: class meetings could be very strenuous affairs. They required a special state of mind, and people unable to get themselves into such a state felt very much out of place.[12] They also required performances, and those who did not excel in such performances might feel upstaged.[13] If one once failed to fulfill the expectations of one's peers in attending and performing in class and in living out the moral implications of the performance, it was humiliating to go back. So intense was fear of judgment and so fragile was mutual confidence, some of these complaints imply, that some might even try to lie about their spiritual condition.

Apologists for class meeting answered such objections in a manner that could hardly have reassured the persons who seriously raised them. Class meetings tempt to falsehood no more than does an oath in court tempt to perjury, asserted one writer, an analogy that must have confirmed the fear that lay behind the question. Other writers suggested that if some did not enjoy the proper state of mind for class meeting it was because they did not cultivate it. Members needed to pray for God's blessing before they went to class, expect to meet him there, and arrive early enough to spend a few moments before starting time "in communion with God only." Another asserted that those who had lost confidence in their fellow Christians had only themselves to blame; they had themselves broken confidence and tended to be suspicious of others. He allowed that objections to speaking in class might arise from "natural diffidence" that, nevertheless, would dissipate with practice. A good "soldier of Christ" ought to get over such squeamishness anyway. He suspected a baser motive, however: a person might object to class meeting out of a "native aversion to the cross of Christ." The sooner the objector crucified "this principle of the carnal mind," the better.[14]

As harsh as this last comment seems, it suggests the essential reason why the class meeting had to be so harrowing an exercise. The pressures and embarrassments were but the inevitable dark side of the benefits that devout Methodists sought and found in class meeting. The point of Methodist ritual practice was to induce and deepen the way of the cross in the soul of the believer. The progress of divine grace in the heart required a mortifying self-knowledge, an awareness of one's specific motives to sin and rebellion. Class meeting created the context of self-awareness and required the self-examination that would produce self-knowledge. Knowledge of the desperate wickedness of the heart led only to despair, however, unless one also knew the promises of salvation in Christ and, more important, saw salvation itself come to living human beings. So class meeting also provided models of religious experience. In telling of God's work in their souls, class members allowed others to know not only their sinfulness but also their hope. If the timid member felt ashamed, foolish, or upstaged, it was one of the relatively small prices to be paid in order to gain the priceless blessings of religion. The sharing of experience generated love among members, and this love helped assure them of their salvation. They invoked the words of the first Epistle of John: "We know we have passed from death unto life, because we love the brethren." People who had not experienced class meetings, testified one writer, could hardly believe the tales believers told of "the happy cementing influence of those spiritual associations" in class meeting.[15] Social shame, then, under carefully controlled conditions, led to spiritual intimacy, and in that intimacy lay the felt assurance of salvation.

It is this linkage between shame and intimacy that sociologist Max Weber missed when he considered Methodism in his classic works on Protestantism and the modern economic and social order.[16] He saw the importance of the strict moral discipline exercised by the local congregation over its members in the interests of maintaining the purity of the "conventicle" segregated from the world. This separatism and discipline, he argued, worked upon the motives of social esteem and the desire to hold one's own among peers to breed the qualities of ascetic righteousness among members, qualities that suited them well for the emerging capitalist and bureaucratic order. He did not sense, however, that the shared sentiment generated in these conventicles was, for the participants, more central to the character and purpose of the groups than was their disciplinary dimension. Where the Methodists sang of the joy of their communion with one another and with God, Weber, who described himself as religiously unmusical, heard only a heavy march step.

Four times a year, Methodists in good and regular standing with their societies had the privilege of attending a circuit-wide celebration of Methodist spiritual intimacy, the love feast. Every quarter the officers and members from the societies making up a circuit would gather for what was usually a weekend of meetings, including business sessions, that generally climaxed on Sunday with the sacrament. Love feast usually came in the morning before sacrament and, unlike the supper, was confined only to members of the Methodist church. Although it varied somewhat, the basic sequence of events in love feast involved the following: (1) an opening with singing and prayer; (2) perhaps an address by the preacher in charge that described the condition of the circuit, including an account of those received into and those excluded from the society during the last quarter; (3) the eating of a small cube of bread and the drinking of some water as tokens of love for one another and of willingness to feed the poor; (4) a time for telling what God was doing for one's soul; (5) a closing by singing and prayer; and (6) perhaps a collection for the relief of the poor.[17]

The center of love feast, and the element that linked it to class meeting, was the time for testimony. In dramaturgical metaphor, class meeting was the rehearsal of the script of experimental religion, love feast the performance. Members arose voluntarily and gave their testimonies spontaneously in love feast, subject neither to inquiry nor to reproof. They did so before a larger audience as well, one that sometimes numbered in the hundreds. Love feast could be a true celebration after the rigors of class meeting. If the performances went awry, however, there were controls available. The preacher in charge was responsible to see that everything was done "decently and in order," and he would speak out when need arose. A less direct method was also available if a member spoke too long, became incoherent, began to preach rather than testify, or otherwise seemed out of line. Frequently the people sang a verse or two between testimonies just to keep the flow of feeling going. The members tuned their music to social control simply by beginning to sing, thus leading the congregation to engulf in its song the voice of an offending member. The practice was called "singing down."[18] Here, as in class meeting, there was considerable potential for comparisons between performances and a similar danger of being upstaged.

One anecdote conveys a sense of the uses and limits of these forms of control. The incident involved James B. Finley as preacher in charge, an Englishman named Babby who was widely regarded as a tiresome speaker, and a devout lady called Mother Fortner who was a "woman of culture" and an especially gifted speaker in social religion. Brother Babby and Mother Fortner rose simultaneously one Sunday morning in love feast, and Babby, oblivious of Mrs. Fortner and of the widespread manifestations of disappointment in the congregation, launched into an overworn rambling account of his emigration from England. No one was more impatient with the tedium than was the Presiding Elder, Brother Finley, who interrupted the Englishman with, "Be short, Brother Babby, be short, many others desire to speak." Babby blandly remarked that Finley could wait until he had finished his tale. A little later Finley interrupted again but got the same response. Having reached the limit of his endurance, Finley began to sing; the congregation joined in with a will; and Brother Babby took his seat—abashed perhaps, but, as subsequent events demonstrated, unsubdued. Mother Fortner rose and spoke of her religious hopes and enjoyments, commanding the eager attention of the people until, near the very climax of her story, Brother Babby began to sing at the top of his voice. "Stop that, stop that, Brother Babby, Sister Fortner is speaking!" blazed the indignant Finley. Babby sang on, unperturbed, until Mrs. Fortner sat down. "The Englishman," observed the chronicler of these events, "had caught up with the presiding elder."[19]

Class meeting and love feast evinced a basic principle by which Methodists and other evangelicals organized their worlds. These meetings were a means to and an evidence of a separation between the religious society and the "world." "It is manifestly our duty," wrote Bishops Asbury and Coke, "to fence in our society, and to preserve it from intruders; otherwise we should soon become a desolate waste." They declared that to allow unawakened persons frequently into these special meetings of the society would be to dampen if not entirely destroy "that *liberty of speech*" that made them such blessed and profitable assemblies for "earnest believers and sincere seekers of salvation."[20] The rule was that sincere persons curious about Methodist practice might be admitted "twice or thrice" before being asked either to join the society or refrain from attending class or love feast again.[21] In the smaller local class meetings, the rule could be enforced by members and the circuit preacher who knew who belonged in the meeting and who did not. For the larger love-feast meetings, the more formal procedure of admission by ticket was adapted from British Wesleyan practice. In America, control of access to love feast was maintained by means of issuing and renewing tickets every quarter for members and for those who gave evidence of interest in religion. The circuit preacher gave out the tickets, but he was urged to give them to no one who had not met in class and obtained the recommendation of the leader or of another reliable person.[22]

Class meeting functioned as a disciplinary hedge principally by winnowing out the worldly minded. An editor of the *Western Christian Advocate* observed that the really galling element for the worldling was the inquiry. Worldly persons might enjoy sermons and sacraments, church duties and positions. They might even endure love feast. They could not abide, however, the close and specific questioning of class meeting. Because class meetings required the exercise of "spiritual feelings," those languid in piety tended to neglect to meet in class; neglect was grounds for exclusion from the church.[23] To John Miley, author of the book-length *Treatise on Class Meetings*, this disciplinary function of class meeting was its primary purpose. Class meetings, he asserted, existed to see "(1) That such as turn aside, or tend to turn aside, from the way of righteousness, may be recovered and restored; (2) That those who cannot be recovered and restored may be separated from the church."[24]

Modern sensibilities might lead us to expect that such a regimen would insure low growth and an intimidated membership for any sect that practiced it. Far from limiting the growth of the church or demoralizing its members, however, enforcement of the disciplinary rules about class-meeting practice seemed, at least to preachers in charge, to result in revivals, increased accessions to the church, moral reform, and unity of spirit.

Peter Cartwright wrote of a revival that dated from "the very day" he managed to get a popular but liquor-drinking local preacher expelled from one local society. Cartwright began his campaign in class meeting after preaching service one Sunday. "Brother W.," he asked the local preacher, "do you drink drams?" Brother W. admitted he did. "Why do you drink drams, Brother W.?" Because it made him feel good, said Brother W. "You drink 'til you feel it, do you? . . . Well, Brother W., there have been reports that you drink too often and too much; therefore, prepare yourself for trial." Cartwright managed to pack a committee of the local society with non-drinkers, and the committee suspended Brother W. until the next quarterly meeting, at which time he was expelled. His family and several friends followed him out of the society. Cartwright followed up on his coup by repeating the ritual by which preachers were to establish societies: he read the rules, exhorted the class leader to be punctual, faithful, and pious, urged the members to attend all the means of grace—especially class meetings, love feasts, and the sacrament, and to have their children baptized. The revival that resulted from Cartwright's show of discipline resulted in the winning back of all the members who had withdrawn from the society plus forty more, "and," claimed Cartwright, "not a dram drinker in the whole society."[25]

This particular drama was only one moment in Cartwright's campaign to tighten the reins of discipline on his circuit as a whole. He had found one hundred and fifty members delinquent in their class attendance, many having been absent for two or three years. Through intense pastoral visitation he recovered about sixty; he felt obliged to drop the rest from membership. "This was awful work," he mused, "it bowed me in spirit greatly." He felt the results worth the pain, however: "[T]here was a stop put to trading in slaves, and the dram drinkers became very few, and many threw off their jewelry and superfluous dressing; prayer meetings sprung up [*sic*], class meetings were generally attended, our congregations increased, our fasts were kept." This surge of disciplined religiosity climaxed in a camp meeting that lasted eight days and added over two hundred persons to the church. "Glory to God!" exulted Cartwright, "Zion travailed and brought forth many sons and daughters of God."[26]

Many preachers reported a pattern of purge-and-grow similar to Cartwright's. They came to circuits "on a downward tendency" and turned things around largely by the enforcement of the rules regarding class-meeting attendance. John Scripps engaged in a "sifting season" in which he recorded as members of the societies only those who attended class. He did this for the first three rounds of the circuit; on the fourth round, he dropped from membership all who were on the old record books but who had not attended. The membership shrank considerably, but the circuit that year still returned a large membership proportionate to the general population.[27] James Finley braved gossip and resentment as he changed "negligent or unprofitable leaders" on one circuit and "started things to work." He claimed that the genuinely pious members were grateful for a return to discipline. In another circuit, he had to break up an unholy team of two class leaders who were fond of drink and managed to keep the local society from delivering a judgment against them in any trial. Finley persuaded the committee of the quarterly conference to expel them. As a result of disciplinary activities, the circuit lost over one hundred members, but evangelizing more than made up the difference as the circuit returned a net increase of fifty for the year.[28]

Clearly the exercise of discipline did not always result in spiritual growth and prosperity. A competitive dynamic existed in the societies that sometimes surfaced in divisive ways. Some accounts of disciplinary action and church trials evinced the spirit of gentry election campaigns or even duels in their concern with insult, reputation, the vindication of honor, and the pursuit of power.[29] In the minds of believers, however, this spirit remained opposed to the spirit of experimental religion. Indeed, Samuel Williams, a prominent Methodist layman, reported that, in the Chillicothe, Ohio, society of 1810, the prosecution of such issues blighted a budding revival. The visible work of grace seemed to die out and leave the young converts complaining of their spiritual deadness. The politics of the religious could seem even more deadly than the politics of the worldly, dealing as it did with judgments of who was to be excluded " 'from the kingdom of grace and glory', or delivered over to Satan." Ironically, the prosecutions and divisions Williams reported arose because some church members objected to participation by other church members in certain political events and associations.[30]

The primary point of class-meeting practice, however, was to prevent or heal such divisions. Methodists saw class meeting as more than an agent of distinctiveness, morality, and evangelism; they experienced it also as a means of securing unity among believers. Where class meetings were faithfully attended, declared a contributor to the *Western Christian Advocate*, there were neither "feuds, nor envying, nor rankling prejudices, but CHARITY." Where they were neglected, the devil came in and bred discord and confusion until the whole society seemed likely to be demolished.[31] Behind the hyperbole of such remarks lay some real evidence of class leaders and class meetings as agents of reconciliation. William Fee's father, a class leader for fifty years, earned a reputation as peacemaker among contending factions in both local societies and families.[32] George Phillips led a class in a season of "examination and consecration" that led him to exclaim, "O that all I have ever offended were here. How I should love to fall before them and ask pardon."[33] Henry Smith felt the blessedness of the peacemakers when he preached to a society riven with disputes and then met the members in class and labored successfully to bring the disputing parties to acknowledge their errors mutually, forgive each other, and live in peace.[34] Henry Kobler reconciled another troubled society by first visiting members separately and conducting an inquiry into the state of their hearts in class-meeting style. He then called them together to exhort them to unity and to appeal to all those who could fellowship with each other to come forward and join in class. Elsewhere on the circuit he persistently met classes, read the rules, urged unity, and inquired to see that all members were working out their salvation. Where he found members doing just such work, he noted that their hearts seemed "cemented and joined in one."[35]

Reflecting from the vantage point of the 1850s upon the Methodism of his early ministry, Finley declared:

> The line of demarcation [*sic*] was much more strongly marked between the church and the world then than at the present time. . . . A profession of religion created a chasm between the professor and the world which . . . was impassable to all but those who would willingly take up their cross and, despising the shame, enroll themselves under the banner of the Prince of Life.[36]

Certainly the class meeting as a disciplinary tool represented in tangible form the line of which Finley spoke. The ordeal of attempting to live out the rules of the Methodist societies under weekly scrutiny by class-meeting inquiry was a considerable chasm to cross. The configuration in which both class meeting and love feast took place evinced this chasm. The "closed-door" policy for class meeting and love feast created a literal spatial separation of the religious society from persons who were identified with the world.

The Methodists defended their closed-door practice against critics on a variety of grounds, but they always conveyed the sense that something essential to their sense of themselves was at stake. One writer mildly observed that the necessity of dealing with delicate matters of discipline and divisions in the society required that members of other churches be kept out of class meetings; nonmembers could not be expected to use the restraint in speaking of such matters that charity and the good of the church demanded.[37] Another argued the pragmatic advantages of separation. It was widely accepted, he observed, that more good in converting souls was done at camp meetings when mourners were segregated and prayed for in the altar area away from the multitude. It ought to be obvious that class meetings and love feasts were established on the same principle.[38] A third writer asserted the necessity of separation in a less conciliatory but more revealing manner. He reported a conversation with a man whom he characterized as an opponent of Methodist discipline. The opponent asked if class meeting and love feast were not the Methodists' best meetings. Assured that they were, he argued that surely sinners and all the world ought to be allowed constant access to the best meetings. The Methodist writer replied somewhat huffily, "It is the peculiar manner in which these meetings are held, by those united in Christian fellowship apart from the world, that makes them better than other meetings: if they were held like other meetings, then truly they would be like other meetings."[39]

This last argument suggests the important link between the closed-door policy and the Methodists' sense of themselves. The spatial separation of class meeting and love feast from the world was a concrete embodiment of the less tangible conception that the church and the world, heaven and hell, and the spiritual and carnal motives of the soul were necessarily separate and incompatible realms. Such conceptions lay behind the eulogy of a class meeting apologist: "No worldly motive, no temporal purposes can have any influence here: shut out from the world and its anxious cares, they [the members] then think and speak only of the concerns of their souls."[40] The "concerns of the soul" stand opposed to the "world and its anxious cares." The proper configuration of the soul was to be an inner calm of spiritual affection fixed upon heavenly objects and impervious to carnal passions excited by the world. The proper configuration of class meeting or love feast was an inner spiritual fellowship separated from the influences of worldly persons. Class meeting and love feast were macrocosms of the soul. Both the soul and these circles of social religion, furthermore, were reflections of the cosmos itself.

The Methodists did not, however, prize exclusivism as an end in itself; they did not seek to be merely a holy club. They were vigorous evangelists. How did their standoffishness square with their stated goal to reform the nation and spread holiness through the land?

We have already seen that maintenance of class meeting as a disciplinary hedge seemed to increase rather than decrease the evangelistic power of the Methodist societies. Numerous anecdotes suggest that the closed-door policy worked in a similar manner. Class meetings in early nineteenth-century America were unusual enough to draw people simply out of curiosity, especially in the new settlements of the Ohio valley. This was also an age in which modern norms of privacy were not fully established, and people did not yet feel compelled, when confronted with novelties happening in private homes, to mind their own business. Sometimes, then, people attended preaching services or prayer meetings out of curiosity or from a yearning for scarce moments of sociability. They found themselves involved in social events unlike any they were used to and were all the more curious when asked to leave the house so that the saints might hold their class meeting. Often the curious onlookers milled around outside the house to get a sense of what was going on.

Benjamin Webb recalled attending a preaching service in which the preacher took as his text, "Set your house in order, for thou shalt die and not live." The preacher then announced class meeting. He invited all who wished to serve God to stay but urged those who did not intend to serve God to go out. Staying, he declared, would only aggravate their misery if they were lost in the world hereafter. Webb and his "companions in wickedness" went out but lingered on the porch of the house to hear what they could. What they heard led to their conviction of sin, a conviction so noisy in its manifestations that the preacher opened the doors. Four of them joined the church that very night.[41] James Finley had to deal with a Lutheran couple in one society who loved to meet in class but who remained tied to the tradition of their upbringing and would not actually join the society. Although the local members were offended with him for it, Finley enforced the rules at his first appointment with this society and made the couple leave. They were "much afflicted." They were sitting there in class again, however, when he met this society on his second round of the circuit. He again insisted they either join the society or leave. This time the wife left, but the husband remained. As the meeting progressed, according to Finley, "the Lord manifested himself to the people in great power and we had a glorious time, so that the old lady, who was an attentive listener on the outside, thrust open the door exclaiming with a loud voice, 'My God, I can stay out no longer!' " The Lutheran couple joined the church that day to the great joy of all the members of the society. The very members he had offended before by his hard line on the rules told him now that he had done just right.[42]

When Finley spoke of the Lord manifesting himself to the people in great power and of the people having a glorious time, he was referring to the shouts of praise from converted saints, cries for mercy from convicted mourners, and perhaps sobs of contrition or of joy from both categories of persons. This noisy worship, a mark of Methodist identity in the early years, drew people into the orbit of Methodist spiritual influence. John Meek, without any apparent embarrassment, narrated the events of the Methodists' first love feast in Cincinnati. The believers so rejoiced in the love of their Savior that their "voice of triumph was heard by the people out of doors, and in the streets. This was something new in Cincinnati." So new in fact, and so disconcerting, that some rushed upstairs and burst open the door to see what it all meant. What it meant to the intruders Meek did not say, but he announced its meaning for the saints. They were rejoicing in hope of better days in Cincinnati.[43]

This was a rejoicing that might well have alarmed worldly sorts, for the Methodist saints used events like love feast as tools of holy aggression. With a certain spiritual craftiness, Charles Hardy gauged the intensity of a love feast over which he presided. When the scene became "quite powerful," he ordered the doors opened to let those out on the porch of the house come in and "see how the Lord was working." In the sanctified melee that followed, Hardy was so transported that he lost consciousness. He awoke some hours later and, lying on a bed to which he had been carried, listened to the cries of penitence and of joy that still sounded around and throughout the house. In all, the evangelistic phase of this love feast lasted over seven hours.[44]

The events of social religion behind closed doors not only attracted people; they also repelled or enraged them. The obvious intent of allowing into class meeting "interested persons" who were not members was to transform them into penitents and finally converts. Although this tactic often worked, sometimes the process short-circuited. One interested person found himself in a very crowded cabin as class meeting began. As the inquiry progressed and he saw what he had got himself into, he became visibly agitated. He rose to leave but found his way to the door blocked by the crowd. He repaired to the hearth, therefore, and scrambled up the chimney onto the roof. Hatless and sooty, he leaped down onto his horse, galloped home, and burst into his house. His wife, startled by his abrupt arrival, asked if the Indians were chasing him. "Worse than Indians!" came his reply.[45]

A prominent whiskey distiller gathered a gang to break into and disrupt one of James Finley's class meetings. Finley, forewarned of impending persecution, posted a sentry at the door to keep it closed against the gang. The class members enjoyed themselves loudly enough to be heard a mile away, however, and the sentry was so caught up in the excitement that he neglected his post for a moment. The distiller broke in. The sentry came to himself quickly enough to shut the others out. Thus did the distiller find himself standing alone, an island of reprobacy in a billowing sea of devotion. Finley stepped up to him and poured on "a warm exhortation." The sinner was enraged, but his rage could not withstand the ocean of love that roared around him. He fell to the floor in conviction, and, at the same moment, the religious excitement reached its peak. To Finley, "it seemed as if heaven and earth had come together." The sentry at the door shouted the news to the distiller's gang outside: "H. is down! H. is down!" They rushed to see the awful sight, and many fell upon one another in the doorway—some, presumably, under conviction as well as under the weight of their comrades. The rest "ran to their horses and fled with the greatest precipitancy and consternation to their homes." The distiller did not experience conversion, but the rules of Methodist membership only required that one show a desire to "flee the wrath to come" in order to join the church. Join the church he did, and never again did he harass a meeting.[46]

In his minor classic *The Damnation of Theron Ware*, Harold Frederic observed that Methodism was a fighting religion. It needed the distillers, the gangs, the scoffers, and the rest of the worldlings because they "brought upon the scene a kind of visible personal devil, with whom the chosen could do battle face to face." Methodism realized itself in the act of conquering the devil by converting the ungodly.[47] It is not surprising, then, to find that distinctive rituals like class meeting and love feast induced love, yearning, or rage but did not allow for mere tolerance or indifference. The penchant for separation and exclusivism must be seen in this light. Separation was not simply retreat; it was rhetoric.

Rhetoric attempts to identify the speaker with the spoken-to, and this identification serves as the basis for the actions the speaker wishes to induce. Inherent in the rhetorical situation is a certain separation that is an essential precondition for all attempts to persuade. If speaker and audience are already unified and no such separation exists, what incentive can there be for appeal? There can be rhetoric only so long as there is division.[48]

Class meeting and love feast were symbolic actions designed both to communicate the identifications and divisions that Methodists felt to be inherent in the cosmos and to move persons into identification with the people of God. The highly visible and audible, yet exclusive, manifestations of religious community awakened people to their identification with the world and their division from God. Some, like Finley's distiller, resented and resisted such an awakening. As creatures of the culture of honor, they marshalled the ritual weapons of banter and bravado, vigilantism and violence, against the Methodists and their usages. They fought a slowly losing battle. Others, the ones who eventually established themselves and their offspring as arbiters of the culture of American Main Street, found in Methodism and similar evangelical churches something vital.

That life-giving thing was more than the opportunity to hold their own in moralistic competition with their peers. Although the competitive impulse clearly obtained, it was secondary, even inimical, to the spiritual communion that frequently characterized the early Methodist societies. That communion and the practice of that which sustained it are the concerns of the next chapter.

7

Fellowship and the Rhetoric of Testimony

Separation from the world, although necessary and difficult to achieve, was not the point for the early Methodists. The point was to be a people of love. There is a story told by an early Methodist itinerant that, although it occurred in the Northeast and thus falls outside the geographic boundaries of this study, communicates the aspirations of early Methodism wherever it was found. Billy Hibbard was one of the pioneer itinerant ministers who took Methodism into New York and New England. Before he became a preacher, soon after he was converted, his wife opposed his Methodist involvements. Only reluctantly did she consent at last to accompany him once to the class meeting that he led near their home. When they returned, he observed that his wife was weeping. He asked her how she had enjoyed the meeting. She answered, "O how they love one another. I never saw such love in all my life." Hibbard replied, "My dear, that is our religion." "Well, I believe it is a good religion," said she, "But I never saw so much love among any people before."[1]

This emphasis on love was manifest in the unity and enlivening fellowship that members enjoyed with one another. And it was the testimonies members gave to one another, and the responses fellow members gave back, that created this fellowship. The experiences of love generated and sustained in shared testimony were the next step, after separation from the world, in the transformations of the self for which class meeting and love feast were designed. We must describe the manifestations of Methodist fellowship and explicate its forms of testimony in order to deepen our understanding of how the rituals of social religion changed people. We will see that testimony equipped the Methodist people to believe that the grace of God, appropriated in experimental religion, was sufficient for them in all circumstances. These circumstances generally had important connections to the vicissitudes of family life. Seeing these connections will enable us to carry forward the argument that social religion disposed members to adopt a new vision of domesticity.

Accounts of Methodist worship and social religion reveal that early Methodists shouted and cried a great deal, either in joy or in penitence. Recall James Finley's frenetic class meeting where, as the whiskey distiller fell to the floor in conviction, the holy noise of the saints could be heard a mile distant.[2] Thomas Mann's terse journal entries note repeatedly that he met the class after preaching or attended love feast at quarterly meeting and that he and the people "had a shout and a cry."[3] Henry Smith organized a class after preaching, and, as he led it, one person "shouted aloud" while the rest "appeared much quickened." After recording this event, Smith observed that he was always at home in class meeting and was "almost sure to come out in class" even if he did not succeed in stirring up the people in his public preaching.[4] Charles Hardy remembered an early love feast where only four or five people were able to testify before the voices of those speaking were drowned "by the cries of the distressed, and the shouts of those that were filled with love divine."[5] Such emotional manifestations did not require large numbers. The future bishop Thomas A. Morris found a tiny group of four people, one a nonprofessor, huddled around a small fire at one his appointments. He stoked up the fire, sang, prayed, preached as if the house were full, and then held a class meeting. "They all wept, one shouted for joy, and the non-professor being seriously affected, we finished with a prayer meeting for her special benefit."[6]

Methodist emotionality was not all high-volume noise. John Kobler recorded a class meeting where the atmosphere was the polar opposite of ecstatic praise. "It was a time of deep feeling," he reported. "Our heads became water and our eyes a fountain of tears."[7] Indeed, for Kobler, these "melting times" were the outstanding image in memory. Decades after recording this event in his journal, he effused over how the "dear people" would go to the classroom and there "with sobbing hearts and flowing eyes" tell over their trials and God's work in their souls in ways so affecting "that the hardest heart could not remain unmoved."[8] The loving sentiment implied by Kobler's remark was, in fact, the sort of emotion that sensitive pastors hoped to cultivate in their congregations. Shouts and rejoicing might be evidence of superficial zeal, but love among the faithful was true spiritual knowledge. As Indiana pastor Isaac Crawford put it, the spiritual work assumed a still better aspect when the "wildfire" was quenched and love was flaming.[9]

Methodist social religion, then, was not simply ephemeral excitement. The creation of these intense moments of communal feeling was intended to issue in something more lasting. It was a good sign, eagerly noted, when societies appeared to be growing in love and unity. In his affectionate letters to his friend Daniel Hitt, James Henthorn blessed God repeatedly for the "solid union" and "share of Divine love" that his class and others enjoyed, although he noted that they had not yet so much life as to make them "flaming Christians."[10] An Illinois pastor noted "a good state of feeling" in one of the societies on his circuit and saw it as "a prospect of better days." "God send salvation," he concluded. At another society he noted a marked improvement in spirituality: "There is now a general spirit of brotherly love among the members." He contrasted this happy state of affairs with a nearby society that was rather sickly due to a "loveless class leader."[11]

Class meeting, love feast, and other forms of social religion appear to have been nodal points in a network of friendship and community. Recall Allen Wiley's celebration of the homes of the people as the best place for religious enjoyment. To meet the class in a good brother's house, he said, was to worship at heaven's gate, the next thing to heaven itself.[12] James Finley remembered a class on one of his early circuits that afforded him some "able and experienced nursing fathers and mothers" to instruct him in experimental religion. "O! how sweet were those days of brotherly love and wisdom," he exclaimed. Love had filled every heart, and persecution had only made the people more faithful.[13] John Scripps chimed in his appreciation for the happiness his people on the circuits conveyed by their "artless civilities," their "open hospitalities," and especially their "frequent piety." "The many precious seasons enjoyed in love feasts, class meetings, and family circles, I retrospect as halcyon days."[14] Scripps's nostalgic retrospection highlights the fact that Methodist community centered around and realized itself in the rituals of social religion. Class meeting, as John Kobler remarked, was the early Methodists' "bond of union," and David Lewis, after traveling much of the nation, observed that nothing contributed more to the unity and spirituality of the entire Methodist connection than love feasts.[15]

When George Phillips spent an afternoon visiting the members of a class in their homes, he remarked that he thought a revival would soon break out among "the friends" because they were all united in prayer for it.[16] In this remark he revealed that revivals and additions to the church were some of the practical, instrumental payoffs of the cultivation of brotherly love among the saints. Because class meetings, love feasts, prayer meetings, and the like were the events where the saints most powerfully realized their good feeling, many instances of conviction, conversion, and joining the church occurred in the context of these moments of social religion. A young man who had attended preaching twice stayed for class meeting the second time and vividly experienced the effects of an evangelical community of feeling: "As I looked about me after the door was closed, I was deeply struck at the solemnity which marked every countenance, and thrilled at the devout aspirations which ascended from every heart . . . the very atmosphere seemed heavenly and divine." He became so agitated as the inquiry progressed that, when the preacher questioned him, he cried aloud for mercy. "This excited the sympathies and prayers of all present in my behalf, and a prayer meeting was appointed for the evening." Apparently the meetings had their intended effect on him; he became a circuit preacher a short time later.[17]

Conversions and accessions to the church were even more frequent in love feast than in class meeting. Allen Wiley experienced conversion during the closing prayer in a love feast. He later included in his history of Indiana Methodism a story of a "high-toned Presbyterian Calvinist" who lost his Calvinism and his prejudices against Methodists in a love feast. The "speaking exercises" brought him to bury his face on his knees and tearfully repeat the prayer, "Lord have mercy upon me! What shall I do!" until he experienced the blessed change.[18] A more striking incident involved a Mrs. John Life, a Lutheran lady of "superior culture" who had married her husband despite his Methodism and remained Lutheran even when her friends disowned her for marrying a Methodist. She attended quarterly meeting with her husband because she wished to please him, not out of any personal spiritual interest. In one love feast, however, after a number had given their experience, a junior preacher felt burdened to ask her to speak. After an uneasy silence, she rose and began,

> "I was baptized in infancy; I studied the catechism in childhood; I faithfully attended the church; I say my prayers; I am a member of the church; I have been religious all my life. My husband is a Methodist, and I do not oppose him; I am a Lutheran, and my husband does not oppose me. . . . I was a Lutheran when he married me; I am a Lutheran still; and expect to live and die a Lutheran." Here she paused, started to resume her seat and had almost reached her chair, when suddenly turning about, her eyes uplifted and arms extended, she cried out—"But, oh, I'm a sinner; O God, be merciful to me a sinner! Oh, my friends, I thought I was a Christian, but I'm not. . . . Oh God, save a poor sinner like me!"

Mrs. Life was converted then and there at that love feast, in the presence of all who managed to crowd into the cabin. She joined the Methodists and became "a helpmeet indeed to her devoted Christian husband." Soon afterward they made their home a haven for the Methodist traveling brotherhood.[19]

To the Methodists, Mrs. Life's story was one of many triumphs of a genuine religion of the heart over the lifeless formalism, worldly pride, and social prejudice they perceived in other denominations. It was important that this triumph led Mrs. Life not only into a new church affiliation but also into a new level of domestic devotion to God, to his ministers, and to her spouse. The point of her story and that of the "high-toned Presbyterian Calvinist" is not simply that they were removed from worldly pride and prejudice; they were moved also into a new style of community life. The

Methodists were not simply a negation of the world; they believed themselves to be a people of love. Their life of love was founded upon the humility of Christian self-surrender, and the cultured Mrs. Life and the high-toned Calvinist had to find such humility before they could know the delights to which it led.

The rituals of social religion were intended to be life-giving realizations of the way of the cross and of the communion it made possible, just as the itinerant holy men of Methodism were supposed to be living symbols of the way of the cross and agents of this communion. Class meeting, love feast, camp meeting, and the like occurred under conditions set apart from the competitive world of materialistic pursuits and class distinctions, the established social structure where selfhood was identified with the persona of role and position. They were separated for the sake of cultivating "Christian fellowship," the evangelical term for a fundamental form of human relatedness, a "generic human bond" on which all other forms of society depend. Such fellowship was precarious, of course. As the previous chapter showed, getting minds and hearts properly separated from worldly attachments and conflicts was a constant struggle. The means of spiritual discipline themselves always risked inviting a censoriousness and false humility that could poison fellowship. When they worked, however, the rituals of social religion evinced a spontaneity, a freedom, and a total absorption of the participants with each other that led them sometimes to lose track of time and to disregard social conventions that discountenanced public shouting or crying, or women speaking in public, or "promiscuous" contact between the sexes. In all these ways, the rituals of social religion provided their participants with many moments of a spontaneous, enlivening mutuality.[20]

Methodist apologists extolled the spontaneous nature of their social religious usages. The saints, claimed one writer, spoke their testimonies "with such a tone of voice, such looks, gestures, simplicity, and native eloquence that even the best-trained orators" could not match the power "of these artless speakers."[21] "Their words were not those of studied eloquence," wrote another; "they were the spontaneous effusion of the heart, when the power of the Holy Spirit was upon them, filling the house with glory, melting, subduing, renewing, and transforming the moral features of the whole." This was indeed a feast of love; for nothing, claimed the writer, was better designed to strengthen Christian fellowship and "cement the hearts of the believers than such principles and facts" as were developed in love feast.[22]

These comparisons to the studied eloquence of the best-trained orators imply the evangelical critique of the political rituals of national liberty around which the American nation was building its identity. Much indeed might be said in praise of the Fourth of July orators who enabled their hearers to relive and reappropriate the great struggle for liberty from Britain. The Methodists believed, however, that the most powerful speakers were those who knew the Christian's liberty from sin and who spoke of it with the spontaneous freedom and power that only the Holy Spirit could impart. This implied contrast of the family of God with the sons of the American Revolution was present by implication every time an evangelical preacher spoke of having liberty in preaching or a local society or congregation understood itself to have enjoyed liberty in worship. The affectionate liberty of Christian fellowship made the competitive brotherhood of independent yeoman patriarchs look like bondage.[23]

Evangelical fellowship was not merely spontaneous, then, it was also ideological; Methodists presented their spiritual community as normative.[24] From a cross-cultural perspective, this kind of community experience can be a potent creative force in human societies. It takes place "outside" routine social structure and often negates it, dissolving its categories, norms, and traditions into an undifferentiated communal unity. As the apologist for love feast put it, the principles and facts developed there cemented the hearts of the believers in fellowship, and the Holy Spirit filled the house, "melting, subduing, renewing, and transforming the moral features of the whole." As old principles melt down, metaphors and symbols emerge that may become models for a transformation and renewal of human life. These new cultural forms may then become the means whereby a group attempts to make of itself a subculture or a whole new society. It will attempt to institute rules to preserve and foster its sense of community. It may also seek to win others to the sense of universal "We-ness" that is essential to the fellowship experience. This new movement, then, promotes not only its own experience of communion but also a vision, however truncated or naive, of a social order in which such communion might flourish.[25]

For believers in the experimental religion of the heart, their experience of "We-ness" was earth's closest approach to the joys of heaven, and, as we have seen, the best metaphors for heaven were sentimental images of family and friendship. For Allen Wiley, the humble cabin where the class met in his early days of ministry was "heaven's gate," and the enjoyments of a love feast were only somewhat less than what heaven's disembodied spirits knew. James Finley spoke and felt as if heaven had come down to earth in some of his class meetings and love feasts.[26] Published apologies reiterated the analogy:

> And if our fellowship below,
> In Jesus be so sweet,
> What height of rapture shall we know
> When round his throne we meet.[27]

As the fellowship experience gave new life and meaning to the idea of heaven, it also suggested new uses of the metaphor of the family. Thus class meeting and love feast came to be represented in the metaphor of family. "How shall we strengthen the cords of Christian fellowship better," queried one writer, "than by sharing with each other, as members of the same Christian family, our mutual hopes and fears, joys and sorrows?"[28] "These little families of love," declared Bishops Asbury and Coke, "mutually weep and rejoice, and in everything sympathize with each other, as genuine friends."[29] The Methodists proclaimed among themselves and to others, then, that in the economy of Methodism one loved and was loved as a member of a family and experienced a kind of heaven on earth. These images and symbols lay at the heart of American Methodism as a movement that attempted to make its own experiences of fellowship normative.

The early bishops of American Methodism had declared that admitting unawakened persons into their special meetings would dampen or destroy the liberty of speech that made the meetings so much a blessing.[30] This characteristic liberty of speech deserves particular attention because speech, specifically the speech of testimony, was the effective symbolic agency in creating the community of feeling so apparent in class meeting and love feast. This ritual speech also seems to have brought many persons to conviction, conversion, and even the elusive experience of perfect love. By setting their moments of spiritual family enjoyment apart from the world, the Methodists aimed to make manifest a sacred inner space that was morally at odds with those on the outside. Such separation implied an appeal to the outsiders to change their moral identifications. By speaking out the inner states of their hearts and the hidden experiences of their lives, the saints went a step further. They expected to endue that inner space with transformative power. Their testimonies were "incantations" of a fellowship that changed those it touched.

Such incantations are effective largely because of their form. Form must be understood from the standpoint of both speaker and audience. A speaker's communication has form when it manifests an identifiable style and arrangement of expression that, in turn, have an identifiable effect upon the audience. This effect may be described in the most general sense as an arousal and fulfillment of desires. Symbolic action—whether written, spoken, or performed—has form if one part of it leads reader, auditor, or witness to expect another part and then satisfies the expectation. The rituals of social religion in Methodism evinced many different types of this general quality of arousal and satisfaction.[31]

The succession of testimonies at the heart of any given love feast or class meeting led audiences to an expectant collaboration with the speakers, a readiness to assent to the general trend or rhythm of the speeches almost without regard to their content. Anyone, asserted one Methodist writer, who sincerely took up the cross of speaking would obtain a blessing; in fact, when the people rose and spoke in quick succession and said just a few pointed words, they hardly ever failed to have a good meeting.[32] James B. Finley's account of his first love feast illustrates the power of this repetitive development of the principles of experimental religion.[33] Stroke after stroke of the gospel of God's grace in the heart fell on him through the testimony of fellow believers. Finley found himself swinging along willingly: "As one after another spoke of the goodness of God, my soul swelled with gratitude and joy, and, being unable to contain myself any longer, [I] sprang from my seat, and shouted the praises of God, with an overflowing heart."[34]

It is, of course, the nature of rituals to be conventional in form; experienced participants know beforehand what sequence of events and style of words to expect. Good Methodists came to their meetings expecting to be gratified by a particular sequence of events in the meeting as a whole and to be fulfilled by particular patterns in the speeches of preachers and people. Isaac Robbins felt the collective power of these expectancies in his first class meeting when, as the door was closed, he looked around and sensed the solemnity on every believer's face. He responded to these signs of devotion with a sort of sympathetic vibration; he reported that he "thrilled with the devout aspirations of every heart." "The very atmosphere," he said, "was heavenly and divine."[35] Thus even the relatively uninitiated might be caught up in the conventional expectancies of devout ritual practice. It was a sign of the decline of class meeting when, in the 1830s and 1840s, apologists writing for church periodicals had to exhort people to work themselves into the right state of mind before they came to class.[36]

One of the best ways to reveal the nature of conventional form is to disappoint or threaten to disappoint its pattern of expectation. If, for instance, a preacher in early Indiana Methodism neglected to meet the class after preaching where there was an established society, he would hear from the people for his breach of their expectations.[37] The young James Finley, before his conversion, was known in his neighborhood as "the Newmarket Devil," and he caused one Methodist class some revealing consternation when he stayed after their prayer meeting to see what their class meeting was like. The believers clearly felt that this devil of a man threatened to disrupt their holy enjoyments. They eyed him very closely, and, Finley recalled, "I could easily tell by their furtive glances that my room would be better than my company." Perhaps their restrained hostility intimidated him enough to allow the rhetoric of their testimonies to sink in, for he reported that he was deeply moved by their words and wept under conviction when the leader, following proper form despite his misgivings, inquired into Finley's religious experience.[38]

The saints' expectations of "a good time" in their meetings could tame some hostilities even more disruptive than those young Finley provoked. While presiding at a love feast later in his career, Finley was outraged by Mr. A., a Democrat and a former member of Congress, who rose and remarked, "Politics is ruining the church . . . for instance, Brother Finley rode into town on Friday afternoon, and refused to put up at my house because I was a Democrat." Finley was an ardent Whig, but he would not stand for his religious motives to be so impugned. "That's a lie," he responded, and the dialogue suddenly took on a contrapuntal form that threatened to lead toward open violence.

> Mr. A. replied, "I say it's a fact;" and Mr. F. rejoined,
>
> "I say it is false, and now, sir, if you have any religious experience to tell, let us have it, but as to your lugging politics in this love feast, it cannot be done."
>
> Mr. A.—"I will talk as I please, sir."
>
> Mr. Finley—"Sit down, sir."
>
> Mr. A.—"I'll sit down when I get ready."
>
> Mr. F. then gathered up a large hickory cane and started from the pulpit toward Mr. A., whereupon Mr. A. seated himself.

What shocked silence, scandalized murmur, or open remonstrance followed this confrontation is not recorded. The exchange was certainly more akin to the machismo of the local tavern or the village commons than to the atmosphere of a love feast. Perhaps some leading members took up the cross to share in proper form their own religious experience and allowed Messrs. A. and F. and the rest of the company to regain their composure. In some way Finley and the former congressman were moved to relinquish or, to use the pious Methodist idiom, to die to, their mutual antagonism. The meeting wound up, we are told, "not only with a shout, but with a general hand-shaking and good feeling; and none met more cordially to greet each other than the irate ex-congressman and the tender hearted Finley."[39]

If the rituals of social religion had a conventional pattern of events as a whole that the saints desired and, evidently, worked to make happen, the particular testimonies they gave also took on a conventional form. Participants got to know one another well enough to expect certain stories from certain members and to be gratified when their expectations were fulfilled. Recall the love feast where the congregation especially desired to hear the former Quaker, Mother Fortner, only to be disappointed by the tiresome Mr. Babby. When she finally did speak, the narrator tells us that the people listened intensely, anxious to catch every word that fell from her lips. Nor did she disappoint them, for they were already deeply moved by the time she was building up to the climax of her remarks. The people's desires and their imminent fulfillment were almost palpable. Then Brother Babby began to sing.[40]

Autobiographical documents of the Methodists show how the form of social religion structured written accounts of the self. David Sullins, for instance, devoted a chapter of his autobiography to "experience meetings," by which he meant class meeting and love feast. After he described them as they were in his youth, he chided himself for talking about experience meetings instead of holding one. He then moved into recounting the details of his own conversion experience, which story fills the rest of the chapter.[41] Virtually all the published Methodist autobiographies center their energy around conversion narratives that resemble each other in essential ways and that certainly answer to the common description of what members shared in class and love feast—that is, stories of what the Lord had done for their souls.

Indeed, Methodism required every member to tell his or her own story, and those stories often became part of a tradition of oral performance in which certain members were expected to give special gratification by telling and retelling their well-known stories. Chauncey Hobart remembered that his mother told for years the story of how God had sent Levin Green to her family in answer to her prayer that her boys would not grow up without religious privileges in their neighborhood.[42] Allen Wiley remembered hearing John Strange tell repeatedly in love feast of how God had pardoned him while he was lying flat on his back.[43] Peter Cartwright's story of the Dutchman and his scolding wife, with which this study began, was one he had heard told repeatedly in love feast. The telling had often melted love feast congregations into tears.[44] And James Finley included in his *Autobiography* a story of a mother and infant daughter who barely escaped freezing to death, a story he had heard both mother and daughter tell in many love feasts with great effect.[45]

From conversion stories in published autobiographies and from the scattered accounts of love feast and class meeting that appear in various published and unpublished documents, it is possible to distill the formal essence of typical testimonies. Class-meeting and love-feast testimonies generally followed the form of the conversion experience whether or not they were actually accounts of conversion. They began with a *contrast* that, like the contrast of one's own sinful state with the demands and promises of God, aroused a desire for change or movement from a condition of disorder-discord-death to a condition of order-harmony-life. In the standard account of the progress of grace in the heart, this beginning part of the story corresponded to the moments of awakening. In the middle part of the testimony story contrast moved into *conflict* in which images and principles of order versus disorder were developed in a narrative counterplay that intensified the polar opposition implied at the outset. In the stages of experimental religion, this conflict corresponded to the struggles of conviction where the subject of God's grace tasted his or her sinfulness to its bitter dregs and agonized between despair and hope. The end of the testimony story involved some principle or image of grace that encompassed the conflicting principles and effected a *resolution* of the conflict through the narrative device of stating them in sequential order, implying a movement from one to the other. For the subject of grace, of course, this was the moment of conversion in which darkness gave way to light, despair to rejoicing, death to rebirth. There were, of course, varieties of stories other than the conversion story, but they all had a similar formal essence. In stories of suffering and danger, the sequence of resolution would be from extremity to deliverance; in stories of reconciliation, discord to harmony; in the final story of every person, earthly death to heavenly life.

In all of these variations there was a peculiar formal device.[46] The stories presented one quality of experience with such intensity as to prepare the mind of the reader or auditor for a contrasting quality of experience. Like the early theory of Alcoholics Anonymous that one must "hit bottom" in order to be ready to give up the bottle, the evangelical testimony narrative required some negative state of feeling to prepare the way for a positive state. In the conversion narrative, images of darkness, pain, guilt, and suffering prepare the way for images of light, comfort, pardon, and joy. In the day-to-day life of the Christian, the pains of mortification led to the peace and comfort of a good conscience and a continuing sense of God's acceptance. The power of the evangelical testimony, then, rested on its capacity to enforce the sense of contrast and conflict between particular conditions of human beings and thus arouse desires to move from one condition to another. The power of the testimony *meetings* rested on the same capacity. The meetings themselves, set apart from the world, manifest in spatial arrangement what the testimonies stated in temporal sequence: "There are two realms of creation and two conditions of human beings—heaven versus hell and life versus death. Therefore choose heaven and life."

This stark, simple formula was a general strategy for encompassing a general situation—a disordered world in need of salvation. The form of the testimony could be adapted, however, to address more specific situations in more concrete imagery. The testimony carved the world up into the fundamental categories of the Christian worldview, but it also conveyed the attitudes implied by those categories, clothing both the categories and the attitudes in images of the people's experience.[47] Concrete situations of sickness and death, migration, politics, wilderness isolation, drunkenness, and just general interpersonal disharmony all figure in testimonies that have been preserved in the documents. All these stories share the basic form of the Christian story, a dying and a rising again, and all focus on the fundamental problem of salvation. They also imply or directly involve another basic human problem: the problem of the family.

It was not uncommon for converts to couch their descriptions of religious experience in terms of sickness and restored health. In so doing they also spoke to the fears, griefs, and yearnings of nineteenth-century Americans who knew so much bereavement and who no longer felt the logic and power of older styles of stoic submission to an inscrutable sovereign deity.[48] Thus one Native American woman who was in the throes of conviction is said to have described herself as sick in her heart. She could not sleep; she could not eat; she could not work; she could only cry. Then the change came. "Now all gone—*no sick*," she proclaimed to her class, "O! no . . . me sing—me well. Now me eat, me sleep, me work. O! me all good. By, by me go up (pointing to heaven) to haba."[49] Having conquered by grace her spiritual sickness unto death, the Native American woman could be assured she would still be "all good" and go to heaven even when temporal illness and death overtook her. This assurance was obviously on the mind of the members of a class whom David Lewis described as rising one after another and declaring their desire to die happy. Apparently Lewis had heard this sort of testimony a bit too often, for he approved of yet another member of the class who rose and declared all *his* anxiety to be over *living* right because he knew he would die right if he had lived right. Christians need not be, Lewis moralized, "through fear of death, all their life-time subject to bondage."[50]

Stories involving sickness and death always implicated family life. Not only did sickness and death disrupt social and economic functioning within families, but, because people generally sickened and died at home, family living space was the center of the attendant existential trauma. When persons did not die at home with family and friends to minister to them in their last hours it was cause for especially poignant comment.[51] Triumph over death, of course, defined the fundamental meaning of the way of the cross, and faithful followers of the way defined heavenly life after death in terms of the restoration of family ties.

The right-living that David Lewis was anxious to do meant being true to sanctified family ties, but there were many subtle ways people might be lured into bondage and ultimate death. The popular politics of the day was one such snare, and a lawyer named William Phillips, speaking in love feast, provided a model for dealing with its allure. He recounted how he had spent the night in "some political feats" and had returned home in "a melancholy state of feeling." His oldest son, an eight-year-old, came into the room where his father had gone to be alone, and remarked that a friend had experienced religion. He then asked his father, "What is religion?" Phillips confessed himself seized with conviction, for he could not answer his child's question, an inability rendered all the more shameful by the fact that his own parents had blessed him with a religious upbringing. He resolved to reform his life and "examine the evidences of Christianity." He joined the church, was converted, and became a local preacher.

The chronicler who recorded this testimony made it clear that Phillips's encounter with his son was the crucial point in a larger familial story. Phillips had been reared by pious parents but had taken up the reading of "infidel authors" that made him a skeptic. His involvement in the "boisterous, stormy sea of political life," furthermore, had ruined his religious impressions and tendencies. Yet his upbringing was too great a barrier to be entirely breached by such worldly chaos; he remained a moral and respectable man.[52] His son's question aroused in him a remorse linked with issues of the sequence of generations. Enmeshed in a self-centered pursuit of worldly honor, he was neglecting the religion that he had received from his parents and that his son, but for the father's infidelity, ought to have understood. Indeed it was this very spiritual influence that, in attenuated form, had sustained him in respectability thus far. Phillips's love-feast testimony dramatized a conflict between spiritual family life and worldly political life. The climax had the father abandoning this threat to religion and family and dedicating himself to building up the church, the institutional steward of the spiritual life that undergirds the sequence of generations. This decision was still understood to have political significance, as we shall see, because Phillips had committed himself to the cultivation of that virtue in his child without which the republic would founder.

Politics was one force in the world's disorder; mammon was another. Although evangelicals did not object to wealth, greed was a soul-destroying passion. James Quinn eulogized the patriarch of the Scioto Valley, White Brown, for accumulating his wealth gradually by dint of persevering effort and frugal habits. In another place, however, he decried the "tide of emigration" onto the rich western lands because it threatened to bear down before it all morality and religion.[53] The point at which emigration allied itself with mammon and threatened to violate the spirit and the letter of the Methodist *Discipline* was the rule against profaning the Lord's day. In their haste to take advantage of better prospects in the West, many otherwise good people failed to reverence their creator by keeping the Sabbath, choosing instead to save travel expenses by keeping on the move. They made such temporal savings, declared one preacher, at the cost of a good conscience. Many who made this foolish bargain bewailed their lukewarmness after such emigration, and many others fell into a worldly and backslidden state.[54]

An entry from John Scripps's journal suggests that another reason for lukewarmness and worldliness among emigrants was simply the disruption of the social support afforded by the religious societies. Scripps reported six consecutive home visits to members on his circuit where he found that the head of the household was either gone or just returned from scouting out new country to which to move his family. Three of the men were class leaders and one was a local preacher.[55] Bishop Thomas A. Morris, writing in the *Ladies Repository* on this and other detrimental effects of traveling, asserted that "there is nothing better for the Christian than to be generally at home." Just following Morris's piece, however, the editor inserted a poem entitled "Impromptu," which registered a caveat against the bishop's strictures. It begins, "Abjuring kindred, friends, and home, / Happy he, whom *duty* bids to roam;" and ends, "Whom Jesus calls o'er earth to rove, / He guides with *light*, and guards with *love*."[56] A church movement founded upon an itinerant ministry could ill afford to discountenance all manifestations of a migratory spirit. Just as wealth was not evil in itself but might be sanctified in service to God, so the roaming urge might be sanctified if dedicated to God.

The testimony rhetoric of one love feast encompassed the ambiguities of migratory aspiration and restlessness by means of the juxtaposition of contrasting testimonies. Two heads of families rose one after another and confessed they were much disappointed in their emigration from the East; their families had suffered illness and death and they were lonely and discouraged. They still aspired to heaven, however, and asked the prayers of their brethren and sisters. A third brother, evidently sensing a wrong turn in the spirit of the meeting, sprang from his seat with a "Glory to God!" and a story of how six months earlier God had called him to sell out his comfortable little Ohio farm and come further west to see what he could do, as a layman, for God and for the Methodist church. He locked the wheels of his wagons each Saturday evening, had glorious Sabbaths with his family, set off again each Monday morning, and arrived in the neighborhood of the love feast to find as good a claim as he could ask. He had family worship all the way, and not one piece of his wagon equipment failed him the whole three weeks of his journey. "I am just as happy as I can be in the body," he crowed; "Glory to God!" This starkly contrasting testimony laid the other brothers properly low. They rose, tearfully confessed they had traveled on the Sabbath, acknowledged God's affliction for their sin, and expressed hopes that God and the brethren would forgive them. Their confessions had a quickening effect, wrote the love-feast chronicler, and that meeting was not soon forgotten.[57] The joyful brother, please note, did not merely keep the Sabbath. God called him to move, and he did his duty. He also held family worship the whole way, his duty as head of the family. Not only itinerant preachers, then, but pious laypersons too might happily, dutifully roam, led by light from Jesus and guarded by His love.

Theorists of the American frontier have suggested that migration fosters privatism because it tends toward a removal of emotional investment from local community institutions and a reinvestment in the immediate family unit.[58] Whether or not domestic privatism actually came about in this way, western families were often isolated from traditional forms of neighborhood support and had occasion to worry over the range of motives evoked by life together. Beyond migration and isolation was the general social and cultural movement away from traditional patriarchal understandings of family relations and toward greater differentiation of family life from other institutionalized patterns of community life. Methodist-style experimental religion, as a significant contributor to this general movement, offered some answers to the inevitable questions about what the new meanings and motives of family life ought to be. The instances of testimony already cited seem to suggest two things: First, people ought to shun the quest for honor and recognition that politics had traditionally offered a community's first families, and concern themselves instead with the rising generation and the religious institutions that would sustain them in virtue. Second, persons who did seek first the spiritual prosperity of the church and their families would find the worldly prosperity they also desired coming to them as a matter of God's grace and providence.

In addition to the issues of the relation of a family to political recognition or economic advancement, however, the quality of the inner life of the family was a major concern. If religious people were people of love, domestic life dominated by experimental religion ought to be an arena of harmony, affection, and mutual solicitude. Recall Peter Cartwright's story of the Dutchman and the scolding wife who was his cross. It is especially appealing for its poignant image of a reconciled husband and wife as well as for its humor. James Finley concluded a story of a prominent inspector-general who was converted through witnessing his wife's conversion at a camp meeting with the observation that husband and wife "embraced with an affection they never knew before; for they were now one in Jesus."[59]

Love-feast testimonies could provide especially appealing evidences of the power of religion to reconcile a husband and wife at odds. Ohio itinerant John Burgess supplied a classic account of a husband and wife who repeatedly transported love-feast audiences with their testimonies of how God had acted in and through them to conquer the demon of drunkenness. The husband told of how he had abused his family under the influence of drink. The death of a friend on one occasion, the destitution of his family on another, and the death of one of his own children on yet another had prompted him to try to reform. All his resolutions lasted only a little while, however, before he was overcome by the influence of friends and the temptations they threw in his path. He finally went to God in despair, confessed his helplessness to stop drinking, and implored help to quit. God heard his prayer, and he found he could quit then and there. "For twenty years," he proclaimed, "I have had no *desire* to touch it. Glory to God! . . . I am now his child, and forever praise the Lord I am happy!" His wife would rise and confirm all her husband had said and add her own tale of triumphant suffering. "The whole congregation was in weeping, yet in a state of rejoicing, under her blessed words and trust in Christ."

At other times the wife would take the lead and tell of her years of struggle in praying for the conversion of her husband. She prayed for seven years, and still he was unsaved. She was tempted to give up and let him be lost, but she went to her closet and promised the Lord to pray for him seven more years if necessary. Those years went by without bringing her husband's conversion. Gloom encompassed her; she began to doubt if God heard her prayer. She repaired again to private prayer and pleaded to be blessed in a special way. God did bless her mightily, and, in her transports of joy, she asked for a blessing for her poor, sinful, dying husband. Lines of a poem came to her mind: "While the lamp holds out to burn, / The vilest sinner may return." She then saw that she had been setting conditions for God to meet in converting her husband, and she yielded them entirely, promising to pray for him as long as he lived. Just a short time later, God made her soul happy by converting him. Her husband would spring to his feet after her story and confirm it all as true, telling of how her prayers and Christian example had at times almost killed him as he had seen his terrible spiritual condition. He had agonized that he was bound for hell while she was on her way to heaven.[60] Both the drunkard husband and the pious wife, however, had had to learn the necessity of unreserved surrender to God before they could find the blessings they coveted.

This husband and wife, like the Dutch couple featured in Cartwright's story, were living proof of the faith they professed. Even if, as one might reasonably suppose, their harmony and mutual love were less than perfect day to day, they still gave "ample evidence" of the power of God in the special moments of social religion. In love feast, as each told his or her story and spouses accompanied each with approving responses, they symbolically reenacted their movement from discord to harmony and carried their fellow believers with them. Thus Cartwright well remembered how the Dutchman had melted whole congregations into tears and, on one occasion "vividly printed" in Cartwright's memory, had led all present to break into a loud shout.[61]

The warm domestic relationships that the Dutchman's audience celebrated had many enemies. The world of the tavern and its drunkenness was just one of them. Believers sensed large impersonal forces of various kinds to which they might fall victim and in the face of which they must construct their sense of themselves. For the earliest pioneers in the West, the wilderness was a potent symbol of a wide range of these hostile forces that threatened the family ties they held dear. James Finley featured a love-feast narrative that addressed this anxiety. It was a story of a mother's struggle against the cold winter wilderness. It provided a model for self-construction with applications beyond the conditions of the frontier.

Polly Boarer was a Roman Catholic by birth and education. Her parents lived across a range of mountains from where she was settled. On January 7, 1800, in bitterly cold weather, she borrowed a horse and rode out with her infant daughter and her dog to visit her parents. She tried a shortcut to their home and lost her way. She wandered until nightfall and then found a place beneath a tree to settle in for the night. "The snow," wrote Finley, "was three feet deep, the darkness profound, and the wind from the north-west broke in a hurricane above her. With no company but her child and no protector but her dog, her condition was lonely beyond the imagination to conceive." This loneliness, however, played an important function in Finley's account of her story. She had been unusually exercised about her spiritual welfare for a week before this journey, and her isolation caused her to feel more acutely her need for God. She called to mind and offered up the prayers from an old prayer book that she had been reading all during the previous week.

During her sleepless night the horse broke its bridle and bolted, leaving her yet more isolated. At dawn, she began a day of wilderness wandering. She left behind some of her extra clothing, apparently in order to walk more freely and carry her child. First she tried to return to the point where she had left the main road. After much exhausting tramping, however, she turned back toward her original resting place, hoping to avoid freezing to death. She left her apron and her handkerchief hanging on bushes as signs of distress, hoping some traveler might see them and try to find her. Upon regaining the place of her last night's lodging, she so dreaded spending another night there that she changed her mind. "Summoning that indomitable spirit of courage peculiar to her sex when in difficulty and danger," she decided on one more desperate attempt to reach a settlement.

She threw off yet more of her apparel in order to be less encumbered and "began again to contend with the snow, rocks, and caverns of the mountains." She came to a deep, narrow gorge that she could not negotiate while holding her child. She hesitated but found no alternative to dropping her child into the snow at the bottom of the gorge. She climbed down and found her little girl unhurt save a for a scratch on the face from the snow crust. She came upon a shelf of rocks where hogs often slept and where she might have found shelter had she not feared that the half-starved animals might return and make food of her and her daughter. As she pressed on, the snow crust lacerated her feet and legs until, bleeding, she yielded the struggle and sat down beneath some pine bushes. The snow beneath the bushes sank under her and "rendered her situation most critical and desperate." She wrapped herself up as well as she could manage, clasped her babe to her bosom, committed herself to God, and slept, exhausted. New snow fell during the night.

She awoke to the sound of livestock in a settlement at the foot of the mountain. She called out loud and long, but the wind blew "violently in a contrary direction" and no one heard her. She discovered that her feet and legs were badly swollen, and, stricken by the sight, she gave herself up to die. She made her own peace with God but could not be at peace while her baby still lived. She tried to lay the child down to freeze to death before she herself died, but she could not ignore her daughter's cries. Her further attempts to attract help by calling and by sending her dog to the settlement with a piece of her clothing wrapped around its neck all failed. She again spent the night in making her peace with God. She later told Finley that she obtained a certainty of going to heaven herself that night, had she died, but she was still in great anxiety over her baby. Only her dog and a blanket of fresh snow kept her from freezing to death.

After her third night on the mountain, she was completely exhausted and frozen to the ground. She called out again. This time two men heard her and set out to search. The echoes of her voice in the mountains deceived them, however, and they hunted all day without success. Just as they were putting up their horses, they again heard her call. "The sun was about an hour high, and the long, lingering beams, striking from the far horizon upon the snow-clad wilds inspired feelings of the deepest gloom and solitude." The men started to search again, but Mrs. Boarer had ceased calling. Just as they were turning in a wrong direction, she felt an "indefinable, mysterious feeling" that seemed to promise help if she would just call one more time. She heeded the prompting, and the men found her. For the first time in her ordeal, she wept. She lost consciousness for a day, and lost several toes as well as much flesh from her limbs.

Finley concluded his rendering of Mrs. Boarer's story with the following observation:

> I have heard the mother and the daughter tell, in love feast, what I have here imperfectly told you. How true, and how applicable in every condition of life—in poverty or in health, in prosperity or adversity, in sunshine or in storm, in plenty or in distress—that declaration of the merciful Keeper of our race, "My grace is sufficient for thee."[62]

This was a story of a divine grace and providence that transcended and even reconciled the conflicting orders of meaning condensed in the two main images: the snowy mountains, and the mother-child pair. The mountains were full of the forces of death: bitter cold, rugged terrain, bloody violence of half-starved hogs, lacerating snow crust, and even contrary wind. The mother and child images, however, imply meanings of "natural" life, affection, and human communion: the recent birth of an infant, the natural desire to bring the child to her grandparents, the courage "natural" to the female sex when in danger, and the natural affection that kept Mrs. Boarer from letting her baby freeze to death. In the Methodist account, however, grace worked a transformation in this mother. In her extremity she became a *praying mother* whose communion with God ultimately saved not only her own soul and body but also the body and, we may infer, the soul of her child. Grace, then, encompassed and made eternal the human affection and communion implied in the mother-child image. Grace effected this transformation, moreover, through wilderness isolation and adversity, through the very forces that seemed inimical to all human meaning. Finley, in his closing remarks, recapitulated and universalized this formal pattern in which opposites were encompassed by transcendent grace.

Mrs. Boarer's testimony, then, is yet another incarnation of the essential rhetorical form of experimental religion. It starts with a *contrast*. An image of a mother and child going to visit grandparents implies principles of domestic order, human communion, and life itself, and this image is set over against an image of snowy mountains and bitter cold that implies principles of disorder, isolation, and death in the extradomestic natural world.[63] The *conflict* begins as the mother loses her way and suffers extreme loneliness. The wilderness is the predisposing ground for her bewilderment and isolation; it misleads and confuses her, leading to her misery. The *climax* is prefigured in her remembrance of prayers from her prayer book and her communion with God. Indeed, this first episode anticipates the form of the entire story: Mrs. Boarer is led to commune with God through the mortification of her natural desires and attachments, a mortification imposed by the wilderness.

The rest of the narrative is an intensification of this basic form. The loss of the horse further isolates her, and the rugged terrain momentarily disrupts her tie to her child. Adversity calls forth her peculiarly feminine courage, and she desperately seeks to reach the settlement. As the mortifying forces of the wilderness cause her limbs to bleed, however, she begins to internalize the principle of mortification; she yields the struggle and sits down. Yet she clings to her twofold communion: she clasps her child "warm to her bosom" and commits herself to God. She clings to God and child even as she despairs of life, finally receiving an assurance of eternal life in the midst of what seems to be her dying hour. The conflict between human life and wilderness death goes on as she hears the sounds of human settlement, and she cries for help only to have her efforts frustrated by contrary wind and deceptive echoes. Indeed her physical salvation is almost prevented by this wilderness disorder as her rescuers are about to go astray and the sun begins to set upon her life with "the deepest feelings of gloom and solitude." The grace of God in her heart, however, prompts her to cry out from the depths of her despair one more time. She is delivered—a fitting climax calling forth a flood of tears.

No doubt the telling of this story by mother and daughter evoked many more floods of tears from love-feast congregations. In the very persons of the narrators, the faithful beheld the outcome of God's saving grace and knew, as Finley suggested in his epilogue, that if grace was sufficient for these women in their great extremity, it was sufficient for all. It is intriguing to pursue in imagination the urge to generalize this story. Someone who had to cope with the "cold, cruel world" of rising nineteenth-century cities might identify with Mrs. Boarer as easily as one who had struggled across the snowy mountain passes as she had. Someone who had left behind family and friends in a trek west might find in Mrs. Boarer's isolation and in her spiritual and parental struggle a model for new meaning and purpose in a life separated from traditional resources of community and culture. A young married woman might find in Mrs. Boarer a heroic model of spiritual independence, able, even in her husband's absence, to brave great hardship to fulfill a mission of saving the rising generation. The rhetorical strategy of the way of the cross might be adapted to a variety of situations and even particular testimonies might have a variety of meanings. The general message of all these stories of experimental religion remained the same: a heartfelt submission to and trust in God overcame the most malevolent of this world's forces and created an eternal community of right feeling. Thus illness and death, politics and mammon, drunkenness and domestic discord, and even fallen natural creation might be made part of a story that glorified God and unified humankind.[64]

8

Methodist Identity

THE WAY OF THE CROSS VERSUS THE CULTURE OF HONOR

The Methodists separated themselves from the world, shared themselves in testimony, and enjoyed what they believed to be the fellowship of love to God and humankind. From the description of these activities, we may distill the patterns of Methodist *identity*. Identity here means basic ways of organizing experience. The groups with which a person identifies provide models of such ways, and individual identity is an appropriation and variation of the group's ways. Identity, then, is both a social and a psychological concept. To know who you are is to know to whom you belong and to know your own distinctive version of your fellows' approach to living. There is also a negative side to identity. To know who you are is also to know who you are not. It is to know the sort of people to whom you do not belong and whose ways of living are not your own.

The culture of honor, of course, represented much of what Methodists knew themselves not to be. It became for most American Methodists the embodiment of the negative side of their identity. There were nevertheless important continuities between the two approaches to living that help explain why they remained linked even as they rejected each other. A comparison and contrast of the social psychology of Methodism with that of the culture of honor will clarify Methodism's basic ways of organizing experience. A clear vision of these patterns at this point in the book will allow us to see later how Methodist efforts to organize family life reflected them.[1]

Claiming an identity and making good the claim takes energy, and Methodism's system of social religion helped supply it. The vicissitudes of living resist the efforts of human beings to organize their experience. People must exert themselves to keep their lives from falling apart into meaningless successions of events and incoherent fluctuations of emotion. James Finley, as a young game hunter on the frontier, had begun just such a process of falling apart before his conversion integrated him into the Methodist community and its rituals. He gained from this change in identification not only a new order in his life but a new energy. Indeed, many witnesses to the effects of class meeting, love feast, and similar rituals spoke frequently of "times of refreshing" or of the people being "much quickened" or "encouraged to go forward." Later in his career Finley used the metaphor of fire to describe how, as a presiding elder, he had energized the official members of the circuits in his district. He had conducted an inquiry in class-meeting style with each group of officials at the various quarterly meetings. "The fire was soon carried out by preachers, exhorters, leaders, and stewards, and by spring the whole church throughout the vast field of labor was in a blaze."[2] When the system worked, penitents and saints who wept and shouted together also endued one another with active properties that gave them strength to be Methodists and to lead others to become Methodists.[3]

These mutually enlivening moments often led ritual participants to feel what they considered to be the presence of God in the meetings. They spoke of heaven coming down to earth, of the Lord being truly with them, or of God being present in power. Some such experience of divine presence is the foundational element of all human ritualization. It harks back to the earliest stage of human development in which the infant looks for the mothering face to communicate a sense of presence that affirms the very being of the child and of the world. Such moments of recognition overcome anxieties over abandonment and fears of self-loss through merger. Rituals that effectively invoke the divine presence assure participants of a "*separateness transcended* and yet also a *distinctiveness confirmed*." Upon this creative paradox is founded the sense of "I," a sense sustained and renewed by the mutual recognition of all "I"s who share a faith in the divine "I Am."[4] In the rituals of social religion, when members shared their inner worlds and found them received with tears and shouts, the experience allowed each person to say "I" with a vitality felt to have its source in God.

The substance of the "I" that the believers claimed when they spoke was a set of dispositions to organize their worlds according to the rhetorical form of the rituals. If they were "much quickened" by their experiences in class meeting and love feast and encouraged to "go forward," where and how they went forward were as fundamental as the quickening they received. Enlivening rituals must do more than simply enliven. If they are to continue to vitalize and bind together a community, they must also organize; otherwise ritual participants are unlikely to come together again.

We have observed earlier that the identity of disciples of experimental religion (that is, their basic ways of organizing experience) may be represented either by a metaphor of place or by the metaphor of story. Speaking in terms of place, the identity of the experimentally religious was within a sacred circle of holy affection set apart from a cold and hostile world. The hostile forces outside the sacred circle were susceptible, however, to the holy love and zeal generated within. This active, rhetorical, evangelistic element becomes all the more evident when one considers Methodist identity in terms of story. Examination of the testimonies spoken in class meeting and love feast reveals the pattern of Methodist identity in a story of death and resurrection, of dying to worldly attachments and disordered living and rising to heavenly affections and well-ordered habits. Unconverted people who heard these stories in the proper context were induced to enter into and live out this story themselves. In so doing, they identified themselves as Methodist evangelicals.

The outward spatial configuration of Methodist ritual events provided the appropriate context for the sharing of the stories of inward feeling and its transformations. The dying life of the way of the cross led away from worldly passions and carnal desires into a virtuous repose where one's renewed soul communed with God and rested happily in the constant witness of the Spirit that one was God's own adopted child. As the inner communal space of class meeting or love feast was to the hostile outer world, so the end state of the Christian soul was to its old fallen nature and its stormy passions; the self-descriptive language of the soul and the actual shape of the ritual context were homologous. In social religion, then, the outer conditions of Methodism and the inner states of Methodists met, ideally, in a single focus.

The spatial configuration in Methodist social religion conveyed more than the ideal inner state of the soul. It also conveyed the Methodists' intent to order and maintain a socially apparent distinction between themselves and the rest of society. They realized this intention through keeping their rules, through the various judicial rituals in which they enforced their rules, and through more subtle social controls like the manipulation of status and reputation in the local church society and the wider neighborhood. One of the more obvious of these social controls involved members' demeanor toward one another and the familial terms of address that signified this demeanor. When they addressed one another as Brother———, Sister———, Father———, or Mother———, they signalled their special relationships with one another and the distinction that obtained between them and the rest of the neighborhood. All these common understandings and corporate organizing efforts marked out a network of relationships where believers might find enlivening encounters to assure them of whom they were. They also learned the avoidances they must practice to assure themselves of who they were not.[5]

In the flux and ferment of the new republic, in the midst of disintegrating forms of traditional patriarchy, and in the rawness of frontier conditions, evangelical religious groups seemed to feel acutely the need to enforce such boundaries. Hence the spirited insistence upon closed doors for Methodist love feasts and class meetings and for closed communion for Baptist celebration of the Lord's Supper. It was not lost upon those excluded that in some way they were judged unfit for the good things reputed to happen within. James Finley was not at all subtle in communicating this message when he discovered some Yankee societies in northern Ohio that were opening the doors of their class meetings and letting all attend who would. He exhorted the Yankees to reform, declaring that Methodists ought not to give that which is holy to dogs, nor cast their pearls before swine.[6]

When the message of negation is made so clear, it evokes great rage. Finley noted such rage in describing how a son of one saintly couple, after he had been kept out of a love feast, tried to break down the door and then smashed in a window, injuring an old man in the process. Finley expressed his own negation in his journal entry: "God's judgments will overtake him before long. I was told he will curse his mother and father to their faces."[7]

Note how filial impiety is evidence, for Finley, of the young man's nearness to God's wrath. A son who curses his parents is not only someone subject to the avoidance of the religious community, he may also become an instructive image of negative identity for the faithful, a powerful example of the sort of person they *must not* be. Methodists belonged to the family of God, and they were to conduct their natural family relations with affection and respect. This violent, profane reviler of parents lent himself readily to the need that the Methodists, like all groups, had to mark the boundaries of their community with concrete embodiments of the evil that members left behind in joining the religious society. The lewd, mocking worldlings who frequently surrounded camp meetings or love feasts served the same function. Even the faults and failings of the saints might function in this way. In the reproof and exhortation of the class leader and in the mourning and repentance of those who fell short of their Christian profession, the believer might discern the appropriate avoidances that were one aspect of the ongoing ordering activity that Methodists sought to induce in one another.

With the social psychology of Methodist ritual and identity laid out in this schematic fashion, some comparison and contrast with the psychology of honor is in order. This comparison is appropriate because the rituals and identities formed in the culture of honor provided so many negative identity images for the evangelicals. Lest we make too much of the opposition between the two, however, at least one basic similarity ought to be noted at the outset: Both the culture of honor and the culture of early Methodist evangelicalism were largely oral cultures. A literate and learned elite did dominate the culture of honor in the eighteenth-century South, and their competence in literate styles of thought and expression helped reinforce the images of a divinely ordained ranking of all creation that legitimated their dominance.[8] Their capacity to get the lower and middling ranks to identify with them, however, depended on their ability to speak and act convincingly in ritual settings of courthouse, tavern, race track, and muster field. The requirement for oral skill in the elite was intensified by the need to win over the common folk to republicanism and revolution.

The nonelite themselves most admired the raconteur, storyteller, or orator. To think was to converse, and both reputation and a sense of community rested on facility in oral performance at gatherings large or small.[9] This special valuing of the good orator or storyteller persisted in the popular evangelical denominations. As we have seen, the records and reminiscences of early Methodism are full of memorable accounts of spoken performances in class meeting, love feast, camp meeting, and other preaching services. The persons who excelled in these performances and the notable moments in their performances were remembered and celebrated in Methodist folklore.[10] The primary medium of early Methodist efforts in organizing experience was the spoken word. That word was spoken in contexts ranging from class meetings, where three or four believers faced each other and spoke of sorrow for sin and God's love in their souls, to camp meetings, where thousands jostled together to hear preachers proclaim God's judgment and mercy.

This essential similarity between early Methodism and the culture against which it reacted made the differences between the two all the more pointed. Both cultures placed high value on performances that were seen, heard, and judged in face-to-face situations; but the types of performances they sanctioned were virtual inversions of each other. The culture of experimental religion demanded self-denial of both men and women. The culture of honor demanded of men a public self-assertion and of women a self-effacing modesty that nevertheless took pride in physical beauty and personal grace as well as in the strength, courage, and skill of their men. On the courthouse green, a man of honor had to demonstrate physical prowess in combat or in a horse race. In the tavern, he had to demonstrate his wit and skill in besting an opponent in playful banter. On the dance floor, both men and women demonstrated their physical comeliness and personal grace. At home among neighbors, friends, and kin, women won pride and honor by their stalwart and uncomplaining management of household affairs. Especially did they demonstrate their raw physical strength and courage in childbearing, an act that fulfilled the fundamental expectation of women: that they perpetuate the family line and name. The rituals of honor conveyed the natural strength of the participants and identified that strength with their inner spirits. The rituals of experimental religion, on the other hand, began with demonstrations of the spiritual weakness of the participants. In class meeting, love feast, or camp meeting, both men and women had to demonstrate their powerlessness in acts of mourning and penitence. Of course in the evangelical cycle of experience the weakness of the natural person gave way to the strengths of God's spirit, but such strength was always founded on the paradox of believers' knowing they were weak in themselves and strong only in God.

Given the evangelical inversion of the very masculine ethos of honor, it is not difficult to understand why women found it more appealing than men. Not only did the rituals of experimental religion transvalue and celebrate the powerlessness that women knew all too well, the rituals also promised a certain social recognition and a mysterious sort of empowerment paradoxically conditioned upon the confession of weakness. This sort of "liberation," however, had inherent limits. Even when those who had been laid low in mourning were raised up in the joy of conversion, their words of testimony still underscored the chasm between their natural weakness and the new strength of the spirit that only the death of their natural self had brought about. For women, this transformation did not in itself obviate their institutionalized inferiority and dependence. Unlike men, they could not lay claim to their natural rights as citizens of the republic; they were *femmes covert*.

For men, the split between the natural and the spiritual self implied a problem of sincerity or authenticity. In the male-dominated culture of honor, the self was regarded as largely identical with its social presentation; public appearance and performance conveyed the character. At least it was supposed to. To question a man's honesty or veracity was to invite vindication by trial of combat—as if knocking down the man who called one a liar demonstrated the invalidity of his questioning. The construction and presentation of self was probably different among women. In the gender-segregated world of love and companionship that Smith-Rosenberg and others have documented, there was possibility of an emotional expressiveness and complexity that allowed deeper, more nuanced self-awareness.[11] This is, perhaps, another reason why some women found the culture of experimental religion more appealing than did men. Among the believers, it was a given that even the most moral and respectable outward behavior did not necessarily signify a genuinely sincere and trustworthy character. True character was a matter of the heart. It was the genius of the rituals of social religion to turn the attention of participants to matters of the heart and to require that such matters be laid out for the affirmation or negation of one's peers in an intimate setting that was neither public nor wholly private. Heart religion required a psychosocial space where one might speak freely of the state of one's heart, where it was possible to express unfeigned sorrow or joy in tears and shouts. Sorrow or joy, tears or shouts were not readily welcomed in the masculine ritual arenas of the culture of honor. Humor or resentment, laughter or curses were more likely.

Parallel to these contrasting locations and presentations of the "true self" were contrasting emphases in the psychology of character and of social control. The contrast may be faithfully rendered in the classic distinction between shame and guilt. The culture of honor emphasized shame, the horror of being seen and exposed as ridiculous, unworthy, cowardly, or simply weak and "lowdown." Honor and shame involve a direct and unmediated equation of self-evaluation and social evaluation; a person is as he or she is seen. Shame, then, is the opposite of autonomy; the self is made to feel dependent and vulnerable to rejection or abandonment. The impulse of a person vulnerable to shame is to avoid or conceal the appearance of any wrongdoing or failure in order to escape the judging, isolating eyes of parents or public and be spared their contempt, for to be shamed is to feel the undifferentiated rejection of the total self. Guilt, on the other hand, implies a separation of deed and doer in which the guilty one fears punishment for discrete acts rather than an experience of total rejection and abandonment. It also discriminates more fully between self and society. Indeed, a true sense of guilt involves a sense of self-condemnation for deeds that others might not judge so harshly or of which they might not even be aware. Guilt looks for punishment; shame hides from it.[12]

In the face of potential shaming, denizens of the culture of honor sought autonomy and shunned dependence. The Jeffersonian ideal of a brotherhood of yeoman-farmer patriarchs reflects this quest. The basic strength or virtue associated with an autonomy that prevails over fears of dependence and shame is the virtue of will, the ability to assert the self with a sense of legitimacy and restrain it with a sense of righteousness.[13] The preoccupation of the early western male pioneers with obtaining their own freehold on which to set up their families and households may be understood in part as a quest for an arena of justifiable self-assertion, the ground upon which all legitimate choice and restraint was founded in their still traditional agrarian society. The corollary of such autonomy and self-assertion for men, of course, was the dependence and self-effacement of their women, whose claims to honor resided in their men and in the family lines they jointly sustained. Men's contest pastimes tested one another's autonomy and willfulness; their charivaris and other rituals of shaming marked the boundaries of acceptable self-assertion. The ethic of this sort of culture could be distilled with disarming simplicity: "A man ought to fear God and mind his business. He should be respectful and courteous to all women; he should love his friends and hate his enemies . . . eat when . . . hungry, drink when . . . thirsty, dance when . . . merry . . . and knock down any man who questioned his right to these privileges."[14]

Methodist preachers and other denizens and promoters of the culture of experimental religion were likely candidates for getting knocked down; for they were quite likely to question a man's right to dance, to condemn his drinking, and, worst of all, to intrude into his business at home and make his wife or children question him too. For her part, the man's wife or daughter would be called to forsake also the dancing, the fashionable clothes, or pride in physical beauty through which she had once demonstrated her honor. In coming forward to the altar, praying aloud in prayer meeting, or standing to testify in love feast, she would have to brave the shaming eyes of many who regarded such performances as violations of the boundaries of feminine propriety. Experimental religion worked to inculcate guilt in the context of a culture sensitive to shame, and it began by a frontal attack on the traditional demonstrations of shame, autonomy, and will. Its central transformative experience was founded upon the sacrifice of the will, that most precious of the virtues of honor. Conversion included an overwhelming experience of total divine rejection. One learned that one was polluted by sin, execrable in the sight of God, and therefore abandoned by him. For the Calvinistic evangelicals, this odious condition precluded any pretense of ever having had free will or autonomy in relation to God. For Arminians like the Methodists, it meant the paradox of choosing and striving to yield the will to God. In either case self-will was broken, and a permanent sense of dependence upon God installed in its place. The experience of God's rejection was followed by an acceptance that felt total even if it turned out to be conditional upon a certain style of life to be lived in the aftermath of conversion.[15]

The implication of such an experience was that the ridicule and rejection from the public and even from one's kin did not matter so long as one had the witness of the Spirit that one was God's child. Certainly acting out one's weakness as a mourner at the altar, braving the exposure of one's life and feelings in class meeting, or acting out one's identification with the despised family of God in the face of the mocking worldlings at quarterly or camp meeting required believers to suffer and overcome the constraints of shame. One readily may see why Methodist meetings were sometimes the object of informal vigilante attacks. Not only did they subvert the sort of willfulness central to the ideals of traditional culture, they also inculcated a certain holy shamelessness, a tendency to defy that culture's modes of social control.

One must hasten to qualify this idea of shamelessness. Evangelical converts might defy the shaming controls of the traditional community only because they had learned a different and much more encompassing repertoire of behaviors and appearances to be ashamed of.[16] In accord with the traditional judgment of character by outward behavior, they still were expected to protect their reputations and the reputation of their new spiritual family, the church. The behavior of church members was as important a reflection on the family of God as was the behavior of any worldling on his or her natural relations. Thus James Finley recalled the family-like surveillance of an early class in Cincinnati, a group he described as closely bound to one another by the natural affinities arising out of their relations to each other as Methodists. "Each one seemed the insurer of the other's reputation, and felt himself [to be] as responsible for his upright character as though he was his special guardian." The slightest sign that any member might be straying from "the path of holy rectitude" aroused "the liveliest apprehensions and interest" in the others. Absence from class meeting occasioned as much solicitude as if some member of a family had been unexpectedly absent.[17] One might readily imagine the shame occasioned by an unjustifiable absence. It is also clear from the complaints about class meeting treated in an earlier chapter that shame over prolonged absence from class kept some from returning. The disciplinary expulsions from the church of wayward members and ministers by quarterly and annual conferences severely shamed those who flagrantly failed to follow God's will and do their duty.

The experimentally religious, then, were far from enemies of social control. They only sought to replace a sense of the sporadic surveillance of the neighborhood with a sense of the omniscient eye of God in the conscience. In order to accomplish this internalization, they had to protect themselves and their new recruits from the immediate watchfulness and judgment of the traditional community. Its shaming power, present in "unawakened persons," might stifle that "liberty of speech" whereby individuals repeatedly discovered to the group and for themselves that Jesus was their own personal and present savior. The process of this discovery revealed to seekers their shame before God as persons polluted by sin. This shame relativized the shame inflicted by the old community of honor and turned attention inward to the struggle for purity of heart, rather than to mere purity of reputation.

The conversion experience also included the conviction that persons were guilty of sinning and subject to God's just punishment. Jesus, they believed, had taken the punishment upon himself and thereby saved them from the guilt and just consequences of their sin. As a result they could now imagine a new life, both here on earth and later in heaven. They could take the initiative to speak of their past sin and weave it into their own individual stories of salvation and hope for better things to come. They did not have to be paralyzed by their trials, temptations, or failings. Instead they could tell them over, turning passive suffering into a sense of active triumph. Thus Mrs. Boarer recounted her harrowing sufferings on the snowy mountainside as a story of yielding her will to God and being enabled by his providential prompting to save her life and her daughter's. The discouraged brethren whose will for wealth compelled them to travel on the Sabbath confessed their sin to their brothers and sisters in love feast, expiated their guilt, and regained their hope and initiative for heaven. Their confessions also had a quickening effect on the congregation. The act of testimony called for initiative. The content of testimony included resolutions to strive for heaven, to act better and differently. The form of the testimony, as of the conversion experiences on which it was modelled, was the symbolic action of moving from a negative condition of passionate helplessness in oneself to a positive condition of loving activity in and for God. On this active condition of the self was founded the distinctive Methodist sense of purpose: to reform the continent and create a holy people. The devotees of experimental religion, in summary, created bounded spaces in which the born-again children of God might verbally play with the raw materials of their experience and fashion them into new stories,

stories that overcame guilt, confirmed initiative, and fostered a sense of purpose.[18]

The right to engage in the verbal play of testimony, however, was bought at significant psychic cost, and the range of such play was narrow. The cost was a sacrifice of the will. Conversion delivered only from the guilt and consequences of sin, not from its pollution. Deliverance from pollution was thought to be the work of sanctification or perfect love, and it was a matter of learning to surrender the will totally to God and let a sense of his love pervade the self. Only then, as George Phillips and Elizabeth Kaufmann made clear in their courtship correspondence, would one be fit for the most extensive usefulness to God's cause. The experimental religion of the Methodists issued in great energy and activity, but only on the condition that such activity be felt and seen as God's will and not one's own. God conferred great strength for doing one's duty, not for doing what one willed. The sacrifice of self-will and, with it, the inner sense of autonomy seem to have left evangelicals with only a slim margin for playful exploration of the self and its world. Strait was the gate and narrow the path that led to their salvation.

In the culture of honor, one learned that moral worth and identity were derived from blood and family name. Purpose was defined in terms of the preservation and glorification of that name.[19] The inner sanctum of that name was the configuration of a vulnerable inner space set over against the world. It was the core of a man's personal and sexual identity as a bearer and propagator of the patronym. The visible symbols of this psychosocial reality were home and property, including the sexual property of wife and generational property of children. This inner space was to be fiercely protected from any intrusion, and those within it—especially the women—were to be kept in their place, firmly under control lest they somehow invite such intrusion and the shame of its attendant pollution. Initiative lay with the patriarch; the residents of inner space were supposed to be passive.

The culture of experimental religion, on the other hand, constructed a sense of greater differentiation between individual and society. It also conferred a more restless sense of initiative. Most important, it attempted to harness the individual's initiative to a broader, more abstract purpose than the preservation and promotion of patronym, clan, and local community. The family of God, of course, was not a natural family and did not serve all the educational, economic, or political functions of natural families. It did, however, confer a general sense of God's calling on each individual who learned to tell his or her story according to the way of the cross. It invested each person with a desire for usefulness and a readiness to sacrifice the self on principle. These attitudes might be carried into a variety of enterprises: religious, benevolent, economic, or even political. They caused a particular bind for women, however, because they were still constrained by the reigning patriarchal assumptions about women's place in home and society. Methodist assumptions about individual personhood and personal salvation were not fully compatible with these patriarchal strictures, and Methodist practices and writings about the family helped free women, albeit in limited and convoluted ways.

In the time of the Second Great Awakening, as we have seen, experimental religion grew up in the midst of ideological and social conditions that were undermining traditional meanings of family solidarity. The movement of Atlantic and much of American culture in the late eighteenth and early nineteenth centuries was away from the definition of persons principally in terms of patronym. Experimental religion must be seen as a part of that general movement. Its characteristic rituals must be regarded as ways of reconstituting the meaning of family life. The way of the cross led home, and it transformed the home it led to. It is to the home, then, that we turn next.

9

The Family of God

An enigmatic, but ultimately revealing, reflection appeared in James Finley's account of the first class he organized in the Cincinnati area:

> The formation of that first Methodist society was the introduction of a new element—not as it was in the old country, to rouse the stagnant forms of religion, and stir them into life, but the introduction of an element into a new and active state of society, growing up under the cold and stereotyped forms of religion from which all animal feeling was excluded, thus destined to rouse or control and adapting itself without changing its principles, to all the phases of social life.[1]

What was Finley talking about? The new element in the new society must have been the culture of experimental religion. The animal feeling excluded by the older forms of religion was the range of human affections and passions that experimental religion was designed to both rouse and control. Experimental religion was emotional religion; it aimed at moving human beings whose natures embraced a world of passion. Those who lost sight of this essential feature of the human constitution were likely to be languid in their religious enjoyments and, as a consequence, unsuccessful in their attempts to win others to the gospel.[2] Such people might as well join the old churches and adhere to their "cold and stereotyped forms of religion."

When he wrote these words, Finley probably had in mind the Presbyterian Calvinism against which he had successfully rebelled as a young man. The new element in Methodism had transformed his own emotional life and provided him with a strong identity well fitted to the new and active state of society in the Ohio valley of the early nineteenth century. The traditional church of his father, on the other hand, suffered significant schism during the great revival in the West and saw many of its members fly off into Shakerism, Campbellism, and other sects. H. C. Northcott, a local preacher of Kentucky and a contemporary of Finley, observed that Presbyterianism lost many to what he called "fanaticism" while Methodism pursued the "even tenor of its way" during the great revival in the West. The reason, he claimed, was that Methodism was essentially revivalistic. From constant experience the Methodists knew how to direct the emotional current of the revival, where to check, and where to augment its course.[3] Methodism, then, seemed to its adherents to have the emotional energy, flexibility, and consistency needed for the new and active state of society. It could, moreover, adapt itself to all phases of social life without changing its principles.

When he made his claims for Methodism's social omnicompetence, Finley could not have been thinking of corporate boardrooms, factory assembly lines, inner-city ghettos, or suburban split-levels. Such spaces and the activities associated with them came after his time. The social realities he knew were rural farming districts oriented to towns that were "island communities" dotting the midwestern landscape. These islands had fairly regular social and economic contact with the nascent cities in their region, but these cities were still communities of mostly merchants and mechanics. The industrialized urban areas that would reach out by railroad and telegraph and reorganize the insular lives of rural and small-town folk were only just beginning to form. The firm distinctions between private domestic life and public occupation and citizenship had not yet been thoroughly institutionalized. Industrialism's separation of work and household was still in the future for most Americans. What most people in the island communities had in common was a deeply felt awareness of themselves as members of the American nation and partakers of an American way of life.

Methodists like Finley aimed to define the American way of life by injecting their "new element" into every region and every community. There was no single American way, of course. It varied from region to region and even from town to town. The Civil War was to provide tragic evidence of the deep cleavages that existed between American ways of life. But the Methodist evangelical concern was for authentic religious feeling, intimate sharing, unity of sentiment, and orderly, self-disciplined living wherever Christians lived.[4] They extended this concern beyond the church to family and friendship, to women and "woman's sphere," and, through them, to the republic itself. In the context of island communities in the first half of the nineteenth century, such concerns with family and nation could seem to encompass virtually all legitimate phases of social life. Methodist evangelicals who pursued these concerns believed they were transforming the whole of social life. I argue that at least they catalyzed a change in the meaning of domestic life.

How did they do it? There were three ways: First, the experimentally religious not only thought and felt themselves to be the heaven-bound family of God but also acted the parts of sister, brother, father, and mother.

The family-of-God metaphor became a ritual rhetoric moving the saints toward newer affection-centered understandings of family ties. Thus the process of change involved a dimension that we might call *metaphorical action*. Second, preachers, class leaders, and rank-and-file believers tried to establish particular ritual patterns in their homes. These patterns reflected the patterns of social religion. They established within the home the ways of organizing experience characteristic of experimental religion. Good Methodist homes became incorporated into the social structure of Methodism. Thus we may speak of another dimension of the change process as the *ritual-organizational* link between Methodism and domestic life. Third, the Methodist popular press, using the network of itinerant preachers as its agents, was unmatched in its efforts to shape the perceptions, feelings, and actions of its audience. The writings of religious leaders in the popular Methodist periodicals were congruent with their ritual efforts to organize group and individual experience in accord with the logic of experimental religion. Thus the final dimension of the change process was *ideological* or *hortatory*. These exhortations in popular print and their congruence with the patterns of social religion and with the logic of experimental religion constitute the final step in the argument.

We deal first with the dimension of metaphorical action. Metaphors are not simply window dressing in human discourse but the very substance of the concepts by which we order our lives.[5] The metaphor of the family of God captured for believers the patterns of pious intimacy and sociability they learned within their rituals of social religion. These patterns contrasted significantly with the sociability of the culture of honor. New norms of friendship arose within the family of God, and it seemed clear that these norms belonged to domestic spaces set at a distance from the world. When the Methodist popular press began to elaborate a domestic ideology, it would echo the patterns of sociability found in the family of God.

A metaphor is an act of persuasion that cultivates greater or lesser degrees of intimacy between those who make the metaphor and those to whom it is addressed. It implies both a certain character in the speakers who employ the metaphor and a certain culture that establishes or supports that character. A metaphor is an invitation to trust the speakers and become, if only fleetingly, part of their culture.[6]

The Methodist editors of the *Western Christian Advocate* must have recognized some of these rhetorical qualities in the metaphor of the family of God when they reprinted a parable entitled "Popularity: A Dialogue." Into a lawyer's office near election time come, one at time, a Presbyterian, a Baptist, an Episcopalian, a Methodist, a Universalist, and a Quaker. The lawyer attempts to speak in the particular idiom of each denomination and pays special compliments to the distinctive doctrines and rituals of each. The entrance of the Methodist is an occasion for a concise evocation of the ethos of Methodist experimental religion:

> How do you do Brother M. I call you brother, because my parents were Methodists. And when I was a child the preachers used to visit our house, and I used to call them all "brothers," from hearing my father and mother call them so. It is singular how strong the impressions of childhood are. Though I do not profess religion, yet I always feel more at home in a Methodist meeting than in any other.[7]

The shyster even throws in an appreciation of the holy noise he had recently heard at a camp meeting, as he rode by. At the end of the piece, however, the simple old Quaker rebukes the politician for his duplicity. The contrast between the world of the Christian churches and the world of politics is manifest for all to see.

Disparaging politics was the purpose of the article, of course; but this imaginary dialogue also communicated some basic facts about each of the denominations represented. About the Methodists it suggests that they, perhaps more than their fellow Christians of other persuasions, identified themselves to one another by the rhetoric of family relations.[8] The passage also suggests the sort of social world in which such modes of address made sense—one in which preachers were constantly in the homes of church members (or at least were remembered to have been there), where the impressions of childhood were given special religious significance and where it was important that religious meetings felt like home.

It might be tempting to regard the terms "Brother" or "Sister" as merely habitual, unthinking usages signifying little. Such an easy dismissal does not square with evidence such as a letter to J. B. Finley from a distraught acquaintance who opened: "Dear Sir[,] You will see by the head of my letter that I no longer address you by the endearing affiliation of Brother—under my present circumstances I dare not claim the privilege." Finley's correspondent had been expelled from his Methodist society for "imprudent conduct in being at the tavern," and it seems he wrote to Finley largely to vent his feelings on the matter.[9] Given his sorrow, outrage, and sense of betrayal—he had shown as much "humiliation" for his indiscretion as he honestly could but still was expelled—his deliberate omission of the "endearing affiliation" was a poignant way to begin his complaint to a friend.

Hannah Bareth wrote to Finley from her father's home after recovering from a severe illness. "Brother Finley," she declared, "your tenderness and affection to unworthy me Shall never be forgotten[.] [Y]ou and sister Filey [*sic*] apears [*sic*] more like near Relations to me than any than else [*sic*]." Bareth had worked with Finley and his wife on a mission station among the Wyandot Indians and intended to go back despite her parents' amazed remonstrances. Surely, they exclaimed, she was not going back there to be killed by Indians. Oh no, she demurely replied, they loved her too well to kill her.[10] For Hannah Bareth, the family of God, even when partially composed of Indians, had become the family that felt most real. Martin Hitt seemed to feel equally the various ties that bound him to his brother and fellow circuit rider, Daniel. He signed himself, "your affectionate and Loving Brother, both by the ties of nature and Grace"; and, on another occasion, "your Loving Brother in a threefold sense."[11]

This latter signature by Martin requires explanation. The Hitt brotherhood and the Methodist Christian brotherhood are clear enough, but what might the third sense of brotherhood be? Another early itinerant, William Burke, pointed to the obvious answer when he described the communion of his colleagues in ministry. "They were like a band of brothers," he recalled, united by their common purpose, "the glory of God and the salvation of immortal souls." When they met in conference, "they had a feast of love and friendship; and when they parted, they wept and embraced each other as brothers beloved."[12] These were the children of God who had left fathers, mothers, brethren, sisters, and homes to become Christ's special wandering disciples. They were mindful of the promise of their master that in return for their sacrifice they would receive a hundredfold more in houses, lands, and family and, ultimately, eternal life.[13] Bishop McKendree, when James Finley wept on his shoulder and complained he was but a poor ignorant child alone in the wilderness with no one to guide him, specified the meaning of that promise to the itinerant brotherhood. He assured the fledgling itinerant that God would provide him with many fathers and mothers in the gospel. Finley's own account of his earliest circuits indicate that faithful lay people partially fulfilled the bishop's echo of Christ's promise.[14] The itinerants themselves, however, also fulfilled the promise for each other; they were a network of fathers and sons as well as a brotherhood.[15]

The early Methodist bishops were especially strong fathers among the preachers. Recall Finley's protest to Asbury over being assigned to a circuit located inconveniently far from where he had settled his wife and children. Asbury had replied with a gentle, patronizing, "Be a good son in the gospel, James," and induced a submission that seemed to penetrate to Finley's heart. Peter Cartwright, another young Kentuckian, wept and pleaded with the bishop to be delivered from a circuit assignment among Yankee settlers in Ohio. "The old man took me in his arms," Cartwright recalled, "and said, 'O no, my son; go in the name of the Lord. It will make a man of you.' " Cartwright was less submissive in mind than Finley and thought to himself that he would just as soon not grow up if he had to do it in this manner. Still, he obeyed. Both sons in the gospel were in their twenties at the time of these encounters and had wives and children. Such was the familial ethos of Methodism and the patriarchal mystique of the bishops, however, that the younger men readily played the part of obedient, deferential sons.[16]

It was, perhaps, a sign of the fading of this mystique when William McKendree failed to impress George Brown with his family-based arguments against lay delegations to the annual and general conferences. Lay delegation, claimed the bishop, would be destructive of the itinerancy. The itinerants were instrumental in the conversion of the lay people; they were their spiritual fathers. Children ought not to rule fathers; the authority of the preachers over the lay people reflected the nature of things. Brown, soon to become a leader in the reform movement that became the Methodist Protestant church, did not dispute the bishop at the time of this conversation. Later, in his written account, he observed that McKendree's argument that instrumentality in conversion gives a right to rule looked like the old doctrine that conquest gives kings a right to rule. The itinerancy ought to perish, he declared, if it could exist only by the destruction of human liberty.[17] The liberty Brown was talking about, though he might not have appreciated the distinction, was indeed *human* liberty, natural republican liberty, albeit claimed in the context of ecclesial politics rather than civil politics. It was not the spiritual liberty of the sinner set free from sin. The Methodist Protestant schism was strong evidence that the culture of experimental religion had yet to find a consistent way to accommodate these two liberties to each other.[18]

McKendree's argument retained plausibility for some people because of the special power that preachers did exert for a time over the people. They were, as we observed earlier, the embodiments par excellence of the way of the cross. Sometimes the overpowering excitement they presided over in the rituals of the religious community could elicit excessive responses to the preachers themselves. One simple, honest soul went forward to join the church at a meeting, and the preacher asked him if he was willing to renounce the devil and the world. " 'I am willing to do anything you tell me,' " he replied.[19] The network of church ritual and community existed to transmute allegiance to a single magnetic personality into loyalty to God and his church.

There remained, however, a special tie between preacher and convert. The use of the phrase "spiritual father" referred to a relation in which the "father" had been the instrument in the "child's" conversion.[20] Even when quite young in the ministry, Peter Cartwright understood his relation to his converts in this way and exploited the tie to frustrate a spiritual kidnapping attempt by the Baptists. He had just formed a society with twenty-three new converts in one settlement and then ridden on toward another appointment. Some Baptists came to these sincere but ignorant converts and convinced them that their next step as Christians ought to be baptism by immersion and joining the Baptists in Christian fellowship. By the time Cartwright got word of the religious raid and had rushed back to the settlement, his new Methodists were about to become Baptists. "I am bereft of my children," he thought at first. Then he got an idea. He offered himself to the Baptist officials for membership in their church, and they gleefully swallowed the bait. On his way to the river he quietly reassured an amazed and tearful Methodist woman of the neighborhood who remonstrated with him; "Dear sister," he soothed, "fear not . . . I hope to retake my children yet." Just as the immersion ceremony got underway, he stepped out from the Baptists-to-be and told the leaders he felt no need to go through with this ceremony because he had already been baptized as an infant. That was no baptism at all, they replied. Cartwright insisted that unless they recognized his baptism, he could not join them. They could not recognize his baptism, and they lost their bid to take his converts. For Cartwright's "children" all declared that he had taught them the way of salvation; if he could not join the Baptists, neither could they.[21]

The father-son relation in the family of God also occurred between those who had no memory of the father directly converting the son. Many male lay members, local preachers, and circuit riders became known as fathers in the societies and played their parts with conviction. White Brown made his home a favorite "preachers' tavern" and provided a camp-meeting ground that became legendary. He served as a class leader for forty-five years and as a steward for forty years. For these and many other virtues, James Quinn styled him "Patriarch of the Scioto Valley."[22] Elijah Sparks of Indiana and Benjamin Northcott of Kentucky were two local preachers who were well known and regarded for the fatherly way they cared for and counseled the younger itinerants who ministered to their circuits.[23] John Sale played father on the circuit to his junior preacher, Moses Crume, and Crume himself later became an itinerant father figure.[24] Many men in the first half of the nineteenth century learned the calling of Methodist preacher in father-son apprenticeship relationships. Nor was occupational direction in the family of God limited to the preachers. Jacob Young's class leader acted a father's part when he broke up an incipient contract between Young and a wealthy, slave-holding Captain Masterman who wanted to make Young an overseer on one of his farms. "He told me, in an authoritative voice," Young remembered, "that it would be my final ruin. He talked to the captain rather severely, and we concluded to dissolve the contract by mutual consent."[25] The young man's impending alliance with the culture of honor was a direct threat to his purity and morals. It is significant that Young's class leader, rather than his parents, played the role of guardian and vetoed his occupational plans.

Jacob Young is an instructive study in the psychological authority that the sons of experimental religion might grant to their spiritual fathers. He committed what he called the greatest blunder of his life in 1808 when, after two years as presiding elder in the extremely trying Mississippi territory, he left to attend an annual conference in Tennessee. Evidently this was a dereliction of duty, a quest for comfort and recognition and a decision to seek a new assignment when he ought to have stayed by his post until the bishops saw fit to relieve him. In any case, he wrote that he grieved the spirits of his friends in the territory by leaving them; he grieved the spirits of the bishops and incurred their displeasure; and, he grieved the Holy Spirit and lost the comforts of religion for many years. The bishops, especially Asbury, were the first to reveal his error to him, and it is difficult not to link this great father's discountenancing to Young's sense of having lost the comforts of religion. He wept much under the lash of the bishop's severe lecture. The rest of the conference he reported to be delightful in many ways but a gloomy time for him; he felt that "Adversity had spread her raven wings" over his future prospects. Only in the ensuing week or two, as he traveled through Kentucky toward his new appointment in western Virginia and encountered many childhood friends who manifested their love for him, was he able to "regulate" his heart. He did his regulating, however, in private reading, praying, and thinking and was very thankful to his heavenly Father when alone. Only by persevering effort was this son in the gospel able to rise above the disapproval of his earthly father in the gospel and find peace with his heavenly Father. Even then, he did not regain for years the concrete, heartfelt sense of the heavenly Father's adoption.[26] Evidently, for some children in the gospel, it took a long time to develop fully the conscience that might grant a measure of independence from the judgments of fellow mortals.

If, in the family of God, the fathers exercised control and the sons submitted and looked for guidance, what may be said of the mothers in the gospel? The fathers acted out a role that echoed the norms of patronage and deference characteristic of the patriarchal culture in which they were reared. The mothers had access to roles in ritual performance that had little or no parallel in the traditional culture of honor. Mary Morriss Smith remembered how a pious Mrs. Holland got happy during a sermon by a local preacher and exclaimed, " 'I must shout [even] if I am in the Courthouse.' " The preacher stopped and let the woman vent her feelings; before she was done, many more felt like shouting.[27] A Mother Williams in Indiana had a reputation for power in prayer to move the hearts of the people. On one occasion, she came forward in church to give her small offering for missions and then turned around and prayed with such moving eloquence for ministers at home and missionaries abroad that the chronicler of the event believed she was under "direct inspiration" from God. "Elect lady, mother in Israel," he called her.[28] Giftedness in such performance might be the basis on which a woman built up significant local prominence and power. Mrs. Sarah Hinton of North Carolina sang, prayed, and even exhorted in public, unashamed by the presence of men of any class or condition. She became known as the chief cornerstone of her Methodist society.[29]

Women with such gifts, so long as they did not presume to preach or assume other so-called masculine functions in the church, seemed at first to be no threat to the Methodist ministers. Some itinerants, in fact, sought them out for wives. D. M. Mitchel boasted about his new wife to his friend and fellow preacher, G. W. Maley. "It is enough for you to know that she is a Christian and a Methodist, that she can pray a pretty good stick in the public congregation when called on and I think her about as great a piece of perfection as you think your Sarah is."[30] Sarah Maley, while still Sarah Enyart, had distinguished herself by the liberty with which she prayed in her Methodist congregation and by the recital of her experience in class and love feast. Many times she melted the hearts of saints and sinners alike. Just a year after she joined the church, G. W. Maley chose her to be his wife. As a preacher's wife, she led many mourners to the altar and prayed over them, organized "female prayer meetings," visited the sick, and led many to greater faithfulness by her godly example.[31] Ministers' wives experienced some pressure to play this role of gospel mother as minister's assistant. When his new wife, Patience Teal Quinn, hesitated to "stir about and exhort others," James Quinn wrote his gospel father, Daniel Hitt, and suggested a word from him might be of service to her.[32] Catherine Walker was socialized into her role when, during her husband's first itinerant year, she stayed with a pious family in Chillicothe, Ohio. The mistress of the house and several other Methodist women encouraged her to take up her "new and responsible duties, as the wife of an itinerant preacher." She became especially active in Sabbath school work.[33]

This range of religious activities was open to all pious women but was expected of the preachers' wives under the demands of what Leonard I. Sweet has termed the "Assistant" model for the preacher's wife. Itinerant preachers' wives also shared with many more traditional women a trying circumstance that underlay what Sweet calls the "Sacrificer" model: they were often isolated, their husbands gone from home and their relatives and friends distant.[34] The general absence of circuit riders from home was an obvious feature of their calling. It is somewhat less obvious to twentieth-century recollection that nineteenth-century men in general, especially those of the rural South, had a strong tendency to travel abroad on business or pleasure. The nearby town with its tavern, green, contest pastimes, and male camaraderie, the fields and forests with their game, the more distant cities with their important economic affairs: all conspired to lure men away from their domestic circles. Even when they were at home, they were ill at ease in feminine company; the norms of male social life and the ascriptions of traditional masculinity were ill suited to relaxed sociability between the sexes. There was little southern women could do about their isolation except bear up under their fate and occasionally register an appropriately feminine, and largely ineffectual, complaint.[35] Thus Mary Campbell of Abingdon, Virginia, pointedly observed to her husband, David, absent in Richmond where he pursued his prominent political career, that he could go about in society as he pleased while she was shut up like a canary with no "power of obtaining society . . . and no employment that I think absolutely necessary to give my attention to, my little domestic concerns being a mere nothing." Her husband's reply was a classic instance of deflection by flattery. She had outdone him with her reasoning, he declared. It was true she was shut in like a bird, but her turn of thought was so elevated, her mode of expression so heavenly, that he could not help thinking that the tyranny of shutting the canary in was somewhat justified by the song it made her sing.[36]

In a limited but real sense, the way of the cross, as applied to the role of preacher's wife, provided a way to turn this traditional isolation of women into something meaningful, into an actively appropriated sacrifice rather than passively accepted fate. Probably the most frequently mentioned virtue of itinerant preachers' wives was that they, by stern fortitude and self-sacrifice, refrained from interfering with their husband's work. Catherine Walker wrote a poem on her sickbed assuring her husband that she could spare him to go preach the gospel while she remained behind, promising to pray for him, "That *you may do* the will of God, / And *I, resigned*, may kiss the rod."[37] Angeline Sears's husband remembered how she wrote him that she felt keenly the lack of his "society" but had resolved that her own claims should never conflict with the calls of the gospel.[38] Elizabeth Kaufmann assured her fiancé, George Phillips, that when she consented to be his wife, she relinquished any right or wish to choose their field of labor. She wanted to go only "where the all wise Disposer of events sees we can 'do the most good, and get the most good.' "[39] Beyond refraining from making claims upon their husbands, good preachers' wives conducted their households with a cheerfulness, competence, and frugal care that caused their husbands to be ever ready to perform their duty. Phillips testified in his diary that his dear Elizabeth showed such cheer combined with Christian meekness that it was impossible to be melancholy in her presence. After their first year, he had yet to hear her complain despite the fact it had been a year of trial. They had gotten only meager financial support from their circuit; but, thanks to Elizabeth's astute management, they had incurred no new debts and had paid off an old one. He was fully convinced that a married minister was better prepared for his work than a celibate one.[40]

Such uncomplaining toughness was expected of women in more traditional households, to be sure. The advantage of the preachers' wives, if advantage it was, lay in the knowledge that they were, in just fulfilling the traditional onerous duties of a wife, contributing to an employment greater than what many women called their little domestic concerns. Then there were the tasks peculiar to an itinerant's wife: speaking in the rituals of social religion, exhorting sinners, Sabbath school work, visiting the sick, or other benevolent tasks. If they combined a wife's traditional virtue with skill and energy in these spiritual duties, preachers' wives might have a sense of significance in their roles considerably greater than that accorded to women in more traditional roles. Thus marrying a circuit rider, for all the hardship and deprivation it seems to have entailed, was still considered by many women a passport to a meaningful life, a life of "usefulness."[41]

Another traditional function of women, providing hospitality and taking care of visitors, took on a distinctive meaning when performed by the mothers in Israel for the wayfaring itinerants. John Burgess remembered how his mother, Lydia, opened her home to the saints gathered for quarterly meeting, giving the beds to the women and laying quilts on the floor for the men. Her home was constantly open to circuit preachers and lay people alike. He thought it likely that his mother had given five thousand meals to the people of God.[42] The spiritual meaning of this sort of hospitality is suggested in a recollection by James Finley of a Mother Stone. Along with the creature comforts that she provided him and his fellow itinerants, she also helped create those social-spiritual enjoyments that built up the family of God. Finley remembered one visit to her house when "she sent for Squire Reese and his wife to spend the afternoon, and we had a comfortable time. We mingled our prayers together, resolved to live for God, and strive for heaven."[43]

In this brief mention and in other allusions glowing through the anecdotes and routine reports that fill Methodist documents, one senses a network of sociability and visiting sustained largely, as traditional roles would lead us to expect, by the women of the church. As Carroll Smith-Rosenberg and others have pointed out, women of the nineteenth century formed networks of friendship in which intense and intimate relationships might thrive.[44] This was a world in which men shared rarely; but, to the extent they did, experimental religion seems to have been a major catalyst for their inclusion. The religion of the heart prospered when its devotees gathered to talk of what God did for their souls and of their hopes and desires for heaven. This outward sharing of inward states was a social skill in which women, due to their distinctive social world, were likely to be much more practiced than men. To find a common ground on which they might converse with men in this more-or-less intimate manner, however, seems to have been a very fulfilling experience not only for the women, but also for those men (generally preachers) who could get themselves into the proper frame of mind. Indeed, the correspondence of some preachers and their friends suggests an intimacy and intensity of feeling approaching that found by Smith-Rosenberg in what she calls the female world of love and ritual.[45]

The terms of spiritual kinship marked the boundaries of the Methodist world of love and ritual. They constituted a rhetoric of address whereby members in everyday contexts identified themselves as belonging to one another and moved one another to act the parts of brothers and sisters, fathers and mothers. The family talk helped the saints to nurture and develop among themselves the moods and motivations they learned and celebrated in the more formal rituals of class and love feast.[46] The relationship was, of course, dialectical. As the spiritual intimacy of social religion radiated out into the everyday relations of the family of God, so the sense of mutuality dispersed through the network of spiritual kinship was most fully realized in the rituals of social religion.

This spiritual sociability of the family of God was opposed in principle to the sociability of the culture of honor. Thus James Henthorn yearned for the days when he and his dear friend Daniel Hitt wandered together "hid from the vulgar eye." How sweet, he rhapsodized, were those "hours of retirement, where none but the spirit of Love and real friend[ship] compose the number of guests."[47] Clearly Henthorn was not talking about the camaraderie of the courthouse green or the muster field; these were the element of men who would have turned "the vulgar eye" upon the spiritual friendship that Henthorn and Hitt enjoyed. To avoid such guests, they went where the spirit of love might prosper unhindered by the spirit of honor. More than forty years after Henthorn wrote to Hitt, Isaac Crawford and five fellow preachers were enjoying one another in "singing and social intercourse" that seems to have been less intense than the love of Henthorn and Hitt but not less opposed to the ethos of the muster ground. The six preachers were aboard a steamboat traveling up the Ohio River when a group of Kentucky volunteers boarded with the blare of martial music. "Farewell to all comfort for the rest of the night," complained Crawford in his journal, "such cursing and swearing I never heard before." Some of the volunteers drank and gambled and swore all night. Crawford and his companions finally left the boat, hired a hack, and found "a Christian welcome" along the way at the home of a Brother McBride. Later they joined with some thirty or forty other preachers to charter a boat and complete their journey upriver; they held a preaching service every evening and family worship every morning.[48]

If the pious abhorred the company of the vulgar men of honor, genteel persons of honor also viewed the pious with some distaste. Young Samuel Williams observed to his cousin that General Worthington of Chillicothe, Ohio, despite his hospitality in allowing a camp meeting on his lands, took his wife away from the altar where she was struggling under strong emotions among the penitent seekers. The general, wrote Williams, "was displeased with these outward manifestations of inward feelings."[49] When the genteel Mary Campbell complained to her husband of being shut up like a canary, she also mentioned she had intended to visit a Methodist class meeting at the Methodists' newly finished chapel in Abingdon, Virginia. Only her sense of the impropriety of going out without some appropriate chaperone prevented her. Her husband took her to task for even thinking of attending a Methodist meeting. "Why would you risk being jostled about in a crowd of fanatics without my protecting arm?" he queried. "[T]he morals of no religious society can be well preserved," he assured her, "where so much irregularity is introduced."[50] He failed to sense, of course, the degree to which his wife's loneliness and boredom made even the society of "fanatics" appear tempting. He was also oblivious to a regularity bordering on the relentless that was implicit in their practices.

Many Methodists held equally censorious attitudes toward the genteel society in which David and Mary Campbell moved. It is commonplace to note evangelical strictures on genteel practices of dancing, fashionable dress, and idle amusements. A devout young Methodist woman revealed a more subtle basis for objections to genteel society. Harriet Stubbs had worked with James and Hannah Finley at the Wyandot Mission near Sandusky, Ohio, but found herself thrust into fashionable company when her father died and his will stipulated that she be placed under her married sister's care in Georgetown, just outside the nation's capital. She found the manners and customs of Georgetown vastly different from what she was accustomed to. "I fear I shall never become reconciled to the change," she confided to Finley. Visits were arranged almost entirely by the sending and receiving of cards—a convenience, she admitted, since it meant one might receive company or not just as one wished. Potential visitors drove their carriages to one's door, sent a servant to inquire if the lady was at home, and understood perfectly if the lady sent word by her servant that she was indisposed or engaged. If the lady did receive them, her servant ushered them into a room, gave them her compliments, and told them she would do herself the honor to wait on them in a few minutes. When the lady appeared, the visitors conversed with her for ten or fifteen minutes and then took their leave. After describing this elaborate protocol, Miss Stubbs remarked that she had been obliged to receive a dozen such visits between the hours of ten and one o'clock, the fashionable time. "*O how I despise such formality*," exploded the simple Methodist woman. She confessed to feeling "extremely awequerd [*sic*] and unhappy" in such company; but she also assured Finley that not all her acquaintances were of that stripe. She was very pleased with the Methodist society in Georgetown and had become very much attached to two or three Methodist families whom she often visited in a sociable way. "After a morning spent in receiving such visits as I have before hinted at," she sighed, "you have no idea of the pleasure and relief there [*sic*] sweet society afford [*sic*] me."[51]

Thirty years after Harriet Stubbs penned her complaint, Bishop Thomas Asbury Morris pilloried in print the fashionable style of visiting. He was explicit, where Harriet Stubbs had only been allusive, about the emotional contrast between fashionable and Methodist styles of sociability. For him, the audience gained through the elaborate process required by polite society was an audience "dearly bought with loss of time and sacrifice of feeling." He much preferred the experiences he had had as a circuit rider when he simply knocked at the door, received "the warm hand of friendship," and felt perfectly at home. Those were the days, he believed, of "simple-hearted, honest friendship, when social life was unembarrassed by the affected and heartless etiquette of modern times."[52] This concern for a simple, heartfelt style of social contact and its corresponding hostility to formality was of a piece with the Methodist concern for authentic outward demonstration of inward feeling in the rituals of evangelism and social religion. True Christian fellowship in class meeting and love feast required a "liberty of speech" freed from the embarrassment that "unawakened persons" might impose. In similar fashion, true sociability among Christians required a simplicity of manners freed from the awkwardness that the unfeeling etiquette of the worldly might create. The culture of experimental religion aimed at the mystery of intimacy; it shunned those circumspect gestures that preserve the mystery of mutual distance.

The experimentally pious were not without their own sense of a necessary distance between persons. For them, however, the fundamental distinction between persons was moral rather than social; distance was to be maintained between the saved and the unsaved, the church and the world. And this distance was only a reflection of a profound internal division between the orderly affections fixed upon heaven and the unruly passions excited by the world. Only those who had died to their passions and had had their affections put in order by the direct personal intervention of heaven could enter into true communion with each other. Such communion did not require an outward circumspection of gesture to preserve the distinctiveness of each person; Christian mortification separated each human self from those motives that threatened to usurp or tread down the selfhood of the other. The result was supposed to be an ascetic but spontaneous harmony, a community of the crucified but risen again.

Such a community could not be constituted solely by the momentary rituals of social religion; it needed embodiment in more enduring social institutions. The church, of course, was one such institution; the family was the other. The family, according to articles carried in the Methodist press, was the most primitive social institution, the foundation of all others. The family and the church, in fact, were the only "societies" that God organized among men "by immediate divine authority."[53]

10

Ritualizing Families for God

If church and family were the only institutions established by divine decree, it was natural for believers to expect that the two work in harmony. They engaged, therefore, in several ritualizing efforts whereby Methodist families became outposts of the Methodist Zion. Family prayer helped secure the souls of the rising generation, fostered the love and unity of both literal and figurative families, and kept them unspotted by the world. The evangelical ritual of the deathbed confirmed the testimony which believers bore to the power of Jesus to save. It also moved witnesses to persevere in their Christian living and to deepen it. These two ritual forms constitute the ritual-organizational link between Methodism and domestic life.

Both rituals evinced the configuration and logic of experimental religion. They reinforced the felt need for the sacred circle of holy affection set apart from and overcoming the world. They also affirmed the necessity of mortifying earthly affections and passions for the sake of partaking of heavenly ones, of dying to self and rising again to Christ. These patterns of perception and response, through the efforts of people like the Methodists, became widely available ways of organizing experience within the family. Once this availability is recognized it will be easier to see how evangelical domestic ideology, which reflected these patterns, made good sense to those whose lives were structured by such rituals.

John Scripps, like T. A. Morris, remembered fondly the "artless civilities . . . open hospitality: but above all . . . [the] fervent piety" he had enjoyed in the western Methodist family of God as an early itinerant. Scripps invoked a trilogy of ritual locations around which Methodist sociability centered. "The many precious seasons enjoyed in love feasts, class meetings, and family circles, I retrospect as halcyon days."[1] Scripps was testifying to a social fact which we noted earlier: the family was a nodal point in the network of rituals whereby the Methodist church communicated the spirit and power of experimental religion to its members. Family circles were on a par with class meeting and love feast as places to enjoy the precious seasons of social religion. His testimony suggests the additional understanding that the family was the center of the pious style of simple, heartfelt sociability unencumbered by the artful formality of the world. The ties that bound natural families to the family of God were tightly woven. They were so tightly woven, in fact, that the figurative and literal uses of kinship language among the pious were sometimes indistinguishable.[2]

This overlap of figurative and literal language reflected an overlap of the figurative family and literal families, an overlap that, in the early years, centered in the class meeting. From 1785 onward, the Methodist *Discipline* urged the religious education of children in a weekly group meeting in a manner analogous to the adult class meeting. Not until 1828 did it speak of Sabbath schools.[3] There is sporadic evidence from the 1790s to the 1840s that some preachers were heeding the *Discipline*'s stipulations.[4] It is likely, however, that most children in the early years, before the spread of Sabbath schools, obtained a good deal of their religious education by tagging along with their parents to the adult exercises.[5] The twenty or thirty or however many individuals who were members of classes on the early circuits usually represented a much smaller number of families. The parents, if they were to attend themselves, frequently had to bring the youngsters along to class. Whatever the effect on order and decorum, these necessities tended to make class meetings family affairs.

Preachers who took seriously the *Discipline*'s instructions to care for the "rising generation" made opportunity of this necessity. According to William Fee, G. W. Maley was a master of the pastoral care of children. Evidently Maley kept his eye on young Fee and initiated him into full membership in the church by way of class meeting and love feast. Fee remembered the small drama when Maley became the first minister ever to "meet" him in class. "After I had spoken with fear and trembling, he asked my father and mother if they had confidence in my religion. They told him they had. He then laid his hand upon my head, and told me that he had too, and prayed God to bless me and make me useful." Maley arranged a more formal recognition of the youngster's religious identity by receiving him into "full connection" with the church at a love feast.[6] For those preachers and class leaders who lacked G. W. Maley's sensitivity, James Finley provided a moral anecdote about a child who joined the church on probation and faithfully attended class only to find that the leader ignored him. The boy went to his grandfather, a former itinerant, and asked why he should be passed over in the class-meeting conversations. At his grandfather's urging and with the old man present, the youngster found courage to rise and give his experience without being asked. In alluding to the neglect he had suffered previously he was so "artless" and sincere that leader and circuit preacher were properly embarrassed for their failure in pastoral care.[7]

William Fee's father, by his son's testimony, exemplified a synthesis of church and family roles which made his spiritual fatherhood and natural fatherhood seem virtually identical. A class leader for fifty years, he was so loved by the young people that they flocked to his class until it had to be divided again and again. He was the friend and counselor of every preacher and a subpastor skilled in the arts of reconciliation. He had an abiding faith that all nine of his children would be saved and saw it rewarded as one after another were converted and joined the church before eighteen years of age. Six of his sons followed in his footsteps and became officials in their respective churches.[8] The elder Fee's pastoral activities among local families were in continuity with the earliest practices of class leaders in visiting the families under their charge. John Kobler described how leaders used to turn the family circle into a special class meeting complete with singing, prayer, and earnest inquiry into the spiritual condition of each family member. Whole families, claimed Kobler, were brought to salvation and into the church in this manner.[9] Pastoral care was family care, and class meeting was one of Methodism's chief ways of providing it.

One of the clearest links between class meeting and family life is evident in Jacob Young's assessment of the church "in every department" in the Ohio District where he had been Presiding Elder for the year 1815:

> I compared our numerical strength to what it was when I came on, and found it, I think, nearly double—our congregations more than doubled; *the attendance in class meetings greatly improved—family religion was on the advance;* our preachers appeared to live more holy, and to preach with more zeal and understanding.[10]

Note carefully the punctuation here. The semicolons divide one department of church affairs from another; the dashes indicate appositional relationships. In the minds of Young and the preachers over whom he presided, advance in family religion seems to have been the result or concomitant of improved class-meeting attendance. The reason for this association was straightforward. Membership in society for heads of families was, in Methodist rules and rhetoric, emphatically conditional upon the holding of family prayer. "This is so plain a case," asserted a church editor, "that nothing need be said in reference to it, except that those who neglect family prayer and will not be reformed must be expelled."[11] Good class leaders and good circuit preachers did not fail in class to inquire of every head of household, "Do you pray in your family?"[12]

Family prayer was a ritual which took one step further the imperative of experimental religion to reorder the inner regions of one's life. Referred to variously as family worship, family religion, family devotion, the family altar, or just family prayer, it consisted chiefly in praying aloud in the assembled presence of all members of the household: adults, children, and servants.[13] If the Methodist culture of experimental religion required a visible weekly testimony to one's personal religious experience in the presence of the local family of God, it also required a visible daily practice of religion in the presence of one's literal family. Just as the testifiers and their audiences mutually persuaded themselves of the truths of religion in class, so heads of households and their dependents mutually reassured themselves of the realities of religion in the midst of their sphere of everyday life. Family prayer was a key element in the effort to ritualize families for God. We might readily expect, then, to find in it parallels with the other rituals of social religion.

Certainly the practice of family prayer, like the performances of class meeting and love feast, seemed to have power to convict and convert those who witnessed it. John Sale, soon after his own conversion, offered to hold prayer in his father's household. His father acquiesced and shortly found himself, his wife, and several of his children awakened and converted to the truths of experimental religion.[14] Just as testimonies in class and love feast moved not just the auditors but also the speakers, so the practice of family prayer tended to convict and convert the heads of families who engaged in it. David Sullins's mother was religious at the time of her marriage, but her new husband was not. His wife's prayers and his father-in-law's exhortations did finally induce him to join the Methodist church as a seeker on probation, but he did not really become religious until children came along. Mrs. Sullins recounted to her son how her anxiety for the spiritual welfare of her children had led her to spend a sleepless night in private prayer. During her vigil, she paused to waken her husband and declare to him that they could never rightly bring up their children without family prayer. Her husband replied, " 'Well . . . what are we to do Becky? I can't pray.' " She insisted that he could and ought to and finally induced him to promise to try by offering to take turns with him in praying. She led out the next morning. That evening she assembled the children and summoned her husband to keep his part of the bargain. He dropped to his knees, stammering and choking, until he began to cry for mercy under a crushing weight of guilt and helplessness. His wife prayed for him until "the comforter came and light broke in and father was converted at family prayers."[15]

To pray in one's family, especially to pray in the extemporary manner which was a hallmark of experimental religion, was to identify oneself as religious amidst those who knew whether this self-presentation was genuine. The human drive to match self-perception to a sense of the perceptions of significant others contributed strongly to the transformation and maintenance of the identity claimed in family prayer. When John B. McFerrin's father was converted at a camp meeting, he promptly went home and held his first family worship. McFerrin's biographer observed that the erection of the McFerrin family altar was a decisive moment for the elder McFerrin because it committed him fully to his new life "in the presence of the dear ones at home." As young John grew up, his father shrewdly called on him to lead in the exercises now and then. " 'This made me more careful of my conduct at home,' " the younger McFerrin recalled, " 'for how could one pray in the family when his spirit and conversation contradicted his profession?' "[16]

Such hypocrisy was, in fact, quite possible, and the pious of the day knew it. Samuel Williams remembered well that his shiftless father's strict attention to outward religious form did not keep him from the dissipation of the muster field and party politics. Nor did it keep him from abandoning his family for almost a decade.[17] Such perceptions caused the experimentally religious to insist strongly upon a religion of the heart and to indulge their hostility to more formal, liturgical worship. William Fee provided a lesson in the futility of high-church formality when he told the story of his grandfather, an Episcopalian whose migration west removed him from the religious privileges of his denomination. Once his family began to grow up, he tried to institute family worship using an old prayer book. He was not satisfied. The arrival of a new prayer book for which he had waited four months did nothing to relieve his uneasiness. Then a neighbor suggested he pray extemporaneously. He was so shy and fearful of humiliation, especially in the presence of his black servant, that he had to pray fervently six times in private before he could bring himself up to the performance. He was converted in the midst of his prayer. Shortly thereafter John Kobler and Henry Smith visited the Fee family and received husband and wife into the Methodist church.[18]

The power of the family altar to propagate and sustain religion extended beyond the heads of households. Peter Doub recounted the story of Dempsey and Sarah Hinton who led in the establishment of an early North Carolina society. As soon as they arrived in their neighborhood they entered into regular family worship. This practice was unusual for their time and place, and Doub judged it to be the "first visible agency to bring about a revival of religion among the people." Thus the Hintons opened the way for the establishment of Methodism in their locale. Their society was soon officially organized by Bishop Asbury himself in 1784.[19] In an age when norms of privacy were lax and boundaries between family and the rest of society were much more permeable than today, family prayer—like class meeting, prayer meeting, or preaching—was indeed a public statement of which the community was likely to take notice.

Celebrations of experimental religion in the family circle did sometimes exhibit the same emotional effervescence which often made events like class meeting hard to ignore. Peter Cartwright offered as a "faint specimen of the way that Western pioneer Methodist preachers planted Methodism" an account of his stay with the family of an old class leader after a cold, wet day's journey. His horse was well cared for, and Cartwright himself was well fed and warm when they began family prayers. The greater part of the family got shouting happy, and one of the old class leader's sons was convicted. They sang, prayed, and shouted together for hours until the young man was converted. Cartwright then retired to bed and, he claimed, slept soundly while the new convert shouted and praised God nearly all night.[20] George Walker's sister Harriet was very likely to shout during family prayer. One time she was so animated as she went round the family circle embracing various relatives that George, his uncle, and several of the hired hands—all unconverted at the time—fled the house as soon as they could get out. The uncle was so confounded by her performance that he gave up his Catholicism and eventually became a member of the Methodist church.[21]

The importance of family prayer which believers most heavily emphasized, as these examples suggest, was its influence over the rising generation. David Sullins fully supported his mother's anxiety to have family prayer in order to bring her children up right. He summarized the careers of his twelve brothers and sisters by claiming that they all had had their own family altars, "fought the good fight," and—save for himself and one living sister—gone home to heaven to be with their own father and mother. He had never heard a profane oath from any of his brothers, and to his knowledge all living children and grandchildren had the altar in their homes and every great-grandchild old enough to know the difference was a Christian. "So much," he averred, "for a faithful family altar."[22] Other children of the family of God, many claiming themselves among the chief examples, were hardly less positive in their claims for the efficacy of family prayer in keeping children from evil and making them religious.[23] The clear expectation, reinforced by exhortations in the periodical press and the testimonies of the saints themselves, was that parents who attended faithfully to family prayer might expect their children to become subjects of the work of grace. One writer reminded his readers of the large numbers of fellow believers who arose in class meetings and love feasts and gave glory to God for praying parents and named family prayer as the cause of their first religious impressions."[24]

The written testimonies of believers brought up under the influence of family prayer indicate that one of its chief meanings was the enforcement of a chasm in experience between the ways of the world and the ways of the family circle and its members. John Burgess remembered a childhood fraught with a "terrible war" between "home religion's influence and the worldly spirit." Only the echo in his memory of his parents' voices at family prayer kept him from evil. John Kiger's memories of the family altar kept him aloof from the "scoffers and blasphemers" among whom he had to live when living away from home as an apprentice after his father's death.[25] They would have readily assented to the wisdom of a "good woman" quoted in the *Western Christian Advocate*. "A family without prayer," she reflected, "is like a house without a roof, exposed to all the injuries of weather and to every storm that blows."[26]

Published exhortations on family religion reflected this sense of the opposition between the world and the family circle at prayer. Family prayer, claimed one writer, "calls off the mind from the deadening effects of worldly affairs" and reminds them of the spiritual world and the life to come. It also upheld the true and right standard of living which was "perpetually in opposition to that corrupt one around and before them."[27] The frequent urging not to let any company or business interfere with the regularly appointed times of family prayer suggests that the practical time and space requirements of the ritual had similar implications for how a family organized its life. The presence of visiting company or of working men hired to pursue the business of the farm or shop evidently was a frequent rationale given for the neglect of family prayer.[28] To interrupt the flow of daily activity and domestic conversation with persons unaccustomed to the solemn ritual of family prayer might require a rather dogged courage. Doing one's duty in such circumstances of course offered an important witness to the unawakened.

It also risked the ridicule and annoyance of those who wished to go about their business without the imposition of unwelcome piety. When the worldly were in the midst of the domestic circle, it was also much harder to enforce the line of separation between them and the family of God. A basic solution to the problem was to keep the worldly out. "Evil communications," went the proverb, "corrupt good manners." Even worse, they corrupted good morals. The company invited to one's home, therefore, ought to consist only of those whose conversation and example tended to strengthen the influence of religion.[29] It would, in any case, be much easier to hold family prayer in the presence of such people just as it was easier to speak with liberty in the rituals of social religion when unawakened persons were excluded. The imperative for family religion constituted a significant force for the creation of a homogeneous social environment, a sphere where only those of sober mind and pious feeling would be welcome and feel at home.

The apologists for family prayer also insisted that it was a major force for creating the love, unity, and order which characterized heaven itself. There was no human influence for binding a family together in peace and love like domestic prayer; it both reminded the family members of their future rest in heaven and united them in efforts of faith and obedience to attain it. Just as class meeting was supposed to insure the harmony, peace, and prosperity of the Methodist society, family religion was "the best bond of domestic peace, the best solace of domestic affection, the best security of domestic happiness." And just as faithful class-meeting attendance developed habits of discipline and an orderly life, so did the faithful performance of family worship where everything was to be done decently and in order.[30] Family prayer also insured the order of parental authority and family government. It gave an impression of the parent as someone next to God; it provided an example of the vitality of religion in the person of the parent; and it reminded the children that even if their parents did not see all their actions and feelings, God did.[31] This mutual reinforcement of parental authority and divine authority laid the groundwork of social and spiritual impressions which, as children grew up, parents expected would issue in the children's conversions.

The distance between the concept of family and domestic life emerging from these evangelical writings and the more traditional understandings of family as an economic and political estate became obvious in a piece by Edward Thomson. Thomson, a doctor of divinity, was president of the Ohio Wesleyan University and also served for a time as editor of the *Ladies Repository*. He described a family where morning worship was held after breakfast, a timing which allowed the children time to kiss the parents and shake hands with the guests and to give everyone opportunity to inquire courteously after one another's health and slumbers. Another, even more important, aspect of this family's religious practice was "an interior altar" where husband and wife, before parting in the morning and after meeting in the evening, held intimate conversation inappropriate for the ears of children, guests, or domestics. Within this doubly inner sanctum, confessions were made, sorrows assuaged, and misunderstandings prevented "as the united spirits become more and more transparent before each other in the presence of their common Father." This practice, observed Thomson, was especially suited to those who live "amid the excitements, the conflicts, the company, and the temptations of a great and guilty city." He then drove home the contrast with older forms of family life: "To parents whose marriage is rather a business partnership than a spiritual union, and whose intercourse is embittered by want of confidence or lack of affection, by repeated misunderstandings or petty offences, I would say: Try it."[32]

Family prayer and the rituals of social religion, in summary, were linked by a common concern for nursing young converts, for securing love and unity among family members, and for keeping all the family unspotted from the world. Within the culture of experimental religion, the imperative for an orderly life drew a line of identification that separated the saved and unsaved. That line became a circle which compassed not only the church but also the home.

The final proof of an orderly life was a happy death. The Methodist saint died as she lived: by the way of the cross. In the culture of experimental religion, dying itself was a domestic ritual which shared elements of purpose and form with family prayer and the other rituals of social religion.[33]

The case of Mary T. illustrates how various ritualizations worked together to form the life and death of "an acceptable member" of the church. Mary T. was only just acceptable. She was naturally "volatile and gay" and fond of similar company. A reluctant recruit, she was led forward to the altar by some friends during a revival and only joined the church on probation when the circuit preacher visited her home and urged her mother to place Mary's name on the membership lists. The class leader was a cousin by marriage to Mary and also boarded in her mother's home. He had access to his young in-law not only in class meeting but also in family prayer, where he sometimes singled her out in his prayers. It took all the "authority and influence" he could command to keep her in line.

At quarterly meeting, possibly in love feast, she was converted. Thereafter, when faithful in her religious duties, she enjoyed communion with God; when unfaithful, she felt cold in piety. This was a common story and did not keep her from being an acceptable member. Her cousin moved away for about a year however and on his return found her backslidden. She had engaged in "too constant and familiar intercourse with the world" and had begun to dress "too gaily." She tried to resist his warnings that she could not dress so and retain her place in the church, but, finding him inexorable, she finally "put away the accursed thing." She began to lament her backsliding and to pray for a return of the comforts of religion. Only during her last illness did she feel God heard her prayers. When her cousin and spiritual preceptor came to see her on her deathbed, he noted that her hands and feet were cold and her speech indistinct. She rose to the occasion, however, when he inquired into her spiritual condition for the last time. "In answer to my inquiries, and with a smile that attested her sincerity, she assured me that she was happy; that she felt the love of God in her heart, that she was going to heaven, and was not afraid to die." She soon fell into her last death struggle, gasping in spasms of pain. He prayed for her, and, as her sufferings came to a close, "a smile of joy lit up the brow of death."[34]

Without the "fostering care and disciplinary restraints" of the church, her cousin reflected, nothing would have kept Mary from the world. The form and concerns of the church's care and restraint were indeed very present up to her last moment. The inquiry to which her class leader subjected her on her deathbed was not very different from the sort he likely conducted when he met her in class. "Sister T.," we may imagine him saying, "do you feel the love of God in your heart? Are you happy in Jesus? If you knew you were to die tomorrow, would you be sure of your prospects of heaven?" This sort of inquiry, as we have seen, occurred regularly in class meeting. It was also a regular feature of the ritual of the deathbed.

Obituary writers sometimes included in their biographical sketches a reminiscence of how subjects loved the usages of the church and of their testimonies in class meeting. Such reminiscence led naturally into accounts of deathbed testimonies which assured all of the continuity and reliability of the dying one's profession of faith.[35] Eagerness to hear this sort of reassurance, tinged with some anxiety, moved friends and relatives to subject their dying loved ones to an inquiry that sometimes continued down to the last breath. Just as Thomas Johnson lapsed into final coma, someone asked, "Is your way clear?" "Clear as the sun," he replied.[36] "Is Jesus precious?" they asked John Kobler just half an hour before the end. "O yes, very precious."[37] Eleanor Ayres had lost the power of speech, but her husband still pressed the inquiry: "My dear Eleanor, if the Lord is with you, and the evidence of your acceptance clear and strong, give me a sign, by raising your hand." The request seems to have revived her, for she raised both hands above her head, clapped them together, and began shouting, "Victory! Victory! thank the Lord, who hath given me the victory."[38]

The deathbed inquiry ought not to be construed simply as an attempt of the witnesses to reassure themselves. Preachers conducted such inquiries because the dying might not be ready and because it was a pastor's duty to see that they were ready. Dying persons ought to be fully aware of their condition and have opportunity to come to terms with God if they had not already done so.[39] On the other hand, some might have firm Christian experiences but still be troubled by doubts or by unaccountable fluctuations in their religious feelings. On such occasions, the deathbed inquiry might lead the dying ones to a clear knowledge of their position with God. Thus Frances Railey felt a sudden darkening of her hopes of heaven and sent urgently for the preacher to ask if he had ever had a similar change in his religious experience. He reassured her that such changes were common and inquired into the grounds of her hope. He asked if she felt any condemnation, and she replied she did not. He asked if she felt she loved God; she beamed and declared she loved him with all her heart. Religion, he told her, was the love of God shed abroad in the heart. She experienced no more of the "darkness" of which she had complained, nor was her sense of the Lord's presence interrupted from that time until her death.[40]

Clearly, in the ethos of experimental religion, one's death was not simply a death of one's own. It was a death for others as well. The testimony one gave to inquiring relatives and friends confirmed them in their faith in a world hereafter. And the ritual drama of the deathbed was larger than just these words. Dying people suffered severe physical and emotional pain. As their bodies failed them, the capricious losses of physical and mental control deprived them of much that had made them feel like themselves. As they anticipated their final dissolution, they were faced with the loss of all those human ties which had made them who they were. In such extremity, religion provided for the dying and for the witnesses—who confronted their own mortality in the dying of their loved one—an affirmation of the persistence of a divinely shaped human character and identity. The dying one and the witnesses together constructed a drama which depicted the triumph of grace over suffering and death.

Persons who died well endured the pain of their illnesses or injuries "with that calmness and patience that becometh a Christian." They often pointed to the sufferings of Christ for their salvation and drew the lesson that their sufferings were nothing in comparison to his and, therefore, they could be borne. Death itself, with all its losses and separations, held no terror for them, for they could feel the merits of Christ's own sacrifice applied to their particular case. All their affections were now withdrawn from earth and fixed upon heaven. They were confident of consummating there all the ties which had been so impermanent and unsatisfying here. They demonstrated these truths for all to see even as pain convulsed their bodies and intermittent waves of delirium carried them out of their minds. When their physical agonies relented for a time and they were able to command their mental faculties, the dying saints, by their peaceful words and patient demeanor, taught the witnesses "an impressive lesson of the efficacy of religion upon the human mind, under circumstances most trying."[41]

Patience and peace were precious evidence of transcendence over physical dissolution and over threatened destruction of earthly consciousness. The struggle that eventually parted body and spirit often stimulated what was taken to be the still greater evidence of ecstasy. Just as the events of Methodist worship and social religion were occasions for singing and shouts, joy and praise, so were some instances of deathbed ritual. Anne Warner was often delirious in her last illness, but when in her right mind, she would clap her hands, shout glory to God, or sing some appropriate verse of a hymn.[42] As "Mother Spahr" passed from the earth and "doubtless to heaven," Joseph Morgan reported, the Lord was present in such power and love that her children forbore to complain but rather shouted aloud for joy.[43] These were the sorts of manifestations which prompted the saints of experimental religion to use the oxymoron "happy death."

The oxymoron encapsulated the rhetoric of the way of the cross. The ritual of the deathbed enforced an intense realization of human frustration in which the mutual attachments and desires of the dying one and of the witnesses were simultaneously evoked and inexorably cut off. This very extremity laid the emotional groundwork for a radical turnabout in mood. The agony of earthly loss turned into the transcendent joy of heavenly fulfillment. Thus when the dying itinerant Isaac C. Hunter greeted his visiting colleague, Maxwell Gaddis, he eagerly asked for some assurance that his brethren in the Ohio conference still loved him and knew of his love for them. His next thought was to ask Gaddis to tell the brethren to remember Mrs. Hunter and their children, soon to be left fatherless and without a protector. Then he fell to musing about how he might still do some good in the church's cause and help his family get on better if only he might live a little longer. His stream of thought reversed its flow, however, as he reminded himself that the church could do without him and that God would take care of his family. With this act of renunciation, his agitated eddy of reflection crested in a flow of emotion. "He cried aloud, 'Bless the Lord, O my soul, and all that is within me, bless his holy name!' " He turned his eyes heavenward and recited the verses of a hymn about the land of pure delight where pleasures banish pain. Then he sat up in bed, clapped his hands, and shouted aloud for joy. " 'O,' said he, 'I feel much better! Thank God, I feel half well!' "[44]

Something like this oxymoronic form of "mournful joy" or "pleasant grief" attended most accounts of deathbed ritual. The image of the dying ecstasies of the saint placed in the midst of weeping witnesses was a transcendent incongruity that pointed the way from earth to heaven. John Stewart wept over his dying daughter during a time at family prayers in which she requested that no one pray for her recovery. She took her turn at prayer and prayed fervently until she fell straightened and trembling back into bed. Supposing her to be at the threshold of death, her parents paused to watch. Suddenly her struggle ceased, her eyes flew open, and her face lighted up with "a heavenly glow." "O what a lovely place!" she exclaimed; "I want to be there." After beholding his daughter as "she seemed to be gazing right into glory land," Stewart declared that he could never doubt the truth of the Christian religion even if he never had any other evidence. He and the friends and family who had witnessed her death "determined that the residue of our days should be spent more resolutely and earnestly in working for the Master and getting ready to join those who had gone before."[45] The way to heaven, for Methodist believers, was the way of self-surrender, and the inducements they felt to deeper and more earnest walking in this way made attendance at the deathbed a privilege for them.[46]

The unconverted, who might regard such attendance only as a duty to kin, did not escape the ritual rhetoric of happy dying. The dying saints frequently exhorted their friends and relatives to seek the Savior and meet them in heaven. David Lewis took full advantage of the opportunity and became, for the moment, something of a class leader, "reproving, exhorting, and comforting as each case required." He bore down especially on a younger brother, giving his dying charge "never to rest satisfied with a mere morality, void of the spirit and power of true religion." Only such a spirit, he testified, could sustain the soul through the crisis of death. When he had finished with his family, he turned to irreligious bystanders and urged them to seek the savior.[47] Such exhortations frequently had their desired effect. At the funeral of a husband and father, Maxwell Gaddis gently reminded the widow of requests her husband had made on his deathbed. He had told her she would be sad and lonely when he died and left her alone with their two children; she would need the religion of Jesus Christ to support and comfort her. He believed she would seek religion and prepare to meet him in a better land. Would she, when she was converted, join the church and have their children consecrated to God in baptism? She experienced religion at a revival just a few months later, joined the church, and took her children to be baptized, just as she had promised.[48]

The ritual drama of happy dying is among the clearest examples available of the basic rhetorical pattern which underlay the culture of experimental religion. The deathbed scene brought together friends and family and evoked all those tender attachments upon which experimental religion built its central metaphors of religious experience. At the same time, the scene centered around the reality of death, loss, and loneliness. It thus highlighted and intensified the feelings of attachment by threatening their frustration. In its inquiries, testimonies, exhortations, and ecstasies, the ritual of the deathbed communicated images of heaven and of domestic ties transposed in order to fulfill the desires it had wrought up. In the process, the witnesses were moved to accept the necessity of mortifying their earthly desires, passions, and affections. They came to understand the need for an active, ascetic, disciplined life as the means to the fulfillment which the deathbed promised. This essential pattern of appeal found its way into a variety of religious expressions having to do not only with death and heaven but also with family life, the nature and role of women, and the destiny of the American nation.

11

The Christian Home in the Republic

The middle of the nineteenth century, argues John Higham, brought a momentous shift in American culture, a shift "from boundlessness to consolidation."[1] Methodism certainly participated in the boundlessness. From the founding of the new American nation through much of the nineteenth century, American Methodism seemed boundless in the pursuit of its mission to reform the continent and spread holiness over the land. It has long been a commonplace of American religious history that the Methodists broke the bounds of clerical elitism, recruiting common men to do their preaching. In this study we have seen how, in the earlier decades of its spread, Methodism subverted the bonds of patriarchal sovereignty in the family and defied the customary boundaries of honor and shame in the neighborhood. It taught all its people, women and men alike, to tell their own gospel stories, and in this tradition of gospel storytelling lay the foundations of Methodist popular preaching. These and other characteristics of Methodism evinced its boundless vision and its boundless energy.

By the 1830s, however, Methodism was beginning a process of consolidation. The generation of preachers who came out of the Great Revival at the turn of the century began to publish their reminiscences. They celebrated the new eminence and respectability of their church and its members but also lamented its loss of early simplicity and zeal. A small but steady stream of articles on class meeting and love feast evinced enough clerical hand-wringing to suggest that these early rituals of social religion were growing moribund. The schism of the Methodist Protestant church marked a hardening of episcopal authority in the parent church and perhaps the beginning of the transformation of the bishops from charismatic fathers of the people into managers of a far-flung ecclesiastical enterprise. A wave of colleges and seminaries—many of them female seminaries—began to appear, and so did a similar wave of Sabbath schools, missionary societies, temperance societies, and the like. The proliferation of church papers for popular reading provided forums for the promotion of the new educational and benevolent enterprises and for the preachers' celebrations and laments. The new explosion of print, while clearly a popular phenomenon, also represented the beginnings of a shift from an emphasis on populist oral patterns of communication to the constraints of textual conventions of communication.

The elaboration of ideologies of Christian republicanism and Christian domesticity was an integral part of this larger consolidation process. It is true that historians have exaggerated and misconstrued the conservative intent of American evangelicals as they responded to the rise of republican nationhood on their continent.[2] The liberalizing and democratizing dynamic of Methodism in particular has been a theme in this study. With liberty came anxiety, however. Freedom could be abused. Citizens of the American republic might lack virtue sufficient to rule themselves. They might create a chaos that invited despotism. Methodist reflections on the roles of the religious community and the Christian home in the republic promoted these agencies as the needed centripetal counterbalance to the centrifugal forces of American liberty. Such advocacy was not a reactionary effort to return to the hierarchy and elitism of the traditional social order. It was, however, a conservative effort to discern order and find one's place in a social landscape made confusing by the absence of the landmarks of patriarchal sovereignty and filial deference, landmarks Methodism had helped to destroy. The ideologies of religion and home in the republic provided a metaphorical map for the setting of new landmarks.[3]

This map charted realms called "religious liberty" and "civil liberty" and spaces called "woman's sphere" and "the world"—which was also man's sphere. It also drew the paths of proper relationship among these realms and spheres. The map reflected the basic organizing pattern found both in the archaic traditions of honor and in the ritual dramas of experimental religion: the configuration of a sacred inner space set over against a threatening world.

The evangelical version of this pattern stressed the contagious communion within this sacred space and the susceptibility of the outside world to its spiritual power. Methodists identified this inner space with various realities: the heart of the individual believer, the church as the family of God, the rituals of social religion, and heaven itself. Of greatest historical significance, however, was their identification of that inner sanctum with church, with home, and with women as the "natural" symbol of religion and domesticity. Within this domestic sanctuary were exercised the rights of religious liberty. The spiritual contagion of that liberty extended its influence into the world to preserve civil liberty by guaranteeing its virtuous exercise.

It seems wise here to disavow again any intent to argue that Methodism originated the popular domestic ideology of the nineteenth century. Western Methodist writers and editors borrowed much of their material on domesticity and "woman" from sources originating in the northeastern United States and even in Britain. It will not do, however, to explain their adoption of such ideology as mere cultural diffusion. They embraced domesticity, under the consolidating pressures of their rising social respectability, as a logical outgrowth of their religious experience and sense of mission.[4]

In order to make as clear as possible this inner connection between religious experience and domestic ideology, it is necessary to restate the emotional pattern of experimental religion and to introduce the notion of the dialectic of social religion.

The emotional pattern of experimental religion was, first of all, to incite desire, typically desire for the communion, joy, and peace of idealized family relations. The second step in the pattern was to enhance the desire by contrasting the desired condition with its negation or opposite, as in a contrast between the warm family of God and the cold and evil world. The third step was to frustrate or threaten to frustrate the desire, a frustration symbolized most perfectly by death, the blight of all human desire and hope. The fourth step was to promise a paradoxical fulfillment of the desire on the condition that one accept a certain kind of death, a denial of the self that willed the desire. The denial of self and the death of desire led, in the fifth step, to their transformation and fulfillment on a new plane, a spiritual plane. The self now willed not its own desires but the desires ascribed to God, which were for the holiness and love of all humankind.

It was in service to what they believed to be God's desires for holiness and love that the Methodists constructed the dialectic of social religion. The dialectic had an *iconic* moment and an *instrumental* moment. At one moment, Methodist believers presented the inner space of social religion, in its seclusion, as an *icon of holiness*, the home of a spiritual liberty deeply affecting to behold and a delight in which to participate. At the other moment, believers also purveyed this inner holiness as a transformative power, an *instrument of morality* generating virtues and activities that would prosper religion and preserve the republic. This dialectic was created and sustained in moments of evangelical communal experience: in class meetings, love feasts, prayer meetings, camp meetings, revivals of various kinds, and always in symbiosis with family circles at prayer. These communual events harmonized the paradox of a religion that required a passive letting go of one's worldly self-will and also required an active, willful propagation of the evangelical gospel as the foundation of true selfhood. In the crucibles of social religion, Methodism had desired to melt down the artificial distinctions of wealth, status, and learning and to unify people into a critical mass. From these fusion reactors of the spirit, it had hoped to release an explosion of spiritual liberty and labor for souls that would transform the whole of humankind into the family of God.

It was inevitable, however, that Methodist energy be contained. The republic, the home, and woman became the social symbols that guided its containment and domestication. Methodist writers in the popular press appropriated for evangelical purposes the themes of republican ideology. The resulting Christian republicanism was a context for a further ideological construction, the ideology of the Christian home in America. These two elements of ideology, Christian republicanism and Christian domesticity, reflected the emotional patterning of experimental religion and the dialectic of iconic and instrumental moments that Methodists learned in social religion. The presence of these rhetorical patterns is prime evidence for the argument that the forms of social religion had laid a foundation in experience for the adoption of an ideology of domesticity.[5]

In the United States, the culture of experimental religion existed within, or at least alongside of, a nascent national culture, a culture guided by republican ideological discourse. As the Methodist movement grew, Methodist Americans had to determine the meaning of their religious identity for their national identity. Reflections on religion and the nation began to pour out of the Methodist newspapers from the 1830s on. This literature generated little that was original; much of it, in accord with the general practice of the day, was borrowed.[6] Their pattern of borrowing suggests that Methodists were developing concerns for the Christian foundations and millennial destiny of the republic that had once been the burden primarily of the New England and Reformed denominations. At about the same time, segments of these more respectable communions began increasingly to adopt Methodist practices and understandings of experimental religion. The result of these reciprocal accommodations was a brand of Christian republicanism that wove certain themes of republican thought into a cord binding the prospects of the nation to the prosperity of the evangelical churches.[7]

Elements of both similarity and contrast between experimental religion and republican political culture played their part in the amalgamation. Both cultures valued a quality of speech and action called liberty, but the liberty of the saints was spiritual. The saints, therefore, felt their Christian liberty to be higher than the temporal liberty of the republicans. Both cultures valued the ascetic virtues of industry and frugality as conditions of liberty, but, for the believers, these virtues were indices of spiritual growth and inner freedom from sin. Believers, therefore, saw Christian virtue as deeper than the virtues that republicans practiced as a hedge against dependence on the temporally powerful. Both cultures identified their liberty with an inner space of feminine sacredness to be defended from the incursions of worldly power, but the inner space of experimental religion was in itself powerful to transform the forces that threatened it. Christian sacredness, therefore, was a wellspring of that eternal life that alone could preserve the merely temporal life generated within republican inner space.

Republican understanding required the practice of the private virtues of industry, frugality, temperance, and the like because only privately virtuous people would be willing to practice the public virtue of sacrificing self-interest to the good of the society as a whole. Only a people willing to transcend themselves in such a sacrifice could sustain a republican form of government.[8] The evangelical insight was that all such virtue depended on the deeper levels of human motivation, the disposition of the affections and passions. Neither republican constitutions, social contracts, nor any other sort of legal machinery was capable of controlling the heart of man, where dwelt envy, malice, covetousness, lust, and all the powerful sources of disorder. These evil motives were vulnerable to "no laws, but those of eternity; no fears but those of conscience; no influences, but those which affect the heart." The theory of experimental religion was that if the affections were pure, "*duty* as necessarily follows as the stream from the fountain, or rays from the sun." Only religion could purify the affections. A pure love of country was political religion. Such religion would prompt true Christian citizens to sacrifice for the public good, to refrain from voting for factional or party interests, and to obtain the knowledge of government they needed in order to exercise their powers for the public good.[9] The inner circle of right affection had to be instilled in the heart before an individual could truly practice public virtue.

Evangelicals repeated this pattern of thought in their conception of the place of institutional religion in the republic. The shape the Methodists saw politics taking in the early republic led them to seek a holy distance from popular political activities. The wild, blind, reckless partisanship and the clamorous hurrahs and vociferous denunciations manifest at political gatherings seemed the very embodiment of the spirit of the world, destined to destroy rather than serve the public good. Such "party spirit" was inimical to moral duty and to the harmony of Christian character. Alongside the stormy passions of politics, furthermore, was the frenzy of speculation, a misuse of liberty in the worship of mammon that threatened both the temporal and the spiritual prosperity of the nation. The licentiousness and drunken debauchery evident in Fourth of July celebrations was an affront to God and a disgrace to the country. All these things were signs that large numbers of the American people lacked the virtue necessary to the preservation of the republic.[10] Only a free, enterprising Christianity untrammeled by political establishment and unpolluted by state policy could remedy this state of affairs. Through a sort of strategic retreat from the worldly realm of politics, Christians might exert the exemplary influence necessary to redeem the nation from its perilous course. Whenever in history, warned a writer on Christian patriotism, a church had become involved in the political movements of a divided nation, her piety had declined, her light had grown dim, and her enemies had become bold to blaspheme the name of Christ. The only reason, in fact, that licentiousness was not more widespread in American society was that religion had lifted the standard of public sentiment and marshaled a "standing army of well-trained consciences" against it. Religion, unsullied by political divisiveness, leavened the mass of American citizens even though most were not professed followers of Jesus.[11] At the heart of that leavening influence was the unity of the believers.

Clearly, separation from party politics or from the raucous political rituals of the earliest decades of the republic did not at all entail entire removal from political concern. Just as unity of feeling among the brothers and sisters in any given Methodist society was a precondition and harbinger of revival and moral reformation in its neighborhood, so, Methodist publicists believed, the unity of evangelical believers undergirded the millennial mission of the nation. "Every sect that is actuated by a supreme love to God," declared Nathan Bangs in 1840, "is contributing its quota toward the civil and political salvation of the country." This united love to God, furthermore, would do much to enable the American republic to spread the blessings of civil and religious liberty over the earth.[12] There was considerable irony in these exhortations to unity. They were elicited in large part by cultural and political tensions between the North and the South that would split the Methodist Episcopal church just four years later. There were some divisions the rhetoric of experimental religion could not bridge.

The saints, nevertheless, developed ritual events that enabled those of similar region and like mind, at least, to feel their unity of sentiment in political religion. A missionary in Indiana reported an 1839 camp meeting in which the believers passed the time united "in sacred harmony." The crowning event was a Fourth of July celebration. "What can be more proper," queried the correspondent, "than the assemblage of the citizens of a great nation in the glorious woods, under the broad canopy of heaven, surrounded by the natural insignia of freedom, to celebrate with religious ceremonies, the anniversary of their political existence, as a free and independent nation?"[13] Methodism had come a long way from the times when a member might be expelled from the church simply for participating in Fourth of July festivities.[14]

Methodist editors and contributors in the 1830s and 1840s rejoiced in the changes in Fourth of July ceremonies, occasions that the previous generation of Methodists had taken as evidence of the vicious character of the American people. No longer beset by drunkenness and revelry, Independence Day celebrations were now times for great Sabbath school jubilees, family gatherings, and pious sociability. The members of the Christian community, rejoiced one writer, "assemble on that day . . . with their families and youth, to sing praises, and to worship and praise God, and to call upon him to continue our national, social, and family blessings, and to teach our children the history of, and duty to their country and their God." It was a day to pray for a union of hearts that would secure the union of states, a day that kindled hope for a time when Christ's perfect law of liberty would become the law of the land, and a day to rededicate oneself and one's children to the sacred trust of bringing civil and religious liberty to all the nations of the earth.[15] Using the Sunday school as their chief instrument, the evangelical churches turned July 4 into the cult day of the Protestant God, American flag, and middle-class domestic circle.[16]

The popular religious weeklies that published such celebratory rhetoric also published evidence of the dark side of evangelical orderliness and harmony. Just as the local instances of community forged in social religion required "the world" and worldlings on their boundaries to symbolize who and what the saints were not, so the national evangelical community needed its symbols of evil. It found them in the Roman Catholic church and its growing numbers of members and institutions in America. Methodists played their part in the sorry story of Protestant nativism and its fevered imaginings of papist conspiracies, licentious priests, and violated nuns.[17] For the purposes of this study it is important to draw the connection between the patriotic meaning of the ideal Protestant family and its negation in the imagined sexual irregularities of the Catholic religious. Both the ideal and its negation evince the evangelical and republican preoccupation with the vulnerable feminine space where life and liberty were nurtured. This space, said Methodists along with most evangelicals, had to be claimed for Christ and subordinated to his way, for the consequences of not doing so would be disastrous in time and eternity.

"The family circle is of divine origin," declared the author of the *Methodist Family Manual*, "and is stamped with signal holiness and beauty."[18] In this cliché, the author introduced the first step in a rhetoric that was derived from the emotional pattern of experimental religion that we noted at the beginning of this chapter. This rhetoric undergirded the Methodist evangelical ideology of the family. The first step was always to create a desire by invoking the imagery and feelings of family affection and to intimate the divine origins of these emotional pleasures. " 'Life's choicest blessings center all at home,' " quoted a young lady. A young itinerant declared that when he remembered his family circle his heart would always vibrate "with supernatural pleasure." He soon moved to the second step, the contrast with the world, when he mentioned how his family circle had "commenced dispersing through an inhospitable world." This world had assaulted him with "storms of persecution" and "waves of disappointment." The evangelical imagination could not picture the heavenly circle of family affection without conjuring up images of worldly unpleasantness to fill the void outside the circle. The contrast was necessary to enhance the interior intimacies. Only those who had to leave home, claimed the young lady, could fully test the truth that all life's choicest blessings centered at home. Then she moved to the third step in the rhetorical pattern: frustration. "Here the scene of the purest happiness, the domestic hearth, must change. For its continuance we have no security." Steps one and two made it clear that home was to be clung to and the world shunned, but step three injected an icy note into the cozy fireside harmony. Domestic felicity, even though God-given, was not to be relied upon; it would not last.

This chilling observation served to move the hearer or reader of such rhetoric to the final steps of the pattern: paradoxical fulfillment of desire after symbolic death by denial of self. If the *best* of earth's pleasures were so transient, and no one could deny that they were, it made sense to turn the mind heavenward where the family circle would be permanent. Thus the young lady continued to weave her sentimental spell: "Here the pleasure of meeting friends is embittered by the reflection that we soon must part; there the family of the redeemed will meet to part no more for ever. O! who can realize the joys of that meeting?" Who indeed but those who choose to sacrifice the pleasures of this world in the effort to get themselves, their loved ones, and as many others as possible into the next? This, of course, was exactly the young lady's point, one that the young itinerant seems to have taken to heart. He, after all, wrote his effusions about the family fireside while on the circuit, separated from all persons he professed to hold dearest, and given over to the pursuit of wandering souls who were unmindful of the blessings of heaven and homeland.[19] Even family ties were to be sacrificed for God's heavenly cause here and for heaven hereafter. The steps of the rhetorical pattern, then, made the mind a stairway from the earthly family to the heavenly one; they also made life an instrument for drawing lost prodigals to the domestic and ecclesial havens at the foot of the stairs.

Two basic imperatives were derived from the rhetoric of domesticity as evangelicals applied it to the specifics of what they termed "family government." The first imperative was to keep the world out of the family and the family out of the world. "God," intoned the author of a *Discourse on Domestic Piety and Family Government*, "has made it the imperative duty of the united heads of families to exclude . . . all influences and examples that would depreciate the . . . worship of God in their house, or that would, either directly or indirectly, vitiate the minds, or morals of any of its members."[20] The second imperative was to practice self-sacrifice. The name "family" was sweet and lovely in itself, declared one writer. Add the modifier "Christian," and it made the name higher and holier, making one think of "the endearing and connecting influences of heaven."[21] But what was the way to make a family Christian? "It is this—you must cultivate a spirit of self-denial. What is the great cause of misery in the heart, and in the family? The worship of that great idol, self-will. What is the readiest way to happiness? For a man to deny himself, take up his cross, and follow Christ daily."[22] The way of the cross, then, not only led home; it also made home heavenly.

The imperative to separate the domestic circle from the world worked itself out in a variety of practical exhortations. "Evil communications corrupt good manners," read a favorite proverb, and not only manners but morals and character as well.[23] Therefore, parents should watch their own conversation that it be sober and godly, while taking care that their children were exposed to no examples or conversation that would adulterate the parents' influence. The places where such adulteration was almost certain to occur included a variety of scenes characteristic of the culture of honor. If sons were allowed to attend horse races and daughters to attend balls and theaters, asserted Bishop Morris, parents' efforts at religious education would be useless.[24] A "fashionable education" with its stint at dancing school led to "light and foolish" society that made home seem a burden rather than a delight. It encouraged drinking, self-indulgent habits, and a neglect of business that could ruin one's temporal prospects. Worst of all it caused the children to despise the heart religion of the parents and turn to infidelity or some empty religion that allowed more self-indulgence.[25]

Simple neglect sufficed to make one's children the subjects of vice rather than religion. Let them choose their own company, mix with the "street rabble," and stay out late at night, and they would associate under cover of darkness with those of whom they would be ashamed by the light of day. Their night sports would lead to night crimes, and those crimes would prepare the way for such neglected youngsters to win a place in the penitentiary before they were old enough for one in the legislature.[26] Children and youth received various warnings against the temptations of the young: corrupt strains of thought and imagination found in novels and the discourses of infidel authors, worldly amusements, bad habits like swearing and drinking, "levity," and "impurity." As hedges against these dangers, young people were to cultivate respect for law, to practice reverence for the Sabbath (the day when worldly amusements were most widely practiced), to develop habits of serious reading and pursuit of knowledge, and to seek religion early in their lives.[27]

Defensiveness against worldly associations might generalize for some into an impulse to wholesale privatization. One writer on "Domestic Peace" insisted that not the slightest incident in the domestic economy or any of its concerns should be exposed by a family's inmates. "None, not even the nearest relations should share in such secrets. . . . Our home is a sanctuary too sacred to be invaded."[28] Perhaps such sentiments prompted the author of the *Methodist Family Manual* to stipulate, right after the standard warning against bad company, the following rule for family government: "Labor to make your children understand that they are a community of themselves, and that they are to depend upon possessions within themselves for happiness here, and not upon the outward excitement of receiving and paying visits, and hearing and sending news, etc., etc."[29]

It is just as likely, however, that this disapproval of exchanges of visits and news reflected the sober subordination of sociability to spiritual usefulness. Recall that the culture of experimental religion valued a certain form of sociability, one that arose from a common experience of grace in the heart. So long as such communion was confined to this earth, however, it could not be an end in itself; it had to be for the sake of heaven. Thus one writer grieved over the hours wasted by believers in "fashionable calls," especially when these same professed Christians pleaded lack of time when called to help in some "benevolent society." How could Christians squander an hour here, an hour there, to talk over "the things of time and sense, rehearse the news of the day, exchange compliments," and nothing more? Better that they bend their steps to "some house of affliction, some bed of death"; better that they expound the Scriptures to someone who never read the book of life; or better that they stay by their own fireside and read the Bible for themselves. One might engage in visiting to God's glory only if it did good to others and made oneself better, only "if the deep things of God were the theme, vital religion the topic." Worldly conversation brought guilt to the soul and reproach to the Christian's profession, causing others to say, "What are ye more than others."[30]

Social religion, after all, had established this order of value. An apologist for class meeting, writing at a time when the usage was virtually dead, entitled his piece "Utility of Class Meetings." He invoked what he called the "social principle." Human beings by nature sought social intercourse, but too often at the sacrifice of the spiritual to merely social enjoyment. Class meeting reversed this order; human longing for social intercourse was "not only gratified but elevated and made tributary to the soul's highest enjoyment here, and eternal felicity hereafter."[31] Even the soul's enjoyments in social religion came in for critical scrutiny from those under the sway of the principle of utility. A contributor to the *Pittsburgh Conference Journal* complained that many fellow Methodists aimed too much at enjoyment at class meeting, prayer meeting, and the like, and too little at action. "Our aim should not be to see how we can best enjoy ourselves, and how we can secure to ourselves the greatest amount of comfort in the Church, but how we can do the most good."[32] The social ties of the family of God were means to the end of benevolence and salvation. The social ties of the families in the family of God were, according to the ideology, to be subordinated to the same ends.

If the Christian way of self-denial mortified all the frivolous desires for unrestrained associations and ambitious quests for a place in fashionable society, it also required a spiritual and, for young children, a physical warfare against inner motives that might disrupt domestic harmony. Disturbances at home were to be expected, one writer sensibly observed. Human beings, whatever their pious aspirations, were not perfect, and the safety and seclusion of home allowed them to show their true characters. If passion rather than virtue ruled them at home, their "general charities" were suspect.[33] Charity began at home.

Methodist family moralists, therefore, counseled husbands and wives to crucify their passions. The author of the *Methodist Family Manual* invoked the text of Ephesians 5:22–23, which counsels wives to submit to their husbands as they would to Christ and husbands to love their wives as Christ loved the church and gave himself for her. This counsel of mutual self-denial comprehended all his rules for husbands and wives. Others wrote of a love that precluded fierce passions and cultivated a patience that made both husband and wife better people. Spouses were to compete to be first in gestures of relinquishment and reconciliation, not in shows of "spirit." This negative "spirit" was born of prideful passion and a "want of feeling."[34]

If husband and wife were to mortify their passions in relation to each other, children were to learn the same self-control from parents through precept, example, and infrequent, but inexorable, force. The family, bound together by the three strands of conjugal, parental, and filial affection, was the "epitome of all rule, authority, and power."[35] For the sake of God, church, and nation, then, parents must secure in their children the habit of implicit obedience at the earliest possible age. Use persuasion and influence "when you *can*," counseled the editor of the *Western Christian Advocate*, but resort to the rod "when you must." The rod would not often be necessary if it were used early, decisively, and once and for all.[36] M. L. Haney, child of a home run on such principles, believed that a watershed moment came in most children's lives that called for the decisive conquest of self-will. "I think my father never had but one such battle with each child," he recalled, "and that generally . . . before it had entered its second year."[37]

The point of the conquest was not the imposition of a strong person's will on a weak person; the point was an insistence on the principle of order, a principle to which strong and weak, parent and child alike were subject. The rules enforced by family government were to be few, clearly understood, suited to the age of the children, and in all other respects reasonable and just. The context of conquest was justice, and justice required parental self-government. "No one governs others well who cannot govern himself." Parents had to be consistent in their enforcement of rules, firm in their decisions, and careful never to promise or threaten what they did not or could not carry through. "Perform what you threaten, else they [your children] will learn lying from your own lips." Correction done in anger communicated a spirit of revenge and was certain to alienate the affections of the child. Such a loss left only fear as a controlling force. "Let the tear of affection, not the flush of anger, meet the eye of the subject of early discipline."[38] Sentimental indulgence was just as ruinous as vengeful correction. The very affections that made family heavenly, such as the tenderness of parent for child, if not chastened by the way of the cross, might prevent some misguided parents from giving " *'a good whipping'* . . . seasonably, calmly, prayerfully *'laid on.'* " Such "false tenderness" only fostered "the corruptions of the heart." It was the sin of Eli, the Israelite priest whose sons died because he did not restrain them from their sins.[39]

Methodists and other evangelicals believed fervently in character, example, and moral influence as tools of discipline, but they felt no inconsistency between such influence and the conquest of the child's self-will, with or without the rod. Although some modern interpreters of religion and family life make opposites out of will-breaking and affectionate moral influence as familial and theological orientations, Methodist experience synthesized the two.[40]

Milton L. Haney provided an excellent example of this synthesis in his narrative of how his mother gave him "the most fearful scourging" he ever received. As a boy he had loved horses, especially a spirited colt that his mother had forbidden him to ride because she feared it might hurt him. He rode it once anyway, on a dare, and was thrown. He limped back to his house to lie down. "Mother," he recalled, "seemed almost omniscient," and he got by her alert questioning only by denying that he had ridden the animal. While he slept off his accident, Mother Haney learned the truth from a neighbor who had stopped by to ask how Milton was. When Milton awoke, he noticed "a well prepared beechrod near by" and a mother coming from her bedroom with eyes red from weeping. He felt "as though the judgment day were nearing." He had to wait through one more of his mother's bedroom prayer sessions before she felt she had light from God. Judgment day broke upon him as he was "invited to accompany her to the barn." She lectured him on the awful character of lying. It was like death to her that her boy had lied to her; confidence in him was destroyed; lying would undermine all that was good, bring the curse of God and the damnation of hell. She prayed and wept and prayed, and then she whipped him. "The procedure of that day," testified Haney, "had much to do with laying the foundation in me for the joy of illimitable years. Mother's love for me was too great to allow me to perish. There was no visible symptom of anger, or revenge in her marred face, but it was the picture of wounded love."[41]

Haney's account of his conversion explicitly invokes his mother and implicitly echoes her scourging. He names his mother as the chief factor leading to his salvation. It is not clear, indeed, that Mother Haney, the Methodist church, or God were sorted out very well in the deeper regions of young Haney's imagination, however well he knew their differences intellectually. The question for him was always how, not whether, he would become a Christian. Here, as in so much else, Mother Haney—or God, or the Methodist church—had her way. Milton Haney was about sixteen when he was converted, but he had received many impressions for several years earlier that he ought *publicly* to renounce a life of sin and join the church as a probationary seeker of religion, just as the Methodist church urged its young people to do. He resisted this impression even as he began to seek religion more intensely at age fifteen. He alarmed his mother by starting to stay home from preaching services. What looked like irreligion, however, was a sort of perverse private religiosity: he spent the time alone with God in prayer. At length he attended a New Year's eve watch night meeting, accompanied by a cousin, from his mother's side of the family, who had often prayed for his salvation. The preaching convicted him to tears, but he did not go to the mourner's bench until another young man put his arm around him and led him there. Mother Haney's scourging image seems to hover clearly about Milton's description of how, as he struggled under conviction at the mourner's bench, "the pains of hell" took hold of him and he was assaulted by such a view of the damnation of the wicked as he could never forget. As the hour grew late and the preacher grew anxious to close the meeting, Milton was still kneeling at the altar. The preacher announced that all who were earnestly seeking religion could be taken into the church by giving their hand and name to him. Milton heard the Holy Spirit suggest, " 'Will you now obey?' " " 'Yes, Lord, I will,' " he replied, and, without rising, turned to the preacher and gave him his hand. In less than ten seconds, he was on his feet "in the new heavens and new earth, God's happy and forgiven child!" When he gave up his last point of disobedience, he experienced religion. He claimed his first urge was to put his arms around all who were present and bring them to Christ. He was full of a new love that flowed back to God and out to universal humanity.

Milton Haney's will was first conquered, one suspects, by a relentless Protestant madonna capable of instilling simultaneously the terrors of hell and the solicitude of wounded love in her son's tender conscience. He never forgot either the terrors or the solicitude. We can easily believe him when he says he found it impossible to shake off the impress of her spirit. "Her care for the company I kept, her scrutiny of my habits, her knowledge of my heart life, her pain when I was perverse, and her hold on God for my eternal salvation made her agency more potent than any other that was human in bringing me to Christ. I can hardly remember a time when I did not desire and intend to be a Christian."[42] This scrutinizing, psychologically intrusive spirit was exactly what parents, as God's stewards and representatives, were exhorted to cultivate in relation to their children. God's eye was all-seeing; no moment of life was beyond his watchfulness and concern. Systematically attentive parents—dispassionate and inexorable in their enforcement of order, faithful in their practice of domestic piety, and affectionately yearning in their inquiries into their children's "heart life"—were God's appropriate vicars on earth. By receiving parental authority, Methodists believed that children would be prepared to receive the authority of the gospel and the Word of God. Through parental precept and example, they thought, children would learn that God was as offended as parents were at children's disobedience, yet even more ready to embrace and forgive.[43]

As a thought experiment, it is instructive to run through Milton Haney's episode with his spirited colt from the perspective of the culture of honor. A father of that culture might have been more inclined to take pride in his son's pluck in attempting to master his horse, that still vital symbol of male prowess and status. On the other hand, if we suppose that father and mother were agreed that the boy was not to ride the horse, the father might have been ashamed and outraged that his son made a fool of himself by getting thrown in public where the neighbors could see. He might then have taken the beech rod to him in anger. The mother might still have had her worries over her boy's physical safety and might have forbidden his riding the colt. Her response to his disobedience would more likely have been on the order of "You got what you deserved for trying some fool trick like that!" and perhaps, for good measure, an unmeaning threat of "If you don't mind, I'll whip the skin off you!" Neither mother nor son would have taken the threat seriously. If the boy were around ten or older at the time, he would have been unlikely to accept his mother's invitation to the barn even if it had been offered, and his mother could not have forced it upon him. It is also unlikely that either parent would have made so much of the boy's lie; in their eyes and his it would have been a relatively harmless, if ineffectual, face-saving tactic. In such households, the child learned not to confess and receive forgiveness but to avoid humiliation. From such a household, Milton Haney might have grown up to be an honorable, hail-fellow farmer who never really "got ahead" in his business, a failing due, as the pious middle-class pillars of his community would remark, to the waste of time and money at horse races down at the county seat. As things actually were, he became an evangelist who helped shape and sustain the middle-class morality that looked askance at lovers of horse races.[44]

One type of psychoanalytic approach to stories like Haney's would characterize the actual Milton Haney as "self suppressed" and the imaginary horse-loving farmer as "self asserted."[45] Such analysis is mistaken in that it tends to disbelieve or ignore the expressions of power and joy in the discourse of persons like Milton Haney. It leads us to expect "suppressed selves" to be so savagely repressed, so beset by inner conflict, so encompassed by fear as to be largely incapable of effective decision and action and to be strangers to the enjoyment of life. Many evangelicals, in fact, were remarkably energetic and willful people who were quite effective in influencing the culture of their times and who knew the joy of their effectiveness, or "usefulness" as they would have called it. We might still question whether it is right or good to war against a child's self-will the way Mother Haney did against Milton's. We must also take seriously, however, Milton Haney's own account of himself and consider that his sense of self and calling were stable and successful enough to warrant the publication of his autobiography at the end of a long and productive life.

It is clear that the Methodists' ideology of child rearing and domestic life was evangelical in the sense that it was an attempt to form the selfhood of family members around the gospel of experimental religion. The family, like the class meeting, was to be a crucible of identity where selves were forged in the heat of an affection made holy by Christian self-denial. This evangelical domesticity, however, was at the same time a republican domesticity. Methodists tied the fate of the republic to their vision of the Christian home using the same logic by which they linked the republic to the prosperity of evangelical religion in general.

That logic centered around the republican theme of virtue. The forging of evangelical selfhood required, first of all, the breaking of the children's self-will as an implementation of an overall principle of self-denial. The parents, by grace, were to have already accomplished this conquering of self in their own characters. People who learned at home the difficult lesson of self-denial laid in their characters the foundations for that sacrifice of self-interest to the common good that was the sine qua non of republican public virtue. Persons reared in such families would make up the sort of citizenry a republic needed in order to survive; persons reared without such family government would make a riotous populace whose "wild, ungovernable passions" only "the iron rod of despotism" could sway. Parents, asserted author John Power, were the republic's alternative to the standing armies that oppress the other nations of the world. If parents proved unfaithful in family government, their children would be unable to govern themselves, and they would betray and murder "social, civil, and religious liberty."[46]

The forging of experimental Christians and virtuous republicans—the former were also invariably the latter—required, as we have seen, the exclusion of foreign matter that might adulterate the molten motives being cast into good habits and refined feelings. Hence, the insistence that the children stay at home. But what were they to do at home? The answer was a time-worn Protestant answer with a nineteenth-century variation: the children were to work and to learn. W. F. King felt rebellious against his parents' restraints, envying the coon hunting and party going of other children his age, but he recalled the two principal advantages of being kept home: it gave him a fine training in various lines of domestic work and an opportunity for reading and study. King reflected that in submitting to his parents he was unconsciously meeting an important crisis; he asserted he was grateful for their requirements and his obedience not long after boyhood.[47]

While King did not specify the nature of the crisis nor why he was later so grateful to his parents, it is likely that he became persuaded of the Protestant moralist's truth: "Idleness is the school of vice, and the way to ruin." Children who were allowed to be idle and to select their own amusements, according to one rehearsal of the familiar theme, were likely to develop indolent habits; no one with such habits ever succeeded in "any calling or profession, either in church or state." The antidote, of course, was to train the youngsters in industrious habits through some regular manual labor. The result would be a patient industry and self-reliance upon which young men could build "a manly, virtuous, and honorable independence." Methodist layman Samuel Williams wrote his brother that he intended to give his boys an education in "some good mechanical" occupation; if, later in life, they found a way into "more agreeable business, or an easier mode of life, let them adopt it." Habits of "industry, economy, and moderate labor, are safeguards to virtue, morality, and stability of character," he asserted; such habits would never be wasted in later life, no matter what business his sons pursued.[48]

These sentiments were fit to warm the heart of any sturdy republican yeoman. Religious families not only inculcated the fundamental dispositions upon which order and authority were built, they also cultivated those virtues that guaranteed the prosperity of the republic. Industry and frugality in the interests of independence were the sterling virtues of republican political economy. Any agency that could establish such virtue in the American citizenry deserved the gratitude of the patriot statesmen who labored so hard to find policies that would accomplish similar ends. In the immodest estimation of the religious, of course, such efforts were bound to fail without the aid of a family piety that alone really got to the springs of virtue.

Methodists were not above citing the personal "pecuniary benefits" incident upon the proper practice of religion and republican virtue. In a chapter headed with the text "Godliness is profitable unto all things" (1 Timothy 4:8), John Power cited such benefits first among four motives for family piety. It was the lowest of the motives, and Power said he mentioned it mainly to counter the enemies of religion who claimed that the churches—in their demands for buildings, ministers, "benevolent institutions," and the like—were bankrupting their members. What really bankrupted people, claimed Power, was the extravagance, excess, indolence, and vice in which irreligious people engaged, as well as the expense of police, prisons, and criminal jurisprudence needed to cope with the crime such habits produced. The infallible remedy to the temporal poverty that followed upon such moral bankruptcy was religion. One of the three reasons Power gave for this claim was the standard observation that religion produced industry and economy. An even greater reason was the abundance of promises in Scripture of God's special blessings upon the labor of his servants.

At the point of this third reason, Power's argument began to trace the peculiar inversions of the way of the cross. The truly pious family, he claimed, derived from its consecration to God the blessing of his presence in their midst. From this presence arose a "refined, intellectual, and spiritual bliss" that earthly amusements cannot impart. With such rich comforts and pleasures at home, the members went abroad not for the joys of earth, not " 'to fill an aching void within,' " but only to fulfill their duty in diffusing among others "the influence of that salvation in which they rejoice." Thus members of the pious family were detached from the objects of earth; their enjoyments were not dependent upon "their position in society . . . , the arbitrary rules of refinement . . . , the profusion of personal decorations, the splendor of parlors, the honors of office, the glories of power, or the delusions of wealth." Instead, they were "filled with the love of God; all their affections sanctified, and wholly concentrated on him, as the exhaustless source of salvation and glory." Only after elaborating this archetypal image of the inner sanctum detached from the world yet diffusing its influence over it, could Power allow himself to dwell on the topic at hand: the pecuniary benefits of religion. To him it was obvious that individuals and families who turned from the world to the service and enjoyment of God "domestically" should rise from material and moral bankruptcy to "important and useful stations in civil society and the Church of Christ." Conversion to Christ and identification with the sacred inner space where Christ and his people dwelt caused old things to pass away and all things to become new. The economic and social-status benefits of religion were merely the external evidence of the fact that in Christ, a person became a new creature.[49]

The nineteenth-century variation on this classic Protestant work ethic had to do with a growing concern for learning and "intellectual culture." It was commonplace to urge parents to provide good reading material in the home in order to keep children from evil and to improve their piety. Some writers promoted it as a means to lead children to a thirst for knowledge in all its branches.[50] The main thrust of such urging was, of course, the anxiety to see the children pious in this world and happy in the next. These exhortations were penned and published, however, during the advent of official Methodist Sunday schools and during the first wave of the founding of Methodist colleges under the sanction of the General Conference.[51] Such advice reflected the first glimmerings of an understanding that middle-class character, in addition to being the outcome of habits of industry and frugality, was becoming a matter of aggressive mental initiative and self-reliance exercised in a career of usefulness. The idea of a career implies a coherently rationalized life course characterized by continuous achievement in the service of universal human needs and interests. Comprehensive knowledge, far-seeing and principled calculation, an inner energy that overcame external circumstances, and a drive to realize all of one's powers were constituents of the character that was capable of following a career. The Methodists were finding their way into what Burton J. Bledstein has called the culture of professionalism. Education, more than manual skills, was becoming the way to cultivate these new dimensions of professional character.[52]

Religion, especially family religion, was just as relevant to these new virtues as it was to the older republican ones. John Power hinted as much when he urged that children, in addition to being constrained to obey their parents, must be educated. He excoriated those parents who were more interested in improving the productivity of their farms or shops than they were in "intellectual culture—the improvement of the minds and morals of their immortal offspring."[53]

The highest motive for faithful practice of family religion was love. Divine love was like natural parental love in that neither was conditional upon the external appearances of its offspring. Both looked past all earthly and superficial circumstances to the intrinsic worth of character. The soul's true value was measured by whether or not it possessed intelligence that loved God or was capable of loving God. The love of God was an active principle that served both the iconic function of being the "ornament and peace of its possessor" and the instrumental function of being the "energy and soul of all active benevolence and Christian enterprise." One's own children, claimed Power, offered the nearest, most practicable field for such loving enterprise. It was a heartless heresy, contrary to God's natural creation, to believe that universal divine love was so impartially universal as to require as much concern for the eternal prospects of strangers as for one's children's salvation.

In his discussion of love, Power provided a rich metaphor for the character of the professional. Such love, he claimed, fixed itself upon "the treasure within—the immortal mind and its endless destiny." He spent four pages, after making this assertion, in extolling the wondrous capacities of the human mind: its "inherent energies—intellect and will," its drive to overcome all obstructions in a quest to comprehend all of God's boundless creation, its reverent contemplation of heaven and God himself. The "expansion of the soul" on earth, however, was but a faint replica of the "incomprehensibly-glorious development of powers, enlargement of capacity, and approach to the perfections of God" that the regenerated soul would attain in eternal life. The point of this apotheosis of human potential was still religious; Power urged the cultivation of scriptural holiness in oneself and one's offspring lest such wondrous capacities be eternally wasted. It takes little imagination, however, to envision how energies mobilized by a call to personal holiness in the service of the eternal expansion of the soul might be deflected into personal character development in the service of the lifelong pursuit of one's career.[54]

The religious content of the work ethic in mid-nineteenth-century America was far from exhausted. The advent of the Methodist Age in American religious history may, in fact, have marked a major step from a traditional to a more modern embodiment of Protestant religious dynamism in visions of economy and social order. The original Puritan vision of work and society saw the calling as a kind of stewardship for God in the context of a limited economy; each person's work served the basic needs of others in a harmonious—and static—community. The calling was twofold: a general calling as a Christian and a particular calling in one's occupation, both of which were determined by God's sovereign ordering, not by personal choice. Usefulness to society and a frugal temperament that made for contentment with one's lot were measures of individual success. Prosperity was promised not to the individual but to society as a whole.

From the time of the First Great Awakening, the "new light" evangelicals in American Protestantism urged the general calling as the key to social harmony and challenged the idea that one served God simply by fulfilling the functions of a particular calling. For them the issue was the root of action in the hearts and affections of humankind; if human beings were to serve the good of the whole, they must have their selfishness rooted out at its base. All of economic life, in this view, might be a spiritual danger because of appeals to covetousness and pride. Particular institutional arrangements, however, mattered less in dealing with these temptations than the emotional quality of relations among persons.[55] This way of thinking may be seen as secularizing in the sense that religion gives no very specific guidance on what callings are appropriate, on the nature of the public good, or on how any particular calling serves the public good.

The implicit social theory that this form of religion did offer was a highly individualistic one that saw social gain or decline as determined by the number of individuals who acquired socially useful moral qualities rather than by the reconstruction of social institutions. Religion and its domestic outpost, the home, were the agencies for the accomplishment of this moral improvement. This belief in the need for agencies, however, reveals an aspect of the evangelical social theory that was not quite so individualistic. In the extension of the opposition of "church versus world" to include "home versus world," evangelicals were recognizing the coldness, impersonality, even cruelty of the emerging capitalist public order of the market and of work. The warmth and care of the church and of the home were supposed to be both compensations for the coldness of that world and leavening influences for its melioration and reform. This theory, some students have observed, seems like an anticipation of twentieth-century functionalist sociology that assigns functions of social integration and personality support to the institutions of religion and family.[56]

Historians of a more radical bent have excoriated this evangelical strategy as a legitimation of the dehumanizing and oppressive order of the capitalist economy. Hence, E. P. Thompson's portrayal of much of the English working class as crucified by the alienating power of Methodist piety and Ann Douglas's mordant account of the narcissism of American women's domestic literature.[57] Other historians have stressed the reformist dynamic implicit in the evangelical gospel that affirmed the spiritual equality of all persons and thus undercut aristocracy, patriarchy, and slavery. Hence, Bernard Semmel's account of a liberalizing "Methodist Revolution" and Timothy L. Smith's linking of revivalism and social reform.[58] In the present study I affirm both emphases in qualified ways. On the reformist side, I have already discussed Methodist communal egalitarianism and its subversion of patriarchy in the traditional ethos of honor. On the legitimating side, I am in the process of discussing the domestication of Methodist communal experience into domesticity and its legitimation of the American nation and of the nation's capitalist order. As Methodist evangelicals increasingly sought "natural" agencies to support and carry on the work begun by their rituals of social religion, this process of domestication and legitimation extended to justifying the legal and social subordination of women. Even in this case, however, such conservative implications were not the whole story.

As I observed at the outset of this chapter, the evangelical love cultivated by Methodist experimental religion had both an iconic and an instrumental quality. As icon it imparted peace and comfort to the soul. As instrument it imparted a burning desire for usefulness supported by energy and independent initiative in the character. This love was indeterminate in its implications. It was readily assimilated to a variety of causes, some socially conservative, others socially progressive. Nothing illustrates this indeterminateness better than the uses made of experimental piety by men for women and by women for themselves.

12

Icons of Holiness and Instruments of Morality

WOMEN IN THEIR SPHERE AND BEYOND IT

During the first half of the nineteenth century, American religion and, more generally, American literary and popular culture became "feminized." Women had for generations outnumbered men in the church pews. They not only increased their numbers during the first half of the century, they also formed the backbone of voluntary religious activity in the local congregations and neighborhoods. Women of the growing middle class consumed ever-increasing amounts of popular literature designed for pious feminine feelings. It was a time of intuitive and heartfelt knowledge of God, of tender and sentimental—even narcissistic—appeal in literature. Simply to promote intuition and feeling as central to religious experience, as Methodism did, was ipso facto feminizing.[1] Inherent in this feminized religion were the doctrines that home was woman's sphere and that both were sacred. We have seen what Methodists made of the home. They also sacralized *Woman*, the center of the home.

Feminist scholars have debated the normative question of whether this doctrine, in its nineteenth-century context, oppressed women or empowered them. They have asked if women's adoption of this ideology was conformist or liberating. Some have described ways in which it was both.[2] A descriptive study like this one is not the place to settle the debate over the oppressive or liberating character of nineteenth-century domesticity. It is an appropriate place to illuminate that discussion by showing the range of motives to which the evangelical cult of womanhood could give rise. At one end of the spectrum was the secluded iconic role in which evangelical men cast sisters, wives, and mothers in order to have a center of inspiration and energy to pursue their own callings. At the other end of the spectrum was the public activist role that some women took upon themselves in order to carry out their callings as instruments of the Christian home whose values, they felt, must permeate the world. All along the spectrum, the assumption was that women embodied Christian self-sacrifice in a special way "natural" to their sex and that their claims to power and recognition were, paradoxically, founded upon their self-sacrificing nature. Very few claimed rights simply as human beings. When they did, they departed from the domestic way of the cross.

Methodist social religion had transcended distinctions of social position and thus helped to subvert the values and social ranking of the culture of honor. It also tended, in a limited way, to transcend distinctions of gender identity. While some in the more respectable denominations were scandalized by the idea of women speaking to public assemblies, Methodists not only allowed but expected women to speak in love feasts, lead in prayer meetings, and exhort sinners at the altar. The wider egalitarian implications of this religious practice, however, were not readily followed up. The leadership roles of women in Methodism were not formalized with ordination to ministry; there were no women circuit riders. Even the licenses to exhort or preach given to local officials were not granted to women until the 1870s, and the giving of such licenses to a few women even then caused such a stir that the General Conference of 1880 revoked from women the right to such licenses.[3] Methodism's tendency to transcend gender constraints was curtailed in a society in which gender categories appeared to be a natural replacement for categories of social class that had lost their legitimacy, if not their empirical reality, as guides for social order.[4] Social religion's dialectic between iconic and instrumental moments was squeezed into the rhetorical mold of the cult of evangelical womanhood. These rhetorical patterns and gender constraints are prime evidence that the way of the cross led home. That it also led some women to leave home for the sake of home is only one more evidence of the paradoxical character of Methodist religious sensibility.

"Every man who knows human nature," asserted a male contributor to the *Western Christian Advocate*, "connects a religious feeling with a softness and sensibility of heart." Furthermore, he lectured, a want of religion in women was proof of that most disagreeable of female faults, a masculine spirit.[5] A generation earlier, James Henthorn had identified the desired center of his religious feeling with a feminine image. After describing in masculine martial imagery his "rigorous combats" with "the adversary," he complained that in such conflicts he felt like "a sinking Peter," "a faithless Thomas," or "the trembling jailer"—discouraging feelings all. Once in a while, however, he was "so happy as to get with Mary at the Master's feet."

This was where he wanted always to be, for his brief Christian experience had taught him that "things go hard when my heart is so; and when that is soft all goes well."[6]

These soft feelings, however, were not simply an exercise in sentimental self-indulgence. Experimental religion was a call to die and rise again, to dissolve one's identity in the inexorable fires of divine love and receive it back newly forged for a life of service and duty. For Henthorn, these soft and feminine states of feeling had the paradoxical power to inspire great energy, aspiration, and resolution to do his duty generally as a disciple of Christ and specifically as a head of a family, a class leader, and a steward in his local society.[7] Mary sitting at the feet of Jesus and communing with her Lord was an icon that motivated a man like Henthorn to enter with alacrity upon his instrumental functions. She symbolized the Christian's ideal contemplative state of mind and feeling, but in that very contemplative passivity she also communicated the active properties needed to live a life in service of this ideal.

Pious women in general were to serve this iconic function for Methodist men. A pair of poems published in the Lexington, Kentucky, *Gospel Herald* vividly captured the complementarity of masculine and feminine roles as constructed in the family of God. "Itinerant Preachers" was a meditation on the apostle Paul's words in Acts 15:36: "Let us go again and visit our brethren in every city where we have preached the word of the Lord, and see how they do."

Dispensers of the Gospel grace,
Visit their flocks in every place,
The state of each to see,
To water what their hands had sow'd
And mark their children's growth in good
In faith and charity.

The church engrosses all their care;
Anxious how every soul may fare,
They every soul attend;
From place to place unwearied go,
Till all their faithful toils below
In rest eternal end.

"Pious Women," printed just beneath "Itinerant Preachers," was a meditation on Acts 16:13, a report on the activity of the apostle after he had acted on his own exhortation: "We went out of the city by a river side, where prayer was wont to be made; and we sat down, and spoke unto the women which resorted thither."

Women, excused from public care
Designed for nobler service seem;
God gives them time, in frequent prayer,

His handmaids to attend on Him:
And more to piety inclined
We always see the gentler kind.

Women we own the foremost still,
Where stated prayer is made to appear;
They first the place of worship fill,
They first the joyful tidings hear,
The welcome messengers receive,
And patterns to the faithful live.[8]

Pious women, the poem suggested, sat like Mary at the feet of God and were therefore the first to hear and welcome the messengers of the gospel. They were the umoved movers who received and energized the preachers and whose holy example moved the rest of the religious people to greater faithfulness. The spiritualized sexuality in these poems is none too subtle. As the itinerant fathers beget spiritual children in the community, pious women are most eagerly receptive to the itinerants' seminal message. Women are also the ones who stay by and nurture the children by their constant presence of persuasive example, while the fathers continue on their frenetic way, providing only intermittent care. One may even infer an awkward and unintentional pun in the poet's assertion that "Women we *own* the foremost still / Where stated prayer is made to appear." Pious women were not the preachers' sexual property in any physical or legal sense, but the poet seems to have made an analogous claim on a different level. Small wonder that many men were hostile to their wives' religion and to the preachers who propagated it.

It will not do, of course, to reduce the spiritual to the physical in interpreting these poems. The spiritual alliance of preachers and pious women in the interests of the family of God is not to be confused with the more mundane alliance of man and woman in the interests, or in the violation, of literal family lines. To be sure, such confusion did happen, on occasion, and led to some sorry violations on the part of Methodist clergy. Such violations incurred strong and swift church discipline.[9] Itinerant preachers, as we have seen, were supposed to be, and generally were, powerful symbols of spiritual communion in the family of God *because* they had sacrificed important traditional markers of their masculine identity: land and, for the earliest itinerants, marriage and family. For women, their Christian self-surrender had a homologous function of spirit overcoming flesh; religion enabled them to transcend a merely sexual identity and lay claim to a moral and spiritual identity as well.[10] Methodism's encouragement of women to take leading expressive roles in worship and social religion and in religious visiting was an example of this expansion of women's role and sense of self in a traditional society that offered them virtually no other opportunities. The transcendence of traditional sexual identities for both preachers and women, then, was real, an expression of a community of feeling that pushed toward the realization of a common humanity in Christ, in whom there was, said the apostle, neither Jew nor Gentile, male nor female, slave nor free.[11] As with most such movements, however, the transcendence was only partial; consolidation ensued predictably.[12]

A significant expression of the consolidating trend in Methodism was the founding of mid-nineteenth-century Protestantism's most successful women's magazine, *The Ladies Repository*, which began publication in Cincinnati in 1841. Joanna Bowen Gillespie describes it as "the emerging voice of Methodist women," but she observes that its original credo was a male expression of the classic doctrine of woman's sphere.[13] One of the tenets of that credo was that Christianity had elevated woman from a degraded level where she was valued only for her physical charms and confined solely to a life of domestic drudgery and sexual slavery. In an oration delivered to pupils of a female seminary and published in the *Ladies Repository*, the story of woman became a type of the story of Christ himself. Paganism, in its worship of Venus, "patron of all licentiousness," had dragged woman from her "high preeminence, and crushed . . . those nobler attributes which linked her to angelic intelligences." When Christ, however, "spoiled the principalities and powers," he rescued woman from the degradation of centuries. She now walks abroad as "a participant in the risen glories of her Lord . . . invested with that moral grandeur which burst upon the world, when the 'Sun of Righteousness arose with healing in his wings.' "[14]

Woman, the archetypal victim, was identified with Christ in a religion that glorified the victim God.[15] Victims are generally weak, and woman's weakness—"delicacy" was the nineteenth-century term—lay close to the heart of her victimage and her consequent elevation to sanctity. Her muscles were of a finer mold, with a greater delicacy and sensibility of nerve. She was like some fair violet that shrank from the glare and rudeness of public life and lived instead to dignify domestic retreat with virtue and softness. Virtues that man had once despised as womanly—love, joy, peace, long-suffering, gentleness, meekness, temperance—were celebrated as fruits of the Spirit in Christianity. Where but in the female heart would such supernatural virtues bloom most naturally and with most grace? It was woman's nature to be patient under trial, tenacious in affection, submissive to denial and want; Christianity exalted and refined the sacrificial traits that were already natural to her. The righteousness of Christ, then, was woman's "fairest ornament"; when piety gilded nature's loveliness, men were constrained to acknowledge that they were "allied to angels on [their] better side."[16]

These angelic icons, however, did more than evoke exclamations of moral admiration from their male literary creators. Their very weakness, retreat, and sacrificial virtue gave them power. Even as Christ, by his self-emptying servanthood unto death, was exalted to lordship over all creation, so woman, by her self-denying retreat to a domestic sphere at the margins of society, attained a pervasive moral sovereignty that was, claimed one, "more absolute than that possessed by the conquering hero or the sceptered monarch."[17] The power of woman's "influence" flowed into society at large through two phases: her roles as peer and companion of men before marriage, and her roles as wife and mother after marriage.

Young women, by their very mildness and moral purity, held sway over young men who desired feminine society. Youngsters who out of a love for display and bravado would defy the commands of older male authorities could be brought into line by the threat of ostracism from female society. Therefore, women could bring about a moral revolution, "a purified public sentiment," if they made it a point to discountenance idleness, drinking, profanity, and impiety. The moral dignity of man and the "consecration of society" depended upon a refined female influence just as the "excellence and lofty aspirations of the soul" depended upon "a pure system of theology."[18] If a woman was a sister to a man, she had yet more intimate opportunities to lead him in paths of good morals and manners.[19]

Woman's most important modes of influence, however, were supposed to be as wife and mother. By industry and frugality that spared the husband financial embarrassment, by fidelity in "the duties of the conjugal relation," by discreet conversation that guarded him from temptation and made home a peaceful retreat from the world, and by that fear and love of God through which she allured him toward heaven, a pious wife might greatly promote her husband's happiness and usefulness.[20] Keeping conversation suitably discreet required that wives refrain from contradicting their husbands, censuring their morals, demanding their attention, wounding their vanity, making them feel they were wrong, or retorting when they were out of temper or abusive. Wives were to rule by the power of mildness, by a mortification of self and self-will that would endear them to their husbands and thus win them an empire of the heart's affections. "Never exact anything," one writer advised, "and you will obtain much."[21]

Anecdotes of wives who seemed to embody this sort of counsel reinforced its credibility. A Brother Winkler, despite his Methodist parentage and serious and thoughtful youth, lived unconverted until he was thirty-three. His wife, however, preserved his character until he was won over to religion: "Had not the unbelieving husband been sanctified by the believing wife, he would in all probability have turned back to the beggarly elements of the world."[22] J. H. Creighton recalled an eccentric Irish uncle of his who did not join the church until old age but always was foremost in his financial support of it. Creighton credited the man's wife, whose "loving heart held this high-tempered wild Irishman in a kind of delightful subjection, that was a fine demonstration of what the gospel can do when fully lived out."[23]

As mother, even more than as wife, woman symbolized the constraining and transforming power of experimental religion. Woman's nature was supposed to be especially suited to the task of child rearing. Her delicacy matched the children's weakness. Association with children suited her "genuine and unsophisticated feelings." Her natural affection most effectively elicited the confidence and affection of the child. This natural maternal affection made woman a stand-in for God himself. Other sorts of affection—those of a friend, brother, sister, husband, or father—depended on circumstances of habit, association, and reciprocity. A mother's affection gushed forth even when it met no return. This self-sacrificing character made maternal love divine. Its distinguishing trait, asserted one writer, was its "ever active desire to reform a wayward child." For this end a mother would sacrifice every material, mental, and emotional resource to the point of "self-immolation." "How awful and overwhelming must be the feelings of that child who thus brings a parent to an untimely grave. . . . how great must be the love of that being who placed this affection in the breast."[24]

Parental love, therefore, especially maternal love, transcended mere private feelings or passive attachments. It was an active moral principle that sought through suffering to accomplish the moral uplift and salvation of its objects. It was the perfect analogy for the love of God in Christ. A poem, "Love's Appeal," asserted the analogy without subtlety. The first stanza portrayed a mother, rod in hand, demanding her child seek forgiveness for some "guilty deed" and eliciting only defiance. The second stanza had her breaking down in tears of grieved affection and her child rushing into her arms to weep "his stubbornness away." The third stanza evoked the image of thunder and lightning at Sinai and the sinner madly swearing that he would dare God's wrath. The next two stanzas spoke of Calvary, of the Son of God bleeding and dying in the midst of a mad, hellish crowd who pierced him in sport. The final stanza sees the stubborn heart overcome by love's meek appeal. Streaming tears told of deeply felt guilt and of a "wayward breast that knew no fears" but "had feelings love alone could melt."[25]

The identification of mother love with God's power to constrain and transform human nature created a host of rhetorical possibilities for nineteenth-century American religion. Men exhorted parents to persevere in prayer for their children's salvation and used testimony to their own mothers' prayers as evidence of the efficacy of affectionate maternal piety. Such solicitude often had to endure years of watching the sons' rebellion before the impressions of childhood deepened into conviction and repentance. The outcome, however, even if the mother never lived to see it, was always sure.[26]

Nor was mother rhetoric only a literary device. One of William Fee's classmates at Augusta College in Kentucky was a nephew to a former governor of Ohio and son of a pious mother who had dedicated him to God before she died. The young man went prodigal, however, choosing to skate on the river rather than to attend a winter evening meeting of the religious students on campus. The next Sunday the president of the College, J. S. Tomlinson, preached with great power, and a Professor Trimble, cousin to the young man, moved in. "By all the memories of the prayers of his loved mother," the professor exhorted the prodigal to give himself to the church. The rebellious youth "looked as unmoved as if he had no soul." The professor's parting shot however struck home: " 'Little did your mother think, when she died, that you would be false to your word and to her teaching.' " As the students walked from church back to their quarters, the recalcitrant one came upon Fee and another friend, took their arms, and said, " 'That allusion to my mother grieves my heart. O, I cannot live this way.' " They held a prayer session together until the prodigal found pardon. When the professor heard the news, he rushed to the new convert's room and took him in his arms. The next day the newborn child of God declared to Fee that God had called him to the ministry.[27]

If mother rhetoric freed a prodigal from sin's slavery, it might also free one from the just consequences of his wicked behavior. James Finley and his fellow Methodists once put down a disruption of a camp meeting. They scattered most of the troublemakers but captured one of the leaders who had pulled a gun on one of the preachers and almost shot him. They held him in a tent until they could get a magistrate to come and deal with him. When he learned that his cohorts had fled and he had no chance of rescue, he pleaded for mercy. He did not deserve it for his own sake, he admitted, but his mother would be heartbroken if she learned of his disgraceful crime. " 'That it should break my mother's heart is more than I can stand. Pity my poor mother, for God's sake,' said he." The appeal to mother moved their sentimental Methodist hearts, and they let him go.[28]

The image of the prodigal son made a natural match with that of the suffering mother. Maternal love, mortified by the blatant wrongs of its object and yet finally winning out over the bent to evil, made an especially affecting variant of the rhetoric of self-denial.[29] One did not need to turn prodigal, however, in order for mother rhetoric to work its guiltiness and salvation. M. L. Haney never turned prodigal. His praying, scourging, weeping, hence overpowering mother saw to that. Maxwell P. Gaddis had hardly time enough to be prodigal before his mother shepherded him into the Methodist fold. He was not quite thirteen when he and his two brothers set out for the camp meeting where Maxwell underwent a conversion that, judging from his account, seems to have been a three-way transaction between God, his mother, and Maxwell himself.

Mother Gaddis saw Maxwell and his two older brothers off to the campground, following them to the gate of their homestead and exhorting, " 'BE GOOD CHILDREN, AND SEEK RELIGION before you return home.' " As Maxwell recalled it in his autobiography, he had no such fixed intention. He had never been to a camp meeting before and was going out of curiosity. He developed appropriately solemn feelings, however, as soon as he entered the campground. These feelings grew into real alarm when he later saw his brother William, the only family member other than Maxwell himself who was not yet a church member, enter a mourners' enclosure that the brethren had formed by joining hands. " 'O, my God,' " he thought,

" 'will father, and mother, and brothers, and sister, and all my relatives, press into the kingdom of heaven, and leave me?' " He rushed to the circle, knelt beside his brother, and soon became engaged in exercises that made him feel like a "great sinner" with a "hard and rebellious heart." He prayed for mercy for six hours; then he ran out of emotional steam. His anguish ceased, his mind became "unusually clear and reflective," and suddenly his heart became insensible: he could neither weep, feel, nor pray. A gloom settled upon him, and "the tempter" prevailed over him for a time with rationalizations that he was not really convicted of sin, only alarmed at his brother's action, that he was too young to become a Christian or join the church. He rose and went back to the sleeping tent.

He got no rest. He kept hearing the cries of the penitents and imagining that he heard his brother's voice among them. At length he went back to the place of mourning, kneeling in despair. As he prayed he heard his other brother, David, at his side. David reassured him that the darkest hour came just before the morning. Then came the appeal to mother.

> O, my dear brother Maxwell, remember how long mother has prayed for your conversion, and how glad she would be if the Lord would make you his child at this meeting. I have no doubt she is praying for you now. And then remember the church is praying, and your bleeding Savior is pleading your cause before the throne of God on high.

Maxwell professed, in his account of these events, to have forgotten his mother's tears and prayers. Now they passed before his mind's eye. He felt at that moment that there was efficacy in prayer and hope in his soul. He looked to the cross by faith and felt in a moment that his burden was gone. "The Sun of righteousness shined into my heart, and I arose and shouted aloud for joy."

David Gaddis had been right about Mother Gaddis praying for her sons. When the boys returned home from the campground and Maxwell had enjoyed an ecstatic reunion with his mother, they learned that she had wrestled in prayer all Sabbath evening to the point of exhaustion. She had been tempted to give up the struggle about the time that Maxwell had left the mourners' circle and gone to his tent. She had resisted the temptation and kept on praying until she felt her prayer had been heard and granted. "Who can tell," reflected Maxwell, "the power and efficiency of a mother's prayer? Her love can only be excelled by the love of God."[30]

The influence of Mother Gaddis's spirit and prayers did not cease with Maxwell's conversion. He went on to become an itinerant and carried with him the knowledge of a prayer covenant with his mother; she promised to wrestle in prayer in her closet whenever she knew or felt he was striving in the pulpit to save souls. He testified that he often "*sensibly felt*" the influence of her prayers as he tried to preach and declared he owed much of his success in saving souls to her intercession. When she died, he knelt at her grave and prayed God to let her "departed spirit" be his "guardian angel in this land of sorrow." A few days after this, he came to feel that the last tie to bind him to earth and to earthly concerns had been severed. He experienced a new and total consecration of himself to God that issued in the experience of sanctification. " '*I am the Lord's forever*!' " he found himself exclaiming repeatedly, " '*I am the Lord's forever*!' " His mother had always prayed that Maxwell be wholly consecrated to God. Now that she prayed no more on earth, her prayers, he believed, found their ultimate fulfillment.[31]

This sort of spiritual symbiosis between itinerant and mother was not unusual. Allen Wiley testified that all preachers might experience a greater exercise of faith and draw renewed energy if they knew that pious friends were praying for them. His chief example supporting his claim was his brother in the itinerancy, Stephen Beggs. Wiley asserted that Beggs owed much of his success in preaching to the prayers of his mother. Since she had died, moreover, Beggs had not been so successful a minister.[32] James Finley provided a sketch of itinerant William H. Raper in which Raper's mother, one of the "matron pioneers of the West," played a decisive role. She had guided him into the Methodist itinerancy when he might have become an army officer. She had sustained him constantly in her prayers. William later declared his gratitude that his mother had led him to become a humble minister of Christ, which was to him a greater honor than if he had become head of the entire American army. He also recalled how he had saved himself once from drowning because of his conviction, which turned out to be true, that his mother had been praying for him at his greatest moment of danger.[33] Whether their needs were spiritual, moral, or physical, it seems that sons found in their praying mothers an ever-present help and inspiration.

It was one thing for Methodist men to make the women in their lives into icons of divine love and constraint and to draw from them inspiration and energy to be the instruments of what they took to be God's will. It was another thing for Methodist women to play the part of icons while also pursuing their own rhythms of spiritual communion and moral action. James Henthorn sought to sit with Mary at Jesus's feet and also to serve faithfully as class leader, steward, and priest of his household. What of the experience of women believers? They also would feel both the yearning to sit at the Master's feet and the drive to be useful in his service. They were expected mostly to sit still, however. Passivity was supposed to be woman's nature, and the prevailing domestic ideology conflated woman's created nature with the redemptive grace that Christians believed flowed from Christ. Women believers were caught in a conflict. On one hand, they were required to act the part of icons for their men. On the other hand, they felt driven to be instruments for their Lord Jesus. The range of response to this dilemma was very wide, and particular positions within it were fraught with pain and paradox.

What is intended here is some illustration of that range of response. There is no claim to statistical representativeness. The limitations of literary sources dictate that the majority of women whose stories are told in the next several pages are not ordinary Methodist women, who left few written records, but wives of preachers. Nevertheless, even the limited sample available evinces varying ways of dealing with the dilemma posed for pious evangelical women by the constraints of their culture's gender categories and the demands of their religion's call to action. At one end of the range were those women who were content with a domestic identity that confined moral instrumentalism largely to a woman's "influence" over her children and husband. Moving toward the other end were those women who found in the way of the cross resources for an increasingly public, even political, feminine identity that was still grounded in domesticity and in the moral power of self-sacrifice. At the far end of the range were those who finally left behind self-denying domesticity altogether and claimed a God-given individuality in their own right. In order to illustrate this full range, it is necessary to move into the middle and later thirds of the nineteenth century in order to see how women of these later periods worked with patterns laid down for them by their forebears in the first third of the century, the main temporal focus of this study. For it seems to be the case that among women reared in the Methodist evangelical milieu, it took a generation or two for the liberating dynamic of the cross to lead very far beyond the home.

Conventional sex role expectations and much of the male-generated ideology of woman directed women to find their sphere of service in the nursery and kitchen, to rear pious children and to woo their husbands constantly to paths of virtue and duty by their winsome self-effacing ways. Some women of piety were content within these confines. We have seen how Elizabeth Kaufmann Phillips and other wives of preachers made no demands on their husbands, managed their households frugally and by themselves, and thus freed their husbands to pursue their careers of holy usefulness. Phillips was a poignant example of a woman who, insofar as she committed herself to paper, presented herself as content with her domestic sphere. Her correspondence shows that even in courtship she resisted her fiance's exuberant expectations that she would supply much-needed female help in his evangelistic work. He ought not to expect too much of her, she cautioned, either as a wife or as an assistant. "You perhaps think more highly of me than I deserve. 'Do not love inordinately.' 'Remember each pleasure has its poison.' " She assured him she was willing to work for the Lord and would doubtless find the work pleasant, but she did not want him to be disappointed in her.[34]

Far from disappointed, George Phillips gave ample subsequent evidence of his delight with his wife. There is little evidence, however, that Elizabeth was active in the various evangelistic and benevolent enterprises that other preachers' wives found central to their identity. Her work was all at home. From her secluded sphere she wrote letters that exuded the spirit of a happy circle of affection in which his absence was deeply felt and his coming eagerly awaited by both wife and children. She guided the hand of their little girl, Fanny Jane, through notes that read like this: "Come home, do Pa, I want to see you very bad. Mother kisses me for you every day. I wish you would come and kiss me yourself."[35] She managed their home and children with quiet competence and, of necessity, without much help from him. She labored to remain resolutely good-humored through his long absences, but, on occasion, she did write of her discouraging moments. One of those moments was during their sojourn in California. The Phillips household was in Stockton, where Elizabeth found the long, dry summer seasons to be terribly oppressive. Sometimes there was not even water sufficient to bathe. "Pray for me," she wrote, "for I need prayers very much. I often feel that my burden is greater than I can bear. I am enduring rather than enjoying life."[36]

Her remedy, or at least compensation, for such low times was the traditional practice of an extended visit to the home of some friend or relative. Phillips wrote her husband from San Francisco, relaying daughter Minnie's message that she was being a good girl and did not want to come home to Stockton. Her friend, Sister Ayers, had also just called, Elizabeth reported, and she sent the message that George should come across the bay to fetch his wife himself; she had not had "half a visit" with Elizabeth yet. Of course, Elizabeth assured her husband, she would enjoy all this much more if she knew he was well and was not too lonely. Therefore, he must write immediately to tell her if he was doing well. Dutifully she added, "We hold ourselves in readiness to come home at any time that your comfort or convenience require it."[37]

Scattered letters by other, nonclergy wives also suggest an acceptance of the constraints and the prerogatives of woman's sphere. Mary Hollingshead resigned herself without complaint to her husband's plans to move to new country away from all their old Methodist friends and religious privileges; she only hoped it was for the best. While she missed her old church family acutely, she wrote feelingly of her husband's heavy load of responsibility, both in the world and in the church, and she prayed the Lord to increase his faith and make him useful. Her husband was class leader, Sunday school superintendent, and circuit steward. Mary herself prayed that she might always sit at the feet of Jesus and desire nothing and esteem nothing but Jesus crucified. She also made brief mention of a female missionary society on whose "feeble efforts" she prayed God's blessing. The encompassing theme of her correspondence, however, was her yearning affection for her friends and fellow Methodists and her hopes to meet them in heaven. Her husband's writing, which sometimes shared the same stationery with hers, was just as pious but more given to reports of how he was managing affairs of church and business.[38]

Ruth Ross portrayed herself as a typical nineteenth-century praying mother. She wrote to Hannah Finley that she had prayed every day for years for her children and still had to endure the anxiety of seeing her older daughter marry destitute of religion. At the recent quarterly meeting, however, "the power that wakes the dead, and bids the sleeper arise, [had] arrested them." Both her daughters and her son-in-law had been convicted of what their mother had always felt was their perilous condition. Her son-in-law had been converted in love feast and his wife soon after; the younger daughter was still praying earnestly for salvation. "Oh, Sister Finley," exclaimed this widowed mother to her friend, "help me to praise the Lord for his tender mercy, for his loveing [*sic*] kindness to me and my dear children." A year and a half later, widow Ross faced the imminent flight of her son from the domestic nest into the world where he was to learn a trade. He was as yet unconverted, and she was "much exercised" over him because of the "ten thousand snares and temptations, which might prove to be his everlasting destruction." She would be ready to give him up, as Hannah had Samuel, had she only the assurance that the Lord had heard her prayers for his conversion. Once again, she received assurance that the Lord did hear and answer her. Her son was converted at camp meeting.[39]

It might seem a rather small step from the private spiritual instrumentalism of a praying mother to the more visible instrumentalism of the publicly active preacher's wife. We have seen how preachers' wives were expected to lead out in exhorting and praying for sinners at the altar, visiting the sick, leading various "female" meetings, Sabbath school endeavors, and the like. The case of one Angeline Brooks Sears suggests that, for some women, the expansion of woman's sphere to such modest dimensions of community usefulness was a daunting and exhausting project.

One of the forces that made her calling difficult for her was her social status. Born in 1817 into the prominent Cincinnati family of Moses Brooks, Esq., Angeline had many privileges, including education at a fashionable boarding school in Philadelphia. It was the sort of upbringing fit for members of the genteel upper class who might expect to shine in society, in fashionable visits and balls. Genteel women, whether pious or worldly, were expected to fill private roles only, not to present themselves boldly in public affairs. The conduct expected of Methodist preachers' wives was largely foreign to women of Angeline Brooks's class.

By the 1820s and 1830s, however, when Brooks was growing up, Methodism was beginning to become respectable and to include a network of prominent families like that of Moses Brooks. Brooks's parents were converted to Methodism after her six-year-old brother died by drowning in the Ohio River. She was eight at the time. Her mother lost her upper-class prejudice against the Methodist people and came to love "the humblest of

[God's] people." She died the triumphant death of a faithful Methodist when her daughter Angeline was fifteen. The Brookses also included among their important connections the friendship of Leonidas and Melinda Hamline. Leonidas Hamline was one of the early editors of the *Ladies Repository* and later a Methodist bishop. Melinda Hamline styled herself "Mrs. Bishop Hamline." She was a leader in the revival of Wesleyan holiness doctrine and practice that swept Anglo-American evangelicalism beginning in the mid-nineteenth century. She became a spiritual mother to Angeline Brooks. She constructed Brooks's biography in 1851 in order to give to the Christian public an example of "a sinner saved 'to the uttermost.' "[40]

The story was of a young woman who was reared among the genteel but who resisted the lure of worldly fashion and opted for the serious Methodist life of holy usefulness instead. For her, as for many women, this life of usefulness was found in marriage to a Methodist traveling preacher.[41] She married Rev. Clinton W. Sears in 1842. Her religion goaded her relentlessly, first, to live up to the high calling of a Methodist itinerant's wife, and second, to press on further to an experience of holiness that made her dying days a powerful witness. Excerpts from her diary and correspondence, which make up the bulk of the biography, reveal a painfully diffident woman. She was full of self-reproach and yearned for that fullness of divine love in her heart that would make her truly joyful and effective in the performance of her role as ministerial helpmeet. "O that I had a zeal," she cried, "a courage, a faith, thus to labor for Him who is worthy!"[42] Although her religion had pried her loose from her early worldly associations, she seemed to have internalized the ridicule and censure that, in her early schooling, had been directed at bold or pious women. Melinda Hamline, however, worked hard to integrate Angeline Sears into the loving female network of Methodism and to school her in the doctrine and practice of what Methodists called "perfect love." With Hamline's aid, Sears turned this doctrine into an engine for the surmounting of a traditionally secluded feminine identity and the building of a more expansive and visible one.

The cultivation of confidence was essential to the task. One is tempted to call it self-confidence. The quest for holiness, however, led to a curiously convoluted sort of self-confidence. It was confidence in calling, in duty, and ultimately in the God who called a woman and who assigned her duty. It was confidence in a self that was no longer a woman's own self, but God's, and that, nevertheless, felt freer and more authentic than she had ever felt simply on her own. Straightforward confidence in self, to pious women like Hamline and Sears, would have had the wrong meaning and the wrong effect. That sort of self-confidence had to be crucified in order that confidence in God might rise in the heart. Hamline, therefore, took pains to assure her readers that Sears never coveted "stations" but only entered into public duties out of a sense of the proper role of a preacher's wife. Confidence in Jesus, however, delivered a person from self-abhorrence, self-doubt, and all other preoccupations with self. Such confidence was a Christian's calling.[43]

A woman who looked thus to Jesus might defy the subtle censuring looks and labels with which the world tried to keep women in their place. Hamline, in one of her frequent glosses on Sears's story, celebrated the example of a sister Taylor whose triumphant death Sears had mentioned in a letter. "Mrs. Taylor was a bright and shining light in Cincinnati," declared the bishop's wife. She had always prayed for and emphatically claimed the rather unfeminine identity of "a soldier of the cross." She was always among the first, in meetings of social religion, to rise and give her testimony. She frequently felt the Holy Spirit in her family worship, as well as in social meetings and in church services, which meant that she commanded the attention of all present as she shouted, wept, or exhorted those present. She was especially visible in her management of "the Female Benevolent Society" through which she served the material needs of the poor and also tried to win them for her religion. Although she moved in some very high and fashionable social circles in both Cincinnati and "a distant city" (probably New York), she appeared in plain Methodist attire. She attended regularly the class meeting and other means of grace and unflinchingly spoke of her religious experience and convictions to the irreligious among whom she visited. Her behavior earned the title "the little Methodist lady from Cincinnati." On her deathbed she was told that she had been called a bold woman. " 'Have I,' said she. 'Well, I am glad of that, for I have prayed the Lord to make me a bold soldier.' "[44]

Angeline Sears also prayed to be a soldier of the cross. But she was not a bold woman. For ten years after her conversion, she was shackled by self-doubt and timidity. She finally won her struggle for spiritual liberty but only, it seems, at the cost of her life.

Sears's health had always been precarious, and she broke it once and for all in December 1847. She had been recovering at her father's home from a bad cold when she heard from her husband that a revival was starting up on his circuit. When she and her husband had first begun their work on that circuit, she had, with boldness unusual for her, exhorted people to accept Jesus. She had felt her own religious experience deepen as a result. When her husband asked her to come again and assist in his evangelism, she eagerly agreed. When he met her after her cold day's journey, she told him that it had been one of the happiest days of her life. She had worked to convert a female stranger, her only fellow passenger, and had felt unusually free and effective. " 'I think I have labored,' " she declared, with a certain sense of finality, " 'in a manner somewhat becoming the wife of a Methodist minister.' " She continued such becoming labor that night and, again, a day or two later. But then she began to feel shooting pains through her chest and had to stop. Heavy rain and snow made her condition worse, and high waters prevented her return to her father's home. On December

17, according to her husband, she announced that she believed she had taken a serious illness from which she would not recover. About a year, she said, would finish her course. Exactly a year later, she died in a manner befitting a Methodist believer.[45] It took that year, however, to prepare her for her part in her own drama.

After the high waters had subsided, she retreated once again to the house of her father, where a daily rhythm of family worship, domestic prayer meetings, and interviews with Melinda Hamline nurtured her into an effective agent for holiness, especially female holiness. She soon obtained the experience of entire sanctification she had so longed for. It was an experience of purification in which she claimed for her own sense of inward moral pollution the biblical promise, "From all your filthiness, and from all your idols, will I cleanse you." She felt "a shock like electricity" and believed it to be the Holy Spirit within her doing the work of cleansing.[46] Her subsequent spiritual course led her, under the prodding of Hamline, through a series of efforts to make her testimony a means for the edification and conversion of others. Her efforts included repeated quasi-public performances in family meetings, with guests present, and letters of testimony and exhortation written to other Christian women. One such letter was published in a holiness periodical. Because illness kept Sears from class meeting and love feast, her published letter, according to Hamline, stood in the place of her public testimony. Sears's letters and diary entries and Hamline's commentary reveal an evangelical female world of love and ritual. That world seems to have been designed to move more and more women—and the occasional man who attended their domestic prayer meetings—to the boldness and liberty that had cost Sears so much to attain.[47]

During her last year of life, Sears struggled to reconcile herself to the prospect of dying and leaving her son and her husband behind. She also worried over how well she would die, whether she might disgrace her profession of faith on her deathbed. A prolepsis of her death occurred when, late in the summer of 1848, she traveled to Brownsville, Pennsylvania, for the hydropathic treatment there. Her husband recorded in his diary that, on parting from her young son, her usual fortitude gave way. "I have hardly ever seen her soul so broken up," he wrote. When he had delivered his wife into the hands of the physicians at Brownsville, he left her to return to his circuit. He reported himself astonished that she would consent to be left without family or friends in a land of strangers. "It was almost Spartan heroism," he mused, "nay, it was more—it was Christian resignation."[48]

It was to be resignation taken to a new and chilling depth. Earlier, when Sears had traveled with her husband to some of their first fields of ministerial labor, she had found that the loss of opportunity both for the regular social prayer meetings and for retreat into private prayer had dulled the acuteness of her religious feeling.[49] At Brownsville, however, she turned further inward and, in her loneliness, settled her spiritual condition. She wrote to her husband that the trial of giving up husband and child was over: "A crucifixion of my will had to be passed through." Upon returning home, she met her friends and even her husband and child with a "cheerful, affectionate smile," but she allowed herself no expressions that might "call back the affections she now had centered in heaven." Her very presence had about it, for Hamline, a "moral grandeur" that seemed to check any "twining sympathy" or expression of grief. She asked her husband to appear more cheerful, reminding him that he had earlier written of his willingness to say, " 'Let the will of the Lord be done.' " " 'Now, be sure to carry it out!' " she commanded.

Hamline assured her readers, "It is not the office of our holy religion to destroy natural affection, but to chasten it." She granted that it might have appeared that Sears's love for her family and friends had been wholly chilled. Just a little conversation with Sears, however, showed clearly that her bearing toward them resulted from "a sense of duty to herself, lest her heart should relapse, and should be weaned again from heavenly things, and her strength be weakened in the way." She still retained her customary kindness and vigilance for the interests and happiness of all around her. " 'You still take care for us all,' " remarked a friend. Sears replied, " 'I never loved human beings as I now do.' "[50]

This new love also brought power. Hamline wrote of the dominion of religion in Sears's person that lighted up her countenance like that of Moses as he descended Mount Sinai. The formerly retiring preacher's wife became the lawgiver. Not long after her command to her husband to stop looking so grief-stricken, she had a further conversation with Hamline while he was in the room. She remarked that her husband was pained at her separation from earthly things, by which she meant her chastened manner toward him. She declared that she wished him to think of her as if she were not. " 'You wish that God may be all in all,' " prompted Hamline. " 'That is it,' she replied, '*that is it*. I do not fear suffering, . . . I do not fear *death*. I can say, "the will of the Lord be done." ' " The clear implication was that she would lose her power over fear should she allow her affections to once again become attached to her husband.

Her resistance to this temptation allowed her an authoritative voice. On the day she began disposing of personal belongings, she held a long conversation with her husband. She gave detailed moral counsel regarding his character and conduct, all in the interests of improving his ministry. His diary entry regarding the interview appeared grateful. Later he suggested that her death might be a blessing to her unconverted sisters. She replied that she expected her *mother's* prayers to avail for them as they had for her. Angeline Sears, however, hoped to be a ministering spirit to her *husband*, as Sears's mother had been to her.[51]

During the months of October and November, when these conversations took place, Sears had been calm and confident but without any great feeling of grace. On November 30, however, in family worship, this calm gave way to the first in a series of ecstatic episodes. In her spiritual transport she declared she felt well, she felt strong. She exhorted her sisters to seek Jesus and declared she felt she could convert the skeptic, so powerful were the blessings to her soul. She wished her husband could see how happy she was. The family sent for him, and when he arrived, she exclaimed, " 'O, my dear husband, how the Lord has blessed me! You have no conception how he has filled me with his love. Such shocks of *power, power, power*! Now it comes again. Now I feel it through every avenue of my poor body.' " It cannot be coincidental that she addressed these claims to "*power, power, power*!" to her male lord. She was beyond his dominion now. She moved toward her final calling. The vocation of the minister's wife never had been entirely her own. The vocation of her deathbed was no one's but hers. She finally died about three weeks after this first outpouring. Her deathbed appeals were effective, as her husband and she had hoped, in converting her three sisters, as well as the youngest sister's husband, who thereafter gave up a law practice to become a Methodist minister.[52]

Other women did not find the call to ministry through marriage quite so agonizing as did Angeline Sears. Sarah Long Stewart, for instance, was Rev. John Stewart's companion in ministry for nearly fifty years and was a stalwart leader in women's ministries. Reverend Stewart wrote once of "her share of the care of the church," in tacit recognition that what he referred to as *his* ministry belonged really to both of them.[53] Sarah Stewart, however, when she was still "Sally" Long, had served an apprenticeship for the role of minister's helpmeet, a training from which a more genteel upbringing had shielded Angeline Brooks Sears. Stewart had had a penchant for religion from at least age seven, when her parents had joined the Methodist church and set up the family altar. As soon as she was converted she was confronted with her duty to bear the cross of prayer and testimony in the public and social meetings of the church, a cross men and women bore equally in Methodist congregations. She felt greatly blessed when she did her duty, but she also was greatly tempted with imaginings that her spiritual transports in these meetings offended many people. Only slowly did she learn the boldness that allowed her to deny herself, take up her cross, and "follow Jesus through good report and bad."

An episode that fixed this conviction in her mind was the time she was called upon to pray during the visit to her congregation of a distinguished Presbyterian gentleman who had a strong prejudice against females praying in public. She wished she might escape the house unobserved, but when the class leader called out, " 'Sister Sally Long, pray,' " she lost awareness of the presence of "any criticising [*sic*] mortal." She felt a "wonderful enlargement of soul" and a "mighty power" resting on the congregation. At the next preaching meeting, the Presbyterian gentleman asked to unite with the church, taking her by the hand and telling her she had been instrumental in removing his prejudice. "I have learned," declared Stewart, "that when the cross seems the heaviest then was it most important for me to bear it, both for my own good and for the good of others."

Around 1815, a revival swept Sally Long's Ohio neighborhood and caught in its refining fire her neighbor and future husband, John Stewart. Sarah Stewart recalled that the local Methodist congregation believed it would be John's duty to become a Methodist minister. John Stewart, not at all coincidentally, had similar impressions and eventually joined the itinerancy in 1816, but not before he had obtained Sally Long's consent to become his wife. As John was riding off on his first assignments, his fiancé's circuit preachers and local congregation were paying her special attention. Preachers called on her to pray after preaching services, and T. A. Morris, later a bishop, chose her to lead a newly established female prayer meeting in the neighborhood. She suffered agonies of self-doubt and embarrassment and tried to avoid the responsibilities, but her fellow believers were firm about what they saw to be her duty. Painfully embarrassed over her lack of education, she took a school to teach small children and used the job as an opportunity to improve her mind. She adopted strict rules for the use of her time, splitting it between study, teaching, and attendance at all the social and public means of grace. She was, as she remembered it some twenty-five years later, preparing herself for responsibilities that might come to her in future life. It was five years before Sarah Long and John Stewart finally married. Sarah Long had redeemed the time, however, and was well prepared for her vocation as minister's assistant.[54]

Ministers' wives seemed to have undergone a process of advancement by humility similar to that whereby ministers themselves advanced into and through the ministry. Just as William Fee had suffered self-deprecation and mental anguish when he felt called to the ministry, and just as James Finley had felt "great depression of mind" as he entered his wider field of service as a presiding elder, so Sarah Long suffered great embarrassment when called to lead out in women's ministries. The logic of Christian self-sacrifice dictated that the higher one rose, the deeper one sank.

Another Sarah came up through her ministerial apprenticeship a generation later than Sarah Long Stewart and with better educational privileges. Sarah Thomas Fee, accordingly, enlarged the sphere of praying mother and preacher's wife almost to the breaking point. Her father sent her to the Putnam Female Seminary, a Presbyterian institution that gave her the best education available to women in Ohio in the 1830s. Catherine Beecher was one of her teachers. Fee's mother saw to it that she was brought up under the influences of Methodist prayers and hymns and the family visits of Methodist itinerants. She was converted at age fifteen and joined the Methodist church. She attended the various means of grace faithfully and never let worldly amusement or inclination interfere with these duties. She began early to speak of her religious experience, to pray in public, to visit the poor, and to try to lead sinners to Jesus. By age eighteen, she was eager to become a missionary among the Indian tribes of the North. No way opened for her or any other single woman to pursue that ambition. God had, as her husband remarked over fifty years later, "other work in another field" for her.[55]

Sarah Fee's subordination to the men in her life may be symbolized by images of her father during her girlhood and by her conversations with her husband at the end of her life. In her youth, she was never allowed to remain at any entertainment after nine o'clock in the evening. Her father would always arrive to escort her home "in the kindest manner." Even when, in times of revival, she lingered into the night around the altar to exhort and pray for penitent sinners, her father stayed by to protect and encourage her despite the fact that he did not profess religion himself. In the last few days of her life, after a long career in which she had acted without escort in many prominent causes, she still expressed a sense of dependence upon her husband when she told him she wished to die before him. She wished that they might walk arm-in-arm together into the presence of Jesus just as they had into their wedding celebration. If they could not die together, however, she wanted to die first, because "I know you would have grace to bear up under my departure, and I do not think I could endure yours." Two days later, he urged her to rest rather than go to a meeting where she, not he, had been asked to deliver the final address and to close with a song. She answered, "My husband, have I not been engaged with you for more than fifty years in your revival work, and have I ever deserted you on any account? . . . Do you think I will desert you now?" Even at the end of her life, she did not openly acknowledge and own the revival to be her work as much as his.[56]

Between her girlhood and her death, however, Sarah Thomas Fee made her own way and her own name for herself, or came very close to it. One of her earliest triumphs came when her husband was assigned to the Guyandotte church in what would become West Virginia, a region seething with hostilities over the slavery issue. They had to stay in a hotel during their sojourn in this unfriendly charge; the wife of one of the church officials told Fee to her face that she was not welcome on that circuit. Unmoved by such animosity, she proceeded to work for the souls of the employees and guests of the hotel, a work that issued in a revival and that converted some seventy-five people. One of her converts became a prominent minister of the West Virginia Conference. Another became, in the words of Methodist Bishop Charles Fowler, " 'one of the most powerful men in the city of Chicago.' "[57]

Fee's greatest moments arose out of clashes with both the powerful and the lowly in the city of Cincinnati. In her twelve years in that city she earned the title of "Mother of the Crusade in Cincinnati." The crusade in question was the women's direct action campaign against the "liquor traffic," a campaign that issued in the founding of the Women's Christian Temperance Union (WCTU). In 1873 and 1874, more and more women were moving their prayer meetings out of their churches and parlors and into the saloons throughout southern Ohio. Sarah Fee and two other women engaged in the first action of the Cincinnati crusade by visiting the Second Street vicinity where dwelt many of the wholesale liquor dealers. They were soon surrounded by a mob of "the roughs of Cincinnati." Some of the liquor merchants gallantly offered the women the protection of their premises, warning them that they might lose their lives in the crush of the mob. Fee and her companions declined to endanger the gentlemen's premises in case of violence and marched bravely out into the crowd, intending to walk to their homes.

The "roughs" yelled at and jostled the female crusaders, pushing them into the middle of the street. They surrounded them and followed them to the Fees's residence adjoining Wesley Chapel on Fifth Street. William Fee saw and heard the crowd "yelling like demons" but professed to have had no idea his wife was among them. As he stood in front of his house, the three women came up to him, "their faces shining with an unearthly radiance." He did not recognize them at first, so great was the change in their appearance. His wife told him the mob had followed them almost from the river. As the crowd came up around them and saw Sarah Fee and her husband together, they fell silent for a moment. Sarah Fee stood up on the steps of the house, waved her hand, and said, "Gentlemen, you have been so kind as to escort us to our home, and it affords me the greatest pleasure to say that you are now excused from any further attention to us." Having heard these brave and courteous words, the crowd of some fifteen hundred men and boys gave three loud cheers and dispersed. They had not, however, seen the last of Sarah Thomas Fee.

As the campaign progressed, she had occasion to be shoved around by an angry and half-drunken policeman, drenched by a saloon keeper wielding a large hose, and finally arrested, along with forty-two other women, for obstructing the streets and sidewalks with their prayer meeting. It was Sarah Fee who led the prayer session for the mayor when he came down to the local police station to survey and speak to the women whose arrest he had helped plan. This encounter with the law earned her and her leading colleagues national and international notice. She was later elected president of the WCTU chapter for the first congressional district of Ohio and delegate to the International Temperance Convention in Philadelphia in 1876, centennial year of the American republic. She and a fellow temperance worker traveled to Philadelphia with their husbands and Frances Willard, who was soon to become the greatest leader of the women's temperance movement. Annie T. Wittenmyer, first president of the WCTU, presided over the Philadelphia temperance convention. She noted the presence of Sarah Fee and her fellow leader and insisted that they come up to the platform so the delegates might have a look at the "two jailbirds." They were received with great applause. Then Wittenmyer introduced S. K. Leavitt and W. I. Fee "as the husbands of Mrs. Leavitt and Mrs. Fee," to similar applause. Reverend Fee, throughout his account of these events, evinced no ill will at being the accessory to his wife's leading role.

The appointing process of the Methodist episcopal system soon made clear the church's understanding of who was accessory to whom. In the fall of 1876, Reverend Fee was transferred to Greenfield, Ohio, and his wife was obliged to follow. She was immediately made president of the temperance chapter for that congressional district. She revived a moribund movement, obtained thirteen thousand signatures to the temperance pledge, and won the allegiance of the congressman for the district as well as that of virtually every lawyer in Greenfield. In the fall of 1877, however, her husband was made presiding elder of the Ripley District in Ohio, much to the dismay of both the Fees and the people of Greenfield. Some of Greenfield's citizens even offered Sarah Fee one of the finest houses in town if only she would stay and nurture the work she had started. As we have seen, however, Sarah Fee was not one to desert her husband in *his* work.[58]

Like many women of her time, Sarah Fee stretched, but did not burst, the sacred sphere of domesticity. Like Sarah Long Stewart, she found her usefulness chiefly as helpmeet to a minister. But her activities took her well beyond the bounds of merely helping her husband or following his initiative. One might in fact describe William Fee's relation to some of his wife's more prominent Christian enterprises in a paraphrase of Milton: "They also serve who only stand and cheer." In another contrast, this time with Angeline Sears, Sarah Fee seemed to thrive on her role as minister's wife and on the public exposure she received in her quest to serve God. She needed no prodding Melinda Hamline to stiffen her resolve or overcome her diffidence. Nothing symbolizes that fact better than the manner of her death.

On the day she died, a Sunday, Sarah Thomas Fee and her husband were concluding a revival campaign in Felicity, Ohio, the place of his birth. Just two days earlier she had had a premonition of her death when she had confided her wish to her husband that she might die before he did. In the afternoon of that Sunday, she led an "experience-meeting" and organized twenty-two children into a home missionary band. It was the closing service of the revival that her husband urged her to forego and that she insisted on attending, refusing to desert him now after over fifty years as his partner in revival work. Reverend E. T. Lane, not her husband, preached the service from the text "Thou are not far from the kingdom of God." "The church," noted Reverend Fee, "was crowded to its utmost capacity." At the end of the sermon she went to the platform and faced the congregation. This was the last time she would see their faces or address them, Sarah Fee began. There were many here who were "out of the ark of safety," she said. "The prayers, the tears, the agonies, of fond parents and dear friends have been in vain. O, will they be lost at last?" Then, for the fond parents who had not properly prayed, wept, and agonized, she concluded her remarks with a story of some wealthy parents from New York City who had given their daughter every fashionable opportunity so that she might shine in the world but who had not labored for her soul. As the beautiful young woman fell mortally ill, she laid on her parents the devastating reproach that their nominal Christian example had left her to face death without Christ and without hope. "How many parents in this audience have neglected the deathless interests of their children?" queried Sarah Fee.

Then she murmured, "I suppose I must sing now." She had planned to sing a song whose first line was "I glory in the cross of Christ." "Doubtless she did sing it," remarked her husband, "but only the angels and redeemed spirits in heaven heard it." She fell forward, her hands grasping the chancel rail. Reverend Fee and two other ministers ran to her. Her husband took her hand; she looked into his eyes, breathed once, and died. He did not include in his account an explanation of what she died of. He only observed that he and his fellow ministers lifted her lifeless body and carried her to the Fee mansion amid the tears of scores who had loved her.[59]

The diffident Angeline Sears had died at home in bed surrounded by weeping family. The bold Sarah Fee died in public on the platform in front of a packed house. Sears's death was instrumental in converting immediate family members. The instrumentality of Fee's death extended beyond traceable limits. For Angeline Sears, the way of the cross clearly led home. For Sarah Fee and others of kindred spirit, that same way seems to have expanded the spirit of the Christian home into wider spheres of self-development and usefulness for women.

Ultimately the spiritual power of the domestic way of the cross overreached itself. The paradox of self-sacrifice for the sake of self-identity, a creative tension for many women, became an intractable contradiction for others. Some women of the nineteenth century felt the contradiction clearly. They simply rejected self-sacrifice and circumscribed domesticity as the basis of selfhood and moral power for women. Before the Civil War, the early feminists had claimed a political and individual selfhood for women founded upon the same natural rights that all male citizens already claimed.[60] Their sisters in conservative religious communities like Methodism, reared on a gospel of "natural" feminine self-sacrifice, did not catch up with them until after the war, and then only with much care and many caveats. By the 1870s, and especially with the emergence of the women's temperance movement, however, Methodist women were beginning to think in ways that transcended, at least implicitly, the constraints of a self that constantly surrendered its publicly valued capacities in order to stay always at home. Important indicators of this newer way of thinking may be found in the later volumes of the *Ladies Repository*, Methodism's elegant and serious monthly magazine that, in its first two decades of publication, was a major purveyor of the doctrine of "woman's sphere." In its last decade, the magazine carried material that addressed the "woman question" in a manner often at odds with the iconic images of earlier years.[61]

In 1870, a writer on "Women's Work" argued that a woman's sphere was not merely marriage and family but, rather, "the limit of the development of her capacities in every direction, mental, moral, physical, spiritual." "Nothing short of full recognition of her claims as an individual" could satisfy such a woman. Work freely chosen was "an inward moral necessity for everyone." The doctrine of domesticity had made a moral virtue out of the female necessity of marriage and child rearing. This writer closed her argument with a contrasting principle: "Work done from necessity may be good work," she granted, "but it never can have the moral power of work undertaken and well carried through from conviction and without outside pressure."[62]

In 1875 and 1876, its last two years of publication, the *Ladies Repository* ran a regular column entitled, somewhat paradoxically, "Women's Record at Home." In fact, the column digested a wide variety of news about women and their activities outside the home: female physicians sent to be medical missionaries by the women's Home Missionary Society, the financial acumen of women in the management of such societies, women speaking capably from the pulpit and other platforms, women studying law and suing when denied admission to the bar, benevolent activities by women for women, the founding and fortunes of female colleges and of professorships at coeducational institutions, proceedings of the WCTU and of various women's suffrage associations, and even some anecdotes of plucky women who thrashed with their bare hands thieves or rowdies who dared to harass them. These last items were adduced in reply to a popular joke that a meeting of a women's suffrage chapter had adjourned without conducting business because someone had let a live rat down through a skylight.[63] Such feistiness on behalf of feminist causes surfaced frequently in this column.

There was an ambivalence, however, to the claims made for women in "Women's Record at Home." This ambivalence appeared clearly in a record of the proceedings of the second annual convention of the WCTU, held in Cincinnati in November of 1875. The column cited with approval a resolution calling for the question of the prohibition of liquor traffic to be submitted to the vote of all adult citizens of the country regardless of sex. The ladies appealed for the right to vote on this issue, they claimed, "not as a means of enlarging our rights, nor antagonizing the sexes, but as a means of protecting ourselves, our children, and homes from the ravages of the rum-power." Not as individual citizens with the same God-given rights as men did they ask for the ballot, but as wives and mothers in need of protection for their domestic sphere.[64] At the same time, the WCTU delegates also exchanged greetings by telegraph with the American Woman's Suffrage Association, an organization that was visibly committed to enlarging women's rights and that seemed to many to antagonize the sexes.[65]

On one hand, women were individuals with rights to self-determination and consequent duties to self-development. On the other hand, women were wives and mothers with duties to the development of others and consequent needs for care and protection. This ambiguity pervaded most discussions of "the woman question" in the *Ladies Repository*. The last few volumes of this magazine did make it clear, however, that the images of "woman's sphere" and its secluded feminine icon were losing their appeal for more and more women.

The magazine printed a series of papers on "The Model Woman" and listed the author as a Mrs. O. W. Scott. Scott ridiculed stock poetic images of woman as the twining vine leaning on the mighty male oak tree. She had seen a tree overgrown with woodbine; "the tree died," she observed. She returned to the timeworn hymn to "a virtuous woman" that ends the book of Proverbs and that preachers frequently used to teach women their place. In Scott's hands, however, "virtuous" was interpreted to mean a woman of "moral courage," "devoted, but not dependent." Women, whether single or married, ought to be trained in business not just because it would allow them to avoid obligatory marriage and to cope with widowhood or other reverses but also because it would make them "tenfold stronger and happier." After all, the wise man of Proverbs had his virtuous woman buying and planting fields, manufacturing and selling clothes.

She quoted Proverbs one verse further than did most male preachers who tended to stop with the part that had the virtuous woman's children and husband praising her. The last two lines were: "Give her of the fruit of her hands; / And let her own works praise her in the gates." She turned the first line into a demand for justice in women's wages and the second line into a damning judgment on another popular poetic image of woman. That image was contained in a verse by British evangelical Hannah More, a verse that had been published more than once in antebellum Methodist papers, including the first volume of the *Ladies Repository*. It read

> So woman, born to dignify retreat,
> Unknown to flourish, and unseen be great,
> Fearful of fame, unwilling to be known,
> Should seek but Heaven's applause and her own.[66]

"Poetry has fearfully beclouded our sky!" cried Scott. The Scriptures, she declared, were more reasonable than the poet. Women must exist, and existing, must be seen. They deserved credit for works well done. If such works were allowed to be admired, examined, and imitated, and if due public praise were given for them, there would be still more women worthy of " 'praise in the gates.' "[67]

In earlier decades, to retreat from the world and to seek only heaven's and one's own applause might have freed not only women, but men also, from the shaming eyes of a traditional community hostile to claims for a wider, deeper individuality. Through their inward turn, evangelicals found, first of all, what they understood to be their lost and sinful natures. But then they also found what they felt were grace and adoption as children of God. Finding God's approval and the affirmation of their brothers and sisters in Christ, they also found themselves in a new way, with new gifts and capacities. They discovered a sense of vocation that many a Methodist preacher expressed with awe and trepidation in the words of Paul: "Woe is me if I preach not the gospel." For a time, women satisfied their sense of calling in local societies on the circuit within the confines of more or less traditional gender roles as "mothers in Israel" and rulers of "woman's sphere." Some of the more gifted or aspiring sought to fulfill their ministry through marriage to preachers. In the latter decades of the nineteenth century, some of the granddaughters and great-granddaughters of the early Methodist mothers in Israel stretched to the breaking point the holy sphere they had inherited.

The direction of the breakout was visible in the insouciant prose of Eliza Woodworth, a minister's daughter whose playful hyperbole revealed great personal ambition and an untamed exasperation at the constraints of her role. Woodworth wrote of two wasted literary opportunities that she believed would have won her great fame if only she had not allowed herself to be preempted by other researchers and writers while she wasted her time doing "this and that and the other little contemptible nonentity." She had a third opportunity, and part of the purpose of her essay was to claim priority in this last matter and so to secure some fraction of the renown she felt was her due. She intended to write an essay that would establish a heresy as a new truth. She was convinced that women in ancient times were no more degraded in relation to men than were women of her day in "enlightened" nations. The version of history given in the standard account of the doctrine of woman's sphere, a history that credited Christianity with progressive elevation of woman, was, she claimed, simply wrong.

Leaving aside whether or not Woodworth merited the glory she sought, what were the contemptible nonentities that had distracted her from her high destiny? She listed things like itinerating with her father's family, dusting parlors to meet the eye of some fastidious wife of one of her father's church trustees, paying and receiving visits, attending mite societies, and teaching Bible classes. In short, she found contemptible all the small ministries expected of a preacher's wife or daughter in support of a husband's or father's usefulness in his calling. Not for Eliza Woodworth were the constraints and sacrifices of woman's sphere. She wanted fame, and she was miffed that her father's occupation and the conventional expectations of small-minded people had kept her from it. After staking out her claim to her heresy about women's history, she ended with an exhortation to women like herself. "Let none bear away your laurels," she warned, "while you wait to perform non-essentials which you fancy duties." If a woman should be so doubly unfortunate as to be a minister's wife or daughter, she should forget all the dusting and visiting and meeting. It might cause great disturbances in her family and in the church. Never mind, said Woodworth. Though it caused heaven and earth to move, a woman with a mission must be true to herself. "*Work your work.* Do your duty by yourself and by your own nature, and He who made you *to be what you are,* will acquit you as to other people and other things."[68]

It is likely that Eliza Woodworth learned either to moderate her rhetoric or to endure some hard knocks in the course of her career in the late nineteenth century. Whatever happened to her later, when she wrote this essay, she parted company with most of her mission-minded evangelical sisters. Rather than merely expand woman's sphere as they tried to do, she burst it entirely.

13

The Family of God Gives Ground to the Salvation Machine

What became of the Methodist church and its distinctive rituals of social religion during and after its adoption of domestic ideology? I have argued that the practice of social religion helped people to transform their visions of themselves and their family life. As the hearts of Methodist believers followed the way of the cross, their eyes turned away from the image of the patriarch: the sovereign over his lineage and estate. Their eyes turned toward the image of home: the secluded and affectionate domestic circle constrained by the self-effacing love of the mother. They appropriated the words of the apostle Paul when he wrote of "the Spirit of adoption" that "beareth witness with our spirit, that we are the children of God." These words from Scripture conveyed their sense that Methodism housed the family of God. The outlooks and sentiments they learned as members of this spiritual family disposed them to evolve a vision of domesticity and increasingly to identify their literal families and home circles with the idea of the spiritual family.

They had another image of the church, however. Methodist apologists took from the prophet Ezekiel the image of wheels within wheels and used it to convey their sense of Methodism as a sublimely efficient machine for reforming the world and making it holy. From the beginning there was an ethos of *organization* in Methodism. American Methodism's first organization, of course, was the church itself, that salvation machine with all its whirling conferences, bishops, elders, and itinerants. Early in the history of American Methodism, the communal ethos of the church as family of God and the activist ethos of the church as instrument of salvation had seemed, if not identical, at least coterminal. As the nineteenth century matured, the growth of the church and the development of American society and economy caused this overlap to differentiate. A new and, to many Methodists, alien choice appeared, the choice between "objective" religious enterprise and "subjective" religious piety. Enterprise, furthermore, was in the ascendancy.

It is impossible to date precisely when this differentiation process began or ended. Russell Richey has found one of its earliest manifestations in the first decade of the nineteenth century. In Richey's reading, American Methodists adopted the camp meeting as a way of preserving the communal dimension of the old quarterly conference while allowing the quarterly meeting to handle the increasing load of church administration that came as a result of the growth of the church.[1] Another important part the process, as noted below, was the proliferation, beginning in the 1820s, of voluntary benevolent agencies connected with the church and requiring the organizing efforts of both laity and clergy. These agencies eventually came to seem like competitors or replacements for the class meeting, the decline of which, again as noted below, was being much decried in Methodist weekly papers by the 1830s. By midcentury, in any event, the differentiation was well established, and by the 1870s, the formal organizational dimension of the church was being touted by church leaders as its most important bond of unity.[2]

This differentiation of family of God from salvation machine can be analyzed from different perspectives. One is the nature of authority. Viewed from this perspective, the emergence of enterprise as the dominant motive in the church involved a change of religious authority from paternalistic to political and managerial. Another perspective concerns the nature of community. A church focused increasingly on enterprise began to value the activity-centered patterns of voluntary associations more than the feeling-centered rituals of social religion. These two perspectives on differentiation should give a reasonably comprehensive understanding of what became of the family of God and the way of the cross as they became domesticated.

First, consider the issue of authority. We have seen several instances of continuity and contrast between the culture of honor and the culture of early Methodist evangelicalism. In patterns of authority, Methodism once again both reacted against and reflected the culture of honor. The form of authority in both cultures was patriarchal. The early Methodist bishops and senior itinerant preachers exerted great, even oppressive, authority over Methodist laity and they did so self-consciously as *fathers* to their people. But their fatherhood was different from that of the gentry patriarchs. They made their claims to authority on a different basis and with a different aim.

The *basis* of Methodist patriarchy was the embodiment of the way of the cross in which the itinerant's self-sacrifice led paradoxically to great spiritual authority. The gentry of the eighteenth century were expected to possess physical strength, manly bearing, martial skill, landed wealth, education, and a variety of other privileges that made their claims to authority seem an expression of the natural order of creation. Early Methodist leaders, on the other hand, presented themselves as marginal patriarchs who were weak in the eyes of this world. They exercised the spiritual powers of the weak in order to symbolize in their persons and promote with their efforts the Methodist community of feeling. The majority of the Methodist people deferred as children to their spiritual fathers out of a sense of the fathers' greater spiritual gifts and sacrifices and out of the sense of family feeling and common interest that the experience of community created in the Methodist movement.

The *aim* of the Methodist patriarchy was instrumental. In the traditional vision, patriarchs exercised authority out of a sense of responsibility to a hierarchical cosmic order; they aimed to sustain the natural order of creation. In the early Methodist transformation of this vision, on the other hand, spiritual patriarchs aimed to promote the individual spiritual growth of their children and the collective advancement of their "Zion." During early conferences the preachers often reminded themselves of their aims by interrupting the business proceedings to hear one another share what God was doing for their souls. These events, in which the itinerant preachers most clearly realized their brotherhood, indicate how the great iron wheel of the itinerancy itself rotated around a hub of social religion. That hub, in turn, elevated the individual telling his story. There was a synthesis of business-like discipline and personal warmth in the brotherhood of preachers and in the church family at large. This synthesis roused in individuals a zeal for growth in grace, for self-transformation, and for the spiritual liberty and usefulness that aimed to transform the rest of the world. Transformation of the self and transformation of the world seemed each to be a function of the other. Religious authority among Methodists was for the sake of this expansive vision, and Methodist leaders saw themselves as instruments of the expansion.

The personal warmth of the family of God allowed leaders to soften their instrumental commands by wrapping them in the velvet of the patriarch's fatherly concern for his children. We have seen how the paternalism of Bishops Asbury and McKendree served to keep some reluctant young itinerants like Peter Cartwright, James Finley, and Jacob Young at their assigned posts. This same paternalism also enabled the early bishops to resist the pressure, which recurred among American Methodists from the 1770s onward, for a more democratic church polity. An example of such pressure was the agitation in the first decades of the nineteenth century for election of presiding elders by the preachers rather than their appointment by the bishops. To one preacher who advocated election, Bishop Asbury replied in the tones of wounded parental love: "I will freely turn my Back [*sic*], and my children shall freely speak against me or my administration. I wish difficulties may be brought. But am I not your Father? What have I said, what have I done?"[3] In the 1820s, the "reform" movement arose and brought together the most concerted effort yet to democratize the church polity. The reformers advocated lay representation to the conferences, rights of representation for local preachers, and election of presiding elders. Bishop McKendree responded to this movement with tones and attitude very similar to Asbury's parental remonstrances. Recall how he lectured reform leader George Brown in familial terms. The laity, claimed the bishop, were the children of the preachers by right of the fact that the preachers had converted the people. Lay representation was wrong because the children ought not to rule the fathers.[4]

Perhaps the simplest way to suggest the outlook that governed the bishops' responses is to say that for the bishops and those who followed them, the Methodist church was not primarily a polity—republican, democratic, or aristocratic. It was a family, and a spiritual family at that. This spiritual family was not a community of legally equal parties entering into a rationally self-interested social contract, nor was it, however much it appeared so to the reformers, a community defined by webs of despotic sovereignty and craven deference. It was, rather, a community of right affection set over against a world of evil passion and dedicated to the spiritual growth, evangelical usefulness, and ultimate salvation of each of the members. The fathers of this great family believed they exerted authority only to defend and extend its boundaries and to sustain its order of spiritual nurture and evangelical mission. To introduce the wrangling, factionalism, and pride of worldly politics into the spiritual family must have seemed a sacrilege to antireform Methodists. Peter Cartwright, himself no bishop and not averse to dabbling in the world's politics, evinced the old-side response to sacrilege in his own colorful use of the family metaphor; he termed the reform movement, "this little radical brat."[5]

The patterns of authority that sustained the Methodist family were rooted in the local society and its class meetings. The class leader was the first link in the long chain of pastoral care and command that reached all the way up to the office of bishop. A local society's shared sense of the legitimacy of a class leader's authority arose out of the subtle interplay of influence between the preacher who chose the leader and the people who submitted to his inquiry and supported his leadership. Prospective preachers, indeed, usually served as class leaders as part of an apprenticeship for their higher calling. Their acceptability as preachers depended in part upon their ability to help create the moving, melting times that people looked for in class meeting. If a man could not move the people, if he could not thereby beget new spiritual children, he could not rise to higher authority in the church family. There were similar tests all the way up the pastoral hierarchy. This reciprocity of influence among preachers, people, and leaders made possible a delicate synthesis of warmth and discipline in class meeting and in other structures of the church, like quarterly or annual conference. The people were, in a sense, disciplining themselves through their preachers and leaders, who embodied the consensus and interests of the family of God much as the patriarchs of the culture of honor were expected to embody the consensus and interests of their households and neighborhoods. The difference was that the community of honor was governing itself according to traditional models of selfhood, while the community of the saints was disciplining itself in systematic methods of individual spiritual transformation and personal self-control.

There was something inherently unstable about the use of patriarchy to inculcate individual self-control. The spiritual children of the Methodist fathers were likely to grow to a point where they no longer desired, and began rather to resent, the fathers' governance. The 1820s' reform movement alluded to above may be seen as a particularly visible eruption of this sort of resentment. Its symbolic significance extended beyond the relatively small number of people who eventually left the Methodist Episcopal church between 1828 and 1830 to form the Methodist Protestant church. It may be seen as an event that contributed to the demystification of Methodism's spiritual patriarchy.

As the reformers assaulted the institution of episcopacy, the bishops did some major political maneuvering to have reform leaders expelled. Many local congregations divided along the lines of reform vs. antireform. The Pittsburgh Methodist congregation had to schedule services at different hours for each side.[6] After all this it was difficult to take for granted that the spiritual patriarchs acted solely for the good of their children rather than for the prerogatives of their own power. The sacrilege had occurred; the leaven of factional politics had openly, visibly infected not only the expelled, but the old side as well. And just as the chain of pastoral care and command stretched from the episcopacy down to the class leader, so the disruption of spiritual family ties proceeded from General Conference meetings down to class meetings. The pressures grew to recognize that the family was not simply a family but also a polity and that the two things were not so easily identified with one another as early experiences of Methodist class meetings and conferences had once suggested. Fellowship was one thing, administration another.

This growing sense of distance between church polity and church family could only have been widened by another trend that changed the character of both the ministry and the local congregation. In the later decades of the antebellum period it became increasingly common for Methodist preachers to be assigned to "stations" rather than circuits; that is, they became pastors to single congregations. Their pastoral superintendence became constant rather than periodic. The pattern of settled ministry brought into congregational life the full-time presence of professional ministers whose main reference group was their fellow ministers, especially their supervisors in the episcopal hierarchy. This presence made the congregation less the lay-run and locally controlled religious community and more a unit in the ecclesiastical organization.[7] One manifestation of this change seems to have been the decline of the class meeting with its leader as lay pastor, who, along with the local preacher and lay exhorter, probably seemed superfluous in the presence of the full-time pastor.[8] Pastors and episcopal administrators might still present themselves as the fathers of the church's family fellowship, but the changing character of community in the church was making this self-presentation less plausible.

As we turn to consider the change in patterns of community in mid-nineteenth-century Methodism, let us observe some historical ironies connected with the church's 1820 General Conference. At this conference, the first specialized American Methodist mission society won recognition, and Bishop-elect Joshua Soule intimidated the delegates into suspending a measure for the election of presiding elders. Soule's move precipitated a decade-long slide into the Methodist Protestant schism. The recognition of a specialized mission agency undermined a longstanding assumption that the Methodist church was itself constituted as a mission agency and had no need to divide itself for the sake of mission. This assumption, and Methodism's lower-middle-class and southern and western center of gravity, had delayed Methodist participation in the great surge of largely upper-middle-class and northeastern Protestant benevolence and reform that influenced much of antebellum America.[9] The establishment of the missionary society, however, marked a trend for increasing Methodist involvement in this aspect of freedom's ferment. The Tract Society, the Sunday School Union, various temperance societies, and assorted other voluntary associations all engrossed the attention of growing numbers of Methodist laity and clergy. At first largely lay-run organizations with ties of communication rather than of accountability to the ecclesiastical structure, these various societies became the occasion for the transformation of the Methodist Episcopal church into a modern corporate bureaucracy in the decades following the Civil War. The first stage of this transformation occurred in the late 1860s and early 1870s when the societies were turned into agencies of the General Conference. One of the ironies of this development was that it made logical and necessary the admission of lay delegates to the General Conference, one of the key demands of the 1820s' reform movement. The greater and more subtle irony lay in the fact that the bishops and the old-side preachers of the 1820s had rejected the divisiveness of the electoral politics favored by the reformers only to admit the beginnings of a different sort of divisiveness. They let in the modern compartmentalizing divisiveness of bureaucracy in which various specialized agencies might each create its own subculture and in which leadership high up in the organization might lose touch with the concerns of laity and others further down the chain of command.

To be sure, there was a unifying dynamic concomitant with this compartmentalizing trend. Activism in benevolence, claimed its proponents, gave the church a sense of common purpose, renewed the "old connectional bonds" of Methodism, and tangibly demonstrated her fraternal love and harmony. Benevolent agencies became the new means of cultivating that "social power" of which class meeting and the other rituals of social religion had made Methodists so profoundly aware.[10] The similarities and differences between these two types of engines of social power are worth contemplating.

Class meeting required members to internalize a regimen of emotional and behavioral self-control that issued in what was felt to be great love and unity among those who suffered through the regimen together. The inner dynamics of this process involved an abiding sense of numinous presence within, the "witness of the Spirit." Such a sense of presence entailed a rather severe constriction of inner autonomy but also issued in restless energy and initiative. These psychological dynamics generated an imperative to usefulness, a usefulness that implied the need to generalize self-control to the control of others. Thus an evangelistic zeal fueled periodic revivals and gave opportunity to initiate others into the same regimen, with all its rewards in feeling and fellowship.

This impulse to generalize self-control to the control of others could not be contained within the undifferentiated revival project. There were too many different kinds of people (children, Indians, "the poor," blacks, immigrants) and too many particular problems of control (intemperance, sexual vice, Sabbath-breaking, gambling) to be encompassed by just one strategy. The process of moving beyond simple revivalism to more complex benevolence required evangelical activism to take precedence over communal fellowship. Class meeting was a dialectic of communion and activism that ultimately subordinated activism to communion. The point of religion, after all, was to get people to heaven, and heaven was seen as an eternal rest in a familial bliss that found its truest reflection in the precious seasons and melting times of social religion. Such times generated activism, to be sure, but such activism was ultimately for the sake of the communion of the saints.

The spirit breathed by the Methodist corporate organization, on the other hand, was relentlessly activist. Alpha J. Kynett, a leader of the move to consolidate Methodist benevolence, declared that the command of Christ and the life-impulse were both "Go," and that the result of both was " 'organized going—the church *as a body* obeying the command of its Master and Head, and the impulse of its life.' "[11] In the bureaucratization of American Methodism, as in the development of Methodist women's consciousness and activity, the way of the cross that had once *led* home was now tending to *leave* home.

It was important, of course, that there be a home to leave. The chief burden of this study has been to show that the spiritual family of God disposed its members, by means of social religion, to see their literal family lives in terms of a sacred home circle set over against a world that was hostile, but also susceptible, to its influences. This affectionate but disciplined Christian home circle, furthermore, was supposed to cultivate the sort of methodical, self-controlled, hard-working, and aspiring character that would, in fact, seek to leave home for wider fields of mission. In short, the early Methodist religious practices helped to create the domestic conditions for the so-called modern mentality, a mentality centered upon "the ambition for rational manipulation combined with expanding aspirations."[12] This modern mentality and its domestic matrix were necessary conditions for the bureaucratic incorporation of the church. The growth of personal independence, rationality, and aspiration, however, was incompatible with the continued paternalistic superintendence over behavior, thought, and feeling that was built into the class-meeting structure.

It does appear that Methodists from about the 1830s onward avoided more and more the close scrutiny and discipline peculiar to class meeting. One way they did this was to keep adding members to existing classes and to resist the efforts of the preachers to divide the class into smaller units. The leaders of large classes, fumed one preacher, "know not whether they [the members] walk upright, on all-fours, or crawl, like the reptile in the filth of sin."[13] Evidently there was safety in numbers for persons who might otherwise writhe like reptiles under the close inquiry that smaller classes made possible. The swollen class memberships resulted in overlong meetings, stilted testimony performances, vague and evasive answers to inquiry, and a general sense of futility that caused many to stay away altogether.[14]

Yet the Methodist people still desired the good times of family feeling that the early class-meeting and love-feast rituals had afforded. To fulfill this yearning a variety of social meetings with names like "general class meeting" or just "speaking meetings" were added in ad hoc fashion to the standard Methodist ritual fare. These events allowed good times without the pressures of close inquiry or the requirement that everyone speak.[15] The diffuse and attenuated fellowship characteristic of these meetings, moreover, eventually was felt to be more appropriate to occasional seasons of revival than to the weekly rhythm of church life. Thus the northern bishops, in their 1856 pastoral address, lamely insisted on retaining the old rules regarding class meeting on the grounds that during revivals, "the class-room, long neglected, is filled with Christians eager to enjoy this means of grace."[16]

No doubt the bishops intended this observation as a telling argument for a return to regular class attendance. At mid-century, however, Methodists had a lot of other things on their minds. Their characteristic communal ferment was bubbling out into many specialized activities of mission, benevolence, reform, and education. A diffuse "fraternal feeling" that seemed to pervade their great church and its voluntary agencies seemed a sufficient, if not wholly satisfactory, distillation of the intense religious community of a half century earlier. In the process, class meeting, originally the generative center of early Methodist community and reform, came to seem like just one more voluntary activity among others.[17] Thus G. W. Maley, a prominent Methodist preacher of Ohio and Kentucky, noted approvingly the 1866 action of the Methodist Episcopal Church, South, no longer to require regular attendance at class meetings. "They are retained as a means of grace, but only as a voluntary association—very right I think."[18]

Class meetings had served, after all, as a major means of resocializing adult converts into the ethos of evangelical self-control. One might expect that the spiritual children of the early Methodist patriarchs would more and more take the lessons of evangelical self-control for granted. They would make these lessons the standard fare of instruction for their own literal children in a school-like context and find less need to resocialize adults in a revival context. This gradual shift from adult to child socialization would have contributed to the decline of class meeting. The formation of the Methodist Sunday School Union in 1827 may be seen, then, as a major marker of this trend.[19] By 1859, the Illinois Conference, while still insisting on the indispensability of class meetings, was recommending that classes meet on weekdays "where Sunday Schools and other religious exercises of the Sabbath require or make it expedient."[20] The mature results of the trend were obvious in the 1878 "Memorial Discourse" of Leonard Gurley, a fifty-year veteran preacher of Ohio, who summarized the differences between early and modern Methodism:

> Early Methodism was *subjective*; personal conversion, personal experience, was the theme of pulpit, class, and love-feast. Modern Methodism is more *objective*: it does not undervalue personal experience, but it devotes its attention more fully to Christian activities. Our people talk less in class, but they work more in the Sunday-school.

Not at all nostalgic, the old veteran judged the modern Methodist Episcopal church to be "better, stronger, and more efficient, than it [had been] . . . in the days of Asbury and M'Kendree; . . . and . . . equally pure."[21]

Not everyone among Gurley's fellow ministers was as sanguine as he. The Southern Illinois Annual Conference, unable to revive the institution of class meeting, institutionalized instead a yearly expression of anxiety over its decline. The Conference *Minutes* include annual reports from a standing committee on class meetings from 1877 until 1913. Even after the reports no longer appeared on the record, the Conference retained the committee on its roster of standing committees until 1919. The 1893 committee did, however, eschew the hand-wringing to affirm what had been obvious for a generation or more: class meetings had been superseded by various specialized agencies.[22] To a committee especially appointed to review the welfare of Ohio Conference Methodism, however, the change affirmed by Gurley was exactly the problem. Working from a questionnaire circulated to the twenty-two stations and fifty circuits of the conference, the committee compiled a detailed and devastating report running to thirteen printed pages. The report ended on an evaluative note very different from Gurley's, but with a descriptive summary similar to his contrast between "subjective" early Methodism and "objective" modern Methodism:

> There is much Church attachment, enterprize [*sic*], and religious sentiment, but little spirituality. . . . The least promising feature for the future of Methodism within our bounds . . . is, that every material and social interest is in advance of experience and spirituality; that we are mare tenacious for our usages, for our doctrines, for our economy than for our progress in Christian experience.[23]

These words were written at the dawn of the age of organization in American society and culture. The Protestant churches, by some accounts, were seedbeds of this cultural transformation that led prominent Americans to see in specialization, centralization, and bureaucratization the promise of unlimited effectiveness in God's service and of unceasing improvement of the human prospect.[24] This age, observed a Methodist editor, was one that required men to be wide awake and ever busy lest they be left behind in the race. The church itself abetted this busyness, leading the saints to overlook the cultivation of personal piety in the social means of grace as they immersed themselves in the rush of religious enterprise for the outward extension of the church.[25] The growth of the church and the concomitant development of society and economy seem to have opened up a choice that was foreign to the consciousness of the early Methodists, who had constructed the stark alternatives of the family of God versus the culture of honor. The new choice was a more subtle one between "objective" enterprises and "subjective" social religion and personal piety. No faithful church person really desired a forced choice between these two sorts of pursuit; subjective social religion and piety were supposed to be the bedrock upon which all objective enterprises rested. In the way Methodists were coming to organize their lives, however, the desired coordination of piety and enterprise was becoming more and more an opposition.

The very domestication of social religion and piety that Methodism had helped bring about, however, encouraged this opposition. In an important sense, the Christian home had superseded the class meeting and other forms of social religion. Class meeting had cultivated a subjective probing and self-examination in a context characterized by seclusion from the world and by intense emotional identification among the participants. Later Methodists found the domestic home circle a better setting in which to cultivate the introspective and autonomous self. The religious home and pious parents, especially the mother, could respond more sensitively to the individual differences of temperament among personalities. Efforts to subject everyone to the same rigors of examination and testimony in class meeting came to seem more and more awkward and oppressive.

The inadequacies felt in the old class-meeting forms were evident in the objections that apologists for the old usages attempted to refute. I have noted these objections earlier and suggested that the threat of embarrassment or social shame which they imply was a condition which led, by the paradoxes of self-surrender, to feelings of inner assurance of salvation and spiritual intimacy in early Methodist social religion. It appears likely, however, that by the time the apologists began to write in the pages of the various *Advocates*, the pressures to conform to expected patterns of performance in class meeting were alienating people from their inner selves more than acquainting them with them. Thus some objected that class meetings encouraged people to tell falsehoods, while apologists replied, "No more than an oath in court tempts to perjury."[26] They obviously missed the point. A people unused to privacy and reared in the oral forms of discourse in the culture of honor might find a court-like inquiry into their inward feelings the sort of shock that jolted them into a new state of self-awareness. A people grown accustomed to such self-awareness and the domestic privacy that went with it might find such inquiry humiliating without promise of relief. Such people did not attend class meeting. They either stayed home, perhaps to pursue more private forms of subjective religion, or they went to the Sunday school or missionary society meeting to pursue the public, objective enterprises of their religion.

There were those within Methodism, of course, who reacted against the bureaucratization of the church. They lamented the demise of class meeting and decried the worldliness and lack of spirituality that seemed to afflict the church as a consequence. They were not ready to assent to domestication of religion if such domestication implied a privatized piety that acquiesced to the worldly operations of "ecclesiastical machinery." They wanted a vital piety that would suffuse the whole of church enterprise and subject all operations to the imperatives they ascribed to the Holy Spirit.

They found in the mid-nineteenth-century Holiness Revival a fitting means to articulate their criticisms of the church and to attempt to restore what they felt had been lost.[27] Their central doctrine was the long-standing Methodist belief in a second spiritual crisis after conversion. The practices whereby they promoted their doctrine gave a central role to testimony, both spoken and written, and to various forms of social religion. There were home meetings for the promotion of holiness, most of them patterned after the famous "Tuesday Meeting" associated with the name of Phoebe Palmer. After the Civil War, these Methodist holiness advocates revitalized the camp meeting and, within its format, the love feast. They also established their own voluntary association, the National Camp Meeting Association for the Promotion of Holiness, that stimulated the formation of many regional and local associations with the same purpose.[28]

This new holiness movement did, in fact, restore certain features of early American Methodism and its rituals of social religion. We have seen how the early Methodist community used these rituals to draw a line of identity between itself and the world. "The world," for Methodism at the beginning of the nineteenth century, was the traditional culture of honor. At mid-century, the new Methodist holiness advocates drew yet another line between themselves and the world, but "the world" for them was the culture of corporate bureaucratic enterprise with its imperatives to rational calculation and specialist expertise. And this new line of distinction ran between individuals and groups who were all ostensibly attached to the mainstream Methodist churches. Schism was on the horizon. That, however, is a story for a different book.

In closing, it is important to observe that this study, especially in its later chapters, has told the story of a fall from Eden. As Russell Richey has so cogently observed, there was an innocent, Edenic quality about the early Methodist forms of community and efforts at reform and a kind of fall in the changes they underwent in the early nineteenth century.[29] This study has corroborated and extended both parts of Richey's observation. Methodists believed they experienced heaven on earth in their class meetings and love feasts and intended to effect a heavenly reform throughout the American continent. Their reforming impulse was readily bifurcated, however, into domestic piety and bureaucratic enterprise. They lost the realization of the harmony they sought "between means and ends, structures and their purposes, business and religiosity."[30] As there was a snake in Eden, so there was ambiguity in Methodism's quest for a holy community.

Several scholars have considered the liberalizing, even radical, implications of the Methodist quest for holiness and have pointed to its reformist, feminist, liberationist aspects.[31] The present study, however, must be seen as qualifying such claims for the socially progressive impulse of Methodist evangelicalism. The impulse was ambiguous. If it created a community of those who identified with the crucified and if it relativized social class distinctions, it also was readily domesticated. Domestication lent legitimacy to the functional compartmentalizing of private and public life and to the new sorts of distinctions between human beings entailed by the growth of modern formal organizations. If it gave common people the opportunity to establish their own religious life, to think and act for themselves, it also catered to their need for charismatic and authoritarian "fathers" who would perpetuate dependence in their spiritual "children" and a nondemocratic ethos in what they called the "family of God." If it freed women to claim their own moral and spiritual identity, it also granted such selfhood only on the paradoxical condition of self-denial. Insistence on self-denial tended to keep women confined to their traditional domestic sphere, however widened in significance that sphere had become. If it freed human beings to become more outwardly self-controlled and more inwardly self-aware, it did so with the demand for a self-constriction that sought the narrow way and allowed little leeway for playful or pleasure-seeking exploration of the self or of the world.

The public, political significance of Methodism must be seen in similarly ambiguous terms. As it fell from its early Edenic state, nineteenth-century

Methodist evangelicalism seems to have become oriented chiefly to the organizing of the inner self and its domestic arena. It claimed social and political significance to the degree that social and political issues strengthened or threatened the preferred organization of either the self or its domestic space. When threats were perceived, as they were in the nineteenth-century temperance movement, a characteristic sort of "cultural politics" was the result.[32] It was a politics in quest of purity that could take on the ugly dimensions of nativism when whole categories of people, such as Roman Catholics or non-British immigrants, became identified with the impure.

It is beyond the reach of descriptive studies like this to argue for normative judgments about early Methodism's adequacy as an ethical vision and virtuous way of life. Here it is appropriate only to point out that the history of Methodist evangelicalism does not lend itself easily to any moral or political agenda, be it progressive or conservative. Rather, understanding evangelicalism in the history and culture of the United States requires an appreciation of the ambiguities involved in a Methodist way of the cross that once led home.

NOTES

When citing works in the notes, shortened entries have been used after the first full reference. Frequently cited works have been identified by the following abbreviations:

CCA	*Central Christian Advocate*
DHL	Daniel Hitt Letters
GSPP	George Shane Phillips Papers
GWMP	George Washington Maley Papers
JBFL	James B. Finley Letters
LR	*Ladies Repository and Gatherings of the West*
PCJ	*Pittsburgh Conference Journal*
S&SWWP	Samuel and S. W. Williams Papers
WCA	*Western Christian Advocate*
WCM	*Western Christian Monitor*

PREFACE

1. Grant Wacker, "Searching for Norman Rockwell: Popular Evangelicalism in Contemporary America," in *The Evangelical Tradition in America*, ed. Leonard I. Sweet (Macon, Ga.: Mercer University Press, 1984), 289–315.

2. The sect, now predictably turned denomination, is Seventh-Day Adventism. Seventh-Day Adventism's founding prophet, Ellen Gould Harmon White, was a Methodist and constructed her religious life in typically Methodist ways. When she was in her teens she and her parents were expelled from the church for their involvement with the premillennial advent movement of William Miller in the early 1840s.

3. Sydney E. Mead, *The Lively Experiment: The Shaping of Christianity in America* (New York: Harper and Row, 1963), 90.

INTRODUCTION

1. Lee here paraphrases Luke 15:27. As in the early American Methodist tradition, however, all direct biblical quotations cited within this book are from the *Authorized King James Version*.

2. Peter Cartwright, *Autobiography of Peter Cartwright*, (Nashville: Abingdon Press, 1984; 1856), 40–41. Cartwright's use of the term "Dutchman" probably reflects a common misunderstanding of the German *Deutsch*.

3. Elie Halevy, *The Birth of Methodism in England*, trans. and ed. Bernard Semmel (Chicago: University of Chicago Press, 1971); Bernard Semmel, *The Methodist Revolution* (New York: Basic Books, 1973); David Hempton, *Methodism and Politics in British Society, 1750–1850* (Stanford: Stanford University Press, 1984).

4. My understanding of social religion as designed to create a "community of feeling" has been crystallized by Sandra Sizer, *Gospel Hymns and Social Religion: The Rhetoric of Nineteenth-Century Revivalism*(Philadelphia: Temple University Press, 1978).

5. Russell E. Richey, *Early American Methodism* (Bloomington, Ind.: Indiana University Press, 1991), 47–64.

6. Edwin Scott Gaustad, *Historical Atlas of Religion in America*, rev. ed. (New York: Harper and Row, 1976), 75–80.

7. Winthrop S. Hudson, "The Methodist Age in America," *Methodist History* 12 (April 1974): 4–15.

8. Gaustad, *Historical Atlas*, 165.

9. C. R. Lovell, *Methodist Family Manual* (Cincinnati: Swormstedt and Poe, 1852), iii.

10. A Young Lady, "Home," WCA, 12 Aug. 1836, 64.

11. Hannah More, "Woman," *LR*, May 1841, 137.

12. D. W., "Woman's Sphere," *LR*, Feb. 1841, 38.

13. Carl N. Degler, *At Odds: Women and the Family in America from the Revolution to the Present* (New York: Oxford University Press, 1980); Colleen McDannell, *The Christian Home in Victorian America, 1840–1900* (Bloomington, Ind.: Indiana University Press, 1986).

14. Mary P. Ryan, *Cradle of the Middle Class: The Family in Oneida County, New York, 1790–1865* (Cambridge: Cambridge University Press, 1981).

15. Edward Shorter, *The Making of the Modern Family* (New York: Basic Books, 1975); Lawrence E. Stone, *The Family, Sex, and Marriage in England, 1500–1800* (New York: Harper and Row, 1977); Randolph Trumbach, *The Rise of the Egalitarian Family: Aristocratic Kinship and Domestic Relations in Eighteenth-Century England* (New York: Academic Press, 1978); Jay Fliegelman, *Prodigals and Pilgrims: The American Revolution against Patriarchal Authority, 1750–1800* (New York: Cambridge University Press, 1982).

16. Donald G. Mathews, *Religion in the Old South* (Chicago: University of Chicago Press, 1977), and "Evangelical America—The Methodist Ideology," in *Rethinking Methodist History: A Bicentennial Historical Consultation*, ed. Russell E. Richey and Kenneth E. Rowe (Nashville: Kingswood Books, 1985), 91–99; Vincent Harding, "Out of the Cauldron of Struggle: Black Religion and the Search for a New America," in *Religion: North American Style*, ed. Patrick H. McNamara (Belmont, Calif.: Wadsworth Publishing, 1984), 252–64.

1. PATRIARCHY AND THE CULTURE OF HONOR

1. Richey, *Early American Methodism*, 47–64.

2. John Mack Faragher, *Women and Men on the Overland Trail* (New Haven: Yale University Press, 1979).

3. Examples of the transformations wrought by Methodist-style evangelicalism in New England culture areas are described in Ryan, *Cradle of the Middle Class*; Paul E. Johnson, *A Shopkeeper's Millennium: Society and Revivals in Rochester, New York, 1815–1837* (New York: Hill and Wang, 1978); and Richard Shiels, "The Methodist Circuit-Rider in the Second Great Awakening in New England" (paper read at conference, Reexamining Revivalism: The Wesleyan/Holiness Perspective, 10–11 June 1988, at Asbury Theological Seminary, Wilmore, Ky.).

4. Rhys Isaac, *The Transformation of Virginia, 1740–1790* (Williamsburg, Va.: The Institute of Early American History and Culture; Chapel Hill: University of North Carolina Press, 1982), 20–21. Isaac's work provides the center of the analysis of gentry culture presented here.

5. In Max Weber's tripartite classification of traditional, charismatic and legal-rational authority, gentry authority was "patrimonial," a subtype of traditional authority. See Max Weber, *The Theory of Social and Economic Organization*, trans. A. M. Henderson and Talcott Parsons (New York: Oxford University Press, 1947; Free Press paperback ed., 1964), 346–48.

6. Isaac, *Transformation of Virginia*, 30.

7. Charles S. Sydnor, *American Revolutionaries in the Making: Political Practices in Washington's Virginia* (New York: Free Press, 1965), 41.

8. J. R. Pole, *Foundations of American Independence: 1763–1815*, History of American Society Series, ed. Jack P. Greene (Indianapolis: Bobbs Merrill, 1972), 163–64; Sydnor, *American Revolutionaries*, 42.

9. Sydnor, *American Revolutionaries*, 66–69, 74–85.

10. Isaac, *Transformation of Virginia*, 308–309; Philip Greven, *The Protestant Temperament: Patterns of Child-Rearing, Religious Experience, and the Self in Early America* (New York: Alfred A. Knopf, 1977), 194–95, 297.

11. This discussion of the more archaic elements of honor depends largely upon the work of Bertram Wyatt-Brown, *Southern Honor: Ethics and Behavior in the Old South* (New York: Oxford University Press, 1982); on the theme of resignation to fate, see 27–33. See also T. H. Breen, "Horses and Gentlemen: The Cultural Significance of Gambling among the Gentry of Virginia," *William and Mary Quarterly*, 3d ser., 34 (1977): 246–47; Faragher, *Women and Men on the Overland Trail*, 146–60; and Lewis Saum, *The Popular Mood of Pre-Civil War America*, Contributions in American Studies, no. 46 (Westport, Conn.: Greenwood Press, 1980).

12. Wyatt-Brown, *Southern Honor*, chaps. 2 and 3.

13. John R. Stilgoe, *Common Landscape of America, 1580–1845* (New Haven: Yale University Press, 1982), 44–58, 71–74, 77–83.

14. Isaac, "Evangelical Revolt: The Nature of the Baptists' Challenge to Traditional Order in Virginia, 1765–1775," *William and Mary Quarterly*, 3d ser., 31 (July 1974): 349–50.

15. Isaac, *Transformation of Virginia*, 58–68; Greven, *Protestant Temperament*, 328–29; Donald G. Mathews, *Religion in the Old South* (Chicago: University of Chicago Press, 1977), 3–10.

16. Isaac, *Transformation of Virginia*, 88–94; A. G. Roeber, "Authority, Law, and Custom: The Rituals of Court Day in Tidewater Virginia, 1720–1750," *William and Mary Quarterly*, 3d ser., 37 (1980): 29–52.

17. Isaac, *Transformation of Virginia*, 94–104; Sydnor, *American Revolutionaries*, 26–27, 44–59.

18. Wyatt-Brown, *Southern Honor*, 39–41; Isaac, *Transformation of Virginia*, 104–10.

19. The idea of rhetoric employed here derives from Kenneth Burke, *A Rhetoric of Motives* (Berkeley: University of California Press, 1969), xii-xiv, 21, 43–46, 131, 141.

20. Sydnor, *American Revolutionaries*, 29, 34; Plebeius [Samuel Williams], "Leaves from an Autobiography," *LR*, June 1852, 223–24.

21. Isaac, *Transformation of Virginia*, 65, 104–14, 131–33; Sydnor, *American Revolutionaries*, 53–59, 61, 67; Carl Bridenbaugh, *Myths and Realities: Societies of the Colonial South* (New York: Atheneum, 1963), 16; Rhys Isaac, "Preachers and Patriots: Popular Culture and the Revolution in Virginia," in *The American Revolution: Explorations in the History of American Radicalism*, ed. Alfred A. Young (DeKalb, Ill.: Northern Illinois University Press, 1976), 147–48.

22. Erik Erikson, *Toys and Reasons: Stages in the Ritualization of Experience* (New York: W. W. Norton, 1977), 87–91.

23. Wyatt-Brown, *Southern Honor*, 74–87; Isaac, *Transformation of Virginia*, 113–14.

24. Wyatt-Brown, *Southern Honor*, 50–55.

25. Isaac, *Transformation of Virginia*, 354–55; Daniel Blake Smith, *Inside the Great House: Planter Family Life in Eighteenth-Century Chesapeake Society* (Ithaca, N.Y.: Cornell University Press, 1980), 61–68; Mary Beth Norton, *Liberty's Daughters: The Revolutionary Experience of American Women, 1750–1800* (Boston: Little, Brown, and Co., 1980), 110–17.

26. Isaac, *Transformation of Virginia*, 70–87; Bridenbaugh, *Myths and Realities*, 25–

26; Edmund S. Morgan, *Virginians at Home: Family Life in the Eighteenth Century* (Williamsburg, Va.: William Byrd Press, 1952), 18–19, 77–82.

27. Daniel Blake Smith, *Inside the Great House*, 55–68.

28. Norton, *Liberty's Daughters*, 100–109. Daniel Blake Smith has a different reading of father-son ties, but it suffers from a tendency to read the present into the past and to ignore the significant differences in the meaning of actions created by the cultural context of honor. See Daniel Blake Smith, *Inside the Great House*, chap. 3. For a more sensitive reading focused somewhat later in southern history, see Wyatt-Brown, *Southern Honor*, chap. 6.

29. Norton, *Liberty's Daughters*, 100–109; Daniel Blake Smith, *Inside the Great House*, 76–79.

30. Daniel Blake Smith, *Inside the Great House*, 69–79; Norton, *Liberty's Daughters*, 4–20, 26–39; Wyatt-Brown, *Southern Honor*, 247–53.

2. REPUBLICANISM AND REFORM

1. Robert Emory, *History of the Discipline of the Methodist Episcopal Church* (New York: G. Lane and C. B. Tippett, 1845), 90.

2. Classic delineations of republicanism in America are Bernard Bailyn, *The Ideological Origins of the American Revolution* (Cambridge, Mass.: Harvard University Press, 1967) and Gordon S. Wood, *The Creation of the American Republic, 1776–1787* (Chapel Hill: University of North Carolina Press, 1969). For the complications that have arisen around the ideological interpretations of Bailyn and Wood, see Robert E. Shalhope, "Republicanism and Early American Historiography," *William and Mary Quarterly*, 3d ser., 39 (1982): 334–56.

3. Bailyn, *Ideological Origins*, 55–60; Wood, *Creation*, 18–28.

4. The reader might question whether these archaic themes would have motivated northern colonists as well as those from the South where the culture of honor seems to have been strongest and most persistent. Wyatt-Brown, the historian of southern honor, believes that popular understandings of honor were widely shared in the North and the South during the Revolution and helped unite the colonies. Only later did the North continue its development of an urban, bourgeois culture where formal law and personal respectability supplanted the norms of honor. See *Southern Honor*, 18–21, 40–41.

5. Wood, *Creation*, 68–69, and "Republicanism as a Revolutionary Ideology," in *The Role of Ideology in the American Revolution*, ed. John R. Howe (New York: Holt, Rinehart, and Winston, 1970), 86.

6. J. E. Crowley, *This Sheba, Self: The Conceptualization of Economic Life in Eighteenth-Century America*, Johns Hopkins University Studies in Historical and Political Science, no. 92 (Baltimore: Johns Hopkins University Press, 1974), 1–12; 50–65.

7. Isaac, *Transformation of Virginia*, 194–98.

8. On the fear of effeminacy, see Greven, *Protestant Temperament*, 335–37, 348–54; and Linda Kerber, *Women of the Republic: Intellect and Ideology in Revolutionary America* (Chapel Hill: University of North Carolina Press, 1980), 31. On the complaint of parental tyranny, see Jay Fliegelman, *Prodigals and Pilgrims*. On the need for frugality in rulers, see Wyatt-Brown, *Southern Honor*, 70–71.

9. Wood, *Creation*, 109; Robert Kelley, *The Cultural Pattern in American Politics: The First Century* (New York: Alfred A. Knopf, 1979), 58–63.

10. For evidence of a "feudal revival" that exacerbated the fears of many colonial Americans, see Rowland Berthoff and John M. Murrin, "Feudalism, Communalism, and the Yeoman Freeholder: The American Revolution Considered as a Social Accident," in *Essays on the American Revolution*, ed. Stephen G. Kurtz and James H. Hutson (Chapel Hill: University of North Carolina Press, 1973), 256–88.

11. Kelley, *Cultural Pattern*, 81–84; 98–99; Fliegelman, *Prodigals and Pilgrims*, chap. 7; Wyatt-Brown, *Southern Honor*, 66–69.

12. Norton, *Liberty's Daughters*, 4–20, 155–70, 195–227; Kerber, *Women of the Republic*, 35–67.

13. Norton, *Liberty's Daughters*, 239–42.

14. Ibid., 242–50.

15. Paul C. Nagel, *This Sacred Trust: American Nationality, 1798–1890* (New York: Oxford University Press, 1971), 13; Benjamin Rush, "A Plan for the Establishment of Public Schools and the Diffusion of Knowledge in Pennsylvania; to which are added Thoughts upon the Mode of Education, Proper in a Republic," in *Essays on Education*, ed. Frederick Rudolph (Cambridge, Mass.: Harvard University Press, 1965), 22; Noah Webster, "On the Education of Youth," in *Essays on Education*, 69.

16. Ruth H. Bloch, "American Feminine Ideals in Transition: The Rise of the Moral Mother, 1785–1815," *Feminist Studies* 4 (1978): 117–18.

17. Norton, *Liberty's Daughters*, 242–50; Bloch, "American Feminine Ideals," 117.

18. Kerber, *Women of the Republic*, 189ff.; Norton, *Liberty's Daughters*, 287–94; Leonard I. Sweet, "The Female Seminary Movement and Woman's Mission in Antebellum America," *Church History* 54 (1985): 41–55.

19. Norton, *Liberty's Daughters*, 263–72; Kerber, *Women of the Republic*, 209–21.

20. Kerber, *Women of the Republic*, 110–11; Bloch, "American Feminine Ideals," 118–19.

21. Kerber, *Women of the Republic*, 99–113; Norton, *Liberty's Daughters*, 177–94, 287–94.

22. Robert Kelley has developed a typology of republicanisms in the Confederation and Constitutional periods which informs this discussion; see *Cultural Pattern*, chap. 3. Such typologies must be taken somewhat lightly. There are always other ways to draw the lines, and inconvenient evidence emerges once they are drawn, as Robert Shalhope's effort to untangle the historiography of republicanism clearly shows. Kelley's typology has the advantage of attempting to encompass all regions of the nation. It also is sensitive to religion as a cultural force.

23. Fred J. Hood, *Reformed America: The Middle and Southern States, 1783–1837* (University, Ala.: University of Alabama Press, 1980), chap. 4.

24. For arguments concerning the early republican sentiments of Methodist leadership, see Nathan Bangs, *A History of the Methodist Episcopal Church* (New York: T. Mason and G. Lane, 1838), vol. 1, 280–88; and James B. Finley, *Autobiography of Rev. James B. Finley*, ed. W. P. Strickland (Cincinnati: Methodist Book Concern, 1854), 392–93.

25. This interpretation follows Richey, *Early American Methodism*, 33–46.

26. Quoted in Emory, *History of the Discipline*, 337.

27. Richey, *Early American Methodism*, 42–44.

28. For excellent analyses of quarterly meeting, camp meeting, and love feast as displays of Methodist community, see Richey, *Early American Methodism*, 21–32; and Richard O. Johnson, "The Development of the Love Feast in Early American Methodism," *Methodist History* 19 (1981): 65–83.

29. On the distinction between utopian and millennial concepts see Leonard I. Sweet, "Millennialism in America: Recent Studies," *Theological Studies* 40 (1979): 520; and Sacvan Bercovitch, *The Puritan Origins of the American Self* (New Haven: Yale University Press, 1975), 137–48.

30. On the oxymoronic compound of affliction and exaltation as the link between conversion and millennium, see James West Davidson, *The Logic of Millennial Thought: Eighteenth-Century New England* (New Haven: Yale University Press, 1977), 129–41, 232–54, 280–97; Nathan O. Hatch, *The Sacred Cause of Liberty: Republican*

Thought and the Millennium in Revolutionary New England (New Haven: Yale University Press, 1977), 118–38, 146–70; and Bercovitch, *Puritan Origins*, passim.

31. Hood, *Reformed America*, 7–26.

32. Ibid., 22–47, 70–81, 85–87, 105–106.

33. Finley, *Autobiography*, 404–405.

34. "Children's Department: A Hymn—L. M.," *WCA*, 24 June 1836, 36.

35. "Independence Hymn," *WCA*, 8 May 1840, 12.

36. See, for example, the aggressive camp-meeting song quoted by William Warren Sweet in his *Religion in the Development of American Culture, 1765–1840* (1952; Gloucester, Mass.: Peter Smith, 1963), 158–59.

37. Hood, *Reformed America*, 88–112.

38. Ibid., 136–68.

39. On the opposition roused by the associations and activities of the Reformed, and for analyses of the social and cultural issues involved, see Hood, *Reformed America*, 138–40; Johnson, *Shopkeeper's Millennium*, 37–94; Ryan, *Cradle of the Middle Class*, 108–27; and Nathan O. Hatch, *The Democratization of American Christianity* (New Haven: Yale University Press, 1989), 170–79.

40. Kelley, *Cultural Pattern*, 84, 96–97; Henry Nash Smith, *Virgin Land: The American West as Symbol and Myth* (Cambridge, Mass.: Harvard University Press, 1950), especially book three, "The Garden of the World."

41. Joseph P. Tarkington, *Autobiography of Rev. Joseph Tarkington, One of the Pioneer Methodist Preachers of Indiana* (Cincinnati: Curts and Jennings, 1899), 72. See also Finley's recollections of his family's preoccupation with the passions of the war in *Autobiography*, 20–21.

42. Theophilus Arminius [Thomas Hinde], "Memoirs and Biographical Sketches to the Late Samuel Parker," *WCA*, 20 Mar. 1835.

43. Finley, *Autobiography*, 253–54.

44. Ibid., 290–91.

45. Faragher, *Women and Men on the Overland Trail*, 112–17.

3. MIGRATION

1. On the general extent, direction, and sequence of migration in the antebellum period, see J. Potter, "The Growth of Population in America, 1700–1860," in *Population in History*, ed. D. V. Glass and D. E. C. Eversly (London: Edward Arnold, 1965), 635ff. and his "American Population in the Early National Period," in *Population and Economics: Proceedings of Section V of the Fourth Congress of the International Economic History Association, 1968*, ed. Paul Deprez (Winnipeg: University of Manitoba Press, 1970), 55–67. See also Ray Allen Billington, *Westward Expansion*, 3d ed. (New York: Macmillan, 1967), 246–51, 294–301.

2. Sweet, *Religion in the Development of American Culture*, 114–19, 129–59.

3. Finley, *Autobiography*, 400–401.

4. On the continuity of economic class and political dominance in the southern regions of the antebellum West, see Thomas P. Abernethy, *Three Virginia Frontiers* (University, La.: Louisiana State University Press, 1940); Sydnor, *The Development of Southern Sectionalism, 1819–1848* (University, La.: Louisiana State University Press, 1948); John D. Barnhart, *Valley of Democracy: Frontier in the Ohio Valley, 1775–1818* (Bloomington, Ind.: Indiana University Press, 1953); Stanley Elkins and Eric McKitrick, "A Meaning for Turner's Frontier II: The Southwest Frontier and New England," *Political Science Quarterly* 69 (1954): 565–83; and Clement Eaton, *A History of the Old South: The Emergence of a Reluctant Nation*, 3d ed. (New York: Macmillan, 1975), 270–90. For similar findings on rural areas, towns, and cities in the Old Northwest, see Barnhart, "The Southern Element in the Leadership of the Old Northwest," *Journal of Southern History* 1 (1935): 186–97; Lewis Atherton, *Main Street*

on the Middle Border (Bloomington, Ind.: Indiana University Press, 1954), 72–76; Richard C. Wade, *The Urban Frontier: Pioneer Life in Early Pittsburgh, Cincinnati, Lexington, Louisville, and St. Louis* (Chicago: University of Chicago Press, 1959), 203–30; Paul W. Gates, "Frontier Estate Builders and Farm Laborers," in *The Frontier in Perspective*, ed. Walker Wyman and Clifton Kroeber (Madison: University of Wisconsin Press, 1965), 143–64; Walter S. Glazer, "Participation and Power: Voluntary Associations and the Functional Organization of Cincinnati in 1840," *Historical Methods Newsletter* 5 (1972): 151–68; and Richard S. Alcorn, "Leadership and Stability in Mid-Nineteenth-Century America: A Case Study of an Illinois Town," *Journal of American History* 61 (1974): 685–702. For the stability of family structure in the West, see Jack E. Eblen, "An Analysis of Nineteenth-Century Frontier Populations," *Demography* 2 (1965): 399–413; and John Modell, "Family and Fertility on the Indiana Frontier, 1820," *American Quarterly* 23 (1971): 615–34.

5. Isaac, *Transformation of Virginia*, 311–12; Richard K. Vedder and Lowell E. Galloway, "Migration and the Old Northwest," in *Essays in Nineteenth-Century Economic History: The Old Northwest*, ed. David C. Klingman and Richard K. Vedder (Athens, Ohio: Ohio University Press, 1975), 167–69.

6. Wyatt-Brown, *Southern Honor*, 43–45, 66, 70–74.

7. Louis Hartz, "A Comparative Study of Fragment Cultures," in *Violence in America: Historical and Comparative Perspectives*, ed. Hugh Davis Graham and Ted Robert Gurr (New York: New American Library, Signet Books, 1969), 110–14. A depiction of authority controlled by the democracy of popular consensus pervades Wyatt-Brown's section on "Structures of Rivalry and Social Control," in *Southern Honor*, 328–493.

8. Abernethy, *Three Virginia Frontiers*, 67–68, 72; Finley, *Autobiography*, 113.

9. Rowland Berthoff, *An Unsettled People: Social Order and Disorder in American History* (New York: Harper and Row, 1971), 203. See also Berthoff and Murrin, "Feudalism, Communalism, and the Yeoman Freeholder," 256–88.

10. Isaac, *Transformation of Virginia*, 301–305.

11. Daniel J. Boorstin, *The Americans: The National Experience* (New York: Vintage Books, 1965), 113–68. See also Stanley Elkins and Eric McKitrick, "A Meaning for Turner's Frontier I: Democracy in the Old Northwest," *Political Science Quarterly* 69 (1954): 341–49.

12. Williams, "Autobiography of Samuel Williams," 101–104, in S&SWWP, Ohio Historical Society, Columbus, Ohio; Plebeius [Samuel Williams], "Leaves," 223–24.

13. Williams, "Autobiography," 98–101.

14. Isaac, *Transformation of Virginia*, 310–22.

15. Cartwright, *Autobiography*, 30.

16. Richard Maxwell Brown, "The American Vigilante Tradition," in *Violence in America*, 154–205; and *Strain of Violence: Historical Studies of American Violence and Vigilantism* (New York: Oxford University Press, 1975); Wyatt-Brown, *Southern Honor*, chaps. 14–17.

17. Fliegelman, *Prodigals and Pilgrims*; Winthrop D. Jordan, "Familial Politics: Thomas Paine and the Killing of the King, 1776," *Journal of American History* 60 (1973–74): 294–308; Edwin G. Burrows and Michael Wallace, "The American Revolution: The Ideology and Psychology of National Liberation," *Perspectives in American History* 6 (1972): 168–289.

18. Finley, *Autobiography*, 127, 147–59.

19. Wyatt-Brown, *Southern Honor*, 327–31.

20. Finley, *Autobiography*, 23.

21. Ibid., 164–65.

22. Ibid., 171.

23. Ibid., 175–76.

24. Ibid., 188.

25. Ibid., 188–89.
26. Ibid., 398–401.
27. Finley, "Experiences and Travels of a Western Preacher," *WCA*, 15 May 1835, 16.

4. EXPERIMENTAL RELIGION AND THE WAY OF THE CROSS

1. See, for instance, John Taylor's accounts of numerous schisms and his hand-wringing over such factionalism in his classic *History of Ten Baptist Churches*, 2d ed. (Franklin Co., Ky., 1828), 49–54, 119–25.

2. Hood, *Reformed America*, 169–76; on further reservations that both Presbyterians and Baptists had regarding the Great Revival in the West, see 204–205, n. 7. See also Mathews's judicious attempt to distinguish the denominational strands of evangelicalism in *Religion and the Old South*, 29–34.

3. For a survey of conversion in different periods, see Jerald C. Brauer, "Conversion: From Puritanism to Revivalism," *The Journal of Religion* 58 (1978): 227–43. For a powerful analysis of the psychology of early American Puritan conversion, see Charles Lloyd Cohen, *God's Caress: The Psychology of Puritan Religious Experience* (New York: Oxford University Press, 1986). Cohen's study provides evidence of important continuities between Puritan and Methodist variants of American evangelical psychology.

4. This account of Methodist religiosity relies on a "family catechism" on experimental religion in Lovell, *Methodist Family Manual*.

5. The autobiographies of James B. Finley, Peter Cartwright, and Jacob Young depict the former sort of minimal spiritual awareness. Examples of those who were sensitized from childhood to their personal spiritual condition include T. D. Welker, *Conflicts and Trials of an Itinerant. Rev. John Kiger, D. D.* (Cincinnati: Cranston and Stowe, 1891), 24–25; M. L. Haney, *The Story of My Life; An Autobiography* (Normal, Ill.: 1904), 6–7; A. Newell, *Biography of the Rev. A. Newell and Miscellanies* (St. Louis: Nixon-Jones Printing Co., 1894), 16; and E. J. Stanley, *Life of Rev. L. B. Stateler, or, Sixty-five Years on the Frontier, Containing Incidents, Anecdotes, and Sketches of Methodist History in the West and Northwest* (Nashville: Publishing House of the M. E. Church, South, 1907), 13–14.

6. On the inadequacy of morality, see John Stewart, *Highways and Hedges; or Fifty Years of Western Methodism* (Cincinnati: Hitchcock and Walden, 1872), 19–20; and Chauncey Hobart, *Recollections of My Life: Fifty Years of Itinerancy in the Northwest* (Red Wing, Minn.: Red Wing Printing Co., 1885), 62–63.

7. Lovell, *Methodist Family Manual*, 109–14, 187–89.

8. Young, *Autobiography of a Pioneer: or the Nativity, Experience, Travels, and Ministerial Labors of Rev. Jacob Young, with Incidents, Observations, and Reflections* (Cincinnati: Swormstedt and Poe, 1857), 38–42.

9. Ibid., 42–43.

10. Lovell, *Methodist Family Manual*, 191–94.

11. Kenneth Burke's category of "qualitative progression" seems to describe the form of the conversion experience. Qualitative progression is a rhetorical form which arouses and fulfills desires by depicting one quality of experience in such a way as to prepare the mind and feelings for another different or contrasting quality. See *Counter-Statement* (1931; Berkeley: University of California Press, 1968), 124–25.

12. Young, *Autobiography*, 43.

13. Hobart, *Recollections*, 49–50.

14. "Meditations on the Happiness of Heaven," *WCM*, Feb. 1816, 57; Mar. 1816, 107; Apr. 1816, 153; May 1816, 196; June 1816, 245.

15. "Meditations on the Happiness of Heaven," 294.

16. James Quinn to Daniel Hitt, 7 July 1803, DHL; typescript held by The Upper

Room Library, Nashville, Tenn.; originals held by Ohio Wesleyan University, Delaware, Ohio.

17. Quinn, "A Journal," *WCA*, 18 and 25 June 1841, 33.

18. James Henthorn to Daniel Hitt, 12 Feb. 1802, DHL.

19. "Re-union in Heaven," *WCA*, 10 Jan. 1840, 149–50. For a similar argument, see the letter of Mary S. Wall to William McKendree, 28 Mar. 1834, in the William McKendree Collection, Special Collections, Jean and Alexander Heard Libraries, Vanderbilt University, Nashville, Tenn.

20. H. Tooley, "Zion Travellers," in vol. 1 of *The Western Methodist Preacher* (Nashville: Garrett and Moffitt, 1835), 189–90.

21. Finley, *Autobiography*, 375–78.

22. Abraham Knicely to George Washington Maley, 5 Feb. 1835, GWMP, Archives of Ohio United Methodism, Ohio Wesleyan University, Delaware, Ohio.

23. James Henthorn to Daniel Hitt, 7 July 1803, DHL.

24. James Henthorn to Daniel Hitt, 19 June 1803, DHL.

25. Benjamin Hitt to Daniel Hitt, 22 June 1795, and Feb. 1796, DHL.

26. See, for instance, Benjamin Hitt to Daniel Hitt, 14 Oct. 1792; Samuel Hitt to Daniel Hitt, 25 Feb. 1791; A. G. Thompson to Daniel Hitt, 20 Mar. 1790; and Seely Bunn to Daniel Hitt, 18 Feb. 1796; all in DHL. See also George Shane Phillips, diary, 11 Sept. 1841, and 22 Jan. 1842; and Sarah Phillips to John H. Phillips, 12 Sept. 1852; all in GSPP, Manuscripts Division, Huntington Library, San Marino, Calif.

27. Benjamin Hitt to Daniel Hitt, 30 May 1790, DHL; Samuel Williams, memoirs, vol. 1, 129–33, S&SWWP; "Vital Religion—No. 1," *WCM*, Jan. 1816, 3–6; "An Elegy on the Death of William Dixon . . . ," *WCM*, Jan. 1816, 45; "Religious Experience—No. 1," *WCA*, 18 July 1834, 45; "Heavenly Mindedness—No. 1," *WCA*, 3 Mar. 1837, 177; "Patience," *LR*, Apr. 1842, 123.

28. Finley, *Autobiography*, 166–68.

29. "Meditations on the Happiness of Heaven," 109, 155, 197–98, 245–47, 292.

30. Maxwell Pierson Gaddis, *Footprints of an Itinerant* (Cincinnati: Methodist Book Concern, 1857), 140–43.

31. Mary Morriss Smith, untitled ms., Mary Morriss Smith Papers, Tennessee State Library and Archives, Nashville, Tenn.

32. "Meditations on the Happiness of Heaven," 245.

33. Kenneth Burke makes the idea of mortification a major implication of his analysis of the rhetoric of Judeo-Christian myth. Mortification is, for him, an extreme form of self-control which involves "the deliberate, disciplinary, 'slaying' of any motive that, for 'doctrinal' reasons, one thinks of as unruly." Mortification is not simply a matter of being frustrated by external circumstances; it comes from within. One part of the self says "No" to another part of the self. See *Rhetoric of Religion: Studies in Logology* (1961; Berkeley: University of California Press, 1970), 190.

34. Miss Polly Jennings to Daniel Hitt, 11 Apr. 1797, DHL. See also James Henthorn to Daniel Hitt, 25 Dec. 1801, DHL.

35. "On the Duty of Self-Examination," *WCA*, 12 Sept. 1834, 77; "Danger of Self-Deception," *WCA*, 12 May 1837, 12; "Think of Death," *WCA*, 15 July 1836, 45.

36. "Danger of Self-Deception," 12.

37. Seely Bunn to Daniel Hitt, 1 Feb. 1803, DHL.

38. Seely Bunn to Daniel Hitt, 26 Aug. 1794, DHL.

39. Lovell, *Methodist Family Manual*, 196–202.

40. "Meditations on the Happiness of Heaven," 246–47.

41. Lovell, *Methodist Family Manual*, 198–201.

42. "Vital Religion—No. 3," *WCM*, Mar. 1816, 103; "Vital Religion—No. 4," *WCM*, 150–51; "Love of God," *WCA*, 5 May 1837, 5.

43. "Vital Religion—No. 4," 151.

44. Joseph and Rebecca Morgan to Daniel Hitt, 27 July 1797, DHL. For similar sentiments more than a generation later, see the letters of Elizabeth Kauffman to her fiancé, George S. Phillips, 23 Feb., 27 June, 27 July 1843, GSPP.

45. "Meditations on the Happiness of Heaven," 292.

46. Learner Blackman, journal, 4, Methodist Archives and History Center, Drew University, Madison, N.J.

47. H. H. B., "Memoirs of the Life, Death and Character of the Rev. James Davidson," *WCM*, Aug. 1816, 362; "The Mourner," *LR*, Feb. 1841, 55–56.

48. James Henthorn to Daniel Hitt, 3 Oct. 1797, DHL.

49. One may trace, for instance, a strange path whereby a tale of woe told in a letter from James Finley to his brother led to a time of rejoicing in the home of the brother. See John P. Finley to James B. Finley, 15 Dec. 1811, JBFL, Archives of Ohio United Methodism, Ohio Wesleyan University, Delaware, Ohio.

50. E. P. Thompson, *The Making of the English Working Class* (New York: Vintage Books, 1963), 365–73.

51. "Christian Holiness," *WCA*, 27 Mar. 1840, 196.

52. Elizabeth Kaufmann to George S. Phillips, 27 June 1843, GSPP; Phillips to Kaufmann, 13 July 1843 and 10 Aug. 1843, GSPP.

53. *LR*, Nov. 1841, 349.

54. "Vital Religion—No. 2," *WCM*, Feb. 1816, 54–55.

55. Lovell, *Methodist Family Manual*, 203–204.

56. Learner Blackman, journal, 7.

57. For examples of Phillips's prayers which link holiness and usefulness, see his diary, 17 Nov. to 6 Dec. 1841 and 22 Oct. 1844. The courtship letters, which show a similar link, are George S. Phillips to Elizabeth Kauffman, 6 Jan., 4 Feb., 12 Mar., 20 May, 13 June, 19 June, and 13 July 1843; and Kauffman to Phillips, 25 Jan., 24 Mar., 1 June, 27 June, and 27 July 1843. Both the diaries and letters are in GSPP.

58. See, for instance, the "Journal of William Hill," in *Religion on the American Frontier, 1783–1840*, vol. 2, *The Presbyterians*, ed. William Warren Sweet (1936; New York: Cooper Square, 1964), 758–61; Christopher and Sarah Houston to Samuel Young, 24 Jan. 1815, Mary H. Kennedy Papers, Southern Historical Collection, University of North Carolina, Chapel Hill, N. C.; Jacob Bower, "Autobiography," in *Religion on the American Frontier, 1783–1840*, vol. 1, *The Baptists*, ed. Sweet (1931; New York: Cooper Square, 1964), 200–203; "The 'Religious Experience' of a Candidate for the Ministry as Related Before the Church," in *The Baptists*, 231–34; J. M. Smith, *A Work on Revivals: Sermons and Sketches in the Life and Preaching of Elder James Smith*, 3d ed. (Indianapolis, 1893), 9–10; and Martin Baskett Letters, Filson Club, Louisville, Ky.

59. Taylor, *History of Ten Baptist Churches*, 62–63.

60. Christopher Houston to Samuel Young, 14 Nov. 1815, and Christopher Houston to Samuel and Sally Young, 5 July 1817, Mary H. Kennedy Papers, Southern Historical Collection, University of North Carolina, Chapel Hill, N. C.

61. Benjamin Nelson, *The Idea of Usury: From Tribal Brotherhood to Universal Otherhood*, 2d ed. (Chicago: University of Chicago Press, 1969), xxiii-xxv, 29–108.

62. J. C. Smith, *Reminiscences of Early Methodism in Indiana* (Indianapolis: J. M. Olcott, 1879), 102.

5. THE SALVATION MACHINE AND THE SUBVERSION OF PATRIARCHY

1. George G. Cookman, *Speeches Delivered on Various Occasions*, quoted in Richey, "The Social Sources of Denominationalism: Methodism," in *Denominationalism*, ed. Richey (Nashville: Abingdon Press, 1977), 163.

2. A well-known Baptist polemic against the Methodist system played upon the imagery of Ezekiel's vision. See J. R. Graves, *The Great Iron Wheel; or, Republicanism Backwards and Christianity Reversed* (Nashville: Marks and Rutland, 1856). See also the Methodist reply by William G. Brownlee, *The Great Iron Wheel Examined; or Its False Spokes Extracted* (Nashville: 1856).

3. Emory, *History of the Discipline*, 178.

4. Cartwright, *Autobiography*, 31–36.

5. Young, *Autobiography*, 35, 40–41.

6. Catherine L. Albanese, "Savage, Sinner, and Saved: Davy Crockett, Camp Meetings, and the Wild Frontier," *American Quarterly* 33 (1981): 482–501.

7. See, for instance, Thomas Scott, "Ohio Circuit, 1793–1794," *WCA*, 8 Nov. 1842, 121.

8. Cartwright, *Autobiography*, 158–60.

9. William I. Fee, *Bringing the Sheaves: Gleanings from Harvest Fields in Ohio, Kentucky, and West Virginia* (Cincinnati: Cranston and Curts, 1896), 34–37. For another example of protracted struggle over the call to preach, see Gaddis, *Footprints*, 78–126.

10. Finley, *Autobiography*, 277.

11. J. C. Smith, *Reminiscences*, 28, 40–41. See also Albanese, "Savage, Sinner, and Saved," 494, on the camp-meeting preacher's power to control his audience.

12. Young, *Autobiography*, 522–23.

13. Finley, *Autobiography*, 253–54.

14. William Beauchamp, *Letters on the Call and Qualifications of Ministers of the Gospel and on the Apostolic Character and Superior Advantages of the Itinerant Ministry* (Louisville, Ky.: John Early, 1849), 25–26.

15. Richey, *Early American Methodism*, 5–11.

16. See J. C. Smith, *Reminiscences*, 35, for a depiction of John Strange as both an apotheosized preacher and a common man.

17. Polly Jennings to Daniel Hitt, 11 Apr. 1797, DHL.

18. Finley, *Autobiography*, 428.

19. *Prodigals and Pilgrims*, especially 12–31, 155–94. Fliegelman makes a clear case for the overthrow of Calvinist orthodoxy as part of the general movement away from patriarchal authority and toward a more affection-oriented and nurture-oriented vision of authority aimed at securing autonomy rather than dependence for children. Because he focuses on New England theology, however, he overlooks the role of Methodist evangelicalism in fomenting the changes he describes.

20. The role of this schism in the process by which spiritual patriarchy transmuted into managerial bureaucracy is discussed in the concluding chapter of this study.

21. Quinn, "Memoir of the Venerable White Brown, a Lay Pioneer and Patriarch of the Scioto Valley," *WCA*, 22 July 1842, 53. For further evidence of lay family leadership in the propagation of Methodism, see C. H. Bonner, "A Condensed History of the Methodism on Miami Circuit, Ohio Conference," *WCA*, 4 Oct. 1837, 93; Zadock B. Thackston, "Historical Sketch," *WCA*, 8 Nov. 1839, 113; and "Piketon Circuit, Ohio Conference, from 1797 to 1840," *WCA*, 20 Nov. 1840, 121.

22. Finley, *Autobiography*, 262–64, 281.

23. Samuel W. Williams, *Pictures of Early Methodism in Ohio* (Cincinnati: Jennings and Graham, 1909), 99–100.

24. Bonner, "Condensed History," 93.

25. Hobart, *Recollections*, 20, 47–48. For similar parental sentiments, see James B. Finley's appreciation of Benjamin Lakin's pastoral visits in Finley, *Sketches of Western Methodism: Biographical, Historical, and Miscellaneous, Illustrative of Pioneer Life* (Cincinnati: Methodist Book Concern, 1854), 183.

26. See, for several examples, Gaddis, *Brief Recollections of the Late Reverend George Walker* (Cincinnati: Swormstedt and Poe, 1857), 71–72; Stewart, *Highways and Hedges*, 19; Haney, *Story of My Life*, 24; Emory Miller, *Memoirs and Sermons* (Cincinnati: Jennings and Graham, n. d.), 16; and Stanley, *Life of Rev. L. B. Stateler*, 14.

27. Tarkington, *Autobiography*, 113.

28. Veteran preacher T. A. Goodwin, in his introduction to Joseph Tarkington's autobiography, observed that Tarkington became class leader, then exhorter, then preacher, which were the normal steps to the ministry in the early decades of the nineteenth century; see "Introduction," in Tarkington, *Autobiography*, 7. For further examples of this sort of pattern of rising to the ministry, see John Burgess, *Pleasant Recollections of Characters and Works of Noble Men, with Old Scenes and Merry Times of Long, Long Ago* (Cincinnati: Cranston and Stowe, 1887), 138ff.; Fee, *Bringing the Sheaves*, 34–42; and Hobart, *Recollections*, 90–102.

29. For an insightful analysis of the norms and motives of southern sociability and hospitality, see Wyatt-Brown, *Southern Honor*, 327–39.

30. Milton Haney believed they did more of this building of foundations than another class of men; see *Story of My Life*, 25.

31. Gaddis, *Brief Recollections*, 24–25.

32. Emory, *History of the Discipline*, 30–35, 50–52, 146–50.

33. Finley, *Sketches*, 95–97.

34. Fee, *Bringing the Sheaves*, 33.

35. Quinn, "A Reminiscence," *WCA*, 27 Dec. 1839, 141.

36. "Annals of Western Methodism: From the Journal of John Kobler," *WCA*, 9 and 28 Aug. 1839, 61, 73.

37. Finley, *Sketches*, 421–22. For other examples of Finley's appreciation for family pastoral work, see his *Sketches*, 318, 357; and his *Autobiography*, 234–35.

38. See Peter Cartwright's appreciation of the prayer meeting in his *Autobiography*, 335.

39. T. A. Morris, "Historical Scraps," *WCA*, 4 Oct. 1839, 93; Emory, *History of the Discipline*, 177–82.

40. Allen Wiley, "Introduction and Progress of Methodism in Southeastern Indiana," *Indiana Magazine of History* 23 (Mar.-Dec. 1927): 175–76.

41. For examples of these sensitivities among Methodists, see Finley, *Autobiography*, 245–46, and his *Sketches*, 339–46; Cartwright, *Autobiography*, 232–35; Scott, "Ohio Circuit," 121; "Piketon Circuit," *WCA*, 20 Nov. 1840, 121. For an excellent treatment of general evangelical concern with the family unit, see Mathews, *Religion in the Old South*, 97–101.

42. Quinn, "Memoir of the Venerable White Brown." Other appreciations of the recruitment power of devout parents are found in Quinn, "Reminiscences of a Good Man," *WCA*, 19 Apr. 1842, 5; "Reminiscences of the Ellsworth Family," *WCA*, 16 Sept. 1842, 85; and "A Journal," 33, 37; See also Bonner, "Condensed History," 93; and Plebeius [Samuel Williams], "Leaves," 97–100.

43. Fee, *Bringing the Sheaves*, 32.

44. Finley, "Historical Sketch," *WCA*, 22 Nov. 1839, 121.

45. Morgan, *Virginians at Home*, 44–45.

46. Cartwright, *Autobiography*, 232–33. For a similar, though less light-hearted, story, see Finley, *Sketches*, 360–71.

47. Finley, *Autobiography*, 177–89; Young, *Autobiography*, 46–49; Gaddis, *Footprints*, 45–65; Williams, "Autobiography," 73–74.

48. Examples of this sort of story may be found in Finley, *Sketches*, 519, 527–29; and in Gaddis, *Brief Recollections*, 61–68, and *Footprints*, 45–65.

49. J. C. Smith, *Reminiscences*, 189–90.

6. DISCIPLINE AND THE RHETORIC OF SEPARATION

1. "Class Meetings," in *Cyclopedia of Methodism*, ed. Matthew Simpson (Philadelphia: Everts and Stewart, 1878), 228–29.

2. In actuality, the number in most American Methodist classes seems to have been many more than twelve. Numbers might range from five or six to a hundred or more. Early Methodist historian Nathan Bangs estimated that most classes were in the twenty to forty range. See Bangs, *History of the Methodist Episcopal Church*, vol. 1, 245. As the society grew, the class grew with it, the members themselves often resisting the division of the class. In many cases, then, the membership of the society was coextensive with the membership of the class, much to the dismay of devotees of strict discipline. This lack of control over numbers was significant for the ultimate fate of the class meeting. On the problems of dividing classes, see "Class and Prayer Meetings," *WCA*, 27 July 1838, 56; "Class Meetings," *WCA*, 25 Feb. 1842; and Jacob Meyers, "Division of Classes," *WCA*, 22 Apr. 1843. For a scholarly, if mildly polemical, treatment of this problem in early American Methodism, see David F. Holsclaw, *The Demise of Disciplined Christian Fellowship: The Methodist Class Meeting in Nineteenth-Century America* (Ann Arbor, Mich.: UMI no. 8009501, 1979), especially 48–71.

3. Emory, *History of the Discipline*, 29, 177–82.

4. "Class Meetings," *Gospel Herald*, Jan. 1831, 130.

5. "On Meeting Class," *WCA*, 17 June 1842, 36. For an examination of the history and significance of band meetings in relation to class meetings in English Methodism, see David Lowes Watson, *The Early Methodist Class Meeting: Its Origins and Significance* (Nashville: Discipleship Resources, 1985), chap. 3. For evidence that at least one group of Cincinnati Methodists formed a band meeting, see Samuel Williams, memoir, vol. 3, 491ff., S&SWWP.

6. Emory, *History of the Discipline*, 184–85.

7. Other samples of questions may be found in John Miley, *Treatise on Class Meetings* (Cincinnati: Poe and Hitchcock, 1851), 202–203, 207–10; and in J. T., "Class Meetings," *Gospel Herald*, Oct. 1830, 56.

8. "Class Meetings—No. 2," *WCA*, 9 May 1834, 5; "Rules for a Good Class," *WCA*, 8 Apr. 1836, 198.

9. On the disciplinary role of the class meeting and class leader see Emory, *History of the Discipline*, 178, 182; "Class Meetings Again," *WCA*, 11 Mar. 1842, 185; and Miley, *Treatise on Class Meetings*, 50. On the "moral courts" of the Methodist church and other popular denominations in the Midwest, see William Warren Sweet's classic, "The Churches as Moral Courts of the Frontier," *Church History* 2 (Jan. 1933): 2–21.

10. Regarding the excessive numbers in many classes, see note 2.

11. This compendium of complaints is drawn from "Class Meetings—No. 3," *WCA*, 16 May 1834, 9; "Attend Your Class Meetings," *WCA*, 28 Feb. 1840, 177; and "Thoughts on the 'General Rules of the Methodist Episcopal Church'—No. 3," *WCA*, 10 Oct. 1834, 93.

12. In one sense, of course, this was precisely the point; those who would not cultivate the right state of mind had to be culled out. See "Disciplinary Advantages of Class Meetings," *WCA*, 19 Nov. 1841, 122.

13. One writer, more sensitive than most, urged class members to be very careful of how they spoke of one another's gifts. See "Class Meetings Again," *WCA*, 11 Mar., 1842, 185.

14. "Class Meetings—No. 3," 9; "Attend Your Class Meetings," 177; "Class Meetings Again," 185; "Rules for a Good Class," *WCA*, 8 Apr. 1836, 198. Other

writers were more ready to fault class leaders and preachers for lack of faithfulness in keeping class-meeting records and in visiting those who failed to attend, reasoning that people who expected to be visited for neglecting class would be less inclined to such neglect. See "Mark Your Class-Books," *WCA*, 1 Dec. 1837, 128; J. A. Reeder, "A Class-Leader's Duty, Once a Week," *WCA*, 27 Dec. 1839, 141.

15. "Class Meetings—No. 4," *WCA*, 23 May 1834, 13; William W. Jones, "Class Meetings," *WCA*, 16 Dec. 1842, 140; J. T., "Class Meetings," 57–58.

16. Weber, *The Protestant Ethic and the Spirit of Capitalism*, trans. Talcott Parsons (New York: Charles Scribner's Sons, 1958), 128–43; and "The Protestant Sects and the Spirit of Capitalism," in *From Max Weber: Essays in Sociology*, ed. H. H. Gerth and C. Wright Mills (New York: Oxford University Press, 1949), 302–22.

17. "Class Meeting and Love Feast," *WCA*, 1 Apr. 1836, 196; "Love Feast," *WCA*, 9 May 1834, 5.

18. Williams, *Pictures*, 98–99.

19. John L. Smith, *Indiana Methodism, Stories of Sketches and Incidents, Grave and Humorous Concerning Preachers and People of the West* (Valparaiso, Ind., 1892), 25–26.

20. Thomas Coke and Francis Asbury, "Extracts from the Notes to the Discipline by Dr. Coke and Bishop Asbury," in Emory, *History of the Discipline*, 304, 330–31.

21. Emory, *History of the Discipline*, 137, 187.

22. As in the case of class meeting, the rules for keeping love feast pure were not always observed. See "Love Feasts," *WCA*, 3 July 1835, 40; "Love Feast Tickets," *WCA*, 23 June 1843, 37. In general, however, there seems to have been much less concern expressed over laxness in regulating love feasts than there was over neglect of class meeting.

23. "Disciplinary Advantages of Class Meetings," 122.

24. Miley, *Treatise on Class Meetings*, 50.

25. Cartwright, *Autobiography*, 128–29.

26. Cartwright, *Autobiography*, 129–30.

27. John Scripps, "Early Methodism in the Far West—No. 3," *WCA*, 13 Jan. 1843, 153. See also Wiley, "Methodism in Southeastern Indiana," 299; Martin Hitt to Daniel Hitt, 1 Sept. 1791, DHL; and George S. Phillips to Elizabeth Kaufman Phillips, 11 July 1847, GSPP.

28. Finley, *Autobiography*, 268–69, 416–17. See also William Burke, "Autobiography of William Burke," in James B. Finley, *Sketches of Western Methodism* (Cincinnati: Methodist Book Concern, 1854), 30, 37; Morris, "Historical Scraps," 93; and Alexander Tolley to Daniel Asbury, 18 May 1815, Daniel Asbury Papers, Commission on Archives and History of the United Methodist Church, Madison, New Jersey.

29. See, for instance, the series of letters from Adam Sellers to James B. Finley, 22 Feb., 3 Mar., 16 June, and 3 Aug. 1852, JBFL. Sellers laments and resents his expulsion from the church and details his efforts to bring countercharges against one Reverend Davis whom he insulted and who led the campaign to have Sellers expelled. His reports of contacts with prominent church members and preachers evoke images of a Virginia burgesses candidate seeking to secure his "interest."

30. Williams, "Autobiography," TS, 170–80, 187–216.

31. Jones, "Class Meetings," 140.

32. Fee, *Bringing the Sheaves*, 16–17.

33. Phillips, diary, 21 Apr. 1842.

34. Henry Smith, "Contributions to the Western Methodist Historical Society," *WCA*, 15 Jan. 1841, 165.

35. John Kobler, "Annals of Western Methodism: From the Journal of John Kobler," *WCA*, 9 Aug. 1839, 61.

36. Finley, *Sketches*, 203.

37. J. T., "Class Meetings," 58.

38. "Class Meeting and Love Feast," 196.

39. "Class Meetings and Love Feasts," *WCA*, 8 Aug. 1834, 59.

40. J. T., "Class Meetings," 58.

41. Benjamin Webb, "Contributions to the Western Methodist Historical Society," *WCA*, 18 Sept. 1840, 85. For another instance of this sort of behavior, see Young, *Autobiography*, 36.

42. Finley, *Autobiography*, 203–204.

43. John Meek, letter, in *Extracts of Letters Containing Some Account of the Work of God Since the Year 1800; Written by the Preachers and Members of the Methodist Episcopal Church to Their Bishops* (New York: Cooper and Wilson, 1805), 32. For a similar event in which such a spirit was incubated behind closed doors in prayer meetings, see "Church Prayer Meetings," *WCA*, 25 Oct. 1839, 108.

44. Charles Hardy, "Contributions to the Western Methodist Historical Society," *WCA*, 3 Apr. 1840, 197. For other examples of the evangelistic use of love feasts, see William Burke, "Autobiography," 76; see also the editorials in *WCA*, 11 Nov. 1836, 115; and 18 Nov. 1836, 118–19.

45. Walter B. Posey, *The Development of Methodism in the Old Southwest: 1783–1824* (Tuscaloosa, Ala.: Weatherford Printing Co., 1933), 116. This story may be more legend than history. Another first-person account, however, by a witness for whom the process finally took, makes clear the symbolic truth of Posey's tale. See Robert Boyd, *Personal Memoirs: Together with a discussion upon the Hardships and Sufferings of Itinerant Life; and Also a Discourse upon the Pastoral Relation* (Cincinnati: Methodist Book Concern, 1867), 31–32.

46. Finley, *Autobiography*, 240–41.

47. Harold Frederic, *The Damnation of Theron Ware*, ed. Everett Carter (1896; Cambridge, Mass.: Harvard University Press, 1960), 234–37.

48. Kenneth Burke, *Rhetoric of Motives*, 21, 43, 46, 271.

7. FELLOWSHIP AND THE RHETORIC OF TESTIMONY

1. Billy Hibbard, *Memoirs of the Life and Travels of B. Hibbard . . .* (New York, 1825), 111.

2. Finley, *Autobiography*, 240–41.

3. Thomas Mann, journal, 7 Apr. 1805 to 14 Jan. 1806, Thomas Mann Papers, Manuscript Department, Duke University Library, Durham, North Carolina.

4. Henry Smith, quoted in Finley, *Sketches*, 199.

5. Hardy, "Contributions to the Western Methodist Historical Society," 197. See also Wiley, "The Introduction and Progress of Methodism in Southeastern Indiana," 394.

6. Morris, "Historical Scraps," 93.

7. Kobler, "Annals of Western Methodism," 30 Aug. 1839, 73. See also Burgess, *Pleasant Recollections*, 374–75; and Isaac Crawford, journal, 17 Jan. 1836, Isaac Crawford Papers, Manuscripts Division, Indiana State Library, Indianapolis, Indiana.

8. Kobler, quoted in Finley, *Sketches*, 174.

9. Crawford, journal, 16 Nov. and 16 Dec., 1837.

10. James Henthorn to Daniel Hitt, 3 Oct. 1797; 25 Dec. 1801; and 10 Jan. 1803, DHL.

11. [Samuel?] Fisk, diary, 27 Sept. 1840 and 1 Aug. 1841, Fisk Papers, Illinois State Historical Library, Springfield, Illinois.

12. Wiley, "Methodism in Southeastern Indiana," 175–76.

13. Finley, "Experience and Travels of a Western Preacher," 8, 12.

14. John Scripps, "Early Methodism in the Far West—No. 2," *WCA*, 6 Jan. 1843, 149.

15. Kobler, "Annals of Western Methodism," 73; David Lewis, *Recollections of a Superannuate: or, Sketches of Life, Labor, and Experience in the Methodist Itinerancy*, ed. S. M. Merrill (Cincinnati: Methodist Book Concern, 1857), 226.

16. Phillips, diary, 22 Oct. 1841.

17. Isaac Robbins, "Contributions to the Western Methodist Historical Society," *WCA*, 20 Mar. 1840, 189. For similar events, see Finley, *Autobiography*, 178–79; and Gaddis, *Brief Recollections*, 58–59.

18. Wiley, "Methodism in Southeastern Indiana," 458–59.

19. John L. Smith, *Indiana Methodism*, 38–39. For other instances of love feast as a means of recruitment, see Gaddis, *Footprints*, 198; Hobart, *Recollections*, 90; Finley, *Sketches*, 25,; Burgess, *Pleasant Recollections*, 312–14; James Henthorn to Daniel Hitt, 19 June 1803, DHL; A. G. Thompson to Daniel Hitt, 25 May 1790, DHL; Ruth Ross to James B. and Hannah Finley, 30 Mar. 1829, JBFP; and Phillips, diary, 3 Apr. 1842, and Feb. 1844.

20. The discussion here is influenced by Victor Turner's concepts of liminality and communitas. See *The Ritual Process: Structure and Anti-Structure* (Chicago: Aldine, 1969), 94–97, 126–29. Turner discusses the spontaneous or existential form of communitas under consideration here in *Ritual Process*, 132; in *Dramas, Fields, and Metaphors: Symbolic Action in Human Society*, Symbol, Myth, and Ritual Series (Ithaca, N.Y.: Cornell University Press, 1974), 169, and in *From Ritual to Theater: The Human Seriousness of Play* (New York: Performing Arts Journal Publications, 1982), 47–48.

21. "Class Meeting and Love Feast," 196.

22. "Love Feast," 5.

23. Here I join Russell E. Richey in diverging somewhat from Nathan O. Hatch's reading of the democratizing impulse of Methodism. Hatch reads denominations like the Methodists and Baptists as evangelical dissenters who adopted republican ideology and championed popular notions of political liberty along with religious liberty in a multivalent rhetoric; see Hatch, *Democratization of American Christianity*. Richey points out that the popular character of Methodism derived more from its native pietist and Wesleyan languages than from its adoption of republican language. See Richey, *Early American Methodism*, xvi–xvii, 33–46, 102 n. 13.

24. Ideological and normative communities are defined by Turner in *Ritual Process*, 132–33; in *Dramas*, 169; and in *From Ritual to Theater*, 48–50.

25. Turner deals with the transformative impulse in movements of communitas in *Ritual Process*, 126–33; and in *From Ritual to Theater*, 48–52. Richey laments the unreflective naivete of Methodist visions of the social order in *Early American Methodism*, 13–20, 44–46.

26. Wiley, "Methodism in Southeastern Indiana," 175–76, 394; Finley, *Autobiography*, 186, 240–41.

27. "Attend Your Class Meetings," 177. For other uses of the analogy, see "Class Meeting and Love Feast," 196; "Love Feast," 5.

28. "Class Meetings—No. 4," 13.

29. Emory, *History of the Discipline*, 329. This passage refers directly to band meetings rather than class meetings. Because class meeting seems to have served in American Methodism the function of the Wesleyan bands, it seems legitimate to cite this use of the family metaphor here. For another use of the metaphor in relation to class meeting, see Miley, *Treatise on Class Meetings*, 166–68; and Finley, *Sketches*, 109.

30. Emory, *History of the Discipline*, 304.

31. These comments draw on Kenneth Burke's theories of rhetorical form; see *Counter-Statement*, 124–28. On the virtual independence of content and form, see Burke, *Rhetoric of Motives*, 58.

32. "Class Meeting and Love Feast," 196.
33. For a definition of repetitive form, see Burke, *Counter-Statement*, 125.
34. Finley, *Autobiography*, 186.
35. Isaac Robbins, "Contributions to the Western Methodist Historical Society," 189.
36. "Class Meetings—No. 3," 9; "Attend Your Class Meetings," 177; "Class Meetings Again," 185.
37. Tarkington, *Autobiography*, 98.
38. Finley, *Autobiography*, 178–79.
39. John L. Smith, *Indiana Methodism*, 184–85.
40. Ibid., 25–26.
41. David Sullins, *Recollections of an Old Man: Seventy Years in Dixie, 1827–1897*, 2d ed. (Bristol, Tenn.: The King Printing Co., 1910), 65–72.
42. Hobart, *Recollections*, 49–50.
43. Wiley, "Methodism in Southeastern Indiana," 433–34.
44. Cartwright, *Autobiography*, 41.
45. Finley, *Autobiography*, 212–17.
46. Kenneth Burke calls it "qualitative progression"; see *Counter-Statement*, 124–25.
47. On the importance and ambiguity of imagery in rhetoric, see Burke, *Rhetoric of Motives*, 86–87, and *Rhetoric of Religion*, 212–15. On the "individuation" of form in rhetoric, see Burke, *Counter-Statement*, 143. On the conveying of attitudes in the symbolic act, see Burke, *The Philosophy of Literary Form*, 3d ed. (Berkeley: University of California Press, 1973), 9.
48. For a brief discussion of these older styles in the South and of the beginnings of their decline, see Daniel Blake Smith, *Inside the Great House*, 260–76. For a more extensive discussion focused on Puritan New England, see David E. Stannard, *The Puritan Way of Death: A Study in Religion, Culture, and Social Change* (New York: Oxford University Press, 1977).
49. Finley, "Experience and Travels of a Western Preacher," 8. For other narrations of experience involving a symbolic illness, see the accounts of William Fee and Maxwell Gaddis of their calls to the ministry in Fee, *Bringing the Sheaves*, 37–38, and Gaddis, *Footprints*, 81.
50. Lewis, *Recollections*, 240–41. On the ritual of happy dying and its links to the rituals of social religion, see chap. 11.
51. See, for instance, Cartwright, *Autobiography*, 234; and George Brown, *Recollections of Itinerant Life; Including Early Reminiscences*, 2d ed. (Cincinnati: R. W. Carroll, 1866), 45–46.
52. Finley, *Sketches*, 486–87.
53. Quinn, "Memoir of the Venerable White Brown," 43, and "Reminiscences of the Ellsworth Family," 85.
54. S. S. Colburn, "Emigration and Sabbath-Breaking," *WCA*, 11 Aug. 1843, 68.
55. John Scripps, "Early Methodism in the Far West—No. 4," *WCA*, 20 Jan. 1843, 157. On the damage which emigration did to settled religious societies, see Bishop Asbury's complaint when James Quinn rejoiced at the arrival in the West of Moses Ellsworth and family. Quinn, "Reminiscence of the Ellsworth Family," 85.
56. Morris, "Traveling," *LR*, Apr. 1841, 104–106; and [Leonidas] H[amline], "Impromptu," *LR*, Apr. 1841, 106.
57. Hobart, *Recollections*, 127–29. Another story which addressed the temptations of mammon was the testimony of the German man who neglected his vows to give money for missions and lost eight hundred dollars and who then fulfilled his vows and got it all back plus the blessing of having his two children converted. See James B. Finley, "The Baltimore and Severn Camp Meetings," *WCA*, 23 Feb. 1838, 176.

58. Everett S. Lee, "The Turner Thesis Reexamined," *American Quarterly* 13 (Spring 1961): 77–83; Ray Allen Billington, *America's Frontier Heritage* (New York: Holt, Rinehart, and Winston, 1966), 193.

59. Finley, *Sketches*, 527–29.

60. Burgess, *Pleasant Recollections*, 259–64. This sort of story, of course, was a cliché of nineteenth-century devotional literature. For a somewhat different tale in which a husband conquered his wife's hostility to religion, see Stewart, *Highways and Hedges*, 201–202. In Stewart's story, the husband was somewhat more aggressive than the saintly wife of the drunkard in Burgess's story; he endured his wife's disruptions of family prayer for a time and then began to pray that God would either convert her or kill her. His prayer was answered when dangerous illness overtook her and seemed to panic her into conversion. Her experience stuck, however, and Stewart reported that she seemed to enjoy hearing her husband tell how grace had triumphed.

61. Cartwright, *Autobiography*, 40–41.

62. Finley, *Autobiography*, 212–17.

63. It might seem strange to identify the seemingly nonmoral wilderness image of the mountains with principles of disorder. Recall, however, that the Methodist writer on the happiness of heaven declared heaven to be free not only from personal and social corruption but from "the misery arising from the disorder of the material world" as well. See "Meditations on the Happiness of Heaven," July 1816, 292–93. Finley himself spoke in other contexts of the "dark and bloody ground" of early Kentucky. Whatever the origins of this phrase, for this renegade turned preacher it meant a wilderness that seemed fallen and evil, a fitting ground for ignorance, discord, misery, and moral disorder. See Finley, *Autobiography*, 145, and *Sketches*, 178.

64. Evangelical rhetoric, as Sandra Sizer has sagely observed, ought not to be taken too literally. Within the logic of their overall rhetorical system, Methodist testimonies were references not just to specific instances of illness, politics, mammon, or wilderness, they were portrayals of the human dilemma as one where individuals are victimized by impersonal forces beyond their control. The present interpretation makes more than Sizer does of the active, even aggressive, element in the rhetoric of social religion; the inimical forces of the world were often transformed by the paradoxical active passivity of the believers. See Sizer, *Gospel Hymns*, 30–44.

8. METHODIST IDENTITY

1. A subtext informs this chapter, as well as the entire book, which it seems wise to make more explicit at this point. The analyses developed throughout the book are not only social scientific but also psychological. This chapter in particular follows the well-known life-cycle theory of Erik Erikson. Readers need not know this theory in order to follow and understand the analysis developed here. Some readers may, however, wish to delve into this analysis with greater theoretical self-awareness. Such readers are invited to attend to several of the notes in conjunction with the main text. Readers who simply want to know more about the Methodists may safely follow the text and ignore the notes. It is important, however, to convey the assumptions which undergird such an approach. The basic assumption is that enduring patterns of human interaction and experiencing are laid down first in particular stages of development and then elaborated and matured in succeeding stages from infancy through childhood and adolescence. In this way of thinking, the stages of the life cycle become categories for the analysis of adult activities. Differences between ways of life are understood as matters of differing emphases on the psychological and social issues that characterize different stages of the life

cycle. Hence my rendering of the ethos of experimental religion as differing from the ethos of honor in its emphasis on the developmentally later issues of guilt more than shame, initiative more than autonomy, and purpose more than will.

2. Finley, *Autobiography*, 347.

3. Erik Erikson has developed the concept of "mutual activation" to speak of the special moments of human contact which seem to generate the energy that enables persons and peoples to claim and sustain their identities. On mutual activation and the strength or virtue it conveys, see Erikson, "Human Strength and the Cycle of Generations" and "Psychological Reality and Historical Actuality," both in *Insight and Responsibility: Lectures on the Ethical Implications of Psychoanalytic Insight* (New York: W. W. Norton, 1964), 109–215.

4. Separateness transcended and distinctiveness confirmed constitute the definition of what Erik Erikson calls the sense of the numinous. See his *Toys and Reasons*, 89–90. See also his *Identity: Youth and Crisis* (New York: W. W. Norton, 1968), 220.

5. On the interpretation of group identity in terms of spatial configurations, see Erik Erikson, *Childhood and Society*, 2d ed. (New York: W. W. Norton, 1963), 111–86. On the need for avoidance as an essential aspect of identity formation, see Erikson's remarks on "reciprocal negation," the opposite of "mutual activation," in *Identity: Youth and Crisis*, 219–20.

6. Finley, *Autobiography*, 386–87.

7. Ibid., 280.

8. On the link between literacy and traditional norms of hierarchy in the eighteenth century and on the necessity of oral competence in translating republican ideology for the nonelite, see Harry S. Stout, "Religion, Communications, and the Ideological Origins of the American Revolution," *William and Mary Quarterly*, 3d ser., 34 (Oct. 1977): 519–41.

9. Wyatt-Brown, *Southern Honor*, 46–48, 330–31.

10. For a lively and informative treatment of the folklore of Methodist circuit riders, see Donald Byrne, *No Foot of Land: Folklore of American Methodist Itinerants*, ATLA monograph no. 6 (Metuchen N.J.: Scarecrow Press, 1975).

11. Carroll Smith-Rosenberg, "The Female World of Love and Ritual: Relations between Women in Nineteenth-Century America," in *The American Family in Social-Historical Perspective*, 3d ed., ed. Michael C. Gordon (New York: St. Martin's Press, 1983), 411–35; Wyatt-Brown, *Southern Honor*, 247–50.

12. This treatment of shame and guilt derives from Erikson, *Toys and Reasons*, 92–103; and Wyatt-Brown, *Southern Honor*, 154–56.

13. On the virtue of will, see Erikson, *Insight and Responsibility*, 118–20.

14. Reuben Davis, *Recollections of Mississippi and the Mississippians* (Boston: Houghton Mifflin, 1889), 20; quoted in Wyatt-Brown, *Southern Honor*, 134.

15. One might argue that the experience of the more Calvinistic converts who believed in the final perseverance of the saints obviated the sense of conditional acceptance. It would seem, however, that some sense of conditionality must have attended the insistence on the part of all evangelical denominations that the believer live an outward life consistent with his or her profession or lose membership in the church. In addition, the Calvinists asserted that those who turned back to the world were never really converted in the first place. This possibility of self-deception in religious experience led to careful questioning of candidates for baptism among the Baptists and to what seems to be more self-doubt among Baptists than among Methodists about the authenticity of religious experience. See, for instance, the testimony of Jacob Bower, "The Autobiography of Jacob Bower: A Frontier Baptist Preacher and Missionary," in *The Baptists*, 196–97; and the pastoral counsel of a Baptist layman to his nephew instructing the younger man how and how not to test his conversion, Martin Baskett to Martin B. Shepherd, 20 Apr. 1825, Martin Baskett Letters, Filson Club, Louisville, Ky. The Calvinist views of conversion might

have changed the character of the conditionality one felt about one's religious experience, but some sense of uncertainty seems to have persisted.

16. According to Erikson, shame is developmentally earlier than guilt and provides its foundations. All human beings are subject in varying degrees to both shame and guilt. It is to be expected, then, that subcultures which emphasize guilt-centered modes of social control will still build upon the dynamics of shame. See *Identity: Youth and Crisis*, 91–122.

17. Finley, *Sketches*, 109.

18. According to Erikson, the problems of purpose, initiative, and guilt in human life reflect the play age of the child. Hedged around by the protections and warnings of parents, the child employs a limited universe of toys and playmates to recreate and correct past experiences and anticipate future roles with the repetitiveness and spontaneity of which all effective ritualization is made. The protective hedge and unity of vision provided by some form of family loyalty is crucial because the child's conscience takes its shape from the example of adults engaged in the common cause of their familial and community pursuits. Those adults communicate the boundaries where play must end and certain acts, thoughts, and feelings be recognized as having irreversible consequences. A strong sense of purpose and a good conscience relies upon at least some general level of consistency in the adult messages. The child's growing capacity to master language at this age is also crucial because a sense of purpose must attach to a reality which is defined by the shared words of conversation. See Erikson, *Insight and Responsibility*, 120–22; and *Toys and Reasons*, 98–103.

19. Wyatt-Brown, *Southern Honor*, 117–25.

9. THE FAMILY OF GOD

1. Finley, *Sketches*, 107.

2. Wiley, "The Introduction and Progress of Methodism in Southeastern Indiana," 26–27.

3. H. C. Northcott, *Biography of Rev. Benjamin Northcott, a Pioneer Preacher of the Methodist Episcopal Church in Kentucky* (Cincinnati: Western Methodist Book Concern, 1875), 43–47.

4. For a powerful evocation and analysis of the Methodist "way of life," see Richey's chapters "Community, Fraternity, and Order" and "Conference as a Means of Grace," in *Early American Methodism*, 1–20, 65–81.

5. George Lakoff and Mark Johnson, *Metaphors We Live By* (Chicago: University of Chicago Press, 1980).

6. Ted Cohen, "Metaphor and the Cultivation of Intimacy"; and Wayne C. Booth, "Metaphor as Rhetoric: The Problem of Evaluation," both in *On Metaphor*, ed. Sheldon Sacks (Chicago: University of Chicago Press, 1979), 1–10; 47–70.

7. "Popularity: A Dialogue," *WCA*, 28 July 1837, 56.

8. The Methodists, of course, had no monopoly on such terms of endearment, and no claim for the exclusive use of family terms is being made here. See, for instance, the Baptist John Taylor's usage in his *History of Ten Baptist Churches*, 11–12, 19, 212–13, 224; and the language of Presbyterian Samuel Wright, "Abstract of Ministerial Labor . . . ," 7, Samuel G. Wright Papers, Illinois State Library, Springfield, Ill.

No claim for exclusive use of family terms needs to be made in order to make the main points of this chapter. Those points are (1) that the rhetoric of family relations was an expression of Methodist personal and social religious experience and (2) that this rhetoric was a formative influence within the Methodist community that disposed them to reconceive the meaning of family life. It is methodologically wrong-headed to suppose that a practice must be unique to a group in order for the practice to be characteristic of the group and influential in shaping other practices of its members. It is equally wrong-headed to suppose that similar discourse in two different groups must have similar meaning. It is possible, indeed likely, that saying "Mother Smith" signified, among Methodists, patterns of action and feeling quite different from those signified by Shakers, for example, who also addressed their female leaders as "mothers."

9. William Blair to J. B. Finley, 29 June 1823, JBFL.

10. Hannah Bareth to J. B. Finley, 24 Jan. 1824, JBFL.

11. Martin Hitt to Daniel Hitt, 14 Nov. 1791, 23 Oct. 1790, DHL.

12. William Burke, "Autobiography," 58.

13. See, for instance, Martin Hitt to Daniel Hitt, 23 Oct. 1790, DHL.

14. Finley, *Autobiography*, 398–401, and "Experiences and Travels of a Western Preacher," 16.

15. Richey provides the most powerful and insightful account available of the brotherhood of early Methodist preachers in *Early American Methodism*, 5–13, 72–80.

16. Richey finds more tension and less submissiveness in his examination of the ordering activities of the bishops. Ibid., 11–13.

17. George Brown, *Recollections*, 116–17.

18. Nathan Hatch points out that it was characteristic for popular religion at this time to blur such distinctions and uses a Methodist preacher, "crazy" Lorenzo Dow, as his chief illustration of this point; see Hatch, *Democratization of American Christianity*, 34–40. It is significant, however, that Dow was not a regular member of the brotherhood of Methodist preachers. It is also important that the majority of Methodists throughout the national and antebellum periods followed leaders like the authoritarian bishops Asbury and McKendree rather than "Republican Methodists" like James O'Kelly, idiosyncratic Methodists like Dow, or "reformers" like George Brown. Once again, the point may be made that the pietistic language of liberty among Methodists did not necessarily align in radical democratic fashion with the republican language of liberty. See Richey, *Early American Methodism*, xvii-xviii, 88–91.

19. Wiley, "Methodism in Southeastern Indiana," 42.

20. See, for instance, the sentimental encounter between James Havens and his "father in the Gospel," which James Finley recounted in John L. Smith, *Indiana Methodism*, 88–89.

21. Cartwright, *Autobiography*, 75.

22. Quinn, "Memoir of the Venerable White Brown," 53.

23. On Elijah Sparks, see Wiley, "Methodism in Southeastern Indiana," 29. On Benjamin Northcott, see H. C. Northcott, *Biography*, 109–10.

24. On John Sale, see Moses Crume, "Reminiscence of Rev. John Sale," *WCA*, 4 Oct. 1839, 93; on Crume, see Wiley, "Methodism in Southeastern Indiana," 142–43.

25. Young, *Autobiography*, 56.

26. Ibid., 245–53.

27. Mary Morriss Smith, "History of the Rise of the Methodist Church in Lebanon, [Tenn.]," Mary Morriss Smith Papers, Tennessee State Library and Archives, Nashville, Tenn.

28. John L. Smith, *Indiana Methodism*, 74.

29. Peter Doub, "Historical Sketches," William Clark Doub Papers, Manuscripts Department, Duke University, Durham, N. C.

30. D. M. Mitchel to G. W. Maley, 22 Feb. 1821, GWMC.

31. G. W. Maley, memoir of Mrs. Sarah Maley, 27 Apr. 1851, GWMC.

32. James Quinn to Daniel Hitt, 7 July 1803, DHL.

33. Gaddis, *Brief Recollections*, 227. See also the account of Sarah Stewart's labors in Stewart, *Highways and Hedges*, 104, 106–19.

34. Leonard I. Sweet, *The Minister's Wife: Her Role in Nineteenth-Century American Evangelicalism* (Philadelphia: Temple University Press, 1983), 44–106.

35. On women's isolation in southern rural culture, see Wyatt-Brown, *Southern Honor*, 247–53, 272–81; Catherine Clinton, *The Plantation Mistress: Woman's World in the Old South* (New York: Pantheon, 1982), 164–79; and Faragher, *Women and Men on the Overland Trail*, 110–28.

36. Mary Campbell to David Campbell, 22 Dec. 1822, and David Campbell to Mary Campbell, 1 Jan. 1823, Campbell Family Papers, Manuscript Department, Duke University, Durham, N. C. For other feminine complaints about the absence of husbands, see Mary Jeffreys Bethell, diary, 7, 21, 24, 32, 33, 44–48, Bethell Papers, Southern Historical Collection, University of North Carolina, Chapel Hill, N. C.; and Jane M. Jones, diary, 5 Jan. 1850, Jane M. Jones Diaries, Tennessee State Library and Archives, Nashville, Tenn.

37. Gaddis, *Brief Recollections*, 271–72. For other examples of self-sacrifice in the face of illness, see the accounts of Sarah Fee in Fee, *Garnered Sheaves from Harvest Fields in Ohio, Kentucky, and West Virginia* (Cincinnati: Curts and Jennings, 1900), 289; and of Mrs. Lakin in "Biographical Department," *Christian Advocate and Journal*, 9 May 1828.

38. Melinda Hamline, *Memoir of Mrs. Angeline B. Sears, with Extracts from Her Correspondence* (Cincinnati: Swormstedt and Poe, 1851), 173.

39. Elizabeth Kaufmann to George S. Phillips, 27 July 1843, GSPC.

40. Phillips, diary, 19–24 Jan., 19 Sept. 1844. See a similar tribute by Philip Gatch to his wife in John McLean, *Sketch of Rev. Philip Gatch* (Cincinnati: Swormstedt and Poe, 1854), 125–26.

41. Julie Roy Jeffrey, "Ministry Through Marriage: Methodist Clergy Wives on the Trans-Mississippi Frontier," in *Women in New Worlds: Historical Perspectives on the Wesleyan Tradition*, vol. 1, ed. Rosemary Skinner Keller and Hilah F. Thomas (Nashville: Abingdon Press, 1982), 143–60.

42. Burgess, *Pleasant Recollections*, 424–25, 457–58. There was also the example of Philip Gatch's wife who provided both temporal and spiritual refreshment to weary itinerants and to whom her husband often sent younger, inexperienced preachers because she was known as the best preacher's nurse. See McLean, *Sketch of Gatch*, 125–27.

43. Finley, *Autobiography*, 281.

44. Carroll Smith-Rosenberg, "The Female World of Love and Ritual," 411–35. See also Daniel Blake Smith, *Inside the Great House*, 76–79; Wyatt-Brown, *Southern Honor*, 247–51; and Clinton, *Plantation Mistress*, 174–75.

45. See, for example, the letters of James Henthorn to his friend Daniel Hitt, especially 7 Jan. 1801, DHL; Aaron Wood to G. W. Maley, 20 Nov. 1823 and 7 Feb. 1824, GWMC; and Adam Poe to G. S. Phillips, 25 July 1854, GSPP.

46. Clifford Geertz, *The Interpretation of Cultures* (New York: Basic Books, 1973), 87–125.

47. James Henthorn to Daniel Hitt, 7 Jan. 1801, DHL.

48. Isaac Crawford, journal, 2–5 Oct. 1847.

49. Samuel Williams to John Widney, 19 Aug. 1810, in "Autobiography of Samuel Williams," 191–92, S&SWWP.

50. Mary Campbell to David Campbell, 22 Dec. 1822, and David Campbell to Mary Campbell, 3 Jan. 1823, Campbell Family Papers, Manuscripts Department, Duke University, Durham, N. C.

51. Harriet Stubbs to J. B. Finley, 13 Sept. 1823, JBFL.

52. T. A. Morris, *Miscellany: Consisting of Essays, Biographical Sketches, and Notes of Travel* (Cincinnati: Swormstedt and Poe, 1852), 92–93. See also Angeline Sears's complaints about the worldliness and dissipation of mind which came with much formal visiting in Hamline, *Memoir of Angeline Sears*, 47–50.

53. "Parental Responsibilities and Encouragements," *PCJ*, 7 May 1835, 57. See also "The Family Constitution," *WCA*, 27 Nov. 1838, 61.

10. RITUALIZING FAMILIES FOR GOD

1. Scripps, "Early Methodism in the Far West—No. 2," 149.
2. See, for example, "Nursing Young Converts," *WCA*, 12 June 1837, 20.
3. Robert Emory, *History of the Discipline*, 147–50.
4. William Burke, "Autobiography," 69; Young, *Autobiography*, 269; "Revival Intelligence," *WCA*, 3 Mar. 1837, 178; "Youth's Department," *WCA*, 8 Jan. 1841, 152.
5. Chauncey Hobart professed to have acquired his idea of conversion in exactly this manner; see his *Recollections*, 19–20.
6. Fee, *Bringing the Sheaves*, 33.
7. Finley, *Sketches*, 350–52.
8. Fee, *Bringing the Sheaves*, 16–17.
9. John Kobler, "The First Class Meeting in Ohio," *WCA*, 23 June 1837, 36.
10. Young, *Autobiography*, 316–17 (emphasis mine).
11. "Family Prayer," *WCA*, 17 Feb. 1843, 173. See also Emory, *History of the Discipline*, 173, and "Thoughts on the General Rules of the Methodist E. Church—No. 19. Family and Private Prayer," *WCA*, 10 Mar. 1835, 181.
12. Tarkington, *Autobiography*, 26; Finley, *Autobiography*, 259, 283; Burgess, *Pleasant Recollections*, 300–301.
13. "Family Religion," *WCA*, 2 May 1834, 4.
14. Crume, "Reminiscence of Rev. John Sale," *WCA*, 4 Oct. 1839, 93. See also Wiley, "Methodism in Southeastern Indiana," 43; and O. P. Fitzgerald, *John B. McFerrin: A Biography* (Nashville: Publishing House of the M. E. Church, South, 1893), 29–30.
15. Sullins, *Recollections*, 24–27. The tactic of bringing the husband into a knowledge of experimental religion by means of family prayer seems to have become a widespread one as the "Methodist Age" took hold in the American churches. See Paul Johnson's account of the Finney revivals in *Shopkeeper's Millennium*, 95–108.
16. Fitzgerald, *John B. McFerrin*, 29–34.
17. Samuel Williams, memoir of William Williams, in vol. 1 of "Memoirs of Samuel Williams," 25–31, 58–60, S&SWWP.
18. Fee, *Bringing the Sheaves*, 13–14. For another instance of a formal religionist being converted as he attended to the duty of family prayer, see John L. Smith, *Indiana Methodism*, 100–101.
19. Peter Doub, "Historical Sketches," William Clark Doub Papers, Manuscripts Department, Duke University, Durham, N. C.
20. Cartwright, *Autobiography*, 289–90. For memories similar to Cartwright's from one who grew up in such scenes, see Burgess, *Pleasant Recollections*, 48.
21. Gaddis, *Brief Recollections*, 77–78. Other accounts of emotional effervescence in family prayer are found in Thomas Mann, journal, 6 June 1805; Learner Blackman, journal, 12; and Crawford, journal, 9 July 1838, 76.
22. Sullins, *Recollections*, 24–27.
23. Burgess, *Pleasant Recollections*, 39–41; Gaddis, *Footprints*, 44; Haney, *Story of My Life*, 26; Stewart, *Highways and Hedges*, 21–22; Welker, *Conflicts and Trials*, 24.
24. "Family Prayer," *WCA*, 25 Aug. 1837, 72. See also Finley, *Sketches*, 446–47; Cartwright, *Autobiography*, 334–35; and "Family Religion," *WCA*, 2 May 1834.
25. Burgess, *Pleasant Recollections*, 39–41; Welker, *Conflicts and Triumphs*, 24. See also M. L. Haney's reminiscences of his father in *Story of My Life*, 26.
26. "Miscellaneous," *WCA*, 16 Jan. 1835, 152.
27. "On Family Worship," *WCA*, 4 Aug. 1837, 60. See also "Family Altar," *PCJ*, 5 Nov. 1835, 164.
28. Cartwright, *Autobiography*, 335; Haney, *Story of My Life*, 26.

29. "Family Religion," *WCA*, 2 May 1834, 4.

30. "Family Prayer," *WCA*, 9 Aug. 1839, 64; "Parents' Department: Family Prayer," *WCA*, 29 Jan. 1836; "Family Prayer," *WCA*, 10 Apr. 1835, 197; "Parents' Department: Family Worship," *WCA*, 8 May 1835, 8; "On Family Worship," *WCA*, 4 Aug. 1837, 60; Lovell, *Methodist Family Manual*, 143–44.

31. Lovell, *Methodist Family Manual*, 178; "On Family Worship," *WCA*, 4 Aug. 1837, 60; "Parents' Department: Family Worship," *WCA*, 5 Sept. 1834, 76; "Parents' Department: The Influence of Family Prayers on Family Government," *WCA*, 10 June 1836, 28; "Parents' Department: Effect of Prayer on the Minds of Children," *WCA*, 24 June 1836, 36.

32. E. Thomson, "Wesleyans—Domestic Worship," *CCA*, 9 May 1860, 76. The piece was borrowed from the *Western Christian Advocate*.

33. John H. Power identified the peaceful, happy death of the Methodist saint as an integral part of the cycle of life in a religious family. See Power, *Discourse on Domestic Piety and Family Government in Four Parts*, ed. B. F. Tefft (Cincinnati: Swormstedt and Poe, 1854), 12, 175ff. In antebellum society generally, of course, dying took place at home. See Lewis Saum, "Death in the Popular Mind of Pre-Civil War America," in *Death in America*, ed. David E. Stannard (Philadelphia: University of Pennsylvania Press, 1974), 30–48. For an interpretation of the Methodist ritual of happy dying in comparison to interpretations of deathbed ritual by Saum and others, see my article, "The Ritual of Happy Dying among Early American Methodists," *Church History* 56 (Sept. 1987): 348–63. Here, as with the issue of the rhetoric of familial address, it is important to stress that no claims to the uniqueness of Methodist deathbed ritual need be made in order to observe that this ritual incorporated the patterns of Methodist social religion into a domestic setting.

34. "Reminiscences," *WCA*, 1 Sept. 1837, 76.

35. For examples of this sort of continuity, see "Biographical Department: Amelia Conway," *WCA*, 9 Oct. 1835, 96; "Biographical Department: Thomas Givens," *WCA*, 27 Nov. 1835, 120; and Gaddis's account of his father's death in *Footprints*, 108, 111.

36. Andrew Carroll, *Moral and Religious Sketches and Collections, with Incidents of Ten Years' Itineracy in the West*, vol. 1 (Cincinnati: Methodist Book Concern, 1857), 107.

37. Finley, *Sketches*, 177.

38. "Biographical Department: Eleanor T. Ayres," *WCA*, 9 Oct. 1835, 96. See also the account of Isaac Hunter's death in Gaddis, *Footprints*, 307–308.

39. See, for instance, James Gilruth's attempt to be faithful to the Wyandot Chief Between-the-Logs in Finley, *Autobiography*, 445–46; and Maxwell Gaddis's faithfulness to his colleague, Isaac Hunter, in Gaddis, *Footprints*, 307–309.

40. "Biographical Department: Frances Railey," *WCA*, 12 Sept. 1834, 80.

41. H. H. B., "Memoirs," *WCM*, Aug. 1816, 360–65; "Biographical Department: Ann Claypool," *WCA*, 26 Sept. 1834, 85; "Biographical Department: Thomas Lakin," *WCA*, 24 Apr. 1835, 205; "Biographical Department: Amanda White," *WCA*, 3 Oct. 1834, 92; "Biographical Department: Joseph Cassel," *WCA*, 2 Oct. 1835, 92; "Biographical Department: Amelia Conaway," *WCA*, 9 Oct. 1835, 96; "Biographical Department: Eliza Preston Thompson," *WCA*, 19 Aug. 1842, 72; Gaddis, *Footprints*, 109–11.

42. M. T., "A Short Account of the Life and Death of Miss Anne Warner," *WCM*, Apr. 1816, 180–81.

43. Joseph Morgan to Daniel Hitt, 17 Mar. 1802, DHL. See also John L. Smith, *Indiana Methodism*, 86.

44. Gaddis *Footprints*, 303–304.

45. Stewart, *Highways and Hedges*, 214–16.

46. Others who were moved by deathbed scenes to greater faithfulness or at least held back from gross sin were Gaddis, *Footprints*, 112; and Finley, *Autobiography*, 26. For more formal reflections on how death strengthened piety, see "Funeral Reflections," *WCA*, 8 Aug. 1834, 57.

47. "Biographical Department: David Lewis," *WCA*, 10 Apr. 1835, 200. See also M. T., "A Short Account of . . . Anne Warner," *WCM*, Apr. 1816, 180–81.

48. Gaddis, *Footprints*, 429. See also the case of Jane M'Neal whose deathbed performance led to the conversion of her father and, perhaps, of her unbelieving physician. Theophilus Arminius [Thomas Hinde], "Reminiscences of the Past," *WCA*, 19 Dec. 1834, 133.

11. THE CHRISTIAN HOME IN THE REPUBLIC

1. John Higham, *From Boundlessness to Consolidation: The Transformation of American Culture, 1848–1860* (Ann Arbor, Mich.: William L. Clements, 1969).

2. Lois Banner has effectively criticized those who exaggerate the concerns of evangelicals for "social control" in her "Religious Benevolence as Social Control: A Critique of an Interpretation," *Journal of American History* 60 (1973): 23–41. Hatch, in *Democratization of American Christianity*, has made the democratizing impulse in popular evangelicalism abundantly clear.

3. Ideological discourse characterizes a society in which the various regions of social experience are, as the sociologists say, "differentiating" and becoming more autonomous social institutions, each with its own more-or-less specialized functions and guiding norms. Ideologies meet, poorly or well, the need for cognitive and emotional orientation in such situations of growing social complexity. See Geertz, "Ideology as a Cultural System," in *Interpretation of Cultures*, 193–233.

4. The evangelical domesticity developed by the midwestern Methodists studied here closely resembled that described by Colleen McDannell in *Christian Home*. McDannell identifies two models of leadership in this domestic religion: paternal and maternal. The Methodist domesticity described here and in the next chapter was closest to the maternal model, though I find among the midwestern Methodist mothers a sterner, less refined form of religious "influence" than McDannell does among the eastern women featured in her sources.

5. Russell E. Richey, whose work is cited frequently and gratefully in these pages, would want to stress a certain discontinuity between the early Methodist community and its views of the nation, on one hand, and the uncritical adoption of Christian republicanism by antebellum Methodists, on the other. Early Methodists, Richey contends, had little in common with the Puritan theocrats who forged the ideological design for America as Christian nation. Early Methodism had an innocent, Edenic quality to its sense of community and its view of America as landscape more than as polity. The alliance of Methodism with American political culture was one measure of its loss of Edenic innocence. See *Early American Methodism*, xi-xiii, 33–46, 88–91. Much of what I have said here about the consolidation of Methodism is in agreement with Richey's judgment. This chapter, however, stresses fundamental continuities of Methodist practice and experience with the ideologies of republicanism and domesticity, continuities that Richey's analysis is not designed to reveal.

6. Wesley Norton, *Religious Newspapers in the Old Northwest to 1861: A History, Bibliography, and Record of Opinion* (Athens, Ohio: Ohio University Press, 1977), 33–34.

7. For general accounts of Christian republican thinking which tend to focus on the northeast, see Perry Miller, *The Life of the Mind in America from the Revolution to the Civil War* (New York: Harcourt, Brace, and World, 1965), 66–72; Banner, "Religious Benevolence as Social Control," 35–39; and Timothy L. Smith, "Righteousness and Hope: Christian Holiness and the Millennial Vision in America, 1800–1900," *American Quarterly* 31 (1979): 21–45.

8. Wood, *Creation*, 53–70.

9. Bishop McIlvaine, "Necessity of Religion to the Prosperity of a Nation,"

WCA, 2 Feb. 1838, 161; "The Minister's Wife," *LR*, Nov. 1841, 337; "Religion Essential to Government," *WCA*, 16 Oct. 1840, 104; "An Address on the Death of President Harrison," *WCA*, 21 May 1844, 17.

10. "Moral Qualifications of Rulers," *WCA*, 26 Jan. 1839, 156; "Christian Patriotism," *WCA*, 31 July 1840, 58, and 7 Aug. 1840, 62; "What Next?" *WCA*, 30 July 1841, 58; "Celebration of American Independence," *WCA*, 1 Aug. 1834, 161.

11. "Duties of American Citizens," *WCA*, 29 Jan. 1839, 156; "Christian Patriotism," 31 July 1840, 58; McIlvaine, "Necessity of Religion," 161.

12. Nathan Bangs, "Motives to Union," *PCJ*, 30 Apr. 1840, 57. This article was one of several published by the *Pittsburgh Conference Journal* in 1840 which are concerned with the need for unity within and among evangelical churches for the sake of both religious prosperity and civil liberty. See Bangs, "Necessity of Union," *PCJ*, 27 Feb., 12 Mar., and 19 Mar. 1840, 24, 29, 35; his "Religious Politicians," *PCJ*, 26 Mar. 1840, 38; and his "United Action," *PCJ*, 26 Mar. 1840, 39.

13. J. N. Maffitt, "Sketches of Missionary Labor—New Albany [Ind.] Camp Meeting," *PCJ*, 28 Nov. 1839, 178.

14. Samuel Williams was expelled from the Chillicothe, Ohio, society on exactly this charge in 1809. See his "Autobiography," 170–80.

15. "Fourth of July," *PCJ*, 14 June 1834, 79; "The Fourth of July," *PCJ*, 18 June 1835, 82; William Hunter, "The Fourth of July," *PCJ*, 26 Nov. 1835, 176; A Parent, "Sabbath Schools—Christmas, New Year's, and the Fourth," *PCJ*, 14 Dec 1837, 186; "Great Sabbath School Jubilee at Pittsburgh," *PCJ*, 16 July 1840, 102; "Fourth of July Sabbath School and Temperance Celebrations," *PCJ*, 25 July 1839, 107; "Celebration of American Independence," *WCA*, 1 Aug. 1834, 55; "Editorial: Fourth of July," *WCA*, 16 July 1841, 50; "Editorial: Fourth of July Visit," *WCA*, 19 July 1844, 55. See also H. C. Northcott, *Biography*, 93; and Allen M. Scott, "Oration Delivered at White Oak Camp Ground, Franklin City, Arkansas, July 4, 1845," in Sion Record, "Diary," Methodist Church Sermon Notes Collection, microfilm no. 693, Tennessee State Library and Archives, Nashville, Tenn.

16. As the discussion in chapter 13 of this study will indicate, the Sunday school seems to have been one of the main agencies which superseded the class meeting in mid-nineteenth-century Methodism.

17. See, for instance, "Nunneries—A New Plan," *PCJ*, 6 Aug. 1835, 112.

18. Lovell, *Methodist Family Manual*, 3–4.

19. A Young Lady, "Home," 64; "Letter," *WCA*, 31 Oct. 1834, 105.

20. Power, *Discourse on Domestic Piety*, 21.

21. "Parents' Department: A Christian Father," *WCA*, 30 June 1837, 40.

22. "Self-Denial," *WCA*, 27 June 1834, 40.

23. T. A. Morris, *Miscellany* (Cincinnati: Swormstedt and Poe, 1852), 38; Power, *Discourse on Domestic Piety*, 38; "Family Religion," *WCA*, 2 May 1834, 4; "Winter Evenings," *WCA*, 15 May 1840, 16.

24. Morris, *Miscellany*, 38.

25. "Parents' Department: Evils of Dancing," *WCA*, 25 Jan. 1837, 72.

26. Power, *Discourse on Domestic Piety*, 33–39; Morris, *Miscellany*, 155–56; Burgess, *Pleasant Recollections*, 39–40; "Parents's Department," *WCA*, 21 July 1837, 52.

27. "Youth's Department: Temptations of the Young," *WCA*, 14, 21, 28 Feb., and 6 Mar. 1840, 172, 176, 180, 184; "Youth's Department: The Young Man from Home," *WCA*, 15 May 1840, 16.

28. "Parents' Department: Domestic Peace," *WCA*, 10 Apr. 1835, 200.

29. Lovell, *Methodist Family Manual*, 177–78.

30. "Visiting," *WCA*, 11 Dec. 1835, 129. The timing of this article, near the start of the holiday season when sociable calling tended to be at its height, may have been intentional. Ten years later and a bit later in the holiday season, Frederick Merrick, a guiding light of Ohio Wesleyan University, echoed the concerns of the

earlier writer. He grieved over "professed disciples of Christ conforming to the foolish practices of the world in making and receiving New Year's calls." The Lord's substance was thereby wasted in "injurious luxuries" and "useless presents," and precious hours were murdered. "What an example to set before an ungodly world," he moaned. Frederick Merrick, diary, 3 Jan. 1845, United Methodist Archives Center, Ohio Wesleyan University, Delaware, Ohio.

31. D. Whitmer, "Utility of Class Meetings," *WCA*, 6 May 1868, 146. A similar utilitarian frame of mind pervades John Miley's introductory chapter on "The Social Principle on Which Class Meetings Are Instituted," in his *Treatise on Class Meetings*, 23–43.

32. "It Is Good for Us To Be Here," *PCJ*, 5 Dec. 1839, 181. For other sentiments of sober sociability see "Recreation," *PCJ*, 10 Aug. 1837, 113; A Parent, "Sabbath Schools—Christmas, New Years, and the Fourth," *PCJ*, 14 Dec. 1837, 186; "Getting into Society," *PCJ*, 11 May 1837, 61. Bordering on the frivolous, but still illustrating the utility to labor of Sabbath rest is a poem by "Journeyman Mechanic" entitled "Saturday Night," *PCJ*, 24 Aug. 1837, 124; see also E. M'Clure, "Imaginary Conversation," *LR*, Aug. 1845, 235–38.

33. "Parents' Department: Kindness at Home," *WCA*, 31 Jan. 1840, 164.

34. Lovell, *Methodist Family Manual*, 173–75; "Rules for Husbands and Wives," *WCA*, 16 May 1834, 9; Bates, "Husband and Wife," *WCA*, 8 May 1840, 12.

35. Lovell, *Methodist Family Manual*, 4.

36. "Editorial: Hints on Family Government," *WCA*, 30 May 1834, 18. See also Morris, *Miscellany*, 32; "Parents' Department: Cultivation of the Infant Mind," *WCA*, 28 Apr. 1837, 4.

37. Haney, *Story of My Life*, 10.

38. "Editorial: Hints on Family Government," *WCA*, 30 May 1834, 18; "Parents' Department: Directions," *WCA*, 17 Apr. 1835, 204; "Parents' Department: My Mother Never Tells Lies," *WCA*, 6 Mar. 1840, 184; "Parental Government," *WCA*, 3 July 1835, 40; "Parents' Department: Influence of Example," *WCA*, 27 Nov. 1835, 120; Morris, *Miscellany*, 32; Power, *Discourse on Domestic Piety*, 26–33, 39–49.

39. "Parents' Department: Ruinous Indulgence," *WCA*, 28 Aug. 1835, 72; "Editorial: Hints on Family Government," 18; Burgess, *Pleasant Recollections*, 76–77. See also Rev. Sears's tribute to his late wife's family government in Hamline, *Memoir of Angeline Sears*, 287–88.

40. Mary Ryan sees the transition from will-breaking to affectionate moral influence as a major theme in the story of middle-class self-definition in the nineteenth century. She correctly associates will-breaking with a conversion experience which required self-renunciation and clearly perceives the Second Great Awakening revivals as subverting traditional patriarchal views of the family and fostering an emphasis on affection as the ties that bind the family. Her association of will-breaking with traditional patriarchy and a hostility to privacy and "individualism," however, seems at odds with parts of her own argument about the role of revivalist conversions in catalyzing the change to a middle-class family centered on maternal affection and conscience. Such a pairing is certainly at odds with the interpretations offered here regarding the evangelical battle with traditional southern styles of patriarchal family and community relations. See Ryan, *Cradle of the Middle Class*, 39–43, 65–103, 155–65, 179–85.

41. Haney, *Story of My Life*, 6–8.

42. Ibid., 26–30.

43. "Children's Department: The All Seeing Eye," *WCA*, 20 May 1836, 16; "Children's Department: Happy Charles—or Impatience Cured," *WCA*, 10 Apr. 1835, 200; "Children's Department: Disobedience," *WCA*, 17 July 1835, 48; "Parents' Department: Happy Parental Discipline," *WCA*, 25 Sept. 1835, 88; "Parents' Department: The Family Constitution," *WCA*, 10 Aug. 1838, 61; "Parental Unfaithfulness

Rebuked," *PCJ*, 24 Oct. 1839, 160. See also John Burgess's recollections of a home not quite so stern as Haney's but just as relentless, in *Pleasant Recollections*, 39–42, 76–77.

44. This exercise in imagination is based on Wyatt-Brown, *Southern Honor*, chaps. 5 and 6, and on what evangelical writers specified as popular, but wrong, ways to govern families. See, for example, Power, *Discourse on Domestic Piety*, 29–39; and "Parental Government," *WCA*, 3 July 1835, 40.

45. Greven, *Protestant Temperament*.

46. "Parents' Department: The Family Constitution," 61; "Cultivation of the Infant Mind," *WCA*, 28 Apr. 1837, 4; "Parents' Department: Instruction of Children," *WCA*, 18 Dec. 1835, 132; Power, *Discourse on Domestic Piety*, 139–55.

47. William Fletcher King, *Reminiscences* (New York: Abingdon Press, 1915), 49–50. For other examples of the work ethic in connection with seclusion from worldly influences in family government, see Haney, *Story of My Life*, 15; and Hobart, *Recollections*, 62–63.

48. Morris, *Miscellany*, 33; "Parents' Department: To Parents—Extract of an Address Delivered in Ohio by D. P. King, Esq.," *WCA*, 9 Sept. 1836, 80; "Early Frugality," *WCA*, 16 Sept. 1836, 84; Samuel Williams, "Autobiography," 502–503.

49. Power, *Discourse on Domestic Piety*, 94–105. For similar understandings of the temporal advantages of religion, see "Take Care How You Get up the Ladder," *WCA*, 23 Sept. 1836, 88; "Parents' Department: Economy in a Family," *WCA*, 22 May 1840, 20; and the reminiscences of William I. Fee, which exuded a remarkable pride in the eminence to which the children of the pioneer Methodist people of the Ohio valley region had risen, in *Garnered Sheaves*, 344–45, 360.

50. "Family Religion," 4; "Parents' Department: Directions," *WCA*, 17 Apr. 1835, 204; "Parents' Department," *WCA*, 10 Jan. 1840, 152; "Parents' Department: Parental Instruction," *WCA*, 28 Feb. 1840, 180; "Parents' Department: Winter Evenings," *WCA*, 15 May 1840, 16.

51. Frederick Norwood's chapter on "Books and Teachers" is an accessible survey of Methodist printing and educational endeavors before the Civil War; see *The Story of American Methodism* (Nashville: Abingdon Press, 1974), 210–22.

52. See Burton J. Bledstein, *The Culture of Professionalism: The Middle Class and the Development of Higher Education in America* (New York: W. W. Norton, 1976), 105–20, 134–36, 146–58. Compare Bledstein's account of character in mid-Victorian culture not only with the language of John Power but also with R. W. Allen, "Independence of Christian Character," *LR*, Apr. 1846, 103–104; and, John R. Burgess's memories of his own schooling and schoolmates in *Pleasant Recollections*, 161–79.

53. Power, *Discourse on Domestic Piety*, 49–54.

54. Ibid., 116–34.

55. Crowley, *This Sheba, Self*, chap. 2.

56. Nancy Cott, following Mary Ryan, makes this observation regarding the integrative functions of womanhood and the family in *The Bonds of Womanhood: "Woman's Sphere" in New England, 1780–1835* (New Haven: Yale University Press, 1977), 69 n.

57. Thompson, *Making of the English Working Class*, chap. 11; Douglas, *Feminization of American Culture*.

58. Semmel, *Methodist Revolution*; Timothy L. Smith *Revivalism and Social Reform: American Protestantism on the Eve of the Civil War* (1957; New York: Harper Torchbooks, 1965).

12. ICONS OF HOLINESS AND INSTRUMENTS OF MORALITY

1. Barbara Welter, "The Feminization of American Religion: 1800–1860," in *Clio's Consciousness Raised: New Perspectives on the History of Women*, ed. Mary

Hartmann and Lois W. Banner (New York: Harper and Row, 1974), 137–57; Richard D. Shiels, "The Feminization of American Congregationalism, 1730–1835," *American Quarterly* 33 (Spring 1981): 46–62. The charge of narcissism is leveled by Douglas, *Feminization of American Culture*, chap. 1. See also Leonard I. Sweet's suggestion that much of late nineteenth-century American culture may be understood as a reaction against such feminizing in *Minister's Wife*, 232–36.

2. Nancy Cott included a balanced assessment of this debate in the conclusion of *Bonds of Womanhood*, 197–206. Ann Douglas (cited above), Nina Baym, and Mary Kelley, writing about nineteenth-century women's literature, have all made important and contrasting judgments in this debate. See Baym, *Woman's Fiction: A Guide to Novels by and about Women in America, 1820–1870* (Ithaca: Cornell University Press, 1978), and Kelley, *Private Woman, Public Stage* (New York: Oxford University Press, 1984). See also Baym's review of Kelley, "Turning Literature into History," *American Quarterly* 36 (Fall 1984): 593–97.

3. Janet S. Everhart, "Maggie Newton Van Cott," in vol. 2 of *Women in New Worlds: Historical Perspectives on the Wesleyan Tradition*, ed. Rosemary Skinner Keller, Louise L. Queen, and Hilah F. Thomas (Nashville: Abingdon Press, 1982), 300–317.

4. This replacement is a theme pervading Kathryn Kish Sklar, *Catherine Beecher: A Study in American Domesticity* (1973; New York: W. W. Norton, 1976).

5. "Female Character," *WCA*, 5 Sept. 1834, 76. See also "Miscellany: Experience," *WCA*, 27 Nov. 1835, 124.

6. James Henthorn to Daniel Hitt, 16 Mar. 1803, DHL.

7. This assertion is based on a reading of the seventeen letters by Henthorn (spanning about ten years) in the Daniel Hitt collection.

8. "Itinerant Preachers" and "Pious Women," both in *Gospel Herald*, Oct. 1830, 70.

9. See, for instance, the samples of church trials involving sexual improprieties in the collection of source materials by William Warren Sweet, ed., *Religion on the American Frontier, 1783–1840*, vol. 4, *The Methodists* (Chicago: University of Chicago Press, 1946), 646–64.

10. Nancy F. Cott's observations on the ideological functions of the idea of women's passionlessness seem appropriate to the western Methodist women under study here; see "Passionlessness: An Interpretation of Victorian Sexual Ideology, 1790–1850," *Signs* 4 (Winter 1978): 219–36.

11. Evidence of such transcendence in a circuit rider lingered in a tribute to an Indiana circuit rider, James Havens, in whom was found the coincidence of many opposites, including the "sturdy passions of a heroic man" and "the gentle and loving spirit of a woman, even the most refined and gentle of her sex." See J. C. Smith, *Reminiscences*, 67.

12. For an analysis of a parallel process of transcendence and consolidation in a different region, see Smith-Rosenberg, "Women and Religious Revivals: Anti-Ritualism, Liminality, and the Emergence of the American Bourgeoisie"; and Nancy Hewitt, "The Perimeters of Women's Power in American Religion," both in *The Evangelical Tradition in America*, ed. Leonard I. Sweet (Macon, Ga.: Mercer University Press, 1984), 199–256.

13. Joanna Bowen Gillespie, "The Emerging Voice of the Methodist Woman: *The Ladies' Repository*, 1841–61," in *Rethinking Methodist History: A Bicentennial Historical Consultation*, ed. Russell E. Richey and Kenneth E. Rowe (Nashville: Kingswood Books, 1985), 152–53.

14. Samuel Galloway, "An Address Delivered before the Pupils of the Oakland Female Seminary, Hillsborough, Ohio," *LR*, Mar. 1841, 65. See also "Woman and Christianity," *WCA*, 24 Jan. 1840, 160.

15. Welter, "Feminization of American Religion," 141.

16. J. S. Tomlinson, "Female Influence," *LR*, Jan. 1841, 28–29; D. W., "Woman's Sphere," *LR*, Feb. 1841, 38–39; J. Adams, "Woman," *LR*, Apr. 1841, 121; Hannah

More, "Woman," 137; "Influence of Religion upon Female Character and Beauty," *Gospel Herald*, Oct. 1829, 41–42; "Parents' Department: The Peculiar Facilities Afforded to Mothers for Training Up Their Children for God," *WCA*, 28 July 1837, 56.

17. D. W., "Woman's Sphere," 38.

18. J. S. Tomlinson, "Female Influence," 194–95; Galloway, "Address," 66–67; J. S. Wilson, "Temperance," *LR*, Dec. 1841, 375–76; "Temperance Department," *WCA*, 30 June 1837, 38.

19. "Sistership," *LR*, Feb. 1844, 42; Dr. Palfrey, "Brother and Sister," *LR*, Oct. 1844, 296.

20. Goodwin, "The Model," *LR*, Jan. 1844, 1–3.

21. "Directions for Ladies," *WCA*, 19 Feb. 1835, 172; "Counsel for Ladies," *WCA*, 8 Sept. 1837, 80.

22. "Biographical Department," *WCA*, 10 Mar. 1837, 184.

23. Joseph H. Creighton and Friends, *Life and Times of Joseph H. Creighton, A. M., of the Ohio Conference* (Lithopolis, Ohio: Western Methodist Book Concern, 1899), 36–37.

24. "Discipline of Childhood," *WCA*, 9 May 1834, 8; "Parents' Department: The Peculiar Facilities Afforded to Mothers for Training Up Their Children for God," *WCA*, 28 July 1837, 56; "Maternal Affection," *LR*, Sept. 1844, 284; "Parents' Department: Love of Parents," *WCA*, 4 Dec. 1835, 128.

25. J. N. M. Hilton, "Love's Appeal," *WCA*, 6 Nov. 1840, 116.

26. J. W., "To Parents," *WCA*, 3 Apr. 1840, 200; A Father, "What Is to Become of Our Children," *WCA*, 17 July 1835, 48; "To a Mother," *WCA*, 2 Oct. 1835, 92; "The Mother's Prayer," *Gospel Herald*, May 1830, 158.

27. Fee, *Bringing the Sheaves*, 42–45.

28. Finley, *Autobiography*, 267.

29. James Finley found it natural to describe one rush of penitents to the altar at a camp meeting as precipitated by "a mother leading a prodigal son." See Finley, *Sketches*, 328. Methodist novelist Edward Eggleston wrote a scene in *The Circuit-Rider* in which his heroine knows, because she too is a woman, that the favorite scripture of a mother tormented by her son's wicked ways is Luke 15:11–32, the parable of the prodigal son. See Eggleston, *The Circuit-Rider: A Tale of the Heroic Age* (New York: J. B. Ford and Co., 1874), 317.

30. Gaddis, *Footprints*, 70–76.

31. Ibid., 125–26, 238–39.

32. Wiley, "Methodism in Southeastern Indiana," 296–97. In the same volume, see also the Dec. 1927 issue, 461, for an account of a local preacher who spoke often in love feast of his mother and her home as a preaching place.

33. Finley, *Sketches*, 466–71.

34. Elizabeth Kauffman to George S. Phillips, 24 Mar. 1843, GSPP. For the comments from George which prompted her cautions, see George S. Phillips to Elizabeth Kauffman, 12 Mar. 1843, GSPP. For further examples of Elizabeth's cautionary mood, see Elizabeth Kauffman to George S. Phillips, 1 June and 27 June 1843, GSPP.

35. Elizabeth K. Phillips to George S. Phillips, 23 July 1847, GSPP.

36. Elizabeth K. Phillips to George S. Phillips, 3 Apr. 1854, GSPP.

37. Elizabeth K. Phillips to George S. Phillips, 23 July 1847, 3 Apr. 1854, and 9 Jan. 1854, GSPP.

38. Joseph and Mary Hollingshead to James B. Finley, 16 Sept. 1832, 15 Dec. 1832, 18 June 1833, 18 Jan. 1834, and 12 June 1834, JBFL.

39. Ruth Ross to James B. and Hannah Finley, 30 Mar. 1829 and 30 Jan. 1831, JBFL.

40. Hamline, *Memoir of Angeline Sears*, 3–4, 13–16.

41. Julie Roy Jeffrey, "Ministry Through Marriage," 143–60.
42. Hamline, *Memoir of Angeline Sears*, 120.
43. Ibid., 42–46, 57–65, 102–104, 123–24.
44. Ibid., 140–44.
45. Ibid., 147–57, 261–63.
46. Ibid., 157–58.
47. Ibid., 173–76, 178–81, 187–88, 193, 200, 204–205, 210–11. Twenty years after Angeline's death Melinda Hamline was still laboring in this network. The *Ladies Repository* published a transcript of a women's class meeting in which Hamline, as class leader, was still encouraging the enlargement of feminine selfhood by urging her "dear children" to be bold in their testimonies for Jesus; see "Woman's Work in the Church: Another Version," *LR*, Apr. 1872, 280–82.
48. Ibid., 161–76, 186–87, 192, 194–200, 202–203.
49. Hamline, *Memoir of Angeline Sears*, 205–208.
50. Ibid., 210–24.
51. Ibid., 224–28.
52. Ibid., 235–43, 246–47, 254–63.
53. Stewart, *Highways and Hedges*, 104, 107, 123–24, 128.
54. Ibid., 97, 106–19.
55. Fee, *Garnered Sheaves*, 6–7, 284–87.
56. Ibid., 6–7, 286–87, 294–96.
57. Ibid., 290–91.
58. Ibid., 510–41.
59. Ibid., 294–300.
60. For a brief account of these radical feminists and the process of their radicalization, see Catherine Clinton, *The Other Civil War: American Women in the Nineteenth Century* (New York: Hill and Wang, 1984), 54–81. Some, like Francis (Fanny) Wright, might be counted among those who were hardly touched at all by the imperative to feminine self-denial and domesticity. Others, like Elizabeth Cady Stanton and Susan B. Anthony, seem to have felt the demand and rejected it.
61. Joanna Bowen Gillespie, in "Emerging Voice of the Methodist Woman," 148–58, perceives a new, more self-fulfilling, voice of Methodist womanhood in the *Ladies Repository* at a significantly earlier date than that suggested here. The evidence Gillespie cites seems much more hemmed in by domesticity than her argument allows.
62. E. Drayton, "Women's Work," *LR*, Jan. and Feb. 1870, 38–42, 91–94.
63. "Women's Record at Home," *LR*, Aug. 1875, 171.
64. On the persistence of this domestic self-presentation even in the midst of very public activities on the part of WCTU activists, see Susan Dye Lee, "Evangelical Domesticity: The Woman's Temperance Crusade of 1873–1874"; and Carolyn DeSwarte Gifford, "For God and Home and Native Land: The W.C.T.U.'s Image of Woman in the Late Nineteenth Century"; both in *Women in New Worlds*, 293–309, 310–27. See also Carl N. Degler's chap., "The World Is Only a Large Home," in *At Odds*, 298–327.
65. "Women's Record at Home," *LR*, Feb. 1876, 172–73. On the antagonism of the sexes, see Mrs. Minna Wright's satirical story, "The Woman's Rights Village," *LR*, Oct. and Nov. 1872, 289–95, 351–59, in which men are allowed into a feminist utopia only by a narrow vote in which married women and young women prevail over the spinsters.
66. See Hannah More, "The Province of Woman," *WCA*, 2 June 1837, 20, and "Woman," 137.
67. Mrs. O. W. Scott, "The Model Woman," *LR*, May, June, July 1874, 347–50, 432–34, 24–27.
68. Eliza Woodworth, "My Three Missions," *LR*, Oct. 1873, 263–67.

13. THE FAMILY OF GOD GIVES GROUND TO THE SALVATION MACHINE

1. Richey, *Early American Methodism*, 21–32.

2. William McGuire King, "Denominational Modernization and Religious Identity: The Case of the Methodist Episcopal Church," *Methodist History* 20 (Jan. 1982): 75–89.

3. Norwood, *Story of American Methodism*, 175.

4. George Brown, *Recollections*, 116–17.

5. Cartwright, *Autobiography*, 114.

6. Douglas R. Chandler, "The Formation of the Methodist Protestant Church," in vol. 1 of *The History of American Methodism*, ed. Emory Stevens Bucke (New York: Abingdon Press, 1964), 659.

7. Roger Finke and Rodney Stark suggest that this change from local to episcopal control made the difference between a "Methodist miracle" of church growth and a "Methodist collapse" that set in soon after the preachers took control. See "How the Upstart Sects Won America: 1776–1850," *Journal of the Social Scientific Study of Religion* 28 (Mar. 1989): 27–44.

8. Norwood, *Story of American Methodism*, 257.

9. Banner, "Religious Benevolence," 29–31.

10. King, "Denominational Modernization."

Writers on class meeting at mid-century made much of the class meeting as an engine of "social power," a mechanistic metaphor which displayed the then-current fascination with rational organization and also obscured the nonrational dynamics and spiritual significance of social religion. See, for instance, I. C. Kimber, "Our Rule on Class Meetings," *CCA*, 30 Dec. 1857, 205; Miley, *Treatise on Class Meetings*, 23–43; and, David Holsclaw's commentary on Miley's paradoxical advocacy of class meeting, *The Demise of Disciplined Christian Fellowship: The Methodist Class Meeting in Nineteenth-Century America* (Ann Arbor, Mich.: UMI no. 8009501, 1979), 98–101.

11. Quoted in King, "Denominational Modernization," 88.

12. Richard D. Brown, *Modernization: The Transformation of American Life, 1600–1865* (New York: Hill and Wang, 1976), 14–15.

13. "Remarks on the 'General Rules of the Methodist Episcopal Church'—2," *WCA*, 3 Oct. 1834, 89.

14. "Class and Prayer Meetings," 56; "Class Meetings," *WCA*, 177; and Jacob Myers, "Division of Classes," 8.

15. Evidence of this trend away from close inquiry is found in a "Report on Class Meetings," in the *Minutes of the Cincinnati Annual Conference, 1853*, 10–11. See also Holsclaw, "Demise of Disciplined Christian Fellowship," 93–94.

16. Quoted in Holsclaw, "Demise of Disciplined Christian Fellowship," 163–64. For other evidence of this pattern see J. Montgomery, "Class-meeting and a Proposition Concerning It," *CCA*, 3 Feb. 1858, 13.

17. On "fraternal feeling" and the engulfing of class meeting in a sea of voluntary associations, see Holsclaw, "Demise of Disciplined Christian Fellowship," 98 n., 120–23, 160, 176–84, 205–208.

18. Maley, journal, 13 Jan. 1866.

19. On Methodist Sunday Schools and the shift from evangelism by revival to evangelism by religious education, see Richard Cameron, *Methodism and Society in Historical Perspective*, vol. 1 of *Methodism and Society* (New York: Abingdon Press, 1961), 271–77.

20. *Minutes of the Illinois Annual Conference of the Methodist Episcopal Church, 1859*, 34–36.

21. Leonard B. Gurley, "A Memorial Discourse Delivered before the Central Ohio Annual Conference of the Methodist Episcopal Church, at Wauseon, Ohio, Sept.

20, 1878, by Rev. Leonard B. Gurley, D. D., on the Fiftieth Anniversary of His Ministry," 12–13; this document is published with the *Minutes of the Central Ohio Annual Conference of the M. E. Church, 1878,* after 338 of the regular minutes.

22. *Minutes of the Southern Illinois Conference of the Methodist Episcopal Church, 1877–1919.*

23. "Welfare of Ohio Conference Methodism," *Journal of the Ohio Annual Conference of the Methodist Episcopal Church, 1875,* 220–32. For milder, but still troubled naggings about class meeting and personal and familial piety, see the pastoral addresses, in *Minutes of the Central Ohio Conference, 1866–1883; Minutes of the North Ohio Annual Conference of the Methodist Episcopal Church, 1878; Minutes of the Ohio Conference of the Methodist Episcopal Church, 1865 and 1866;* and the "State of the Church" report, in *Minutes of the Illinois Conference of the Methodist Episcopal Church, 1870,* 56–57.

24. Robert H. Wiebe, *The Search for Order, 1877–1920* (New York: Hill and Wang, 1967); Ben Primer, *Protestants and American Business Methods* (Ann Arbor, Mich.: UMI Research Press, 1979); Peter Dobkin Hall, *The Organization of American Culture, 1700–1900: Private Institutions, Elites, and the Origins of American Nationality* (New York: New York University Press, 1984).

25. Joseph Brooks, "Editorial: Class Meetings," *CCA,* 14 Mar. 1860, 42; "Why Piety Is Superficial," *CCA,* 28 Mar. 1860, 49.

26. "Class Meetings—No. 3," 9; J. Montgomery, "Class-meeting and a Proposition Concerning It," 13.

27. Two important scholarly overviews of this movement are Charles Edwin Jones, *The Perfectionist Persuasion: The Holiness Movement and American Methodism, 1867–1936* (Metuchen, N.J.: Scarecrow Press, 1974); and Melvin Easterday Dieter, *The Holiness Revival of the Nineteenth Century,* Studies in Evangelicalism, no. 1 (Metuchen, N.J.: Scarecrow Press, 1980).

28. For valuable contemporary accounts of the Tuesday Meeting and of the activities of the National Camp Meeting Association, see George Hughes, *Fragrant Memories of the Tuesday Meeting and the Guide to Holiness and Their Fifty Years' Work for Jesus* (New York: Palmer and Hughes, 1886); and *Days of Power in the Forest Temple: A Review of the Wonderful Work of God at Fourteen National Campmeetings from 1867 to 1872* (Boston: John Bent and Co., 1873).

29. Richey, *Early American Methodism,* xii-xiii.

30. Ibid., xiii.

31. Timothy L. Smith, *Revivalism and Social Reform: American Protestantism on the Eve of the Civil War* (1957; New York: Harper Torchbooks, 1965); David Moberg, *The Great Reversal: Evangelism versus Social Concern* (Philadelphia: J. B. Lippincott, 1972); Semmel, *Methodist Revolution;* Donald W. Dayton, *Discovering an Evangelical Heritage* (New York: Harper and Row, 1976); Hatch, *Democratization of American Christianity.*

32. For a systematic analysis of the connections between evangelicalism and republican politics in the nineteenth century, see George M. Thomas, *Revivalism and Cultural Change: Christianity, Nation Building and the Market in the Nineteenth-Century United States* (Chicago: University of Chicago Press, 1989), especially 66–102. For an insightful discussion of recent manifestations of these connections in relation to pro-life and antifeminist issues, see Wacker, "Searching for Norman Rockwell," 289–315.

BIBLIOGRAPHY

PRIMARY SOURCES

Manuscript Sources

Asbury, Daniel. Papers. Commission on Archives and History of the United Methodist Church, Madison, New Jersey.

Baskett, Martin. Letters. Filson Club, Louisville, Kentucky.

Bethell. Papers. Southern Historical Collection, University of North Carolina, Chapel Hill, North Carolina.

Blackman, Learner. Journal. Methodist Archives and History Center, Drew University, Madison, New Jersey.

Campbell. Family Papers. Manuscripts Department, Duke University, Durham, North Carolina.

Crawford, Isaac. Papers. Manuscripts Division, Indiana State Library, Indianapolis, Indiana.

Doub, William Clark. Papers. Manuscripts Department, Duke University, Durham, North Carolina.

Finley, James B. Letters. Archives of Ohio United Methodism, Ohio Wesleyan University, Delaware, Ohio.

Fisk. Papers. Illinois State Historical Library, Springfield, Illinois.

Hitt, Daniel. Letters. Typescript held by The Upper Room Library, Nashville, Tennessee. Originals held by Ohio Wesleyan University, Delaware, Ohio.

Jones, Jane M. Diaries. Tennessee State Library and Archives, Nashville, Tennessee.

Maley, Rev. George Washington. Papers. Archives of Ohio United Methodism, Ohio Wesleyan University, Delaware, Ohio.

Mann, Thomas. Papers. Manuscripts Department, Duke University Library, Durham, North Carolina.

Merrick, Frederick. Diary. United Methodist Archives Center, Ohio Wesleyan University, Delaware, Ohio.

Phillips, George Shane. Papers. Manuscripts Division, Huntington Library, San Marino, California.

Sion Record. Diary. Methodist Church Sermon Notes Collection, Tennessee State Library and Archives, Nashville, Tennessee. Microfilm no. 693.

Smith, Mary Morriss. Papers. Tennessee State Library and Archives, Nashville, Tennessee.

Williams, Samuel and S. W. Papers. Ohio Historical Society, Columbus, Ohio.

Wright, Samuel G. Papers. Illinois State Library, Springfield, Illinois.

Published Sources: Periodicals

(St. Louis) *Central Christian Advocate*

(New York) *Christian Advocate and Journal*

(Lexington, Ky.) *Gospel Herald*

(Cincinnati) *Ladies Repository and Gatherings of the West Pittsburgh Conference Journal*

(Cincinnati) *Western Christian Advocate*

(Chillicothe, Ohio) *Western Christian Monitor*

Published Sources: Books, Pamphlets, Minutes

Bangs, Nathan. *A History of the Methodist Episcopal Church*. Vol. 1. New York: T. Mason and G. Lane, 1838.

Beauchamp, William. *Letters on the Call and Qualifications of Ministers of the Gospel and on the Apostolic Character and Superior Advantages of the Itinerant Ministry*. Louisville, Ky.: John Early, 1849.

Boyd, Robert. *Personal Memoirs: Together with a Discussion Upon the Hardships and Sufferings of Itinerant Life; and Also a Discourse Upon the Pastoral Relation*. Cincinnati: Methodist Book Concern, 1867.

Brown, George. *Recollections of Itinerant Life; Including Early Reminiscences*. 2d ed. Cincinnati: R. W. Carroll and Co., 1866.

Brownlee, William G. *The Great Iron Wheel Examined; or Its False Spokes Extracted*. Nashville: 1856.

Burgess, John. *Pleasant Recollections of Characters and Works of Noble Men, with Old Scenes and Merry Times of Long, Long Ago*. Cincinnati: Cranston and Stowe, 1887.

Carroll, Andrew. *Moral and Religious Sketches and Collections, with Incidents of Ten Years' Itineracy in the West*. Vol. 1. Cincinnati: Methodist Book Concern, 1857.

Cartwright, Peter. *Autobiography of Peter Cartwright*. With an introduction by Charles L. Wallis. New York: Abingdon Press, 1956.

Creighton, Joseph H., and Friends. *Life and Times of Joseph H. Creighton, A. M., of the Ohio Conference*. Lithopolis, Ohio: Western Methodist Book Concern, 1899.

Eggleston, Edward. *The Circuit-Rider: A Tale of the Heroic Age*. New York: J. B. Ford and Co., 1874.

Extracts of Letters Containing Some Account of the Work of God Since the Year 1800; Written by the Preachers and Members of the Methodist Episcopal Church to Their Bishops. New York: Cooper and Wilson, 1805.

Fee, William I. *Bringing the Sheaves: Gleanings from Harvest Fields in Ohio, Kentucky, and West Virginia*. Cincinnati: Cranston and Curts, 1896.

———. *Garnered Sheaves from Harvest Fields in Ohio, Kentucky, and West Virginia*. Cincinnati: Curts and Jennings, 1900.

Finley, James B. *Autobiography of Rev. James B. Finley*. Edited by W. P. Strickland. Cincinnati: Methodist Book Concern, 1854.

———. *Sketches of Western Methodism: Biographical, Historical, and Miscellaneous, Illustrative of Pioneer Life*. Cincinnati: Methodist Book Concern, 1854.

Fitzgerald, O. P. *John B. McFerrin: A Biography*. Nashville: Publishing House of the M. E. Church, South, 1893.

Frederic, Harold. *The Damnation of Theron Ware*. Edited by Everett Carter. Cambridge, Mass.: Harvard University Press, 1960 [1896].

Gaddis, Maxwell Pierson. *Brief Recollections of the Late Reverend George Walker*. Cincinnati: Swormstedt and Poe, 1857.

———. *Footprints of an Itinerant*. Cincinnati: Methodist Book Concern, 1857.

Graves, J. R. *The Great Iron Wheel; or, Republicanism Backwards and Christianity Reversed*. Nashville: Marks and Rutland, 1856.

Hamline, Melinda. *Memoir of Mrs. Angeline B. Sears, with Extracts from Her Correspondence*. Cincinnati: Swormstedt and Poe, 1851.

Haney, M. L. *The Story of My Life: An Autobiography*. Normal, Ill., 1904.

Hibbard, Billy. *Memoirs of the Life and Travels of B. Hibbard. . . .* New York, 1825.

Hobart, Chauncey. *Recollections of My Life: Fifty Years of Itinerancy in the Northwest*. Red Wing, Minn.: Red Wing Printing Co., 1885.

Hughes, George. *Days of Power in the Forest Temple: A Review of the Wonderful Work of God at Fourteen National Campmeetings from 1867 to 1872*. Boston: John Bent and Co., 1873.

———. *Fragrant Memories of the Tuesday Meeting and the* Guide to Holiness *and Their Fifty Years' Work for Jesus*. New York: Palmer and Hughes, 1886.

King, William Fletcher. *Reminiscences*. New York: Abingdon Press, 1915.

Lewis, David. *Recollections of a Superannuate: Or, Sketches of Life, Labor, and Experience in the Methodist Itinerancy*. Edited by S. M. Merrill. Cincinnati: Methodist Book Concern, 1857.

Lovell, C. R. *Methodist Family Manual*. Cincinnati: Swormstedt and Poe, 1852.

McLean, John. *Sketch of Rev. Philip Gatch*. Cincinnati: Swormstedt and Poe, 1854.

Miley, John. *Treatise on Class Meetings*. Cincinnati: Swormstedt and Poe, 1851.

Miller, Emory. *Memoirs and Sermons*. Cincinnati: Jennings and Graham, n.d.

Minutes of the Central Ohio Conference of the Methodist Episcopal Church, 1866–1883.

Minutes of the Cincinnati Annual Conference of the Methodist Episcopal Church. 1853.

Minutes of the Illinois Annual Conference of the Methodist Episcopal Church, 1859, 1870.

Minutes of the North Ohio Annual Conference of the Methodist Episcopal Church, 1878.

Minutes of the Ohio Conference of the Methodist Episcopal Church, 1865–1866.

Minutes of the Southern Illinois Conference of the Methodist Episcopal Church, 1877–1919.

Morris, T. A. *Miscellany: Consisting of Essays, Biographical Sketches, and Notes of Travel*. Cincinnati: Swormstedt and Poe, 1852.

Newell, A. *Biography of the Rev. A. Newell and Miscellanies*. St. Louis: Nixon-Jones Printing Co., 1894.

Northcott, H. C. *Biography of Rev. Benjamin Northcott, a Pioneer Preacher of the Methodist Episcopal Church in Kentucky*. Cincinnati: Western Methodist Book Concern, 1875.

Power, John H. *Discourse on Domestic Piety and Family Government in Four Parts*. Edited by B. F. Tefft. Cincinnati: Swormstedt and Poe, 1854.

Simpson, Matthew, ed. *Cyclopedia of Methodism*. Philadelphia: Everts and Stewart, 1878.

Smith, J. C. *Reminiscences of Early Methodism in Indiana*. Indianapolis: J. M. Olcott, 1879.

Smith, J. M. *A Work on Revivals: Sermons and Sketches in the Life and Preaching of Elder James Smith*. 3d. ed. Indianapolis, 1893.

Smith, John L. *Indiana Methodism, Stories of Sketches and Incidents, Grave and Humorous Concerning Preachers and People of the West*. Valparaiso, Ind., 1892.

Stanley, E. J. *Life of Rev. L. B. Stateler, Or, Sixty-five Years on the Frontier, Containing Incidents, Anecdotes, and Sketches of Methodist History in the West and Northwest*. Nashville: Publishing House of the M. E. Church, South, 1907.

Stewart, John. *Highways and Hedges; or Fifty Years of Western Methodism*. Cincinnati: Hitchcock and Walden, 1872.

Sullins, David. *Recollections of an Old Man: Seventy Years in Dixie, 1827–1897*. 2d ed. Bristol, Tenn.: The King Printing Co., 1910.

Sweet, William Warren, ed. *Religion on the American Frontier, 1783–1840*. Vol. 1, *The Baptists*. New York: Cooper Square, 1964 [1931].

———. *Religion on the American Frontier, 1783–1840*. Vol. 2, *The Presbyterians*. New York: Cooper Square, 1964 [1936].

———. *Religion on the American Frontier, 1783–1840*. Vol. 4, *The Methodists*. Chicago: University of Chicago Press, 1946.

Tarkington, Joseph P. *Autobiography of Rev. Joseph Tarkington, One of the Pioneer Methodist Preachers of Indiana*. Cincinnati: Curts and Jennings, 1899.

Taylor, John. *History of Ten Baptist Churches*. 2d ed. Franklin Co., Ky., 1828.

Tooley, H. "Zion Travellers." In vol. 1 of *The Western Methodist Preacher*, 189–90. Nashville: Garrett and Moffitt, 1835.

"Welfare of Ohio Conference Methodism." In *Journal of the Ohio Annual Conference of the Methodist Episcopal Church*, 220–32. 1875.

Welker, T. D. *Conflicts and Trials of an Itinerant. Rev. John Kiger, D. D.* Cincinnati: Cranston and Stowe, 1891.

Wiley, Allen. "The Introduction and Progress of Methodism in Southeastern Indiana." *Indiana Magazine of History* 23 (March, June, September, December 1927): 3–62, 130–216, 239–332, 393–466.

Williams, Samuel W. *Pictures of Early Methodism in Ohio*. Cincinnati: Jennings and Graham, 1909.

Young, Jacob. *Autobiography of a Pioneer: Or the Nativity, Experience, Travels, and Ministerial Labors of Rev. Jacob Young, with Incidents, Observations, and Reflections*. Cincinnati: Swormstedt and Poe, 1857.

SECONDARY SOURCES

Abernethy, Thomas P. *Three Virginia Frontiers*. University, La.: Louisiana State University Press, 1940.

Albanese, Catherine L. "Savage, Sinner, and Saved: Davy Crockett, Camp Meetings, and the Wild Frontier." *American Quarterly* 33 (1981): 482–501.

Alcorn, Richard S. "Leadership and Stability in Mid-nineteenth-century America: A Case Study of an Illinois Town." *Journal of American History* 61 (1974): 685–702.

Atherton, Lewis. *Main Street on the Middle Border*. Bloomington, Ind.: Indiana University Press, 1954.

Bailyn, Bernard. *The Ideological Origins of the American Revolution*. Cambridge, Mass.: Harvard University Press, 1967.

Banner, Lois. "Religious Benevolence as Social Control: A Critique of an Interpretation." *Journal of American History* 60 (1973): 23–41.

Barnhart, John D. "Southern Contributions to the Social Order of the Old Northwest." *North Carolina Historical Review* 17 (1940): 237–48.

———. "The Southern Element in the Leadership of the Old Northwest." *Journal of Southern History* 1 (1935): 186–97.

———. *Valley of Democracy: Frontier in the Ohio Valley, 1775–1818*. Bloomington, Ind.: Indiana University Press, 1953.

Baym, Nina. "Turning Literature into History." *American Quarterly* 36 (Fall 1984): 593–99.

———. *Woman's Fiction: A Guide to Novels by and about Women in America, 1820–1870*. Ithaca, N.Y.: Cornell University Press, 1978.

Bercovitch, Sacvan. *The Puritan Origins of the American Self*. New Haven: Yale University Press, 1975.

Berthoff, Rowland. *An Unsettled People: Social Order and Disorder in American History*. New York: Harper and Row, 1971.

Berthoff, Rowland, and Murrin, John M. "Feudalism, Communalism, and the Yeoman Freeholder: The American Revolution Considered as a Social Accident." In *Essays on the American Revolution*, edited by Stephen G. Kurtz and James H. Hutson, 256–88. Chapel Hill: University of North Carolina Press, 1973.

Billington, Ray Allen. *America's Frontier Heritage*. New York: Holt, Rinehart, and Winston, 1966.

———. *Westward Expansion*. 3d ed. New York: Macmillan, 1967.

Bledstein, Burton J. *The Culture of Professionalism: The Middle Class and the Development of Higher Education in America*. New York: W. W. Norton, 1976.

Bloch, Ruth H. "American Feminine Ideals in Transition: The Rise of the Moral Mother, 1785–1815." *Feminist Studies* 4 (1978): 101–26.

Boorstin, Daniel J. *The Americans: The National Experience*. New York: Vintage Books, 1965.

Booth, Wayne C. "Metaphor as Rhetoric: The Problem of Evaluation." In *On Metaphor*, edited by Sheldon Sacks, 47–70. Chicago: University of Chicago Press, 1979.

Brauer, Jerald C. "Conversion: From Puritanism to Revivalism." *The Journal of Religion* 58 (1978): 227–43.

Breen, T. H. "Horses and Gentlemen: The Cultural Significance of Gambling among the Gentry of Virginia." *William and Mary Quarterly*, 3d ser., 34 (1977): 239–57.

Bridenbaugh, Carl. *Myths and Realities: Societies of the Colonial South*. New York: Athenaeum, 1963.

Brown, Richard D. *Modernization: The Transformation of American Life, 1600–1865*. New York: Hill and Wang, 1976.

Brown, Richard Maxwell. "The American Vigilante Tradition." In *Violence in America: Historical and Comparative Perspectives*, edited by *Hugh Davis Graham and Ted Robert Gurr*, 154–205. New American Library. New York: Signet Books, 1969.

———. *Strain of Violence: Historical Studies of American Violence and Vigilantism*. New York: Oxford University Press, 1975.

Burke, Kenneth. *Counter-Statement*. Berkeley: University of California Press, 1968 [1931].

———. *The Philosophy of Literary Form*. 3d ed. Berkeley: University of California Press, 1973.

———. *A Rhetoric of Motives*. Berkeley: University of California Press, 1969 [1950].

———. *Rhetoric of Religion: Studies in Logology*. Berkeley: University of California Press, 1970 [1961].

Burrows, Edwin G., and Wallace, Michael. "The American Revolution: The Ideology and Psychology of National Liberation." *Perspectives in American History* 6 (1972): 168–289.

Byrne, Donald. *No Foot of Land: Folklore of American Methodist Itinerants*. ATLA Monograph no. 6. Metuchen, N.J.: Scarecrow Press, 1975.

Cameron, Richard. *Methodism and Society in Historical Perspective*. Vol. 1 of *Methodism and Society*. New York: Abingdon Press, 1961.

Chandler, Douglas R. "The Formation of the Methodist Protestant Church." In vol. 1 of *The History of American Methodism*, edited by Emory Stevens Bucke, 636–83. New York: Abingdon Press, 1964.

Clinton, Catherine. *The Other Civil War: American Women in the Nineteenth Century*. New York: Hill and Wang, 1984.

———. *The Plantation Mistress: Woman's World in the Old South*. New York: Pantheon, 1982.

Cohen, Charles Lloyd. *God's Caress: The Psychology of Puritan Religious Experience*. New York: Oxford University Press, 1986.

Cohen, Ted. "Metaphor and the Cultivation of Intimacy." In *On Metaphor*, edited by Sheldon Sacks, 1–10. Chicago: University of Chicago Press, 1979.

Cott, Nancy. *The Bonds of Womanhood: "Woman's Sphere" in New England, 1780–1835*. New Haven: Yale University Press, 1977.

———. "Passionlessness: An Interpretation of Victorian Sexual Ideology, 1790–1850." *Signs* 4 (Winter 1978): 219–36.

Crowley, J. E. *This Sheba, Self: The Conceptualization of Economic Life in Eighteenth-century America*. Johns Hopkins University Studies in Historical and Political Science, no. 92. Baltimore: Johns Hopkins University Press, 1974.

Davidson, James West. *The Logic of Millennial Thought: Eighteenth-Century New England*. New Haven: Yale University Press, 1977.

Dayton, Donald W. *Discovering an Evangelical Heritage*. New York: Harper and Row, 1976.

Degler, Carl N. *At Odds: Women and the Family in America from the Revolution to the Present*. New York: Oxford University Press, 1980.

Dieter, Melvin Easterday. *The Holiness Revival of the Nineteenth Century*. Studies in Evangelicalism, no. 1. Metuchen, N.J.: Scarecrow Press, 1980.

Douglas, Ann. *The Feminization of American Culture*. New York: Alfred A. Knopf, 1977.

Eaton, Clement. *A History of the Old South: The Emergence of a Reluctant Nation*. 3d ed. New York: Macmillan, 1975.

Eblen, Jack E. "An Analysis of Nineteenth-century Frontier Populations." *Demography* 2 (1965): 399–413.

Elkins, Stanley, and McKitrick, Eric. "A Meaning for Turner's Frontier II: The Southwest Frontier and New England." *Political Science Quarterly* 69 (1954): 565–83.

———. "A Meaning for Turner's Frontier I: Democracy in the Old Northwest." *Political Science Quarterly* 69 (1954): 321–53.

Emory, Robert. *History of the Discipline of the Methodist Episcopal Church*. New York: G. Lane and C. B. Tippett, 1845.

Erikson, Erik H. *Childhood and Society*. 2d ed. New York: W. W. Norton, 1963.

———. *Identity: Youth and Crisis*. New York: W. W. Norton, 1968.

———. *Insight and Responsibility: Lectures on the Ethical Implications of Psychoanalytic Insight*. New York: W. W. Norton, 1964.

———. *Toys and Reasons: Stages in the Ritualization of Experience*. New York: W. W. Norton, 1977.

Everhart, Janet S. "Maggie Newton Van Cott." In vol. 2 of *Women in New Worlds: Historical Perspectives on the Wesleyan Tradition*, edited by Rosemary Skinner Keller, Louise L. Queen, and Hilah F. Thomas, 300–17. Nashville: Abingdon Press, 1982.

Faragher, John Mack. *Women and Men on the Overland Trail*. New Haven: Yale University Press, 1979.

Finke, Roger, and Stark, Rodney. "How the Upstart Sects Won America: 1776–1850." *Journal of the Social Scientific Study of Religion* 28 (March 1989): 27–44.

Fliegelman, Jay. *Prodigals and Pilgrims: The American Revolution Against Patriarchal Authority, 1750–1800*. New York: Cambridge University Press, 1982.

Gates, Paul W. "Frontier Estate Builders and Farm Laborers." In *The Frontier in Perspective*, edited by Walker Wyman and Clifton Kroeber, 143–64. Madison: University of Wisconsin Press, 1965.

Gaustad, Edwin Scott. *Historical Atlas of Religion in America*. Rev. ed. New York: Harper and Row, 1976.

Geertz, Clifford. *The Interpretation of Cultures*. New York: Basic Books, 1973.

Gifford, Carolyn DeSwarte. "For God and Home and Native Land: The W.C.T.U.'s Image of Woman in the Late Nineteenth Century." In vol. 1 of *Women in New Worlds: Historical Perspectives on the Wesleyan Tradition*, edited by Rosemary Skinner Keller and Hilah F. Thomas, 310–27. Nashville: Abingdon Press, 1981.

Gillespie, Joanna Bowen. "The Emerging Voice of the Methodist Woman: The Ladies' Repository, 1841–61." In *Rethinking Methodist History: A Bicentennial Historical Consultation*, edited by Russell E. Richey and Kenneth E. Rowe. Nashville: Kingswood Books, 1985.

Glazer, Walter S. "Participation and Power: Voluntary Associations and the Functional Organization of Cincinnati in 1840." *Historical Methods Newsletter* 5 (1972): 151–68.

Greven, Philip J. *The Protestant Temperament: Patterns of Child-Rearing, Religious Experience and the Self in Early America*. New York: Alfred A. Knopf, 1977.

Halevy, Elie. *The Birth of Methodism in England*. Edited and translated by Bernard Semmel. Chicago: University of Chicago Press, 1971.

Hall, Peter Dobkin. *The Organization of American Culture, 1700–1900: Private Institutions, Elites, and the Origins of American Nationality*. New York: New York University Press, 1984.

Harding, Vincent. "Out of the Cauldron of Struggle: Black Religion and the Search for a New America." In *Religion: North American Style*, edited by Patrick H. McNamara, 252–64. Belmont, Calif.: Wadsworth Publishing, 1984.

Hartz, Louis. "A Comparative Study of Fragment Cultures." In *Violence in America: Historical and Comparative Perspectives*, edited by Hugh Davis Graham and Ted Robert Gurr, 110–14. New American Library. New York: Signet Books, 1969.

Hatch, Nathan O. *The Democratization of American Christianity*. New Haven: Yale University Press, 1989.

———. *The Sacred Cause of Liberty: Republican Thought and the Millennium in Revolutionary New England*. New Haven: Yale University Press, 1977.

Hempton, David. *Methodism and Politics in British Society, 1750–1850*. Stanford: Stanford University Press, 1984.

Hewitt, Nancy. "The Perimeters of Women's Power in American Religion." In *The Evangelical Tradition in America.*, edited by Leonard I. Sweet, 233–56. Macon, Ga.: Mercer University Press, 1984.

Higham, John. *From Boundlessness to Consolidation: The Transformation of American Culture, 1848–1860*. Ann Arbor, Mich.: William L. Clements, 1969.

Holsclaw, David F. *The Demise of Disciplined Christian Fellowship: The Methodist Class Meeting in Nineteenth-century America*. Ann Arbor, Mich.: UMI no. 8009501, 1979.

Hood, Fred J. *Reformed America: The Middle and Southern States, 1783–1837*. University, Ala.: University of Alabama Press, 1980.

Hudson, Winthrop S. "The Methodist Age in America." *Methodist History* 12 (April 1974): 4–15.

Isaac, Rhys. "Evangelical Revolt: The Nature of the Baptists' Challenge to Traditional Order in Virginia, 1765–1775." *William and Mary Quarterly* 31 (July 1974): 345–68.

———. "Preachers and Patriots: Popular Culture and the Revolution in Virginia." In *The American Revolution: Explorations in the History of American Radicalism*, edited by Alfred A. Young, 125–56. DeKalb, Ill.: Northern Illinois University Press, 1976.

———. *The Transformation of Virginia: 1740–1790*. Chapel Hill: University of North Carolina Press, 1982.

Jeffrey, Julie Roy. "Ministry Through Marriage: Methodist Clergy Wives on the Trans-Mississippi Frontier." In vol. 1 of *Women in New Worlds: Historical Perspectives on the Wesleyan Tradition*, edited by Rosemary Skinner Keller and Hilah F. Thomas, 143–60. Nashville: Abingdon Press, 1982.

Johnson, Paul E. *A Shopkeeper's Millennium: Society and Revivals in Rochester, New York, 1815–1837*. New York: Hill and Wang, 1978.

Johnson, Richard O. "The Development of the Love Feast in Early American Methodism." *Methodist History* 19 (1981): 65–83.

Jones, Charles Edwin. *The Perfectionist Persuasion: The Holiness Movement and American Methodism, 1867–1936*. Metuchen, N.J.: Scarecrow Press, 1974.

Jordan, Winthrop D. "Familial Politics: Thomas Paine and the Killing of the King, 1776." *Journal of American History* 60 (1973–74): 294–308.

Kelley, Mary. *Private Woman, Public Stage*. New York: Oxford University Press, 1984.

Kelley, Robert. *The Cultural Pattern in American Politics: The First Century*. New York: Alfred A. Knopf, 1979.

Kerber, Linda. *Women of the Republic: Intellect and Ideology in Revolutionary America.* Chapel Hill: University of North Carolina Press, 1980.

King, William McGuire. "Denominational Modernization and Religious Identity: The Case of the Methodist Episcopal Church." *Methodist History* 20 (January 1982): 75–89.

Lakoff, George, and Johnson, Mark. *Metaphors We Live By*. Chicago: University of Chicago Press, 1980.

Lee, Everett S. "The Turner Thesis Reexamined." *American Quarterly* 13 (Spring 1961): 77–83.

Lee, Susan Dye. "Evangelical Domesticity: The Woman's Temperance Crusade of 1873–1874." In vol. 1 of *Women in New Worlds: Historical Perspectives on the Wesleyan Tradition*, edited by Rosemary Skinner Keller and Hilah F. Thomas, 293–309. Nashville: Abingdon Press, 1981.

McDannell, Colleen. *The Christian Home in Victorian America, 1840–1900*. Bloomington, Ind.: Indiana University Press, 1986.

Mathews, Donald G. "Evangelical America—the Methodist Ideology." In *Rethinking Methodist History: A Bicentennial Historical Consultation*, edited by Russell E. Richey and Kenneth E. Rowe, 91–99. Nashville: United Methodist Publishing House, Kingswood Books, 1985.

———. *Religion in the Old South*. Chicago: University of Chicago Press, 1977.

Mead, Sydney E. *The Lively Experiment: The Shaping of Christianity in America*. New York: Harper and Row, 1963.

Miller, Perry. *The Life of the Mind in America from the Revolution to the Civil War.* New York: Harcourt, Brace, and World, 1965.

Moberg, David. *The Great Reversal: Evangelism Versus Social Concern*. Philadelphia: J. B. Lippincott, 1972.

Modell, John. "Family and Fertility on the Indiana Frontier, 1820." *American Quarterly* 23 (1971): 615–34.

Morgan, Edmund S. *Virginians at Home: Family Life in the Eighteenth Century.* Williamsburg, Va.: William Byrd Press, 1952.

Nagel, Paul C. *This Sacred Trust: American Nationality, 1798–1890*. New York: Oxford University Press, 1971.

Nelson, Benjamin. *The Idea of Usury: From Tribal Brotherhood to Universal Otherhood*. 2d ed. Chicago: University of Chicago Press, 1969.

Norton, Mary Beth. *Liberty's Daughters: The Revolutionary Experience of American Women, 1750–1800*. Boston: Little, Brown, and Co., 1980.

Norton, Wesley. *Religious Newspapers in the Old Northwest to 1861: A History, Bibliography, and Record of Opinion*. Athens, Ohio: Ohio University Press, 1977.

Norwood, Frederick A. *The Story of American Methodism: A History of the United Methodists and Their Relations*. Nashville: Abingdon Press, 1974.

Pole, J. R. *Foundations of American Independence: 1763–1815*. Edited by Jack P. Greene. History of American Society Series. Indianapolis: Bobbs Merrill, 1972.

Posey, Walter B. *The Development of Methodism in the Old Southwest: 1783–1824*. Tuscaloosa, Ala.: Weatherford Printing Co., 1933.

Potter, J. "American Population in the Early National Period." In *Population and Economics: Proceedings of Section V of the Fourth Congress of the International Economic History Association, 1968*, edited by Paul Deprez, 55–67. Winnipeg: University of Manitoba Press, 1970.

———. "The Growth of Population in America, 1700–1860." In *Population in History*, edited by D. E. C. Eversly and D. V. Glass, 361–88. London: Edward Arnold, 1965.

Primer, Ben. *Protestants and American Business Methods. Studies in American History and Culture*, no. 7. Ann Arbor, Mich.: UMI Research Press, 1979 [1977].

Richey, Russell E. *Early American Methodism*. Bloomington, Ind.: Indiana University Press, 1991.

———. "The Social Sources of Denominationalism: Methodism." In *Denominationalism*, edited by Russell E. Richey, 163–79. Nashville: Abingdon Press, 1977.

Roeber, A. G. "Authority, Law, and Custom: The Rituals of Court Day in Tidewater Virginia, 1720–1750." *William and Mary Quarterly*, 3d ser., 37 (1980): 29–52.

Rudolph, Frederick, ed. *Essays on Education*. Cambridge, Mass.: Harvard University Press, 1965.

Ryan, Mary P. *Cradle of the Middle Class: The Family in Oneida County, New York, 1790–1865*. Cambridge: Cambridge University Press, 1981.

Saum, Lewis. "Death in the Popular Mind of Pre–Civil War America." In *Death in America*, edited by David E. Stannard, 30–48. Philadelphia: University of Pennsylvania Press, 1974.

———. *The Popular Mood of Pre–Civil War America*. Contributions in American Studies, no. 46. Westport, Conn.: Greenwood Press, 1980.

Schneider, A. Gregory. "The Ritual of Happy Dying among Early American Methodists." *Church History* 56 (September 1987): 348–63.

Semmel, Bernard. *The Methodist Revolution*. New York: Basic Books, 1973.

Shalhope, Robert E. "Republicanism and Early American Historiography." *William and Mary Quarterly*, 3d ser., 39 (1982): 334–56.

Shiels, Richard D. "The Feminization of American Congregationalism, 1730–1835." *American Quarterly* 33 (Spring 1981): 46–62.

———. "The Methodist Circuit-Rider in the Second Great Awakening in New England." Paper read at conference, Reexamining Revivalism: the Wesleyan/Holiness Perspective, 10–11 June 1988, at Asbury Theological Seminary, Wilmore, Kentucky.

Shorter, Edward. *The Making of the Modern Family*. New York: Basic Books, 1975.

Sizer, Sandra. *Gospel Hymns and Social Religion: The Rhetoric of Nineteenth-century Revivalism*. Philadelphia: Temple University Press, 1978.

Sklar, Kathryn Kish. *Catherine Beecher: A Study in American Domesticity*. New York: W. W. Norton, 1976 [1973].

Smith, Daniel Blake. *Inside the Great House: Planter Family Life in Eighteenth-century Chesapeake Society*. Ithaca, New York: Cornell University Press, 1980.

Smith, Henry Nash. *Virgin Land: The American West as Symbol and Myth*. Cambridge, Mass.: Harvard University Press, 1950.

Smith, Timothy L. *Revivalism and Social Reform: American Protestantism on the Eve of the Civil War*. New York: Harper Torchbooks, 1965 [1957].

———. "Righteousness and Hope: Christian Holiness and the Millennial Vision in America, 1800–1900." *American Quarterly* 31 (1979): 21–45.

Smith-Rosenberg, Carroll. "The Female World of Love and Ritual: Relations between Women in Nineteenth-century America." In *The American Family in Social-Historical Perspective*, 3d ed., edited by Michael C. Gordon, 411–35. New York: St. Martin's Press, 1983.

———. "Women and Religious Revivals: Anti-ritualism, Liminality, and the Emergence of the American Bourgeoisie." In *The Evangelical Tradition in America*, edited by Leonard I. Sweet, 199–231. Macon, Ga.: Mercer University Press, 1984.

Stannard, David E. *The Puritan Way of Death: A Study in Religion, Culture, and Social Change*. New York: Oxford University Press, 1977.

Stilgoe, John R. *Common Landscape of America, 1580–1845*. New Haven: Yale University Press, 1982.

Stone, Lawrence E. *The Family, Sex, and Marriage in England, 1500–1800*. New York: Harper and Row, 1977.

Stout, Harry S. " 'Religion, Communications, and the Ideological Origins of the

American Revolution' " *William and Mary Quarterly*, 3d ser., 34 (October 1977): 519–41.

Sweet, Leonard I. "The Female Seminary Movement and Woman's Mission in Antebellum America." *Church History* 54 (1985): 41–55.

———. "Millennialism in America: Recent Studies." *Theological Studies* 40 (1979): 510–31.

———. *The Minister's Wife: Her Role in Nineteenth-Century American Evangelicalism*. Philadelphia: Temple University Press, 1983.

Sweet, William Warren. "The Churches as Moral Courts of the Frontier." *Church History* 2 (January 1933): 2–21.

———. *Religion in the Development of American Culture, 1765–1840*. Gloucester, Mass.: Peter Smith, 1963 [1952].

Sydnor, Charles S. *American Revolutionaries in the Making: Political Practices in Washington's Virginia*. New York: Free Press, 1965.

———. *The Development of Southern Sectionalism, 1819–1848*. University, La.: Louisiana State University Press, 1948.

Thomas, George M. *Revivalism and Cultural Change: Christianity, Nation Building, and the Market in the Nineteenth-century United States*. Chicago: University of Chicago Press, 1989.

Thompson, E. P. *The Making of the English Working Class*. New York: Vintage Books, 1963.

Trumbach, Randolph. *The Rise of the Egalitarian Family: Aristocratic Kinship and Domestic Relations in Eighteenth-Century England*. New York: Academic Press, 1978.

Turner, Victor. *Dramas, Fields, and Metaphors: Symbolic Action in Human Society*. Symbol, Myth, and Ritual Series. Ithaca, N.Y.: Cornell University Press, 1974.

———. *From Ritual to Theater: The Human Seriousness of Play*. New York: Performing Arts Journal Publications, 1982.

———. *The Ritual Process: Structure and Anti-structure*. Chicago: Aldine, 1969.

Vedder, Richard K., and Galloway, Lowell E. "Migration and the Old Northwest." In *Essays in Nineteenth-Century Economic History: The Old Northwest*, edited by David C. Klingman and Richard K. Vedder, 167–69. Athens, Ohio: Ohio University Press, 1975.

Wacker, Grant. "Searching for Norman Rockwell: Popular Evangelicalism in Contemporary America." In *The Evangelical Tradition in America*, edited by Leonard I. Sweet, 289–315. Macon Ga.: Mercer University Press, 1984.

Wade, Richard C. *The Urban Frontier: Pioneer Life in Early Pittsburgh, Cincinnati, Lexington, Louisville, and St. Louis*. Chicago: University of Chicago Press, 1959.

Watson, David Lowes. *The Early Methodist Class Meeting: Its Origins and Significance*. Nashville: Discipleship Resources, 1985.

Weber, Max. *From Max Weber: Essays in Sociology*. Edited by H. H. and Mills Gerth, C. Wright. New York: Oxford University Press, 1949.

———. *The Protestant Ethic and the Spirit of Capitalism*. Translated by Talcott Parsons. New York: Charles Scribner's Sons, 1958.

———. *The Theory of Social and Economic Organization*. Translated by A. M. and Parsons Talcott Henderson. New York: Free Press, 1964 [1947].

Welter, Barbara. "The Feminization of American Religion: 1800–1860." In *Clio's Consciousness Raised: New Perspectives on the History of Women*, edited by Mary Hartmann and Lois W. Banner, 137–57. New York: Harper and Row, 1974.

Wiebe, Robert H. *The Search for Order, 1877–1920*. New York: Hill and Wang, 1967.

Wood, Gordon S. *The Creation of the American Republic, 1776–1787*. Chapel Hill: University of North Carolina Press, 1969.

———. "Republicanism as a Revolutionary Ideology." In *The Role of Ideology in the American Revolution*, edited by John R. Howe. New York: Holt, Rinehart, and Winston, 1970.

Wyatt-Brown, Bertram. *Southern Honor: Ethics and Behavior in the Old South*. New York: Oxford University Press, 1982.

INDEX

A. GREGORY SCHNEIDER is a professor in the Department of Behavioral Science of Pacific Union College.